A History of Conservative Politics since 1830

John Charmley is Professor of Modern History and Head of the School of History at the University of East Anglia.

His previous publications include *Chamberlain and the Lost Peace* (1990) and *Churchill: The End of Glory* (1993).

A History of Conservative Politics since 1830
Second Edition

John Charmley

British Studies Series
General Editor: Jeremy Black

First edition *A History of Conservative Politics 1900–1996* published in 1996
Second edition published in 2008 by
PALGRAVE MACMILLAN
Houndmills, Basingstoke, Hampshire RG21 6XS and
175 Fifth Avenue, New York, N.Y. 10010
Companies and representatives throughout the world.

PALGRAVE MACMILLAN is the global academic imprint of the Palgrave
Macmillan division of St. Martin's Press, LLC and of Palgrave Macmillan Ltd.
Macmillan® is a registered trademark in the United States, United Kingdom
and other countries. Palgrave is a registered trademark in the European
Union and other countries.

ISBN-13: 978–0–333–92974–2 hardback
ISBN-10: 0–333–92974–8 hardback
ISBN-13: 978–0–333–92973–5 paperback
ISBN-10: 0–333–92973–X paperback

This book is printed on paper suitable for recycling and made from fully
managed and sustained forest sources. Logging, pulping and manufacturing
processes are expected to conform to the environmental regulations of
the country of origin.

A catalogue record for this book is available from the British Library.

A catalog record for this book is available from the Library of Congress.

10   9   8   7   6   5   4   3   2   1
17 16 15 14 13 12 11 10 09 08

Printed and bound in China

To Rachael

Contents

Acknowledgements

The first version of this book appeared in 1996 as *A History of Conservative Politics 1900–1996*. This book updates the material in that volume, but takes the story back to Peel and forward to David Cameron, and in that sense (as well as others) is quite a different version; there are many reasons for this, including the exponential expansion of books on the Conservative Party over the past 10 years; whatever the electorate might think, the party continues to fascinate historians.

I remain grateful to those whose comments informed the first version, my old colleague, Professor Geoffrey Searle, Andrew Roberts, and the now, alas, late Alan Clark. I should also like to thank two current MPs, Keith Simpson and Richard Bacon, at whose side I learned a great deal about Conservative politics.

I am extremely grateful to Felicity Noble and Sonya Barker at Palgrave Macmillan for bearing with me whilst this volume was completed. I would like to thank one of Palgrave Macmillan's anonymous readers for his advice, which has saved this volume from some of the more egregious errors of its predecessor. I am grateful to my secretary at the University of East Anglia, Judy Sparks, for her help in getting the book ready.

On a more personal level, and at a professional one, I am very grateful to my son, Gerard, who not only read the whole volume with a critical eye, but provided much of the material on which the final chapter is based. To my wife, Rachael, without whose encouragement and care this volume could not have been complete, my gratitude is beyond the power of words to express.

Harleston, Norfolk

1   The Conservative Tradition

The Conservative Party exists to conserve; it is the party of the status quo. Unfortunately for it and its adherents all things change – 'the flower withereth and the grass fadeth'. In another world perhaps these things are restored and made new, but in this world the process of change poses a fundamental challenge to Conservatism as a political force. Many of those who vote Conservative do so because of an instinctive distaste for the consequences of change, but for a Conservative Party some accommodation with this process is inevitable – if only to ensure political survival. There is, then, a tension between instinctive Conservatism and expediency. Because of this, all Conservative leaders have faced charges of opportunism and betrayal; but historians have generally judged them by their success in adapting to change. Since the Conservative Party has existed for nearly 200 years, during which time Britain has changed beyond recognition, historians are agreed that the Party has been a great success; visceral Conservatives are less easily convinced. Even in 2005, after three successive election defeats, there were those in the Party who argued that its sufferings were due to its failure to abide by traditional values. This 'Tory Taliban' tendency, as one wag called it, has existed in every age, and its song has ever been the same: it harkens back to some bygone golden age, and calls its party to repentance and reformation of life. It might be unkind to point out that in the last golden glow of aristocratic rule, before the country went to the dogs, the Conservatives were, for the most part, in opposition, and that it was only with the advent of democracy that they came to dominate British politics; this always puzzled Marxists, since it ran counter to their theoretical model, but since 1989 those remaining disciples have had other things to distract them from this little local difficulty.

The twentieth century dominance of the Conservative party has created a misleading historiography, best expressed in Lord Blake's highly readable and influential history of it.[1] Robert Blake wrote with elegance and a focus that can only be admired by lesser lights. He knew the importance of having a strong narrative line, and his *History of the Conservative Party*, in its many editions, told a good story. In so far as it had a hero, it was Sir Robert Peel, whose moderate, judicious, sensible conservatism was a model to be emulated; that this version of

1

Peel chimed with Lord Blake's own conservatism was not, perhaps, wholly coincidental. If the reader drew from the tale the moral that all good Conservative leaders should be mild, and sensible, and good as him, then Robert Blake would not have been displeased. Lord Blake sketched the alternatives facing the Tories after their debacle at the 1832 General Election: the Ultra Tory option of resistance; the Tory Radical option of an alliance with the lower orders; and the Peelite option of adaptation to circumstances. The first of these would lead to death (no doubt glorious) in the last ditch; the second was the unfeasible dream of the young Disraeli, and fell at the first fence of practicality (the lower orders did not have the vote); and so it was that Peel's moderate Conservatism came to replace the less flexible Toryism of Wellington – which was why a new word was needed, although the old one remained in use. On the back of this strategy, and with a new emphasis on party organisation through the founding of the Carlton Club in 1839, the Conservatives came into their inheritance in 1841, only to be deprived of the fruits of Peel's foresight and moderation by disputes over the Corn Laws. The great minister fell from power, but not public and political esteem, whilst his block-headed supporters were condemned to a quarter of a century in the political wilderness before the prophet Benjamin (Disraeli) brought them back to the Promised Land by adopting a Peelite approach to the great issue of the day. The success of the Disraeli/Peelite strategy could be seen in the fact that between 1874 and 1905 the Conservatives were in office for all but eight years – a startling reversal of fortunes. This happy state of affairs was brought to an end when the party, or rather the leader of its Liberal Unionist allies, Joseph Chamberlain, raised the thorny issue of reintroducing Protection through the ingeniously named 'Tariff Reform'. Leaving the broad road of pragmatism for the dense thickets of principle, the Conservatives found themselves so entangled in the mire that they once again lost disastrously at a General Election, and from 1905 until the First World War, they languished in opposition. It was only with the advent of the sensibly moderate Stanley Baldwin, so well-attuned to the necessities of the new politics of democracy, that the Conservatives returned to winning ways: Winston Churchill, Anthony Eden, Harold Macmillan and Edward Heath were all dedicated followers of the middle way, and so it was that the Conservatives thrived.

For those who thought that what might be termed 'Blake's law' (i.e. moderation is always the right way) did not apply after 1979, and who would see in the success of Mrs Thatcher proof positive that 'leading from the Right' was the way forward in the modern age, the years after

1997 suggested reasons for caution; indeed, they even suggested that Blake's law might apply on both sides of the political fence, since it was only by bringing their party in from the wild left that Neil Kinnock and Tony Blair made it electable. To the objection that the Tory party prospered by being on the far Right, several ripostes could be made: the first would be that Mrs Thatcher's rhetoric was far to the right of her practice (which in itself, was too right-wing for those on the left); and the second would be that she owed her ascendancy as much to the fractured nature of the opposition as she did to any virtues of her own; a majority of the population always voted against her. Those who doubted such diagnoses were to have many years to ponder their truth after 1997.

Robert Blake was a shrewd observer of the political scene, but he was also a Conservative of the post-1945 vintage, who identified his party's success with Macmillan's liberal conservatism; his book pointed a moral to adorn a tale, and Mrs Thatcher's success surprised him, as much as it did Ted Heath, whom he much admired. But unlike Heath, Blake was a congenial, even jovial man, and he possessed, almost to genius, the Conservative quality he most admired, that of adaptation to circumstances. He was largely untroubled by questions of Conservative philosophy; to adapt a phrase of Herbert Morrison's, he believed that Conservatism was what Conservative governments did. This was tested to the limit by Mrs Thatcher. Academics take a great interest in political philosophy, traditions and consistency; Blake's Conservatives took all these things as they could find them, but placed most emphasis on the politics of the possible. Conservatives succeeded because they were pragmatists, not ideologues. Those current Conservatives who wish to argue otherwise would be more convincing if they did so from a position of electoral success; Blake's law stands the test of time.

Academics and students like their politicians to be men of conviction and consistency, but in the real world of politics most political beliefs are situational as much as they as dispositional; that is they are 'determined at least as much by circumstances as by deeply held moral convictions'.[2] It is true that there are politicians for whom this is not the case, but this takes us to the debate that has been at the heart of all Conservative politics: the tension between visceral Conservatism and political necessity. The Tory who stands on principle will declare that without it, power has no purpose; his colleague who professes pragmatism will interject that principles without power are doomed to sterility; they are, of course, both correct, and the Conservative Party has been at its most successful when it has possessed a leader who could run with the tension between the two positions – just as it has been at its least successful when that tension has torn the party apart.

It is, in part, the need to manage this tension that places the focus of this book where it lies, on the machinations of the key players at Westminster. This is not the only way to read the history of Conservative politics, but it is one that seeks to address the issues of the Conservative frame of mind and the temperament associated with it. What did Conservative leaders understand themselves to be doing? How did they understand political conservatism? Did it differ from that visceral conservatism we have already noted? For those in search of an institutional history of the Conservative Party, there are the six monumental volumes in the Longman series, and the splendid one-volume history by John Ramsden; but for those who want to know what Conservative leaders understood themselves to be doing, and therefore how they articulated a Conservative politics in circumstances not of their own choosing, there is an interpretation offered here which may offer insights into what being a political Conservative has implied across the past two centuries.

It is fitting in this context that the location of the origins of the Conservative Party should be problematic. The name came into use in the early 1830s, but it did so to describe a phenomenon that was at least a generation older. In its modern form, the hostility to change that is at the heart of Conservatism focused upon events in France after 1789. The results of applying 'Reason' to politics in France suggested to Edmund Burke and his English admirers that a little less of that quality and a lot more respect for what had grown organically might be called for. As would ever be the case, admirers of the philosophy behind the Revolution declared that there was nothing wrong with its principles; it was just that the practice of them was imperfect. For Burke this was missing the point on a grand scale. Utopian political visions would always be undeliverable because the vehicle through which delivery would have to take place was itself defective; the fallen nature of mankind lies close to the heart of Burkean conservatism. Even when not explicitly Christian, Conservatism is sceptical of projects of social improvement; except, of course, when pragmatics call for a rhetoric which suggests the opposite; politically this did not happen between the 1790s and the 1830s.

The military and political threat posed by France, whether revolutionary or Napoleonic broke the Whig Party and created a governing coalition around the iconic form of the Younger Pitt, in which Burkean Whigs joined Pittite Tories in the great patriotic war. Because they were all gentlemen in an age of aristocratic politics, no draconian measures were taken against the Whig leaders such as Charles James Fox or Earl Grey; it was only when the war was over and the lower orders seemed to be revolting that recourse was had to the iron glove; and then it was applied only to those outside the arena of Westminster.

The government of Lord Liverpool, which contained within it five future Prime Ministers, serves to illustrate the variety of political options that could be concealed within one amorphous 'Tory' Party. Its most politically imposing figure after 1822 was George Canning; he was also its most divisive figure, and in a perverse way deserves the title of the man who made the Conservative Party possible. Then there was Liverpool's chancellor of the exchequer, Frederick Robinson, who would, as Lord Goderich, briefly and ingloriously occupy the premiership; an illustration of a phenomenon too often repeated in Conservative history, but rarely so perfectly – namely that the temptation in an emergency to reach for the nearest suitable nonentity usually ends in tears. Its most famous minister was the great Duke of Wellington, whose distrust of reform was as visceral as his willingness to carry it out if ordered to by his sovereign; another common Tory trope. The emerging man was the red-haired and industrious Home Secretary, Robert Peel, the scion of the new wealth created by the Industrial revolution. The rising hope of those stern unbending Tories whom he would, one day, disgust, Peel seemed to represent an alliance between tradition and change which offered a way to the future for the Tories; this might, or might not, have been an illusion. Lower down the pecking order, and invisible as Secretary at War to all but his vast social circle, lay the man with whom the future really lay, Henry John Temple, second Viscount Palmerston, who, even more than Peel, would show how the future of Toryism could lie in a Liberal direction.

It is in the destruction of the Liverpool government and the disper-sal of these talents that the origins of the Conservative Party may be seen to lie. Historians record and explain what happened, but they are wise if they incorporate into their narrative what contemporaries expected to happen, since that often contains the key to why people acted as they did; Canning's career in 1827 is a good example of this. Liverpool had been ill during 1826, and he might well have gone then, save for the fact that his obvious successor was Canning. The flamboy-ance of the liberal foreign secretary, in an age when neither adjective was a passport to Tory approval, had made him a multitude of enemies; nearly all within the Cabinet – although the Whig leader, Earl Grey, was an exception to this, since he loathed Canning without becoming a Tory to do so. That there had been wisdom in Liverpool's prevarication was shown by events following his incapacitation with a stroke in

February 1827. Wellington and Peel, the Tory road to the future, along with Lord Chancellor Eldon, the Tory road to the past, rebelled at the idea of serving with Canning, and seceded from the administration. This left Canning having to look to the opposition benches for support, and in so doing he managed to put together the ideal solution to the political chaos which threatened to break on Westminster.

Canning's government was that fabled beast of future myth – a centre party. At its head was the most talented orator of the day, a man whose foreign policy made him the scourge of the absolutists, but whose stance on the controversial issue of Catholic emancipation made him more than acceptable to the liberals; that he was agnostic on the other great reform question – that of parliament – made him an ideal leader of the centre ground. Moreover, his administration attracted to it a range of talents that included three future Prime Ministers: one of these was Palmerston, who would, within the year, stake a claim to be Canning's heir; another was the brother of Palmerston's mistress, William Lamb, who within the year would become Lord Melbourne following the death of his putative father; the third was the youthful Edward Stanley, getting, at the age of 28, his first taste of office. Stanley was the scion of an ancient Whig house, but his association with Canning ought to be borne in mind in assessing his political trajectory; very Whig of very Whig he may have been born, but the centre ground where he first found a political toehold, would be for him, as for his son, his natural habitat.

The 'what might have beens' of British political history contain few such intriguing puzzles as the question of what would have happened had Canning not died in August 1827. Had he lived even a few years more, Grey's career would have ended in the sands of political exile, where, on the opposite shore, he would have been joined by Wellington. The great issue which wrecked Wellington's career and which came close to destroying Peel's, Catholic emancipation, would have been passed by a Canningite administration with no harm done; the other issue which became great thanks to Wellington and which made Grey's name, parliamentary reform, would have been dealt with in another, incremental and less dramatic way, and progress might even have been made upon Ireland. All these delectable prospects were ended by the virus which infected Canning as he stood in Westminster Abbey in February 1827 at the Duke of York's funeral; Prime Minister in April, he was dead by August, the centre would not hold; the worst were certainly filled with passionate intensity.

That ageing and dissolute roué, George IV, would not have Grey at any price, and who balked at 'King Arthur' (as he called the great Duke when he was pouting, which was frequent by this time), told Lord Goderich that he was Prime Minister. Goderich put together the shadow of Canning's friends, but without that master spirit holding the sinews of government taut, all became flabby, not least the will of the new premier; in December he fled without ever meeting parliament. King George turned to King Arthur, who did the business and made Peel his right hand man; there were those who thought Peel aspired to more than that, but Peel knew how to wait.

The Wellington administration was the last Tory government; but it would be a mistake to see it as the precursor of the Conservative Party. It may have helped beget the Conservative Party, but it would be more accurate to see in it the detritus from which the right-wing of the Conservative Party would form itself. It failed to prevent the Russians from winning a great triumph in the Eastern Question; it failed to prevent the Catholics from being emancipated, having tried to do so, and, in the attempt, lost its right-wing supporters like the Duke of Newcastle; and when the Duke tried to rally his troops by declaring 'no surrender' on the issue of parliamentary reform, he found he had actually nailed his trousers to the mast of a sinking ship.

As the ship went down, only a few months after George IV had performed a similar feat, the new King, William IV, turned to Grey and the Whigs. It was from the events of the next three years that the Conservative Party would emerge.

Only the Russian Tsar and Lord Eldon could see in Grey the spectre of the Jacobin revolution; but others could see in those behind him the shadow of the Jacobins; men such as Lord Durham and Lord John Russell held ideas on issues of Church and State which outraged those who held to normative views on Anglicanism and its relations with the state. Grey's actions in pursuing a radical reform bill, and then in moving in on the Church of Ireland, ensured that the rabble on the bench opposite would huddle together – whilst simultaneously wracking his own government with unbearable tensions. From these tensions the Conservative Party would emerge.

With scarcely 150 opponents after the 1833 election, Grey seemed set for life. The great reform bill debates had produced speeches of note, not least from Peel, who established himself as the towering figure on the opposition benches. Those who had learned to hate him because of his change of stance on Catholic emancipation, learned to need him on the issue of reform. His speeches were those of a statesman. He knew he would lose the vote, but he put the intellectual case against such an extreme measure of reform so well that those who cheered him missed the corollary, which was that a more moderate and timely measure of reform would have been preferable. It was upon the twin bases of this mutual misunderstanding about Peel's views on reform, and the Tory need for an articulate leader, that the conservative alliance was formed; and then only just in time.

As Grey's government staggered after the effort of producing the Reform Act, a battle for its future was fought out. Grey himself feared the extremists such as his son-in-law, Durham, and Lord John Russell, and he looked to the youthful 'Rupert of debate', Edward Stanley as his putative successor. Stanley saw a bigger prospect – the chimera of the Canning coalition reborn. Why should he not, he mused, attract to his moderate Whig position, Tory moderates such as Peel? In early 1833 he left the Whig government, disgusted by Russell's policy of despoiling the revenues of the Irish Church for lay uses; it was an issue on which he could hope to attract the Tories, and keep moderate Whig support. As the King dismissed Melbourne, Grey's successor, and called Wellington to office, Stanley's hour seemed to have struck; with the future lying between the radical Whiggery of Russell and the blockhead Toryism of Wellington, the ground was clear for the annunciation of what, out of deference to his ancestral home, Stanley called 'the Knowsley creed'. It was true that Wellington had stood down in favour of Peel, but there seemed no reason not to announce his new line in December upon his installation as rector of Edinburgh University. It was with more than a little annoyance that he read in the press of Peel's 'Tamworth manifesto'. Like the 'Knowsley Creed', it was a play for the centre ground; and unlike Stanley, Peel was Prime Minister and leader of a party.

Peel's followers seemed happy to be identified with a policy which promised no enmity to moderate and judicious reform; it was wonderful what unity could be induced by the spectacle of a Whig government which looked like it was going to attack the Church. Instead of leading a centre party, Stanley became the driver of the 'Derby dilly', which went no-where. Peel's stance did not win the 1835 election, but it showed the Conservatives, as they were coming to be called, were back in business. Fortune favoured Peel again in 1837, when the death of William IV precipitated an election five years sooner than would otherwise have been the case; this enabled the Conservatives to make up more electoral ground – and for the final building blocks to be added to the party in the form of Stanley and his supporters.

Stanley's career had stalled after 1835. His slashing rhetorical style had led him into making comments his old colleagues would not forgive, whilst Peel's steady hand ensured that the Conservatives occupied the central ground of opposition to an increasingly incompetent set of Whigs. Stanley's pride and his tongue barred the road back; Peel's moderation and encouragement provided him with an alternative road forward; henceforth Stanley and his supporters would vote with the Conservatives.

For those with a discerning eye, such as the Whig minister and historian, T. B. Macaulay, Peel's Conservatives were less impressively monolithic than their opposition to the government made them appear. Reviewing the first work of a young Conservative MP first elected in 1832, William E. Gladstone, Macaulay called him: 'The rising hope of those stern unbending Tories' – a phrase forever quoted by Gladstone's biographers, who usually omit the rest, and more telling part of the description: 'who follow reluctantly and mutinously, a leader whose experience and eloquence are indispensable to them, but whose cautious temper and moderate opinions they abhor'. In that comment is the germ of the explanation of the strange fate of Peel's government.

Peel's government was the first Conservative administration, and it exemplified in stark form the conflict between principle and expediency. For the 'stern unbending Tories' the election victory of 1842, the first time a General Election had led to a change of government, signified that the Promised Land had been reached; what more was there to be done save protect the Church and the aristocratic settlement? Peel provided the answer, as he brooded over what contemporaries called 'the condition of England question'. Industrialisation had proceeded apace with urbanisation, but the new towns and cities were often grim places in which to live, and the prosperity and even the survival of their inhabitants depended heavily on the price of food, not least of bread; the duties payable to the Treasury designed to protect home agriculture, kept food prices higher than they should be – or so claimed the first great middle-class pressure group, the anti-Corn Law League, led by two radical MPs, Richard Cobden and John Bright. Trade languished, the economy was sluggish, the national exchequer was in a parlous way; the Whigs had been quick enough to reform when it came to their old constitutional and religious preoccupations, but to the new challenges posed by industrialisation and urbanisation, they had no answer. As the state of their own personal finances might have suggested, economic management was not the strongest Whig suite.

The tensions that would mark all Conservative governments were swiftly and starkly apparent. For the majority of Peel's followers the task of government was to preserve aristocratic government and the position of the Church; many of them came to doubt Peel's commitment to these first principles. In fact, Peel was as firmly committed to these causes as the most mutinous of his MPs; where they differed was over tactics – and here Peel's leadership was defective in the extreme. Facing the economic and social distress of the 'hungry forties', Peel divined correctly that remaining indifferent to it, whilst seeming concerned only to protect its own privileges, would be injurious in the extreme to aristocratic rule. The middle-class activists like Cobden were claiming that an aristocratic parliament would never act against its own short-term economic interests in the wider interest of the nation; Peel was correct to see that the best way of tackling such a charge was to act in the national interest. However, in the highly charged political atmosphere created by the social distress of the early 1840s, where the Chartists and the Anti-Corn Law League competed to see who could turn up the heat most, Peel's technocratic approach to the problems facing him was less helpful than might have been thought.

One of the disadvantages of the fact that so much political history is written by academics is that they tend, perhaps unconsciously, to create the politics which they admire; thus Peel comes close to the *beau idéal* of the academic historian. He was something of an intellectual; he made a good speech and penned a succinct letter; he expressed a clear view of a politics of the national interest which commands admiration and respect; he took a firm stand on that position in defiance of the more partisan sections of his own party: a national, rather than a party leader. Most of this has something to be said for it, but it presents a distorted picture of politics. Arthur Balfour, who was another of those politicians academics admire, showed himself more aware of realities than his admirers when he declared that he would not 'be another Sir Robert Peel to my party'. His uncle Salisbury took a similar view in 1885, much to the chagrin of Gladstone, who could not see why, for the third occasion in his life, the Tories should not solve a national problem at the expense of their unity.

It is not just a modern cliché to call politics a 'rough old trade'. The fourteenth earl of Derby, whose preoccupation with his sporting activities has drawn forth some academic scorn, recognised better than his critics that a political party and a hunt had much in common, and when the moment came, in 1852, he knew that he must show his party some sport, or it would fall apart. The boys on the backbenches needed a good ride in pursuit of their prey, a head of speed and the momentum it brought could take the horses over hedges they would balk at in cold blood, and a view to a kill in the morning, like the sound of the hunting horn, could lift the spirits like nothing else; whether or not the prey was brought to book was not as relevant as the chase itself. In this aspect of party leadership Peel was totally inadequate, and for all the admiration of his academic fan club, this made him ultimately a political failure.

Blake's analysis of the 1841 election victory is correct but seriously misleading. It is true that 1841 was the sole occasion between the reform acts when the Conservatives won as many as 111 of the small boroughs, but the vast majority of their seats came in the counties (124). In the most urbanised seats Peel's Conservatives had only 13 out of 45, which hardly amounted to a mandate to govern in the interest of their inhabitants. One of the many ways in which nineteenth-century politics differed from its twentieth-century successor (except in parts of Ireland and Wales) was the importance attached to religion. The evangelical Tory and son-in-law of Palmerston, Lord Ashley, argued that 'our great force has been Protestantism'; one might make some allowance for his own religious obsessions by adding agricultural protection to the list – before noting that according to surviving poll books, five out of every six Anglicans voted Conservative. In these circumstances, for Peel to embark of reforms which seemed to threaten the Church and agricultural protection was, to put it mildly, unwise; for him to do so in the manner he chose to adopt was disastrous to his party. Those historians who praise the national leader and take the view that free trade was well worth breaking up the Conservative Party for, miss several points, including the central one that by this period, party was becoming the essential vehicle through which politics was conducted.

That Peel's administration should have received a favourable press from history is hardly surprising. If not an assemblage of all the talents, there were few it omitted. It contained five past and future Prime Ministers: Lord Ripon (Goderich as was), Lord Aberdeen, Edward Stanley and Gladstone; it tackled the economic problems besetting the country with a boldness that commanded admiration; it made a real effort to engage with the Irish problem; it attempted to legislate on the 'condition of the people'; and in falling, it inaugurated the great period of free trade which was to coincide with an unprecedented rise in national prosperity and power. The question is whether it could have done these things without wrecking the Conservative Party; and here, although the answer must, of necessity, be ambiguous, it has to be admitted that Peel's style of leadership was a major handicap.

At first sight this might seem surprising. Even his sternest critics, Disraeli, admitted that 'In the Senate he was the easiest, most flexible, and adroit of men. He played upon the House of Commons as on an old fiddle.' His speaking manner, like that of Walpole before him or Baldwin afterwards, was conversational and tended towards the dull. As Disraeli put it: 'His flights were ponderous; he soared with the wings of the vulture rather than the plume of the eagle; and his perorations, when most elaborate, were most unwieldy. In pathos he was quite deficient.' But Peel was an executive politician of the old school. He had entered the Commons in 1809 as MP for the Irish rotten borough of Cashel, and had, from the start, been on what would now be called the fast track to high office. He had first held major office in 1812, when he was appointed Chief Secretary for Ireland, and since then he had been in office continuously whenever his party had been in power. It had been around his political experience and prowess that the demoralised Tories had gathered in the 1830s, and so, in his own mind, Peel had a 'doctor's mandate'; that is a clear run to do what he thought best for the country. That was how men like the Younger Pitt had proceeded.

Peel had served his time, but he was of that class of politician who expected not only to rule, but also for others, less brilliant, to follow him. The Commons was, after all, made up of two types of MP: there was the vast majority who were there because of their local position, men such as the MP for Kings Lynn, Lord George Bentinck who, by his own admission, had 'sate in eight parliaments without having taken part in any great debate'; and then there were the Peels and the Pitts; and Peel was conscious of the proper relationship between the two types: the one existed to vote for measures which the other thought right. As one commentator put it: 'They followed him wherever he led them in blind obedience, and he accepted their allegiance without question, as a tribute justly paid to his masterful intelligence.' Sir Edward Knatchbull, a staunch agriculturalist Tory MP for Kent, noted both the fact of Peel's ascendancy, and its limitations: 'I never in my time saw a minister who possessed more absolute power in the House of Commons than Peel ... In the House he is everything – but there his power ceases. If he was the same in Council, and in all his intercourse with mankind, he would exceed anything this country, or perhaps any other, ever saw, but I fear he is not equal to the situation he fills, and to the times in which he lives.'[3] Harsh though this verdict was, and discount it as we may as coming from one of Peel's severest critics, it must be acknowledged to contain the kernel of truth.

Whether the measures Peel thought himself forced to adopt to the challenges he faced could have commanded the allegiance of the majority of his supporters might be doubted; that they would not, given the manner in which he presented them, became increasingly likely after 1842. His first major act was to introduce the Income Tax. Previously only used during the Napoleonic Wars as an emergency leisure, Peel gave notice of how he regarded the country's economic situation by bringing it in as a temporary measure; no government since that date has been able to dispense with it, despite a noble attempt to promise to abolish it by Gladstone in 1874. This was payable only by those with an income of £150 or more a year, but since all Peel's MPs and supporters fell into this category, it was an admirable example of putting one's money where one's rhetoric lay; the pleas of urgent necessity reconciled Conservative MPs to the measure, but it did nothing to cheer them up.

By setting the level of the income tax as high as he did (Pitt's had been £60 per annum), Peel was showing his increasing conviction that a shift from indirect to direct taxes offered the best remedy for the problems facing the country. Deeply impressed by the distress in the cities and industrial areas, Peel was less so by the grumblings of some of his followers; by May he was telling Gladstone that he would have problems ever again defending the Corn Laws in principle. In a sense this was typical of Peel's virtues – and of his defects. William Gladstone was a bright young politician in his own mould. Another scion of the new wealth created by the Industrial Revolution, Gladstone too had excelled at Oxford and had entered the House early, bound for high ministerial office. Peel admired his talents but wondered about his temperament, and was trying to educate him to the realities of power; this was admirable, but he would have done better to have taken others into his confidence. As Lord Ashley put it: 'Peel has committed great and grievous mistakes in omitting to call his friends frequently together to state his desires and arouse their zeal. A few minutes and a few words would have sufficed';[4] but this was not done. Peel preferred to treat his party as a squadron of troops to be drilled into following orders; and that produced mutiny.

The Duke of Buckingham, known as 'the farmers' friend', resigned from the Privy Seal as early as 1842, in protest against the income tax, and there were grumblings from the agriculturalists about the decision to remove the prohibition on the import of cattle. In 1843 there was a mini-revolt against the proposal to lower the duty on Canadian corn, although, partly thanks to the spirited advocacy of the Colonial Minister, Edward Stanley, the government secured a majority of 83. None of these things was, by itself, a serious threat to Peel's dominance, but each of them helped demoralise the troops and to create a situation in which when he needed to call upon their reserves of loyalty, he would find them wanting. In March 1844, when the government brought forward legislation on working conditions in factories, Lord Ashley brought in an amendment to limit the hours of work for women and children to ten hours a day; a palpable hit at the sanctimonious middle-class factory owners who were funding the anti-Corn Law League, Ashley's bill was passed with the support of 95 Conservatives.

Peel was furious. This went further than he thought judicious, and he demanded another vote to give his followers the chance to recant; they did so – but the grumbling grew. In June 1844, when the government introduced a proposal to lower the duty paid on sugar imported from non-slave sources, Peel faced a major revolt. Many Conservatives recalled that, as part of the bargain by which slavery had been abolished in the British colonies in 1833, it had been promised that West Indian sugar producers, whose costs had been thereby increased, would receive protection from foreign competition; this, it was argued, was a blatant breach of faith. A Conservative amendment to the bill to reduce the duty on colonial sugar was passed, with 62 of Peel's MPs voting in favour of it. Peel, as in March, let it be known that he would resign unless the vote was rescinded, and three nights later the vote was reversed – but only after a tremendous speech from Stanley – his last in the Commons.

It would be easy and tempting in retrospect to read into this a narrative of disintegration, not least because that is what it became; but at this point all was far from lost. It seemed as though Conservative MPs were demanding to be heard by their leaders, and it was by no means the case that they were willing to bring the great minister down. The problem was that Peel was not only not listening, he showed no sign of any willingness to do so on any future occasion; most worrying of all, for those with eyes to see, was the divide opening up between the Cabinet and the party. On both the Factory and the Sugar legislation, the Cabinet voted with Peel, but the backbenchers were, in the majority, on the other side. Having offended the protectionist susceptibilities of his followers, it was unfortunate that circumstances pushed Peel into offending their other main shibboleth – Protestantism.

Of all the baleful effects of the 1801 Act of Union, that upon the government of the day ought to receive a special mention: Ireland brought down Pitt himself in 1801; it effectively destroyed the credibility of Wellington's government in 1829; it precipitated the downfall of Grey's administration in 1833; and in 1845 it provided the occasion for the destruction of Peel's Conservative Party; its later effects, in 1885, 1886, 1911 and 1921 will be noted in due course. Peel, like all British Prime Ministers who had to deal with it, found the Irish question vexing in the extreme; but it was his peculiar fate to have to deal with it at a time of supreme crisis.

It was typical of Peel's cerebral approach to politics that his proposals for Ireland should have ignored the growing economic difficulties confronting a country whose population was rising at a greater rate than the resources available to feed it, and instead have concentrated on the problem of persuading the Irish to identify themselves with the British state; it was also unfortunate, since the former were about to become so overwhelming that they would destroy whatever feeble chance there might have been of achieving the latter. Peel determined to bring forward legislation which would endow the Catholic seminary at Maynooth with an annual grant that would make it possible for it to undertake the task of training priests for the whole island of Ireland. His Protestant critics were horrified.

It was recalled that Peel had, as it were, 'form' on this issue. Known early in his career as 'Orange' Peel because of his defence of the Protestant Ascendancy, his decision to support Catholic Emancipation in 1829 had drawn forth the vitriol of his former admirers: 'Oh member for Oxford, how you shuffle and wheel, you've changed your name from R. Peel to repeal', went one of the less offensive verses penned against him; this was remembered with advantage against him in 1845. If his party was becoming sick of him, the feeling was, it seems, reciprocated. In January 1845 Peel spoke to Gladstone: 'I wish to speak without any reserve. And I ought to tell you it [Maynooth] will probably be fatal to the Government.'[5]

It was a hitherto politically unimportant Conservative backbencher, Benjamin Disraeli, who, in addition to accusing Peel of being a political tyrant, first pointed out what would soon become clear to all. Stating in debate on 28 February 1845 that he had been sent to support a Tory administration, Disraeli jibbed: 'Whether a Tory Ministry exists or not I do not pretend to decide; but I am bound to believe that the Tory majority still remains.' From this observation he drew one startling conclusion: 'I do not think that it is the majority that should cross the House, but only the Ministry.'[6]

2 Stanley and the Protectionists

The success of the free trade lobby was twofold: in 1846 it persuaded Peel and a political majority that its case was unanswerable; ever since, it has persuaded most historians and commentators of the same thing; this had had two effects: in 1846 it broke the Conservative Party; and ever since it has 'produced a widely-held view of the protectionists as mere *révanchistes* and political untouchables'.[1] That both their contemporary opponents, and Peel, took such a view of them, and that one of their own leaders, Disraeli, was sometimes scarcely more flattering, and tried to drop their cause as soon as possible, has served to reinforce such a view of the Protectionists. That there is such an orthodoxy is evidence not of its truth, but of that 'absence of historical sympathy' which usually accompanies studies of the political right. The fact is that there was a very good case in favour of agricultural protection in the 1840s – and there continued to be one for a good deal of time after that. If these things are not appreciated it becomes difficult to understand why the party split in 1846, and why Protection continued to be a popular Conservative cause until the 1850s.

In the past few decades historians have been digesting the impact of the views of Boyd Hilton, who, in a series of important studies, has revolutionised our understanding of the phenomenon of 'liberal Toryism'; it is a measure, perhaps, of the difficulty of summarising his arguments that they have failed to percolate through to the world of the general survey; here, however, it is crucial that this should be done.[2] Where some historians, most notably Peel's most influential modern biographer, Norman Gash, have seen Peel as a pragmatist, Hilton sees him as something of an ideologue; our understanding of this has been limited by our failure to comprehend the nature of the ideology; this, in turn, has been conditioned by our failure to locate Peel within the context provided by contemporary evangelical Christianity. For Hilton, Peel's version of Christianity made him predisposed to see in 'laissez-faire' economics an instrument for the fulfilment of God's will; on this reading the free market was nothing more than the actions of the Holy Spirit, and social and economic paternalism were, therefore, impediments to the wishes of the Divinity. These views were widespread, not least amongst those who supported Peel, such as Sir James Graham and Gladstone, but they were not universal, and they were not shared by many Conservatives, who saw in economic protection a way of preserving a way of life in which values other than those of the market might yet prevail. To see Peel as the paladin of reason with the future on his side is, effectively, to endorse a free market economic view of the world; this may, or may not, be a reasonable thing to do, but it is assuredly not the only view that could be taken. To do this is to at least assume that the Protectionists were motivated by something more than economic and social self-interest; although, of course, just like their opponents, they were *also* moved by such considerations – the saintly politician is a rare phenomenon, and will not trouble us much in these pages.

That there was a coherent and sensible Protectionist case, and that it was central to an understanding both of the nature of early nineteenth-century conservatism, and of the split of 1846 has been established in Anna Gambles' ground-breaking *Protection and Politics* (1999). When the Conservatives opposed to Peel pointed out the connection between the repeal of the Corn Laws and the desire of the manufacturers to reduce the wages of their labourers, they were doing more than making a point about the hypocrisy of Cobden and Bright (although it might be admitted that there is something about the sanctimony of both men which invites such treatment), they were contributing to an argument on the role of government in both welfare and social order. It was commonly accepted that the burdens both of government and of taxation fell upon the owners of land; this was accepted in return for the privileges enjoyed by those who owned the land – a species of social contract, if one liked. But what of the capitalists, those who either owned little land, or whose primary source of income was not thereby derived; their wealth carried with it no responsibilities; was it right for them to press for protection to be taken from the land just so that they could make more money by lowering the wages of their employees? At the heart of the Protectionist critique was the question of how capitalism, commerce and agriculture should coexist, and what their relationship should be to labour. Should Cobdenism prevail, then the capitalist and the consumer would triumph over the landowner and the employee; by the time the consumer remembered that he was also an employee, the capitalist would have taken his dividend and transferred his money to somewhere else where labour was cheaper.

Protectionism recognised that it is only in the short term that everyone seems to benefit from market economics. Conservatives argued that it was an abrogation of real conservatism to ignore the long term, in which, contrary to the pronouncements of the childless economist

Lord Keynes, we may have been dead, but our children would still be living. This view of the present generation as stewards for the future, came naturally to a party of landowners, who deplored the selfish individualism which the capitalists espoused. It was, Bentinck and company argued, real Conservatism to query the liberal economics increasingly espoused by Peel by raising questions about the sort of society that was being created by the new wealth coming from urbanisation and industrialisation; for their pains they would be dismissed as blockheads by Peel, and be subject to the condescension of posterity. Yet, in Dr Gambles' words: 'Conservatives met the challenge of Richard Cobden and the Anti-Corn Law League with a public philosophy of protection as a viable panacea for food policy, stable and sustained manufacturing advance and balanced economic development.'[3]

The Conservative understanding of the constitutional settlement of 1832 helps to explain much of their anger in 1846 – even as their understanding of what happened in the 1911 Parliament Act helps explain their growing resentment before 1914. Before 1832 all types of property had been represented at Westminster: the great and smaller landed properties, upon whose owners fell so much of the burden of governance and financing it; and shipping and colonial interests, through the old pocket boroughs. The Great Reform Act had replaced this unsystematic agglomeration of interests with the enfranchisement of individuals; how were the wider interests of the state to be served in such a system? It was true that it could be argued that Peel's introduction of the income tax reasserted the link between property and the interests of the state, but for the Protectionists that just reinforced the need to retain those fiscal duties which protected the economic interests of property; after all, Cobden and Bright and their ilk had opposed the income tax – showing clearly what their conception of the function of the state should be. Peel's tariff reforms of 1842 were welcomed by many Conservatives as part of a necessary rebalancing of the various interests which needed protecting; they were not against the idea of some easement for the manufacturers in times of distress, but it was all a question of balance. It was here that Peel, in their view, went wrong in 1845–46, when he shifted, in a most unbalanced manner, in the direction of the Anti-Corn Law League; that was not what not many Conservatives had stood for in 1842 – and they would not stand for it now.

Disraeli accused Peel of using the Irish famine as an excuse for repealing the Corn Laws, arguing that he had already come to that opinion some time before; this is hard to refute. Peel's growing conviction in the arguments advanced by the Anti-Corn Law League meant that the issue was not one of if he would repeal the Corn Laws, but rather when he would do so; here the Irish famine came as an unwelcome prod in the right direction.

The timing was bad for Peel in a number of ways. In the first place he was physically very weary. When, at the end of the summer session 1845 Gladstone congratulated him upon his robustness, Peel 'shook his head and complained of the pressure of a sense of *fatigue* upon the brain, I mean a physical sensation.'[4] The concomitant of playing the role of Prime Minister in the way he had chosen had come close to exhausting Peel; this further reduced his already limited ability to act as party leader. He had, as we have seen, always expected his followers to come to heel at his command, now he demanded it; the Irish famine gave to his discourse a sense of urgency which simply served to irritate his opponents all the more. In the second place, although Peel was convinced of the case for repeal, it is by no means clear that he had come to a decision upon its timing. There were good political reasons to wait for a general election before declaring his position of the Corn Laws, and since there did not need to be one of those before 1848, time might have been on his side; but again, Ireland altered the timetable. There were, it was true, arguments that could have been advanced for a temporary suspension of the Corn Laws to help the Irish, but not only were these not very convincing – as Stanley argued, the starving Irish peasantry was hardly in a position to buy any grain, however cheap – they would have meant passing up the opportunity to do something which he was convinced was needful; that was never Peel's style. It was, however, still not inevitable that the Conservative Party would split under the pressure of the Corn Law debate, and there is no reason to suppose that Peel thought that it would. Historians may recoil in simulated weariness from the fierceness of the debates of 1844 and 1845, and, with the wisdom of hindsight declare that a split was inevitable, but to Peel it all showed how robust his party was. There were heated arguments in Cabinet throughout November 1845, and although most ministers were reluctant to push their disagreement with Peel to resigning point, there was one notable exception – Edward Stanley.

The former leader of the Derby dilly had seen his political fortunes stagnate under Peel. His abilities and reputation, as well as his position, secured for him a high place in Cabinet, but he and Peel were never close, and Stanley's talents, being mainly in the oratorical line, were not the sort the Prime Minister most appreciated. For his part, Stanley, dogged by the early onset of the gout that would plague him for the rest of his career, found the business of departmental administration a grind; and he never cared for that sort of thing. In August 1844, pleading the need to bring some assistance to the ageing Duke of Wellington, who nominally led in the Lords, Stanley took advantage of the constitutional convention which allowed heirs to a peerage to seek translation to the Upper House in the lifetime of their father by taking one of the family's lesser titles; so it was as Baron Stanley of Bickerstaffe that Edward Stanley left the Commons in the summer of 1844. It was a fortuitous transference. Ironically, had he remained in the Commons, those oratorical talents, which had been at a general discount for most of Peel's administration, would have been invaluable; being the man he was, Stanley would have been bound to have taken up a partisan position, and had he done so on the side of the Protectionists, he would surely have incurred as much of their wrath as did Disraeli, and, instead of being a possible figure around whom reunion could occur, he would have been almost as divisive as his future deputy. As it was, Stanley was able to state his case in the privacy of the Cabinet and the dullness of the Lords.

Stanley declared that he was perfectly willing to put aside all considerations of consistency, capacity and even foresight: 'but I must bear in mind that our support of the Corn Laws has been our main inducement to others to give us ... support.' He took the view that to repeal them in the present circumstances would be to give the impression of 'hasty flight from our position, in consequence of clamour, aided by most unfortunate but temporary circumstances'. Stanley's position was consonant with the general protectionist position. As the heir to a great estate, he knew that aristocratic leadership rested, ultimately, upon consent. He sat in the Cabinet as a representative of the wider interests of the community, and for him, the question was 'whether the legislative power is to rest with the land and those connected with it, or with the manufacturing interests of the country'. On the one side he saw that network of interconnected interests which made up the common good; on the other a bunch of avaricious capitalists who wished to put their interest above all others – and who did not scruple to stir up a popular unrest in pursuit of their selfish aims. Stanley was also asserting the importance of a lesson which Peel had sought to impress upon his followers – that in the circumstances of modern politics, party mattered, and leaders ought not to act in a way that failed to command the confidence of their followers. Peel had been in favour of such a doctrine since the 1830s – but now he was to find it being cited against him. Faced by Stanley's threat to resign, Peel decided that the whole government should quit instead; he asked the Queen to find an alternative Prime Minister.

What followed was something of a farce. Queen Victoria turned to the leader of the Whigs, Lord John Russell. Russell was evidently much embarrassed, and inclined to agree with his former colleague Lord Minto, who wrote to him on 18 December 1845 that: 'The more calmly I contemplate the prospect before us, the more strongly do I feel the inexpediency of your undertaking the government, if it can be honestly avoided; and I cannot but think it much more for the public advantage – and in a party sense, much more to your advantage – that Peel should be compelled to bear the burden ... .'[5] Perhaps fortuitously (or not) an 'honest' excuse presented itself in the form of an unseemly personal dispute between Lord Grey and the former Foreign Secretary, Palmerston. Grey took the view that Palmerston's return to the Foreign Office would have a fatal effect upon Britain's foreign policy, and refused to serve any government which placed Palmerston there; since Palmerston declined to serve in any other position, Russell declared the whole thing impossible and threw in a hand he had never wanted. The Queen turned again to Peel, who accepted office, despite Stanley's refusal to serve.

Views upon Peel's action varied according to one's prejudices. Palmerston, always the most conservatively inclined of Whigs, told Russell on 5 January 1846 that he thought that: 'Peel has on the whole mended his position by resigning, for he has gained some good recruits for his Cabinet, and, having taken the benefit of the act, he is free from his former engagements and sets up business as a new man.' He was not convinced by those who argued that 'Peel's new government cannot last three months, so great is the furies of the Tories against him';[6] not for the last time, Palmerston's sanguine temperament rendered him unable to understand the passions of others. For Lord George Bentinck, who was coming to the fore as one of those determined to oppose his titular leader, there was something puzzling about Peel's 'motives in resigning', and then returning: 'I incline ... to think it all a trick to make it more easy for him to carry on the government upon his new principles'; he suspected that Peel hoped to frighten 'a great body of the Landed Aristocracy into submission' by brandishing the spectacle of a Whig administration.[7] If Peel had thought that such a prospect would have the effect it had had throughout the previous decade, that of uniting the party, he was very wrong; as Bentinck told his father on 2 January 1846: 'the cry of "No Surrender" seems very general.' Peel may have believed in Free Trade; his party did not.

Peel's party was wrecked by a fatal combination of circumstances: his own conception of the function of party came into conflict with his perception of the national interest, and whilst the latter won, for his followers there was no such conflict, which was why they were willing to lose him and most of the Cabinet; this was exacerbated by the emergence of a triune leadership for the Protectionists, which both rallied the opposition to him, undermined him, and provided an alternative to him. Of all the correctives that need to be made to the Blakean picture of the Conservative Party, the one most needful concerns the roles of the triumvirate who deposed and replaced Peel. The need for the restoration of what might be called 'the view from Knowsley' will be an ongoing theme of this chapter and the next, and will be considered in its place; Bentinck and Disraeli, however, need to be considered here.

Blake takes the common view that Bentinck (or 'the Jockey', as he was known because of his racing interests) was an entirely destructive force, a hitherto obscure backbencher, who briefly and devastatingly erupted onto the scene in 1846, only to die, fortuitously for his party, in 1849; his role was to act as guarantor for Disraeli, and to rally the country gentlemen of England to the 'Jew'. More recently, however, emphasis has been placed on the centrality of Bentinck to the case being made against Peel. Bentinck 'was a whig of 1688 … modified by all the experience of the present age'.[8] A younger son of the Duke of Portland, he had sat as MP for King's Lynn almost for time out of mind, without ever troubling the House over much. He belonged to that class of MP thought of by men like Peel as lobby fodder. A Canningite by family connection (his mother's sister was married to Canning), Bentinck had followed his relative and then rejected Wellington and Peel in 1828. He had followed the Canningites into the Whig coalition in 1830, before climbing aboard the Derby dilly in 1833, by which he was conveyed into the Conservative ranks. As early as 1841 he took the view that 'in honour Sir Robert Peel can not … break that bargain' that he had made by pledging to keep agricultural protection, and by 1846, seething with rage, he shouted on the floor of the House that Peel's 'political lying and pledge-breaking', would fatally undermine public confidence in aristocratic government. Lord George Bentinck was one of their own, and his language and his bluntness appealed to the gentlemen of England who felt 'sold out' by Peel. The most recent and thorough account of Bentinck's role concludes that: 'the fall of Peel is often seen as a joint operation in which Disraeli's philippics complemented Bentinck's influence on the rank and file. In reality Bentinck was throughout the dominant partner without whom the job might not have been done.'[9] It was Bentinck who dictated the tactics that kept the party in relentless pursuit of Peel's destruction, Bentinck who best expressed and injected into the political bloodstream the vitriol felt by his kind against Peel, and Bentinck who argued that Protection was a coherent and viable system which worked in the national, rather than the sectional interest.

To accept this is to begin the process of reassessing the role played by Disraeli. The early death of Bentinck and the accidents of history which produced no major biography of the fourteenth earl of Derby before the twenty-first century, have, along with the intrinsic fascination of his own character, propelled Disraeli to the centre of the stage at least a quarter of a century before he really occupied that position. History, like nature, abhors a vacuum, and in the absence of serious studies of either Bentinck or Stanley (who did not become the fourteenth earl of Derby until 1852), historians have rushed in to give Disraeli all the credit he always claimed for himself. This makes for a good story, but bad history.

This is not to deny the role Disraeli played between 1844 and 1846, merely to place it into its proper perspective. His novels, *Sybil* and *Coningsby* did, indeed, hold Peel up to ridicule and provide historians with a quarry from which to hew fragments which could be fitted together into a Disraelian memorial, but without Bentinck and what he represented, Disraeli would have remained a marginal figure. The revolt against Peel was the product of a genuine grass-roots Conservative movement – the so-called 'Anti-League', which developed across more than a hundred constituencies during 1843 and 1844; coordinated by the Duke of Richmond's Central Protection Society; it was this body which provided the votes which not only sank Peel, but which ensured the survival of the Conservative Party.[10]

Their Conservative message, enunciated by Bentinck and Stanley was the call for a genuinely national creed that would protect both landowners and workers from the selfishness of the free trade clique. Disraeli's function was somewhat different. His message was the secondary theme of his leaders – that of the role of party, and Peel's failure to live up to his own conception of what that should be. As he put it in the Commons on 11 April 1846: 'If you are to have a popular government, if you are to have a parliamentary administration, the conditions antecedent are, that you should have a government which declares the principles upon which its policy is founded, and you can then have on them the wholesome check of a constitutional opposition.' In a series of sarcastic and cutting speeches, he ridiculed Peel and shook his hitherto unassailable hold on the Commons. 'The right hon. Gentleman', he declared in February 1845, in a phrase what would become immortal, 'caught the Whigs bathing, and walked away with their clothes'; *The Times* noted 'much cheering and great laughter', at this sally, and in truth, this was Disraeli's greatest contribution to the Protectionist cause – to raise morale and to show that Peel could be bested. These were important contributions, and they raised Disraeli to a parliamentary prominence he was never to lose; but he was neither trusted nor liked, and for the next quarter of a century his existence would be parasitic on the one man of undoubted ministerial calibre on the Protectionist side of the debate – Lord Stanley.

Bentinck's tactics during the first half of 1846 ensured that Peel would not be able to dissolve Parliament and go to the country. On 25 June 1846, 69 Conservatives voted with the Whigs against the government's Irish coercion bill; it was a blatant attempt to do what it did – namely to bring Peel down in a manner that would oblige the Whigs to replace him. As Lord John Russell now, mysteriously, managed to form an administration with little trouble, the Protectionist party looked to the future – and that meant Stanley.

The centrality of the role of Edward Stanley to the history of the Conservative Party in the nineteenth century is firmly established in Angus Hawkins' masterly two-volume study, which is one of those rare studies that revolutionises its field. It rested on three pillars: position; talent; and experience. Stanley had been identified as the 'coming man' as early as 1830, and it was only thanks to a mixture of ill fortune and bad judgements that his political position had become becalmed; he remained one of the great orators of the age, and was, after 1846, the only man of Prime Ministerial calibre on the Protectionist benches. Stanley was the heir to the earldom of Derby, one of the oldest peerages in the country; he owned thousands of acres and had an annual income of more than £100,000; although his grandson was sometimes known as 'the king of Lancashire', this description could have been more accurately applied to the fourteenth earl of Derby, as he became in 1852. Stanley had brains, talent and wealth – and in the context of 1846 this would have been more than enough to secure him the leadership of the Protectionists; but he had something equally valuable – the qualifications to reunite the party.

Stanley was not at all sure that he wanted to lead the Protectionists; indeed, although they had wanted him as their leader before the defeat of Peel, it was only afterwards that he accepted the position – and then largely because he saw himself as the person best suited to reunite the party. Gladstone, whose quixotic decision to resign over the Maynooth grant on the grounds that it contradicted an opinion he had expressed in his book, but which he no longer held, had kept him out of the Commons during the bitter philippics over the Corn Laws, was quite happy that those who followed Peel should support the new, minority, Whig government, but as he told Peel himself: 'if so much confidence is due to them, much more is it due towards friends from whom we differed on the single question of Free Trade'.[11] That this 'single issue' contained within itself a host of differences, was something which would become apparent only over time. To men looking for reunion, Stanley was the ideal man; immensely experienced; a man of political substance; he was also the sole leading Protectionist who had not raised the political temperature during the Corn Law debates by insulting Peel. There was no alternative to Stanley – which left Stanley with no alternative.

The historical fate of the House of Stanley in the nineteenth century is a curious illustration of the workings of fate. In Blake's account, as in most others, the fourteenth earl of Derby stands in Disraeli's shadow – which is an exact reversal of contemporary reality; the reasons are not, however, far to seek. Disraeli sought publicity in his lifetime and he was the subject of two extremely good biographies at either end of the twentieth century; the massive six-volume official biography begun by William Flavelle Monypenny in 1910, and finished by George Buckle in 1920, was replete with copious quotations from Disraeli's extremely quotable writings, and fixed him firmly as the apostle of Tory Democracy; and, in 1966, Robert Blake published what was to become the classic modern life, which refashioned Disraeli for the age of Harold Wilson and Ted Heath, presenting him as the supreme political tactician. Both biographies were firmly based on the mass of Disraeli's papers; both were well written, and both presented a Disraeli for their times. Contrast the fate of Derby. His son, Edward, sponsored no biography, nor did his second son, Frederick, who became the sixteenth earl in 1893. A pot-boiler by the Tory hagiographer, T. E. Kebbel, in 1892 would be followed in 1958 by another study by William Devereux Jones, but since neither had access to Derby's papers, nor those of most of his contemporaries, the view remained the one from Disraeli's vantage point. Robert Blake undertook to fill this historiographical chasm after his *Disraeli* appeared, but the book was hardly begun, let alone finished. Had it not been for Robert Stewart's excellent volume on *The Politics of Protection* (1971), and his volume in the Longman's history of the Conservative Party, *The Foundation of the Conservative Party 1830–1867* (1978), Derby's role might have gone quite unheralded. It is only with Angus Hawkins' triumphant two volumes on Derby (2007 and 2008) that he can now take his proper place on the historical stage.

Stanley, or Derby as he became in June 1851, was simply the dominant figure on the Conservative side of politics from 1846 until his retirement in 1868. His wealth and social standing gave him an unshakeably solid position, which was bolstered by his pre-eminent talents as an orator and politician. It was, perhaps, part of his misfortune at the hands of posterity that the first of the political diaries of his era to be published, as early as 1885, was that of Charles Greville, who loathed him. Greville was one of those minor figures on the fringes of politics whose name is secured by his diaries, which are full of witty malice and gossip; his dislike of Stanley stemmed from the way in which the latter condescended to Greville, and he took his revenge in his diaries, portraying him as an amateur politician, addicted to the pleasures of the turf and the shoot; modern academics, little disposed to either pursuit, have proved easy dupes. Stanley certainly was an habitué of the turf, as were so many of his contemporaries, and it was there, and on the shooting stand that he won the confidence of the average Conservative MP; he was one of them. And so he was, but raised to a much higher power. Far from being a distraction from his political position, Stanley's sporting interests were a support for it; even the most inarticulate Protectionist could see in Stanley those things he admired most; breeding and the sporting temperament. That he could turn from the turf to politics in a moment was evidence not that he was a dilettante, but that he was one of the commanding figures of mid-nineteenth-century politics.

For all that, however, Stanley's career never quite went where he wanted it to go. He had failed to establish himself as the leader of the political centre in the 1830s because of Peel, and his second attempt so to do in the period after 1846 came to grief on the same rock. Stanley's reasons for staying out of the Cabinet Peel formed in December 1845 have already been recorded; in his eyes, repealing the Corn Laws was incompatible with his own personal honour, which meant that it would bring discredit on him, and the rest of the Conservatives, to follow Peel's lead. That did not mean that he meant to break with Peel permanently. His aim was to try to preserve the Conservative Party as a force against the sort of radicalism represented by Cobden and Bright. He told his old friend Ellenborough in December 1845 that: 'though it is difficult to foresee the future, my own opinion is that my official life is over, and I am well content that it should be so. The political current seems steadily setting in a direction which leaves me high and dry on the breach.'[12] Too much should not be read into this last comment. Stanley was much given to moments of gloomy melancholia – usually when the gout was upon him, or the tides of politics were against him. In December 1852, after his first administration had fallen, he told his son and heir Edward that: 'I knew as long ago as 1845 that I was playing a losing game: I said so then: I thought I was left high and dry forever: the tide has risen once, high enough to float me again, which was more than I expected: it will never do so again: the game is lost, but I think it ought to be played, and I will play it out to the last.'[13] This pose as the last of the Romans, holding the citadel against the inevitable barbarian victory, was a fancy which pleased Stanley's classical, and gloomy, caste of mind, and there were, no doubt, moments when it represented how he really felt; but few multi-millionaires with a range of other diversions devote a quarter of a century to playing a 'losing game'.

To call Stanley the accidental leader of the Protectionists is true at a number of levels, but it misses an important truth. Certainly he had never aspired to lead the Protectionists. His friend Malmesbury noted that when a group of Protectionist peers decided to 'look upon' him as their leader, Stanley was 'much pleased and flattered';[14] but, not so pleased that he accepted. Stanley knew he was born to leadership, and if he condescended to take on the leaderless Protectionists, it was so that he could weld together the old fragments of the Conservative Party and make it new. So often portrayed as a gloomy dilettante who presided over the Protectionists until Disraeli could take over and move things forward, Stanley was, in reality, central to the survival of the Conservatives, and he was a skilful and determined politician who, despite increasing ill-health, ruled his party with the authority which attached to his lineage, wealth and political skills. For 20 years he was the key figure on the Conservative side of the House, and it is a mark of his determination that neither poor health nor political ill-fortune drove him from his path, and that, at the end, when the chance fell to him to change the destiny of his party, he seized it.

As one who had been but tangentially involved in the late unpleasantness over the Corn Laws, Stanley was in an ideal position to unite the party – being the only figure respected by both its wings; but he was frustrated in these hopes by the attitude of the fallen ministers. As Gladstone later recalled: 'from 1846 to 1850, Sir Robert Peel and Sir James Graham adopted as the leading principle of their action the vital necessity of keeping the Protectionists out of office'. He did not think that 'in this course of action they were moved by personal animosity', opining that it 'sprang entirely from a belief' by Peel that once in power, the Protectionists would 'endeavour to establish a policy in accordance with the designation of their party'.[15] One might discount a little Gladstone's first comment, since it is clear that Peel in particular did nurse some unchristian sentiments towards those who had destroyed his government, and he would, indeed, have had to have been a candidate for canonisation not to have done so; but his second comment is a reminder of something that historians have sometimes forgotten – that Protection remained a force in British politics for the next five years.

For as long as he lived, Peel took the view that whatever their defects, it was better to have the Whigs in power than to let the Protectionists in; with nearly 120 supporters before the 1847 general election, this was easily done; and even with about half that number afterwards, the 'Peelites' as they became known, remained numerous enough to keep the Whigs in office. He told Gladstone: 'I foresee a tremendous struggle in this country for the restoration of Protection; and he knew where he and his followers must stand in such an event. But this attitude of Peel's was combined with a 'determination to hold himself aloof from party and not to contemplate the resumption of office', which effectively made his followers political eunuchs. But however much younger men like Gladstone might wish to enter into 'arrangements of convenience' with 'some other section of the House of Commons', he, and the other 'Peelites', 'all felt the great and special difficulty' which Peel's attitude caused. He was willing to go so far as to let his followers constitute themselves into a voting bloc in the House, but beyond that he would not go.[16]

This was part of the reason Stanley's hopes were frustrated. He had hoped that after the 1847 election there might be movement toward reunion; but Peel's attitude effectively vetoed it. The other reason there was no progress towards unity was that Peel was correct in noting the increasing importance of the Protection issue. If the argument is accepted that 'Protection' covers a Conservative mindset quite different from the liberal-conservative attachment to Free Trade, then it was only to be expected that the politics of the late 1840s should be dominated by the struggle between the two positions. The parliamentary arithmetic was not so decisive as to rule out a reintroduction of the Corn Laws, which, in any event, would not be totally abolished until 1849. The Conservatives who followed Stanley won about 243 seats in July 1847, more than half of which were county constituencies; there were about 89 Peelites, and on the government side 324 MPs; Conservative reunion could deliver another period in power – but on what terms?

It is a function of hegemonic discourse that it forecloses on certain ways of thinking; thus historians have generally written about Protection after 1846 as though it was something that Stanley was anxious to dump as soon as possible; this is based upon three misleading readings of events: it accepts the Free Trade version of history, which presents 1846 as the moment at which the reactionaries were confined to the margins as Britain forged ahead to the Free Trade future; it ignores the full range of meanings contained within the 'Protectionist' label; and it treats Disraeli's disreputable opportunism of 1849, when he did indeed argue that protection should be dumped, as normative; a different reading is offered here.

In the first place, it was by no means clear in 1846 that Free Trade had won the day – or that it was a good thing if it had. The repeal of the Corn Laws would not be complete before 1849, and almost immediately, a series of bad harvests hit English agriculture hard, making Stanley's followers even more certain that they had been correct in seeing free trade as heralding the ruin of the landed interest. Blake and others are correct to see a desire for consistency as part of the reason that Stanley stuck with Protection; but it was not, as they sometimes suppose, the only reason. When he presented a petition from Lancashire to the Lords in July 1850, Stanley showed how wide was the constituency upon which he could call: certainly, as one would expect, the landowners were there calling for the reintroduction of Protection, but so too were manufacturers, tradesmen and artisans;[17] Protection was not construed as a purely agricultural issue. As the Conservative journalist and propagandist, Sir Archibald Alison argued, in accepting the repeal of the Corn Laws Peel had 'made himself not the representative of a nation, but of a section of the nation'. Free Trade, it was argued, benefited one part of the country – the cotton, iron and wool exporters – at the expense of the nation as a whole; the power of the consumer to purchase manufactured goods would, it was claimed, decline; agricultural depression from 1848 to 1852, and the sluggish performance of the manufacturing sector of the economy in 1848–49 all reinforced such arguments. For historians to laud Disraeli's attempt in 1849 to drop Protection as a sign of his far-sightedness, is to miss the elephant in the room, so to speak; downstream it may, indeed, have become necessary to discard Protection, but to try to do so in 1849 showed how little Disraeli understood his own party.

The main weakness of the Conservatives after 1847 was not its voting strength in Parliament, nor yet its main cause – it was its leadership in the Commons. Bentinck was a good man to lead the hunt against Peel, but as a party leader he was hopeless. Opinionated and quick-tempered, he was a difficult man with whom to work, and it occasioned little surprise and even less regret when he resigned in 1847. It was typical of Bentinck that he should have done so because of his liberal stand on the Jewish disabilities bill; a Canningite to the end, he could not, he said, bear to stay when 'the great Protectionist party' had 'degenerated into a "No Popery", "No Jew" party.'[18] Lord George remained, however, a potent talisman, and when, at the beginning of the 1848 session Stanley allowed the Whips to send a circular to those who were 'Conservatives', it drew forth a typically brutal response from Bentinck: 'I know nothing of *this* "Conservative Party", I gave my adherence to the "*Protectionist Party*" and to no other ... I acknowledge nothing in the

"*Conservative Party*" but an "Organised Hypocrisy".'[19] The author of that phrase, Disraeli, was not, however, even considered for the place vacated by Bentinck; that was designated for the Marquis of Granby, a man who was, to adopt a much later phrase, indubitably 'one of us'. Heir to the Duke of Rutland, Granby was an amiable fellow liked by all, but so aware of his own shortcomings that he declined to take the lead in the Commons.

During the debates of 1848 Disraeli showed his undoubted talent as a parliamentarian, but as Derby noted 'superior ability and power in debate' would 'not alone do'; he well knew that 'personal influence' was essential and that 'in this respect Disraeli labours under disadvantages which I do not think he can overcome'.[20] That Disraeli was able, two decades after this was written, to become leader of the whole party, owed much to Derby's leadership, which enabled him to partly overcome his 'disadvantages'.

3 Derby's Conservatives

Recent scholarship, in particular Angus Hawkins' magisterial study of Derby, and Geoff Hicks' revisionist account of Conservative thinking on foreign policy in the 1850s, helps pave the way to a more balanced view of the Conservative Party during its wilderness years; this, of necessity, involves a recalibration of the role played by Disraeli.[1] Interesting as he is, and fascinating as he remains, and significant as his leadership was, Disraeli does not take centre stage before the 1860s, and to write as though his (sometimes rather odd) views were Conservative policy before that date betrays the paucity of historical accounts that would enable him to be placed into his proper context.

When Stanley wrote about Disraeli's 'disadvantages', they included his 'superior ability and power'. Harold Macmillan was apt to comment that he had had to live down the reputation of being an intellectual in order to become the party's leader, and it is hard to think of any other party in which being called 'too clever by half' would be considered a devastating put down, as it was when 'Bobbety', fifth Marquess of Salisbury applied those words to Iain Macleod. The best compliment a Conservative can be paid is to be called 'sound'. Baldwin, who was preeminent in that, if in no other quality, spoke for the party as a whole when he told Lord Birkenhead (amongst whose many great qualities no one would have included soundness) that the country preferred 'second-class intellects with first-class characters, to first-class intellects with second-class characters'; there were plenty who would have considered the ascription of even a second-class character to 'Dizzy' too much of a compliment.

For all the attempts by some to play it down, there can be no real doubt that Disraeli's Jewishness was a factor in the distrust he aroused; it can be called endemic and even mild, but of the existence of a strain of anti-semitism in the attacks made on Disraeli there can be no doubt. It was not just that he was a Jew, it was that he was a very Jewish-looking Jew; nor was this the end of it. He was a disreputable Jewish literary fellow with a highly questionable past, appalling taste in tailors, and a glib line in political patter; to the average Conservative, he was to be distrusted on sight. Even Stanley was not immune to this visceral feeling. Writing in February 1846, he told his colleague, the earl of Wilton: 'I know Disraeli has the feeling I dislike

31

him … [and] I certainly have no personal prepossession in his favour.'[2] Back in 1832 Stanley had suspected Disraeli of entangling his brother, Henry, into some disreputable company, and whatever the truth of the matter, it was thought to be entirely plausible that this might have been the case.[3] Disraeli had become heavily indebted even before he reached his majority, and his ability to stay one step ahead of the bailiffs was, as everyone knew, greatly enhanced by his election as an MP in 1837; MPs could not be imprisoned for debt. His marriage to a wealthy widow kept both wolves and other predatory beasts from the door, but did nothing to quiet those who thought Disraeli a designing rogue who had married an older widow solely for her money. It was typical of his chutzpah to later admit the offence, but to add that if he had to marry her again, he would do so for love; such comments caused almost as much offence as the behaviour they related to. His novel writing was hardly a help to his cause. The early productions were lightweight society novels which, in truth, said more about his aspirations to be in Society than they did of his experience of it; whilst the great novels of the mid-1840s may have been cutting satires on Peel's management of his party, they hardly suggested an orthodox mindset. That was only fair, since even on the rare occasions he tried, Disraeli had the greatest of difficulty in being an orthodox Conservative.

Ability may not be everything, or even, at times, anything, in the Conservative Party, but the ability to speak on the floor of the Commons is not given to everyone, and he who has it wields a formidable weapon; through its use Gladstone overcame the doubts about his character, as did Winston Churchill; and however distrusted he might have been as Lord Birkenhead, the young F. E. Smith made his way towards the 'glittering prizes' with the sharp sword of his oratory; so too did Disraeli. It was this talent which brought him to the attention of Bentinck, who found him an admirable partner. One of the things his flamboyance served to conceal was the hard work Disraeli put into his politics; in the age of the amateur, he was supremely professional. He made himself the master of the arcane procedures of the Commons, and his assiduity in attending debates won the reluctant admiration even of some of his critics. But it was the cutting edge of his tongue and the readiness of his wit which made him feared; and fear commands a type of respect. As Bentinck noted with satisfaction in March 1848: 'Cobden writhes and quails under him just as Peel did in 1846 [and in spite of] … Lord Stanley … it will end before two sessions are out in Disraeli being the chosen leader of the party.'[4]

Bentinck's support did much to make Disraeli less unacceptable to some MPs, and before his early death in 1849, Lord George had taken one important further step towards making Disraeli acceptable; with the aid of his brother, the Duke of Portland, he had been able to help raise a mortgage to buy Disraeli a small country estate at Hughenden in Buckinghamshire. At least, as the squire of Hughenden, Disraeli could start to look like the sort of chap who might lead the Conservatives in the Commons – provided, that was, that one was spared the sight of him trying to pretend to ride to hounds. To the end, Disraeli remained a figure of the salons and the smoking rooms – which was why he always needed Stanley who, uniquely, was as at home on the hunting field as he was in the drawing room or the debating chamber. Disraeli started by being the parliamentary equivalent to a hired hand, a man whose oratorical skills made him necessary; slowly, by his assiduity in parliamentary affairs, he made himself indispensable to Derby, but he remained Derby's 'man of business', and it was only during the political drama of 1866 and 1867 that he showed he had the stature needed by a party leader; and even after that there remained grave doubts about him. There can rarely have been a Prime Minister who had so many colleagues join his Cabinet in order to keep him in check.

The prevailing mistrust of Disraeli can be seen even in early 1849 when it was becoming clear that the Conservatives could not do without his debating talent in the Commons. Stanley thought it sufficient to suggest to him that he should form part of a triumvirate with Granby and that antediluvian survivor from the days of Liverpool, J. C. Herries; there was a depth of hurt in his refusal: 'I am Disraeli the adventurer and I will not acquiesce in a position which will enable the party to make use of me, and then throw me aside.' But Stanley would have none of this melodramatic self-pity, and pointed out to Disraeli that 'the lead of the Commons was a question to be decided by the party in that house' and not by him, and that it had 'raised strong objections' to Disraeli. When Disraeli had another flounce and threatened to go away and write more novels, Stanley's response was typically robust: 'All this is very well, but the position is one which you cannot hold. Peel has tried it, and you see how his influence is gone'; he warned Disraeli that if he did take himself off, he would lose his position altogether. He declined, he said, to apply the epithet 'adventurer' to Disraeli: 'but this I will say, that certain feelings exist, call them prejudices if you will, that will make many of our friends desire, in the man who is to lead them, a degree of station and influence which circumstances have not as yet enabled you to acquire.'[5] It was good advice – but Disraeli always had trouble taking good advice.

Although Stanley had not mentioned it, high on the list of the disadvantages of having Disraeli in a leading position was the fact that 'he was the most powerful *repellent* we could offer to any repentant or hesitating Peelites.'[6] Disraeli continued to formally decline the position he had been offered, but in practice, throughout the 1849 session he worked with Granby and Herries, and no one who thought about the shape of a future Conservative government could doubt which of the three would lead it in the Commons; as early as March, Herries was declaring his willingness to give way.

One of the concomitants of Disraeli's character was that those who doubted it seldom had long to wait for ammunition. In October 1849 Disraeli decided that the time had come to bury Protection since it was an obstacle to power and place; Stanley's response was a magisterial rebuke telling him to recant: 'I am firmly convinced that the public mind is beginning to be impressed with the conviction that Free Trade has proved a delusion ... Our hold on the public mind is our adherence to the principles for which we have contended'.[7] As would be the case throughout their collaboration, once Stanley had spoken, it was his view that prevailed.

Read backwards, history is lived, as it were, forwards, and whilst we know that the two decades after 1846 would be ones of frustration and opposition for the Conservatives, at the time it seemed quite otherwise. From 1846 through to 1852 the governing combination was not even a coalition, and Russell's feeble and palsied leadership gave every hope to those opposing him; without Peel the Whigs would have faltered. Nor were the coalitions forged first by Aberdeen and then, more lastingly, by Palmerston any more stable. Had the cards fallen slightly differently, Stanley's hopes of power would have been realised. As it was, his opponents, whilst fumbling the ball several times, never quite managed to lose it – despite Russell's ingenious attempts to do so in the early 1850s.

For all that his survival depended upon Peelite support, Russell managed to effectively alienate it during 1850. First came the infamous Don Pacifico debate in June 1850, when Russell found himself having to support his belligerent Foreign Secretary, Palmerston, against charges that he had behaved in a heavy-handed way in a dispute with Greece over its treatment of a Gibralterian Jew who claimed British citizenship. Palmerston defended himself in the only great oration of his career, claiming the right of British subjects to imitate the Roman of old to hold himself immune from foreign persecution by claiming 'civis Romanus sum'. Gladstone, in particular, found the arrogance of Imperial pride in such a statement impossible to support, and heavily criticised Palmerston; as did Peel, in what turned out to be his last appearance in the Commons; on the way home he fell from his horse and died of the injuries he sustained.

Leaderless they may have been, but the Peelites knew well how to respond to Russell's attempt to recapture public support with an outburst of anti-Catholicism. In an effort to regain the initiative, Russell had recourse to what might be called ancestral prejudices by taking up the cause of 'no popery'. In 1850 Pope Pius IX created Archbishop Wiseman Cardinal-Archbishop of Westminster and 'restored' the Roman Catholic hierarchy in England, dividing it into 12 sees with territorial titles. Admittedly Pius IX had been, even by his standards, monumentally tactless in his Papal Brief, describing the Church of England as 'the Anglican Schism'; and it ought also to be admitted that Wiseman, in his enthusiasm, had outdone his pontiff in a flowery epistle 'From the Flaminian Gate'; and it ought to be remembered that only five years before the Vicar of St Mary's, Oxford, John Henry Newman, had gone over to Rome, sparking fears that the Oxford Movement was nothing more than the Roman equivalent of a Trojan Horse; but even when all these things are taken into account, Russell's reaction was so extreme as to be inexcusable: as Talleyrand had said on another occasion: 'It was worse than a crime, it was a folly.'

If Pius IX and Wiseman were writing epistles, why so too would that doughty Protestant champion Lord John Russell. So it was that Maltby, the bishop of Durham, found himself in receipt of one of the oddest letters to come from the pen of a British Prime Minister; in it Russell denounced papal 'insolence', and staked his claim to be the defender of Protestantism and its institutions. Now this might have been pleasing unto the eyes and ears of those frequenters of Nonconformist tabernacles who looked to Lord John to do the work of another and greater Lord, but it was a little ripe for many of his fellow Whigs, whose ability to take a relaxed tone on such matters amounted to part of their group identity; they, however, might have been expected to take an indulgent view towards the foibles of their leader. The Peelites shared neither an hereditary fondness for the House of Russell, nor the habits of the conventicle-haunters, and priding themselves upon their religious tolerance were disturbed by Russell's opening sentences; reading on, some of them were appalled, for the Prime Minister went on to lambaste the Puseyite and the Tractarians, calling them 'unworthy sons of the Church of England' who were trying to restore the superstitious mummeries of Popery. Since Gladstone was himself that way inclined, it was no wonder he described it as 'disgraceful', but Sir James Graham, who was not, spoke for many when he called it 'hasty, intemperate, and ill-advised'.[8]

Lord Stanley, whose Churchmanship was of a similar hue to Russell's on this issue, thought rather well of the 'Durham Letter', which was probably wise given the views of many of his followers. Disraeli was usually a good barometer of the views of the average Conservative MP on Church matters since, lacking any real feel for them, he tended to fall back on what he took to be the popular view. Writing to that pillar of old Toryism, Lord Londonderry in November 1850, he commented, apropos of the restoration of the Catholic hierarchy that: 'The people are very much alarmed in this country. Even the peasants think they are going to be burned alive.'[9] Such feelings made Russell temporarily immensely popular – in every quarter save the one that mattered in terms of parliamentary arithmetic. His introduction in 1851 of an Ecclesiastical Titles Act, which forbade the Roman Catholics to adopt the titles of any existing Anglican Sees, lost him the support of the Peelites just when he needed it most. In February 1851 he lost a vote on a motion to equalise the borough and country franchises, and, worn out by his labours, and the constant struggle with his domineering Foreign Secretary, Palmerston, Russell resigned his office; this time, however, it was the Conservatives who declined to take the poisoned chalice, handing it back to Lord John until the very dregs were consumed.

Lord John advised the Queen to send for Stanley. If evidence were ever needed that the proximity of power makes politicians behave in strange ways, the comings and goings of February 1851 could stand as a proof-text. Asked for his view by the Queen, Stanley advised her to send for the Peelite leader, Lord Aberdeen. 'It is', he told his son, 'a bungling fisherman who strikes at the first nibble: I shall wait till my fish has gorged the bait, and then I am sure to land him.'[10] Under the impression that he was being summoned to form a government, Aberdeen was correspondingly (and characteristically) glum when he realised that the Queen wanted him to attempt a 'junction' with Lord John; this, he told her, he could not do because of the disapproval of his colleagues for Russell 'Durham Letter'.

Stanley also refused to consider giving up Protection. To do so, he told the Queen and Prince Albert would so damage his party and his own reputation for honour and consistency, that it would destroy his position in politics. Stanley was bound to try to achieve his objective of bringing the Peelites back, and Disraeli even offered to stand aside as leader of the House if it would help net the biggest fish of all, Gladstone. This was either an act of uncharacteristic generosity, or one calculated on the assumption that it would be declined – as it was. Gladstone recorded coolly that he was surprised that Stanley had wasted time 'in proposing to me to join a Cabinet which was to propose a fixed duty on Corn'.[11] Gladstone made it plain that even had they been inclined to join Stanley they would have acted as a 'band'. It was fortunate that no junction took place, since, as Edward Stanley noted it 'would have been one of the weakest [governments] ever formed'. The putative Prime Minister was as relieved as his son and heir. 'It is bad enough to deal with mere sticks instead of men; but when these sticks all fancy themselves great Ministers, what can one do?'[12] The answer was, as it would be so often, to wait upon events – and opposition disunity.

Forced back into office by Stanley's refusal to undertake the Queen's commission, Russell's government was soon overwhelmed by its internal dissentions. A touchy and insecure figure, Russell had come to dislike Palmerston, whom he correctly divined as a threat to his own position. He would have liked to have been able to have obliged Prince Albert and the Queen by dismissing him, but getting rid of the only popular figure in his government because the Crown objected to his habit of sending off despatches without showing them to the Queen would have alienated his own radical supporters – and precipitated Palmerston into the arms of the Conservatives. However, when the bellicose Foreign Secretary decided to recognise the *coup d'état* of Louis Napoleon in December 1851, Russell calculated it was safe to sack him; the radicals were alienated by his support for a coup; the patriots outraged by the return of a Napoleon to the French throne; and the Queen and her husband were again demanding action. So Palmerston went, but Russell had been correct to apprehend that his dismissal would lead to trouble. In February 1852 Palmerston moved an amendment to the government's Militia Bill which was carried by 136 votes to 125; it was effectively a vote of no confidence, and Russell resigned. Those, such as Lord Clarendon, who thought that there would be a repeat of the events of 1851 were proved wrong, and Derby, as Stanley had become in June, following his father's death, accepted the commission to form a government.

The first Derby government has been permanently saddled with the sobriquet of the 'Who? Who? Ministry'; this is a reference to the comments made in the Lords by the aged and deaf Duke of Wellington, who, as the names of the members of the new government were announced, asked 'Who? Who?' never having heard, it is said, of most of them. Whether true or not, the story captures a deeper truth – which is that the names were not those associated with executive office; with the Peelites refusing to join him, Derby was thrown back on his own resources. Derby himself was the only man with senior executive experience, and it was not until the first Labour government of 1923 that so many ministers had to be sworn in as members of the Privy Council. As the mainstay of the debating strength in the Commons, Disraeli was awarded high office – although there were those who wondered, in the anti-Semitic way of the time, at Derby's finding the only Jew in history with no financial acumen, and then appointing him Chancellor of the Exchequer. To Disraeli's disclaimer of any talent for figures, Derby responded with the splendidly Whiggish statement that 'they give you the figures'.

The circumstances in which the government had come to power meant that although Derby remained committed to Protection, he would be unable to do much to enact it since the majority of the Commons was firmly committed to Free Trade. In fact, with the revival of agricultural prices, the old sense of crisis had begun to pass, and the momentum for the reintroduction of Protection was fading. At the election in June 1852, Derby remained committed to Protection in principle, but his party emphasised its Protestant credentials even more – thus solidifying the division between it and the Peelites – some of whom lost their seats to Protectionists. Although the Conservative improved their position in the Commons, gaining about 20 seats to give them nearly 300 MPs, it was not enough to give them a majority over all the other parties. By September 1852 Russell could write confidently that Aberdeen did 'not think the fusion of the Peelites with us at all unlikely or distant', but that 'it must be brought about by circumstances rather than by stipulation.'[13]

The exact circumstances were rather dramatic, and their outcome not at all what Russell had expected. Disraeli's budget was an ingenious attempt to compensate the agricultural interest for the loss of the Corn Laws by remitting the tax on Malt, and making up the revenue thus lost by extending other types of direct taxation; his opponents disliked this, and the Peelites took particular exception to his distinction between the rates at which earned and unearned income should be taxed. Still, given its unorthodoxy, Disraeli got through his budget speech in good order, and as he sat down, at just after one o'clock in the morning, he had reason enough to feel confident of success. Then, in defiance of parliamentary tradition, an MP rose to answer the Chancellor. Stanley noted that: 'Gladstone's look when he rose to reply will never be forgotten by me: his usually calm features were livid and distorted with passion, his voice shook, and those who watched him feared an outbreak incompatible with parliamentary rules.'[14] Gladstone's pent-up frustration at not being able to defend Peel in 1846 broke out in a vehement defence of his fiscal legacy, and he damned Disraeli's budget.

When the House divided at 3 a.m. the budget was lost by 19 votes; it was all over.

Derby was philosophical about his experience: 'I knew as long ago as 1845 that I was playing a losing game: I said so then: I thought I was high and dry for ever: the tide has risen once, high enough to float me again, which was more than I expected: it will never do so again: the game is lost, but I think it ought to be played, and I will play it out to the end.'[15] Derby was given to such elegiac statements, but they should not be invested with too much importance, since he remained committed to the 'game' for the next decade and a half; and even declining health would not prevent him forming a government in 1866. Gladstone's performance over the budget did not make Derby despair of the chances of winning him and some of the Peelites, and he disbelieved in the permanence of any alliance between them and the Whigs, not least because of the simmering quarrels between Palmerston and Russell. He remained committed to providing a constructive Conservative alternative to the unstable radicalism which looked to Russell and Palmerston; but, as Derby well understood, this could be achieved as easily in opposition. On this subject he and Disraeli would never agree.

Derby tolerated his assistant in the Commons, but there was not much warmth in their relationship. Disraeli was avid for office, forever looking for opportunities and combinations, whereas, as Edward Stanley noted in January 1853: 'The Captain [Derby] does not care for office, but wishes to keep things as they are, and impede "Progress".'[16] This created tensions between the two men, and Derby felt obliged to warn Disraeli: 'You must not build upon any possible union between me and the Ultra-Whigs, such as Lord Grey, or the Manchester School. Such an union is simply impossible.'[17] Edward Stanley had let drop hints that such, indeed, were Disraeli's thoughts, and 'the Captain', ever solicitous for his reputation and honour, would have none of it.

It was not surprising that Disraeli, who had neither the private means that would allow him to disdain the salary which office would bring, nor yet much of a reputation to lose, should have found Derby's high-mindedness intensely irritating; but it is a mark of the nature of their relationship that he accepted (sometimes grudgingly) whatever decision Derby reached. This was especially hard in 1855 when the Aberdeen government resigned after losing the confidence of the House of Commons in January. The Queen asked Derby to form a government, and he immediately turned to Palmerston, offering him the lead in the Commons. Derby well knew that he was the key to the parliamentary situation; if he came across the House, he would bring with him enough liberals to create a Conservative majority, which would, in turn, allow him to see through a war with Russia; but the likelihood was that he would not, since, by staying where he was, he was likely to find himself Prime Minister; and so it proved.

Palmerston's tactics at this juncture were extremely skilful. Unwilling to incur the odium of seeming to block Derby's chances through his own selfishness, Palmerston said that he would join the government if Gladstone and Herbert would also come in; when they declined, Palmerston was free to blame them. Derby wrote to the Queen on 31 January telling her that: 'He had no men capable of governing the House of Commons, and he should not be able to present an Administration that would be accepted by the country'; he advised her to send for Palmerston.[18] Disraeli thought this a 'ruinous' mistake, and sulked mightily.[19] His view was that if the Tories had taken office they could have held it for a decade, but he was always an incurable optimist. Derby saw clearly that without support from some of the Peelites and/or Palmerston, he would be doomed to another minority administration, and that, he was sure, was no way to fight a war. Palmerston duly became Prime Minister, saw the war through to a conclusion that could be considered successful, and seemed set fair to remain in office as long as he liked – as his triumph in the 1857 election seemed to show.

The view that Derby was an apathetic and lacklustre leader of the Opposition is a function of the way in which Disraeli has dominated the historiography, not an accurate representation of the historical reality. Disraeli continued to grumble, but Derby remained firmly committed to his long-term strategy, which was to provide a Conservative alternative to the unstable Whig-Liberal coalition; the experience of 1852 suggested to him that actually being in government might not be the best way of frustrating the radicals. As ever, it was Derby's word that was law. Whenever, as in February 1857, the party met to discuss parliamentary tactics, Derby was received with overwhelming approval. The newly elected MP for Leominster, Gathorne Hardy, who came into the House in early 1856, spoke for many such when he wrote that the policy of watching and waiting was 'the only mode in which we can safely act'.[20] Derby's immense political experience and judgement were respected by most of his followers, few of whom stood in quite such need of a ministerial salary as did Disraeli, and historians would do well to discount his grumbles. The wisdom of Derby's policy was shown in early 1858 when Palmerston, who had risen on the back of that bellicose patriotism which would later be called jingoism, fell by the same force. His misjudgement over the Conspiracy bill, which he brought in to try to deal with the issue of refugee terrorists, resulted in a parliamentary revolt, and in February 1858 Derby was, once again, asked to form a government.

In truth the Conservatives were even less well-placed than they would have been in 1855, having only about 260 seats, but as Derby explained, to have declined the Queen's commission would have been 'the signal for the utter & final dissolution of the party'. He remained, as always, mindful of the need to give the 'hounds' a good run, and the second Derby administration did much to scotch the notion that the Conservatives were unfit for government; but he still failed to make the vital breakthrough of attracting any of the Peelites, or of persuading Palmerston to join him.

One of the problems Derby faced was that the 1832 electoral system was biased against the Conservatives. It took about 1477 voters to elect an MP for a borough constituency, but 3335 to do the same in the counties – and the Conservatives were the party of the counties.[21] There were only two things that could overcome such a disadvantage, and Derby tried them both: one was the fabled junction with the Peelite remnants, and whilst Gladstone would condescend enough to accept a diplomatic mission to the Ionian Islands from Derby, he would not join the Cabinet – despite his intense distrust of Palmerston; the other was some measure of parliamentary reform, but the Conservative bill of 1859 was never likely to win the support of a House in which liberals of various shades remained in the majority. There was, to be sure, a variant of the first option, which was to try to extract some of the traditional Whigs, such as Earl Grey, away from some of the radicals who infested their party – but no one was likely to suspect a party led by Palmerston of being a vehicle for radical reform.

In accordance with what was becoming the accepted pattern, the Conservatives minded the shop long enough for the Whigs and their allies to agree to bury the hatchet – which found its habitual resting place in the back of the Conservative government. In June 1859, at a meeting of Peelites, Radicals, Whigs, Liberals – and Lord Palmerston – the forces of liberalism assembled at Willis' Rooms to oppose what they suspected was the Conservative desire not to support the forces of Italian nationalism in the war of Italian unification. Here, at least, Gladstone could agree with Palmerston. That the Conservatives were not proposing to do what the Liberals said was, somehow emblematic of the new Liberal Party. On 12 June the Conservatives lost a motion of no confidence by 13 votes, and Palmerston was invited to head the first Liberal government.

The elections of April 1859 had seen a slight revival in fortunes for the Conservatives, who had lost 23 country seats, but it had come in the smaller boroughs, where they had gained 15 seats; the evidence suggested that the Conservatives would remain strong enough to oppose the government, but there were no signs that they would become the

governing party. Derby disbelieved in the permanence of the new
Liberal coalition. Palmerston was a genial figurehead under whose ageing leadership the forces of moderate liberalism and radicalism could
jockey for influence and power. He resented what he saw as the fac-
tional cynicism that had driven him from office, and looked forward to
the day when the tensions inside the government ripped it apart. By
supporting the conservative Palmerston against the radical instincts of
some of his followers, Derby was able to act as an effective bulwark
against any attempts to subvert 'the institutions of the country'.[22] As
Edward Stanley noted in 1861 when recording the discontent felt by
some Conservatives with their continued exclusion from office: 'Ld. D.
is well known to prefer the indirect and irresponsible power which he
holds in the Lords, to office.'[23]

Such an attitude was entirely understandable from Derby's point of
view; it suited the needs of a man who was increasingly a martyr to the
gout that had first attacked him in the 1830s; and it suited the needs of
a Conservative statesman for the reasons he gave Disraeli in July 1865:
'Our game must be purely defensive and we must be ready to support
the moderate portion of the Cabinet, and watch for every opportunity
of widening the breach between them and the Rad[ical]s.'[24] A Liberal
victory in the general election of July 1865 suggested Derby was correct
in his calculation that there was nothing to be done whilst Palmerston
lived. On 13 October it was reported that 'old Pam' was unwell; on
18 October he died. What a world of relief there was in Disraeli's cry:
'the truce of parties is over. I foresee tempestuous times, and great vicis-
situdes in public life.'[25]

Once more, it is necessary to revise the balance of the historical
account in Derby's favour. There can be no doubt that Disraeli played
a notable and major part in the events which led to the passing of the
second reform act in 1867, but it ought to be borne in mind that the
broader strategy of which this was part was, yet again, that of the Earl of
Derby. The events of late 1865 and early 1866 were the vindication of
Derby's policy. The aged John (now Earl) Russell became Prime
Minister, but the driving force in the new government was Gladstone,
whose new reform bill was too much for the more conservative Liberals
to take, which led to its defeat in June 1866. There was a general expectation that this might lead to a realignment of parties, after all, the issue
was not a party political one, and it might be a good thing if the old
guard all withdrew from the scene at once, as it were, with Russell,
Derby, and perhaps Disraeli, all taking a well-earned retirement; it was
mooted that the respected Whig figure of Lord Clarendon might
become Prime Minister, with Derby's heir, Stanley, becoming leader of

the House in a 'fusion' government. Had Derby been the dilettante of legend, it was a perfect opportunity for him to stand aside.

The party was uncertain what course to take, but the voice that had guided it for the past two decades spoke out in its accustomed tones: as Gathorne Hardy noted: 'Lord Derby spoke strongly about his views of office. He would never hold a subordinate place. He would never be a minister on sufferance again.'[26] He rallied his forces, faced down those who wanted him to go, and, at the age of 67, became Prime Minister for the third time. As usual, Derby tried to expand his reservoir of ministerial talent by inviting others to join his Cabinet, and he was sore at the refusal of Whigs such as Clarendon and Lansdowne, taking the view that 'as they had mainly caused the position in which I found myself, I might fairly look to them for assistance'.[27] His policy, he told the Lords on 9 July was one of 'safe and steady progress', strengthening rather 'than subverting the institutions of the country through a legislative response to the temper and character of the times'.

It was in this spirit that Derby's government tackled the question of parliamentary reform. Derby himself favoured a slow and considered approach, not least because it would give time for the divisions on the Liberal side to widen; but Disraeli's instinct was to 'cut the ground entirely from under Gladstone' by bringing in a Conservative reform bill. However, once the prospect for early action faded, Disraeli became rather more cautious – just at the time, ironically, that Derby decided that 'there is a genuine demand *now* ... in favour of the acceptance of a moderate and conservative measure.'[28] Disraeli remained doubtful, fearing that any Conservative bill would reunite the Liberals, but Derby was determined that 'we cannot escape doing something'. As he told Disraeli firmly on 9 October: 'I come myself more and more to the conclusion that in some shape or another we must deal with it, and that immediately.'[29] As Hawkins' biography makes clear, it was Derby, as usual, who gave the decisive lead on the reform issue; he not only insisted on pressing forward with the issue, but drew up the original resolutions. His plan was to commit the Cabinet to a bill whilst keeping away from the sort of detail that might unite his opponents – and alienate those Conservatives who might dislike anything more than a minor alteration in the franchise; a series of resolutions, followed by a Royal Commission, would allow time for a consensus to develop. Derby's preference was for 'household suffrage, with a plurality of votes',[30] and it was on that basis that plans were drawn up to take the resolutions to the Commons in early February 1867.

Derby's authority had kept his party together and prepared the ground for a moderate and cautious approach to reform – but the demands of parliamentary politics soon threatened to wreck his careful plans. Disraeli's lacklustre performance in the House on 11 February was followed by clear indications that the Liberals were liable to unite against anything which threatened to slow down the reform process, which led him to suggest on 14 February that the government might bring in an immediate bill. Good tactics though that was in terms of keeping the Liberals at bay, it produced a crisis in the Cabinet. General Jonathan Peel, the Secretary of State for War (and brother of Sir Robert) disliked the notion of household suffrage, and others had their doubts, including Lord Carnarvon and the young Lord Cranborne. The government's plan was to be given to the Commons on the afternoon of 15 February; that same morning Derby received two letters from Cranborne and Carnarvon offering their resignations. Over breakfast, Derby wrote to Disraeli: 'The enclosed, just received, is utter ruin. What on earth are we to do?'[31]

The Cabinet met at 12.30, and it was the stormiest of Derby's long leadership. There was much argument and even more recrimination, but ten minutes before a meeting of the parliamentary party, the Cabinet agreed on a £6 rating franchise. It was clear to Derby that most MPs did not like the idea, but in order to keep the Cabinet together, he agreed to let the so-called 'Ten Minute' bill go before the Commons that evening. Disraeli did his best with it, but it offered such an easy target that all sections of Liberal opinion could condemn it, and the following day the Conservatives dropped it; as Lord Stanley noted: 'there was in fact no alternative'. It was the great crisis of Derby's leadership. He had devoted the past two decades to trying to unite the Conservative Party, and now he was faced with the 'utter ruin' of his plans; it was little wonder that his health deteriorated. But Derby proved his mettle, and he determined to revert to the principle of household suffrage, even at the cost of ministerial resignations. At a long and acrimonious Cabinet on the afternoon of 2 March, Derby announced his decision, asking each minister whether he accepted the policy; Cranborne, Carnarvon and Peel all refused. As they left the room Derby sighed, closed his red despatch box and sighed: 'The Tory party is ruined.'[32]

The daily meetings across the next two weeks drained the already ailing Derby, and on 11 March he fell ill; he would never fully recover his strength. But it was his determination to proceed with a bill, and his backing for Disraeli, that kept the Conservatives in line. On 14 March the Cabinet decided to make household suffrage its base-line, with some so-called 'fancy franchises' added to appease more conservative souls. The following day, overcoming excruciating pain from his gout,

Derby addressed a large Conservative meeting at Downing Street, emphasising the importance of the party staying together; Cranborne, Carnarvon and Peel could not agreed – but they were, it turned out, almost alone in this view. It was almost Derby's last great service to his party.

Disraeli introduced the bill on 18 March, and on 26 March the second reading was passed without a division; it was a great personal triumph for the man who had been so distrusted by his party for so long. Derby's generous letter of congratulation showed how far both men had come: 'I cannot let the day pass over without offering you my cordial congratulations ... I hear from all quarters that it was the finest speech you ever made ... In fact you have won our game for us.'[33] Disraeli's triumph could not have been better timed, especially from the point of view of his own fortunes. Just as Disraeli ascended to Olympian heights in the House, Derby's health failed him; henceforth it would be to Disraeli that command over the strategy and tactics of reform would pass; it was a foretaste of things to come.

Disraeli's tactics unsettled the opposition – and some of his own party – as he cheerfully jettisoned most of the 'fancy franchises'. Derby was (literally) wheeled out on 6 May to steady the nerves of those Conservatives who wondered whether they should really be conceding household suffrage in the boroughs. He served the same essential function on 19 July with Conservative peers, threatening to resign if there was any attempt to amend the bill; it would, he warned, lead to a repeat of what had happened in 1846. The ailing Derby summoned up his final reserves of strength in a speech on 22 July in which he introduced the second reading of the bill in the Lords. He declared that he did not 'intend for a third time to be made a mere stop-gap until it would suit the convenience of the Liberal party to forget their dissentions and bring forward a measure which would oust us from office.' A Whig attempt to amend the bill in committee brought the ailing Derby back to the House for one last time on 6 August – when he delivered the famous words which came to sum up the whole crisis over reform: 'No doubt we are making a great experiment and taking a leap in the dark, but I have the greatest confidence in the sound sense of my fellow-countrymen.' Derby's hope that 'the extended franchise which we are now conferring upon them will be the means of placing the institutions of this country on a firmer basis', was actually a more accurate summary of his motives.

In this version of events, with Derby restored to something like his proper place, we can see past Disraeli's tactical genius to the conservatism which underlay the second reform act. Derby had always distrusted the stability and nature of the Liberal coalition; he saw in it a means by which, unless otherwise checked, radicals would undermine the stability of the country's institutions; this was the job of the Conservatives. He had discharged this duty in two minority governments and by supporting Palmerston against his own radicals; but given a chance to reach a settlement of the reform issue on firm ground, he had done so. Only the future would tell whether he had extricated the Conservatives from their role as 'stop-gaps'. The myths about Derby's lackadaisical attitude to power and office totally fail to explain why the tough old statesman hung on to both until the new year; indeed, it was only when it became clear to him that he would be unable to come up to London for the opening of Parliament in February 1868 that Derby decided that the time had come to retire. He wrote to Disraeli with the news on 19 February: 'I trust, however, that if Her Majesty should send for you, which, under the circumstances, I should think most probable, you will not shrink form the heavy additional responsibility.'[34] It was hardly likely that, after overcoming his various 'disadvantages', Disraeli would decline, and nor did he, although, having learned the importance of proper form, he did tell Derby: 'All I will say is that I never contemplated or desired it.' Any one who believed that would, as they say, believe anything.

4 Disraeli on Top

In rectifying the balance in the existing historiography of the Conservative Party by restoring the 'view from Knowsley', it has been necessary to revise the Disraelian mythology which has distorted our view of Derby's leadership; due credit has been given to Disraeli for the part he actually played – that of Derby's (sometimes) loyal lieutenant; but from February 1868, Disraeli must take centre stage.

The historiography of Disraeli deserves a monograph of its own. He is one of the few politicians to leave a mythology, which has been of use to generations of successors. From soon after his death in 1881 he became a name to conjure with. Lord Randolph Churchill enlisted him as the tutelary deity of something called 'Tory Democracy', and the picture of him that emerges from the six-volume official life begun by Monypenny and finished by Buckle is one of the prophetic seer who discerned the Conservative working man as the sculptor does the angel in the marble: a biography begun in 1910 and finished in 1920 might well have needed a Conservative of this kind, and from thence, until the 1960s, Disraeli found favour. By the time Robert Blake was writing in the 1960s, governments and Prime Ministers were assessed according to their legislative achievements; it was the heyday of the nationalised industries and of 'big' government. By these standards Disraeli fared badly; he was an orator, a tactician, an opportunist. However, by the late 1990s, when the importance of such things could not be denied, Disraeli was back in fashion as a master of presentation and political imagery – as befitted one who denied that 'politics and government were primarily a ratiocinative activity.'[1] Perhaps each age remakes Disraeli in its own image; it is a sign of the protean nature of his legacy that this should have been so.

Disraeli's greatest legacy to the Conservatives was to make them the 'national' party. From the late 1870s the Conservatives were able to wrap themselves in the Union Jack, and, when all other tactics failed, they were able to identify themselves with a strong foreign and defence policy: whatever else changed between Disraeli and Thatcher, that, at least, remained the same; for this, Disraeli must take the credit. There was no intrinsic necessity for this to have happened, after all, under Palmerston it had been the Liberals who had been able to claim that they upheld the rights of British subjects across the globe, and who were identified with a strong foreign policy; indeed, Palmerston's stock-in-trade had been the projection of a bellicose patriotism. Historians have, at least until recently, paid little attention to Conservative foreign policy under Derby, but thanks to the recent work of Geoff Hicks we now have a better idea of how the Conservatives looked at foreign affairs in the period before Disraeli; to put it mildly, it was in a very undisraelian way.[2] Derby, like Aberdeen and Castlereagh before him, had favoured a policy of physical non-intervention combined with diplomatic cooperation with the other Great Powers; bellicose sabre-rattling had been left to the likes of Canning and Palmerston. With Palmerston's death in 1865 there were no obvious successors to this line of politics. Even before his death, his methods and style seemed to be going out of fashion. The great days of his Don Pacifico speech of 1850 were well behind him. The Crimean War, with its revelations of aristocratic incompetence and the lacklustre performance of the British army, had sated the national lust for military glory by emphasising its cost. The Schleswig-Holstein crisis of 1864 had finally seen Palmerston's bluff called by a master of the new diplomacy, Bismarck, and most people seemed to concur with John Bright's view that that 'foul idol' the 'balance of power' had been thrown down.[3]

Whilst Britain had been preoccupied with the reform bill, Prussia had been fighting and defeating Austria. Derby had articulated the Conservative view of all this excitement in Europe when he told their Lordships on 9 July that: 'the Conservative party consists, in a great measure, of men who have the greatest interest and the largest stake in the country; they are the men upon whom the consequences of a war would fall the most heavily; they are the persons who have the greatest interest in the peace and prosperity of the state'; this, he emphasised, made the Conservatives 'the party who are least likely to be carried away by that popular enthusiasm and those popular impulses which may hurry even a prudent government into the adoption of courses – I might say, into the adoption of Quixotic enterprises – inimical to the welfare of the country.'[4] This was a definition of Conservative foreign policy as it had existed in Derby's time, and it was a view taken by his son, Lord Stanley, who was Foreign Secretary from 1866 to 1868, and who held the office again from 1874 to 1878; there are few signs that many Conservatives disagreed with such a line. Since the same was true on the Liberal side of the House, there was something like a bipartisan consensus that expensive foreign commitments were to be eschewed. This did not mean that a policy of 'isolation' was pursued, since Britain was part of the Concert of Europe and was consulted as a matter of course on any major diplomatic problems. During the Austro-Prussian war Stanley was in constant contact with the French and the Russians, and, had the war not finished so swiftly, Britain might well have joined the other Powers in seeking to mediate between the Austrians and the Prussians.

Occasionally it was necessary to indulge in foreign wars in a small way, and Disraeli's first premiership was marked by just such a war – against Emperor Theodore of Abyssinia. It had all the classic ingredients of a popular Victorian 'small war'; a mad African despot holding European hostages and defying the British Crown; a campaign in impossible terrain which took the derring-do of a resourceful British general to overcome; and a great triumph. All irresistible – and if it was a trifle expensive, then by the time the bills came in, Disraeli was gone. He had, however, noted the popular acclaim – if only because there was so little of it by the end of his premiership.

For all Derby's hopes that the Conservatives could escape from being the 'stop gaps' whilst the Liberals sorted out their internal disputes, that was precisely what happened in 1868. Disraeli's great triumph over the 1867 Reform Act had made him the inevitable Prime Minister; it was the one occasion in his career to date when that could have been said. Gladstone proved terrible on the rebound, and anyone who thought his career broken by his failures in 1866 and 1867 had failed to get the measure of the man. Derby had feared that the Liberals might bring forward the issue of Irish disestablishment, and his fears were realised in March 1868 when Gladstone came out in favour of it. It was just the cause to reunite all sections of the Liberals, bring the Irish across to his side, and to diss Disraeli. A more respectable Conservative leader might have found room for manoeuvre, but such was the distrust in which he was held on Church issues that Disraeli had to take his stand against disestablishment. Derby made one last service to his party by leading the opposition in the Lords to Gladstone's proposal to suspend Irish ecclesiastical appointments in July, but it was clear that if the Liberal leader brought forward proposals to disestablish the Irish Church in the next parliamentary session, Disraeli's government would lack the authority – and the votes – to defeat it, unless the general election, due in November, produced the first Conservative majority since 1841.

Derby had the satisfaction of seeing Lancashire return 19 out of 32 possible MPs, and of seeing Gladstone go down to defeat in South West Lancashire; all three Liverpool seats were taken by the Conservatives; but nationally the picture was disappointing. The Conservatives lost about 20 seats, ending up with 279 to Gladstone's 379; it was their worst performance since 1835, and hardly suggested that the new electorate was very grateful to those who had given them the vote. Disraeli's instinct was to abandon the usual practice of waiting to be defeated in the House, and he resigned at the end of November. Gladstone became Prime Minister for the first time, determined to disestablish the Church of Ireland and to establish a Liberal ascendancy.

The election showed how fortunate Disraeli had been in the timing of Derby's resignation; as the former Prime Minister he remained leader of his party, a role he might not have won had Derby stayed on until the election. As it was there was a great deal of discontent over the next few years. Without the reassuring presence of Derby, who died on 22 October 1869, Disraeli seemed to lack authority. Disraeli himself told the new Earl of Derby that: 'though still willing to exert himself for the benefit of the party if necessary, his interest in it was diminished, he had obtained his object, and if he never held office again, he should not feel that his life had been a failure.'[5] That was all very well, but there were many of his colleagues who began to feel that his leadership was, indeed, a failure. Gladstone's government swept all before it, disestablishing the Irish Church against what was generally acknowledged to be a feeble Conservative opposition. By early 1872 there was a general feeling among senior Conservatives that it was time for a new leader.[6]

A gathering of leading Conservatives at Burghley House, the seat of the Marquess of Exeter, in January 1872, agreed that the new Earl of Derby would be the ideal man to lead the party. Although he lacked the oratorical talent of his father, the fifteenth Earl was a man who commanded a wide degree of respect. Not only was he an extremely intelligent man, he was a serious politician who could be expected to attract those Liberals becoming worried by Gladstone's radicalism. As Gathorne Hardy recorded in his diary: 'Cairns boldly broached the subject of Lord Derby's lead & the importance of Disraeli's knowing the general feeling.' However, as with Churchill in the late 1940s, 'we all felt that none of his old Colleagues could undertake such a task as informing him.'[7] Only Disraeli's old friend from 'Young England' days, Lord John Manners 'professed ignorance of the existence of the feeling in or out of doors'. The Chief Whip, Gerard Noel, said that he thought that having Derby as their leader would win them 40 or 50 seats at the next election, and there was general agreement that such a development was devoutly to be desired; it was, however, the inability to agree on a way of achieving it that secured Disraeli's leadership – for the moment. It seems more than a coincidence that later that year Disraeli should have broken cover to give two rousing public speeches, which established beyond doubt his willingness to soldier on.

In truth, Disraeli's unwonted quietness was probably his best tactic. As the Conservatives discovered in 1906, 1945 and 1997, reforming governments swept to power with a large majority are not to be fruitfully opposed; the public has given its opinion, and since it clearly wanted to hear as little as possible from the Conservatives, it is usually wise to oblige them – and wait for better times. All reforming governments contain within themselves the seeds of their own destruction. The new Prime Minister is apt to have given the impression at the election that utopia is at hand, and when that fails to materialise, problems begin; expectations that the Archangel Gabriel might have trouble meeting return to haunt prime ministerial hubris; and so it was for Gladstone by 1872. His great Education Act of 1870 had thoroughly annoyed his more radical nonconformist supporters, including a newcomer to the national scene, the former mayor of Birmingham and apostle of 'municipal socialism', Joseph Chamberlain; his licensing bill had alienated the brewers and publicans; whilst his insistence on not only going to international arbitration over the *Alabama* incident, but on paying the compensation suggested to the Americans over the depredations of that gunboat in the late civil war, outraged public opinion generally. It is at such moments that the wise leader of the Opposition strikes – which is what Disraeli proceeded to do.

Too much should not be made of Disraeli's two notable speeches of 1872. At the Manchester Free Trade Hall (and with what exquisite irony he must have spoken there) he mocked the government as a 'range of exhausted volcanoes', scarified their shortcomings, and assured his audience that he would maintain a policy of 'proud reserve' towards Europe; lest this have been too specific, he declaimed that: 'The programme of the Conservative party is to maintain the Constitution of the country'; not many hostages to fortune were given. The same was true of his oration to the National Union of Conservative Associations at the Crystal Palace on 24 June, although here he was bolder in asserting the Conservative claim to be a 'national' party. Liberalism was, he claimed, an 'attempt ... to establish in this country cosmopolitan idea', whereas the Conservatives stood for 'those national principles' which had made Britain great. He called his party 'the national party', declaring that it was dedicated to maintaining the institutions of the country, upholding the empire, and elevating the 'condition of the people'. This identification of Liberalism with 'cosmopolitan ideas' which would lead to the disintegration of the Empire, was to be a constant theme over the next eight years – and it was one which was to pay dividends – in the long run.

In the short term, it was Gladstone's unpopularity and the incapacity of his government which offered Disraeli inviting targets at which to aim his invective; and the public mood, as evinced in the by elections of 1872, where the Conservatives won seven and lost none, had turned against the Liberals. In March 1873 Gladstone attempted to serve up yet another episode of the long-running saga, whereby the Conservatives minded the shop whilst the Liberals regrouped, by resigning when his bill to reform the Irish universities was defeated. But Disraeli had learned not to snatch, and declined the poisoned chalice. It is some index of how much he was still distrusted that the prospect of office should have given rise to renewed questions about whether or not Derby would be a better bet for the leadership. Everything, clearly, depended on the results of the next election; another defeat would see the end of Disraeli's career.

In late January 1874, with his government limping from crisis to crisis, Gladstone announced an immediate dissolution of Parliament – and declared that if returned, he would abolish the income tax. Such a bold move threw Disraeli onto the defensive, and even the devoted Buckle had to admit that his election address was of a 'negative character.'[8] But the results surpassed all expectations, for the first time since 1871 the Conservative won a clear majority in the Commons, with 352 seats; the Liberals dropped to 243, with 57 Irish MPs making the balance. Stunned by the extent of his success, Disraeli became Prime Minister for the second time.

Delighted though the Conservatives were at their success, not all of them were enamoured of the prospect of Disraeli as leader. The third Marquess of Salisbury, as Cranborne had become in 1867, liked 'Dizzy' no more than he had done when he had resigned from the Cabinet in 1866. Good government, he thought, depended 'upon the respect [with] which the Chief's intellect or power in the country is held', and by that standard, given the lack of respect for Disraeli, Derby would have made a better leader. As he told his former step-mother, now Mary, Countess of Derby: 'if Lord Derby were prime minister I should find no difficulty in accepting office without emphasis as to prospective policy: for I think I know his mind'; the same could not be said for Disraeli.[9] Lord and Lady Derby both emphasised to Salisbury that he would be in a better position to restrain Disraeli from within the government, and, perhaps knowing that if he declined at this juncture, his career was effectively over, Salisbury graciously consented to join the Cabinet as Secretary of State for India. He need not have worried about 'the Chief's prospective policy', since he did not have one; it was enough for Disraeli that he was in power.

In many respects the Cabinet was as much Derby's as it was Disraeli's; he it was who had insisted that his protégé, Richard Cross, should go to the Home Office; he who brokered the deal whereby Salisbury came into the government; and, as Foreign Secretary, he was clearly the second man in the government; junior to the ailing Disraeli by more then 20 years, Derby was the rising sun. It is true that Derby did not wish to lead the Conservative Party, but equally plain that, had Disraeli died at any stage before 1877, he would have been hard put to it to have avoided replacing him. Had that happened then it is unlikely that the Conservatives would have become the 'national party' in the way they did; that happy event owed its genesis to the same phenomenon that destroyed Derby's career – the recrudescence of the Eastern Question in 1875.

One of the consequences of the hegemony of the Disraelian version of the history of the nineteenth-century Conservative Party is that it underplays the contingent nature both of Disraeli's triumph, and of his eastern policy. It is traditional to write off Derby as an odd-ball with Cobdenite tendencies and a habit of stealing spoons, who, thankfully resigned from office in 1878; this ignores almost everything that actually matters about Derby, Disraeli, and the crisis of 1875 to 1878.[10] In the first place, as we have seen, Derby was widely regarded as the next leader of the party, and one whom many would have preferred to Disraeli in the early 1870s. Secondly, the line of policy preferred by Derby was entirely consonant with the previous tradition of the party. Indeed, so much was this the case that it took extraordinary efforts by Disraeli to discredit and then dislodge Derby in 1878; efforts that would hardly have been required had Derby's policy lacked support.

Derby would have been quite happy to have joined with the other Great Powers in pressing on the Turks the reforms suggested by the so-called Berlin Memorandum of May 1876, but Disraeli, feeling that he had been snubbed in not being consulted about its contents, declined to be a party to it; to Derby's surprise, this turned out to be a very popular gesture, with the press contrasting it to the supine way in which Gladstone had proceeded in such circumstances. It may have been popular, but it did nothing to help the deteriorating situation in the Ottoman Empire, and by the summer of 1876 the press was full of stories about 'atrocities' committed in Bulgaria. In his last speech in the Commons, Disraeli played down the rumours – only to find to his chagrin that they seemed to be true. Public opinion took the side of the massacred Bulgars, and a great 'atrocitarian' agitation excoriated Disraeli, now ennobled as the Earl of Beaconsfield, for his levity and lack of moral tone; it was rather late in the day to notice these things.

Disraeli's retirement to the Lords was the only alternative to outright retirement. Suffering from acute respiratory problems, Disraeli broached

By December 1877, with the Russians at the gates of Constantinople, Disraeli was desperate to take some sort of action; he had, after all, given the electorate to understand that he would take a firm line in defence of British interests, and there he was doing nothing. The reason for this was plain: the Cabinet did not back him. At a heated Cabinet on 17 December, Disraeli even threatened to resign, and, for a while no one was even sure whether the government still existed. However, since Derby would not take a decided lead of the sort that would have allowed his colleagues to have turned to him as the alternative to Disraeli, and since Disraeli would not give up his opinions; there was a complete deadlock at the heart of government.

In an attempt to break it, Disraeli reached out to his old enemy, Salisbury, seeking his aid as a man of the world in a 'private' matter; he revealed to him that he suspected Lady Derby of being the source through which secret information was passing to the Russians. Relations between Salisbury and his former step-mother were already complicated by the belief that she had begun her affair with Derby during his father's lifetime, and Disraeli, a master of such gossip, would have known of the likely effect on Salisbury of a new infidelity. Salisbury was a busy man that Christmas, in addition to the Prime Minister's blandishments, he received a letter from Derby. Relying on the unspoken assumptions of a common Conservative view on foreign policy, Derby told Salisbury that Disraeli 'believed thoroughly in "prestige" – as all foreigners do'. He would, Derby warned, 'be willing to spend £200 millions on a war if the result was to make foreign states think more highly of us as a military power'; whilst 'intelligible' such ideas were, Derby stated, 'not mine, nor yours.'[16] That was, in a sense, what was at the heart of the matter.

From Castlereagh's time, with the exception of Canning, Tory foreign policy had been marked by the characteristics which Derby invoked during the Great Eastern Crisis; a concern for British honour, certainly, but also a desire to avoid the grandiloquent gesture that might lead to war. Derby doubted that Disraeli actually wanted war, but thought that his policy might lead to one by default since 'he fears above all things the reproach of a weak or commonplace policy.' For Derby, public opinion consisted of the sound common sense of the enfranchised middle classes, which is why he noted that Disraeli 'lives among people ... who lead him to believe the public feeling much more warlike that it really is.'[17] Disraeli's 'people', were those who flocked to the Music Halls to see the 'Great MacDermott' sing 'We don't want to fight, but by Jingo if we do, we've got the ships, we've got the men, we've got the money too ... the Russians shall not have

Constantinople!' With his feel for the importance of symbol and image in politics, Disraeli knew instinctively how to appeal to this 'Jingo' tendency; Derby hardly recognised its existence.

In the end Derby had to threaten to resign before Disraeli would back away from threatening to send the British fleet through the Dardanelles. Disraeli, informed at first by the Whips that Derby's resignation could be coped with, was inclined to accept it, but on the rumour sweeping Whitehall that he had actually gone, the Whips changed their mind and threatened dire electoral consequences; so, having resigned on 24 January, with no answer from Disraeli Derby found himself 'back' two days later. Salisbury would later claim that from that point, through to Derby's resignation in late March, foreign policy was carried on by himself, Disraeli and Lord Cairns; there are no grounds for believing this story – which has not stopped generations of historians repeating it. Men often reveal more about themselves by the lies they choose to tell than they do by telling the truth.

During February and March there was a campaign against Derby in the more vulgar parts of the press, and rumours about his drinking and his nerves multiplied with the telling. These stories found their place in history through Salisbury's retailing them to his nephew Arthur Balfour, through whom they passed into the official biography and thus into wider circulation; but the weak point in them was surely the fact that Disraeli and Salisbury, having had the chance to dump Derby in January, invited him back? This flaw was covered by the story of the mini-committee of public safety, which is, itself, believable only if one accepts Salisbury's biased account of Derby's state of mind. This asks us to believe that a man who had been Foreign Secretary for more than five years would not have noticed the red boxes drying up, and that Derby, who had returned only to keep Disraeli in check, would have consented to remain a figurehead; it also requires us to ignore Derby's meticulously kept diary, which records him doing business as usual.

From late January until March, Derby worked hard to keep Disraeli from making any flamboyant gesture that would lead to war with Russia; he rested his policy on reassurances from Count Shuvalov, the Russian ambassador, that Russia's peace terms with Turkey would be reasonable, and here he made his greatest mistake. When the terms of the Treaty of San Stefano were known in March, it was clear that the Russians were intending to impose a harsh peace, and British public opinion would demand action. Disraeli, with the support of Salisbury, determined to give them what they wanted – and Derby resigned – to be succeeded at the Foreign Office by Salisbury.

The politics of the Eastern Crisis were crucial for the future of the Conservative Party in a number of ways. In the first place, by removing Derby, the crisis opened up the question of the future leadership of the party itself; he had been heir-apparent for so long that there had been no point in anyone else coveting the post; but now he was gone, and with Disraeli clearly on his last legs, the contest was on for who would replace him. Here Salisbury had done wonders for his chances by changing sides in January to back Disraeli. As Foreign Secretary he had a high profile at the Berlin Congress that settled the crisis in June 1878, and he settled into the role of Disraeli's right-hand man almost as easily as he had that of his chief critic. Of course, nothing was settled, Gathorne Hardy saw himself as a possible contender, as did the Chancellor, Sir Stafford Northcote; but whoever it was, it would not be Derby.

Equally, if not more crucial in the long term, the crisis saw the triumph of Disraeli's Jingoism. It is clear, from the support Derby received until the end, that many Conservatives were uneasy with it, but its clear success at Berlin, from which Disraeli and Salisbury returned bringing 'peace with honour', stilled their doubts; henceforth, the Conservatives would, indeed, be the 'national party'.

If this legacy was successful in the long term, in the short run it was near disastrous. Salisbury's concern that an absence of the 'peace' part of the 'peace with honour' might lead the electorate to wonder about the 'honour' turned out to be justified. Encouraged by the Imperial tone set by Disraeli, the Viceroy of India, Lord Lytton, encouraged a 'forward' policy in Afghanistan, refusing to learn from the lessons of the disasters of 1842; the result, as usual, was a fresh disaster, with a British mission being massacred in Kabul, and the sending of a relief force under General Roberts to punish the malefactors. South Africa also saw a set-back for those of an Imperial caste of mind, when the attempt to take a hard line with the Zulu led to the massacre at Islandhlwana; by 1879 there was neither much peace, nor any honour.

On the home front, although later Conservatives would claim to discern in Disraeli's policy the glimmerings of 'Tory social reform', they must have been looking particularly hard, since contemporaries saw little more than a few necessary measures, such as tidying up Gladstone's licensing legislation and reforming his trades union laws. By the time the election hove into view in 1880, the country seemed to be in the grip of an agricultural depression, and in March Disraeli decided to go to the country; he lost, and lost heavily. The Conservatives ended up with 238 seats, fewer than at any time since 1832; the Liberals, with 352 seats, were swept back to power. The only cheering note for Disraeli was that Gladstone's part in the election victory meant that although he had officially retired in 1875, he was the inevitable Prime Minister; and whilst there was Gladstone, there was always hope.

At first it seemed as though the mid-Victorian Liberal domination had resumed its sway, and that the brief interlude of 'Beaconsfieldism' had passed away like a bad dream. Disraeli himself died in early 1881, and with him, it seemed, had passed away a whole era.

The death of Alexander the Great was followed by the wars of the Diodarchi – the struggle to succeed to his Empire by his lieutenants; there was a similar, if less bloody battle to succeed Disraeli. Northcote, as leader in the Commons and repository of Tory soundness, had many advantages, but the ability to win over the electorate seemed to be lacking; in power he would perform tolerably well – but how would the Conservatives ever acquire power under him? To this two answers were offered. On the one hand was Salisbury's massive pessimism. Although philosophically glum, his lordship had developed a nice line in pragmatism since the days when his 'jibes and flouts and jeers' had been used by good Liberals to frighten their children.

Salisbury allowed his nephew, Balfour, to join the 'Fourth Party', a ginger group, led by Lord Randolph Churchill, which, whilst ostensibly attacking Gladstone, actually helped undermine Northcote, if only by revealing how the job of tackling the 'Grand Old Man' should be done. He also took the labouring oar in the negotiations which led to the passage of the 1884 Reform Act, which equalised the borough and county franchises. All of this, combined with Northcote's obvious inadequacies, made Salisbury the obvious figure to send for when, once again, the Liberals fell out with each other in May 1885. At first it seemed as though it was the old story, so familiar from the days of Derby and Disraeli, and the results of the election marked only a partial recovery, with Salisbury, at the head of 250 Conservatives, facing 334 Liberals and 86 Irish Nationalists. But this result concealed much confusion.

The Liberals had left office in their usual state of disarray, and Gladstone, anxious to find a rallying cry, looked to Ireland to provide it. Conscious, however, of the potency of that issue, he hoped that Salisbury would provide a bipartisan approach by favouring the policy of Home Rule. If Salisbury had given the impression that he was not wholly against the notion, it was only to flush Gladstone out, and in January 1886, he committed himself and the Liberals to the cause of Irish Home Rule. Salisbury immediately resigned, but although he was able to form a government, Gladstone was unable to bring all his colleagues with him. In the event, Joseph Chamberlain and his followers on one wing of the party, and Lord Hartington and his Whigs on the other, all declined to adhere to a policy which seemed to presage a break up of the Empire, and with the defeat of his Irish bill, Gladstone resigned in July 1886, leaving Salisbury free to form a second administration. The election in July 1886 saw the Conservatives emerge as the largest single party, with 316 MPs, whilst the Liberals, split between 191 Gladstonians and 78 Liberal Unionists, were out of the running. Of course, the Liberals might reunite – but for the moment, Salisbury was in office – and power.

Gladstone's decision to go for Home Rule marked a decisive step in the emergence of the Conservatives as the national party; it was not just that they opposed his weak foreign policy, they had become the party of the Union itself. This, as it turned out, suited Salisbury well enough, not least because it allowed him to face down the main challenge to his own position – Lord Randolph Churchill. Ever since Disraeli's death, the erratic Lord Randolph had been declaring his willingness to wear the mantle of Elijah. In practice this meant talking a lot about 'social reform', and buttering up the local Conservative Associations as a way of intruding his unwelcome presence into the heart of Conservative councils.

Lord Randolph lacked judgement, even as he lacked morality and good taste. His rhetoric was vulgar in an age when the aristocracy was expected to provide a good rather than a bad example. His ideas, such as they were, were inchoate and second-hand, and he provided himself the best definition of what he meant by 'Tory democracy' – opportunism mostly. But if 'Tory democracy' was a device for persuading the democracy to vote Tory, then it was something of which the party stood in need. Churchill's banging of the Disraelian drum of social reform, and the obvious support he enjoyed from the constituencies, all suggested another line of approach which lay open to the Conservatives: 'One Nation' Toryism, which would convince the masses that it was from the Conservatives that they could expect practical social reforms – and without the usual Liberal sermons.

Whilst there were some positive reasons for the long Salisburian ascendancy, they did not account for it. The main reason for the success of the Conservatives under the third Marquess was the condition of the Liberal Party. Salisbury provided reasons for not voting against the Conservatives – and Gladstone provided reasons for not voting Liberal. It is true that social trends, combined with the effects of the 1885 Redistribution of Seats Act, all helped the Conservatives. The creation of single-member constituencies, especially the suburban seats around London and other big cities, provided a socially conservative electorate who only needed Gladstone's encouragement to become politically so. The Whigs, alienated by Gladstone's Irish land legislation, took themselves off in 1886, but the split went deeper than that. The Liberal Party could have coped with the defection of a group of conservative aristocrats, men whose prestige and income were greater than the votes they could command or the ideas they espoused; but the secession of Joseph Chamberlain and his radical allies was a greater blow.

Gladstone may have had little time for the brash Chamberlain and his espousal of 'constructionist' legislation, but 'Radical Joe' brought many votes along with some interesting ideas into the alliance with Salisbury. It is a mark of how eclectic the great Marquess was prepared to be that he should have been willing to embrace, at least in electoral terms, a man he had once stigmatized as 'Jack Cade'; but then, since Chamberlain was equally shameless in the expediency of his alliance with the Conservatives, the whole business just went to prove how far the Unionist allies would go to preserve the Union – and to keep out Gladstone and the Irish.

Churchill and Chamberlain were natural allies. To their many enemies they were vulgar opportunists with an eye to the main chance – which was another way of saying that they were successful at the hustings. They had something else in common too; both men were impatient with the old liberal nostrums and wanted to utilize government to deal with the problems facing the country. The eventual consummation of a union between Chamberlainite radical Imperialism and Churchillian 'Tory Democracy' in the years after 1922 was to provide the foundation stone upon which the modern Conservative ascendancy came to rest, but Churchill himself put paid to any chance of it happening in his lifetime. He resigned from the Exchequer in December 1886 and fell, like Lucifer in his pride, never to rise again. But his son, Winston, was right to suspect that the Conservatives had lost something by Lord Randolph's fall. Despite his electoral success, Salisbury never did find any positive reason why the electorate should vote Conservative. There was, of course, the Disraelian legacy of imperialism, and he added to it the cause of the Union. Indeed, although few realized it at the time, the two were powerfully connected. The Empire gave purpose to the Union, as the Scots, Welsh and Irish (at least those who wanted to) could combine in the Imperial enterprise. But beyond this Salisbury could not go. It was a sense of the dead hand of Cecilian Conservatism which caused the young Winston Churchill, then a Unionist MP, to declare: 'I hate the Tory Party, their men, their words and their methods.'[18] Writing in 1903, Churchill discerned an England beyond the reach of the Northcote-style competence of the Conservative Party, one which Salisbury's essentially negative political legacy was unable to reach; nor was he the only one.

Lord Randolph's old partner, Joseph Chamberlain, found association with Salisbury equally frustrating. It was not that the Marquess was
inclined towards political reaction in his policies, but rather that his attitude remained that of a mid-Victorian. Back in 1883 Gladstone's Private
Secretary, Edward Hamilton, had commented that the Conservatives,
unlike the Liberals, would not be worried by Irish obstruction of legislation since it 'does not matter so much for them. It is not their
game.'[19] Salisbury's success in making the Unionists the party of most
of the men of property demanded a continuation of Victorian 'small
government', with a correspondingly small tax base.[20] But this imposed
severe limits on what the Unionists could do in the spheres of social
reform and Imperialism; the electorate may have said it wanted both,
but there was no sign that it was keen to bear the cost. Salisbury
accepted these limitations with equanimity. Where legislation was possible and cheap, in the area of local government, or where spending
came from local authorities, as with housing acts, Salisbury would spon-
sor it; although even in this area, the increasing cost of compulsory
education was creating a problem which would help scupper his
successor. Where large sums of money would have to come from the
taxpayer, whether for Imperial adventures or for old age pensions,
Salisbury scouted the notion. Since these last two were both dear to
Chamberlain's heart, it is not surprising that he was frustrated. But if
the 'Hotel Cecil' (as the government was called by its critics, who
thought there were rather too many members of the clan in it) thought
that they had boxed Chamberlain into a corner, they had reckoned
without his formidable talent for changing the political weather.

Hatfield, the ancestral home of the Cecil clan, offered recondite and
historical reasons for voting Conservative, but its resources for handling
change were limited. Salisbury dealt with the changing international
situation by throwing scraps to Britain's competitors in the expectation
that they would never agree among themselves and mount a concerted
challenge to British interests; he adopted much the same principle for
dealing with domestic politics. Salisbury's nephew and heir-apparent,
Arthur Balfour, was more conscious of the challenges to the status quo
at home and abroad than his uncle, but he was no more fertile in suggesting answers to them. For that it was necessary to look to Highbury –
the home of Joseph Chamberlain. The aristocracy might look at
Britain's affairs with a mixture of complacency and pessimism, but
Chamberlain belonged to the thrusting, optimistic entrepreneurial
class which had made Britain the 'workshop of the world'. Conscious of
the challenges being mounted to Britain's status abroad, Chamberlain's
background in municipal politics also gave him an acute awareness of

the state of the people. British political leaders generally fall into two categories – the active and the passive; if Salisbury belonged to the second category, Chamberlain was most emphatically in the first. The 1900 election, fought in the middle of the Boer War, showed Chamberlain's talents as an electioneer. The Liberals loathed him, which was just another reason for his admirers to adore him. Salisbury may have run the government, but 'Joe' made the political weather.

In an age where the main medium of communication to the electorate was through the electoral meeting or the newspaper report, Chamberlain's appeal is understandable. Winston Churchill who, unlike many modern historians, believed in the concept, commented that 'one mark of a great man is the power of making lasting impressions upon people he meets – [and] so to have handled matters during his life that the course of after events is continuously affected by what he did'; by these standards, Chamberlain was a great man.[21] To Mr Gladstone's type of Liberal he had seemed a portent of socialism to come – an opinion shared by Salisbury. The popular press, who adored or hated him passionately, often depicted him as a boxer – the 'Brummagem Pet'. This is not surprising. Chamberlain fought for everything he had. Unlike Gladstone he could not live off the rentier income of the labours of his father; unlike Salisbury he could not rely upon the accumulated treasures of centuries; what 'Joe' had, 'Joe' had earned. In retrospect he was the pioneer of a new type of Unionist. A successful manufacturer, who gravitated naturally towards the mid-Victorian Liberal Party because he was a dissenter, but who was eventually repulsed from it by Gladstone's obsession with Ireland, Chamberlain represented on the national stage a phenomenon which was occurring frequently on the more parochial one. Because of his background Chamberlain could make an appeal to the average elector which no one else could do. Although a wealthy man, he was a self-made one and his concern for social reform was no mere persiflage. As a reforming Mayor of Birmingham he had practised what others called 'municipal socialism' – paving the streets, providing sewers, sanitation and electricity for the second city of the Empire. His hold on Birmingham never slackened – all seven of its MPs followed him in the Home Rule split, and by the time of his death in 1914, all seven seats were still in Unionist hands. It was not until 1895 that Chamberlain finally sat in Cabinet with Salisbury, and although the two men cooperated for electoral reasons, it could not be argued that their alliance was close.

On foreign affairs, where Salisbury had reigned supreme in the previous administration, he found himself under siege from Chamberlain, who wanted a more active diplomacy, in Africa, the Far East and

Europe.[22] The same pattern repeated itself in domestic matters. Chamberlain's own base in municipal politics dictated the lines of his politics – and nothing in his background disinclined him from putting further burdens on the landed classes. His antennae were tuned to a different wavelength than Salisbury's – and few politicians had an acuter sense of what the time demanded.

Did 'social researchers' like Booth reveal that there was dire poverty in the heart of the capital of the greatest empire the world had seen since Rome? Why then, came the cry from the 'New Liberalism', Fabianism and the trades unions, let the State intervene to put things right. Such was the confidence in their own ability of the likes of Beatrice Webb that it would have seemed inconceivable to them that three-quarters of a century later their successors would be demanding still more expenditure on 'social' problems which seem to be rooted in human nature rather than, as sociology would have us believe, society itself. This line of thinking began to capture the mainstream of the Liberal Party in 1891 with the adoption of the Newcastle Programme by the Party Conference. This may have included such Liberal chestnuts as Irish Home Rule, Welsh Disestablishment and Scottish Disendowment and Disestablishment, but alongside them was an agenda which would have satisfied Chamberlain at his most radical. There were calls for an increase in the power of local authorities to take into their control land which could be used to provide allotments, smallholdings and working-class housing. The Liberal Conference also endorsed demands for a 'thorough reform of the land laws' which would include the repeal of the law of primogeniture and entail the 'just taxation of Land Values and ground rents', the taxation of mining royalties, the equalization of death duties as between real and personal property, as well as an extension of the factory acts and a direct popular veto on the Liquor traffic. To ensure that the House of Lords did not differentiate between measures which would be popular and those which would simply allow self-obsessed 'faddists' to dictate their own personal preferences to others, the Upper House was to be 'ended or mended'.

This was as comprehensive an assault as could be asked for on what some Liberals called 'feudalism', but what was, in fact, the structure which had provided the English ruling class for generations. Precisely because it was such a broad-based attack it was difficult for the Unionists to defend at all points, and it served to highlight the divide between the two parts of the Coalition. A national system of unemployment insurance and old age pensions remained on Chamberlain's political agenda, and were thought likely to prove popular with his own electorate. But paying for these things would add an extra burden to the landed classes, who were always the object of Salisbury's solicitude. This was not simply self-interest, but rather a reflection of his fears for the future. In 1888 he had written that: 'the incomes of country gentlemen are not now obtained without difficulty or trouble, and there is no doubt that for some time to come the possessors of land in this country will have to attend to their own affairs very much more than they have in times past, and probably therefore will be less prominent themselves in attending to public affairs'.[23] It was a commonplace complaint amongst agriculturalists within the Conservative Party that its leadership did nothing for agriculture and refused to reverse the situation which had obtained since Peel had first deprived them of the special protection to which they felt entitled. Now faced with possible impositions which were bound to be popular with those who would benefit without having to pay for them, the landowning classes looked to Salisbury's party for relief.

It is perhaps unfair to chide the Marquess with failing to come up with an answer to a problem he had diagnosed even before 1867. There was no way in which an electorate which contained a majority which would either benefit, or at least not suffer, from an extension of State control and activity, could be prevented from getting it. This may account for the sense of gloom with which Salisbury went about his task. Whilst Gladstone still dominated the Liberals and sought to polarize politics around issues such as Ireland which did not divide the country on class lines, Salisbury could happily concur, for it had always been the claim of the Conservatives that they were a national party, and they could proclaim themselves, with their Liberal Unionist allies, as the nationalist party of Great Britain. But with Gladstone's political enfeeblement and demise, and the advent of the Newcastle Programme and the imposition of death duties by Chancellor Harcourt, it was not surprising that Salisbury should have been told by his Chancellor, Sir Michael Hicks-Beach, that he doubted 'whether the country can be governed nowadays by persons holding opinions which you and I should call even moderately Conservative'.[24]

Faced with a challenge from a Liberalism which held obvious appeals to the dispossessed and dissatisfied, Salisbury's party came up with three answers, none of which really served his purpose and one of which he would hardly have approved of had he lived to see its efflorescence.

One possible strategy has already been mentioned, that of finding an issue which transcended class boundaries, but issues like Ireland did not grow on trees, and the next best thing, the Boer War, cost a fortune and meant that taxation had to be raised. In 1901 Hicks-Beach told his colleagues that a 'real check' had to be placed on expenditure, whilst

Salisbury warned not long before his death that 'some very drastic reforms will be necessary in order to bring back our finance into a healthy state'.[25]

A second possible strategy was to erect what might be called bulwarks against the encroachments of Liberalism and collectivism. Here the Conservatives enjoyed more success, but for reasons not entirely under their control and which they understood but imperfectly. It had always been part of Salisbury's intention that the Conservatives should be the party of property of all types, and the Home Rule split in the Liberal Party, electoral changes in 1884, and the effects of demography and growing prosperity all helped to bring about something close to Salisbury's wishes. Until 1884 the Conservatives had been the party of the shires and of agriculture, and the Liberals the party of the great boroughs and the cities, but demographic and electoral changes after 1880 helped to alter this situation. Despite the attention which historians have lavished on the poor the dispossessed and the outcasts of society, late Victorian England saw an increase in general levels of prosperity, yet the growth of suburban England and its inhabitants with their petty snobberies and parochial mentality has had little appeal to modern historians; but to its inhabitants the Conservative Party came to have a natural appeal. The movement of the more prosperous out to suburbs created a late-Victorian equivalent of the 'Essex man' so-beloved of journalists a century later. Lord Randolph Churchill may have mocked the owners of the pineries and vineries, and Lord Salisbury may have referred to the *Daily Mail* as a paper 'written by office boys for office boys', but the office boy vote, the votes of the clerks and of the professional classes in their neat suburban lives, were waiting for the Conservative leader who could project an image of confident authority and ruling competence – something at which Salisbury excelled. That the Conservatives became the party of suburban England during the tenure of the last great aristocrat to lead the Conservative Party is not the least of the ironies of the history of England during this period.

If the suburban vote helped to buoy up Conservative fortunes, it did nothing to answer the cries for State intervention which came from the political left. The low tax policies of the Conservatives may have made a natural appeal to the landowners and to the suburbs, but there were not enough property owners to make this strategy an election winner – although one of the ironic effects of greater State intervention would be to create a situation by the 1980s where this would be the case. When faced with the plight of the poor and the dispossessed, it was natural for the enemies of the Conservatives to portray them as heartless landlords intent on grinding the faces of the poor. The rootless intellectual of the late nineteenth and early twentieth centuries knew little of the ties that bound agricultural society together. More often than not he was a creature from an urban, or even suburban environment, ill-equipped emotionally or by experience to observe the unifying effects of religion, hierarchy and village life. Yet Conservatives were not, despite the charges of their enemies, heartless, and sympathy, clothed in the Disraelian myths which gave their party credit for pragmatic social reform, provided a third mode of combating collectivism, especially when it meshed with some of the ideas injected into the Conservative bloodstream by the advent of Chamberlain and the Liberal Unionists.

Chamberlain shared neither the pessimism of Salisbury nor yet his scepticism about the possibilities of the state taking action; what the two did have in common was a commitment to a low taxation economy which would allow British commerce and industry to enrich the nation in the next half-century as it had in the previous 50 years. As a businessman himself, Chamberlain was well aware that the State had not created the national wealth and he was reluctant to see it spend too much of what it had not made. On the other hand he had no theoretical qualms about using the powers of the State to help the less fortunate, and he had a pragmatic attitude towards social reform which was to have a long history in the Conservative and Unionist Party, not least through the medium of his second son, Neville.

Chamberlain's attitude towards social reform has been called 'principled opportunism', which is not a bad description.[26] His Radical comments about the 'insurance' which wealth had to pay for the continued enjoyment of its privileges were capable of being developed in a Conservative direction. Chamberlain's Whiggish leader, Hartington, could have told him, had he not already known it, that a cardinal tenet of Whiggery was to enact timely reform in order to avert future extremism. During the 1890s he sought to meet demands from the trades unions and the Liberal left for wholesale labour reform by coming up with an essentially conservative package which included old age pensions, industrial arbitration and employers' liability, as well as local authority loans for working-class housing. But 'Joe's War' put Joe's pensions at risk. The costs of the war meant hostility from the Cabinet to any measures which would increase the tax burden, and it was partly out of this dilemma that Chamberlain's tariff reform ideas were to emerge.

The Salisbury administration employed all three strategies – principled opportunism; the expression of sympathy; and the erection of bulwarks against collectivism – during the 1890s. The allotments acts of 1887 and

1890 permitted local authorities to buy land for tenants, and rating reforms and a compensation act gave the allotment holder tax advantages and compensation for any improvements he made. As with the Employers' Liability Bill of 1897, the intention was to pass legislation which would take the sting out of Liberal proposals whilst showing how sympathetic the party of Disraeli was to social reform. Continuity in office, however, depended upon Unionists continuing to preside over general prosperity and retaining their reputation for competence in government. This did not happen.

The interruption of this happy state of affairs owed much to Chamberlain. His war increased taxation at a time when Britain was already beginning to suffer from the competition from American and German industry. Ever the activist, Chamberlain's fertile mind came up with a solution which was designed to square every conceivable circle – 'Tariff Reform'. In theory the idea could hardly have appeared more attractive. How were higher defence bills to be met at the same time as old age pensions and other measures of social reform, and how were these things to mesh with the perceived need for a closer union of the Empire? – Why, by Tariff Reform. It would be the 'foreigner' who would pay for these things by levying taxes from the goods which he 'dumped' in Britain. At the same time Imperial unity would be enhanced by bringing the Empire together as a low tariff zone. It was a bright idea and entirely in the tradition of pragmatic opportunism, but it carried two problems with it: the first was that it implied an increase in the price of food – which hardly made it an election winner; and the second was that the idea split the Coalition in a number of directions. The man who had broken the Liberal Party in 1886 now went on to repeat the trick – this time with the Unionists.

Salisbury had presided over the creation of a new Unionist alliance which had dominated British politics since 1886. But the question of how far that dominance was due to the appeal of Unionism and how far it was the product of Liberal inadequacy was about to be tested. Unfortunately for the Unionists, by the time the test came the great Marquess was dead and it was left to his nephew and political heir, Arthur Balfour, to meet the heavy weather stirred up by Chamberlain.

5 Balfour in Trouble

Lloyd George said of Balfour that he was 'not a man but a mannerism'. Other contemporaries, like F. E. Smith and Winston Churchill, said of him that his was the finest intellect which had devoted itself to politics in their time; for this there is much evidence. The comparative failure of his leadership perhaps serves to show the limited uses which politics finds for ratiocination. It was once said that Franklin D. Roosevelt possessed a 'second-class intellect with a first-class temperament'; Balfour's first-class intellect was accompanied by a political temperament which perhaps failed to match it. It is usual, when considering his career, to contrast the initial verdicts that he was a lightweight figure – known to some as 'Pretty Fanny' – with the sternness he showed as Secretary for Ireland, where he earned the sobriquet 'Bloody Balfour'; but taking his career as a whole, it is by no means clear that the first opinions were wholly wrong. There is, about it, a curious inconsequence. What Balfour demonstrated in Ireland was not a sternness of resolve, but rather the absence of any human sympathy, a trait which he extended to the rest of his relations with mankind; it was easy to mistake indifference for firmness. But those who trusted Balfour, from Lord Randolph Churchill to Lord Curzon, always found that he let them down; he did so with exquisite politeness, but he did so just the same. It took another exceptionally vain Scotsman, Ramsay MacDonald, to get Balfour right: 'He saw much of life – from afar.'

A cerebral bachelor, Arthur James Balfour was a fine example of the results of Salisbury's nepotism; his prowess owed much to the fact that Salisbury was his uncle. What he did not owe to this he owed to another fact which was, in the end, to cost him dear – the lack of talent in the Salisburian party. It is customary for journalists, commenting upon current Cabinets, to lament the decline in quality from some age when political giants trod the stage, but not even the most opaquely rose-tinted spectacles can make much of most of Balfour's colleagues. Of those who impressed contemporaries, the two great figures in Cabinet after Salisbury himself had both begun their political life elsewhere, and the Duke of Devonshire was a wasting asset, whilst the other was Joseph Chamberlain. Of the rest, at best only Lansdowne at the Foreign Office, and Selborne at the Admiralty have attracted favourable notices from historians. Probably the best of the bunch was

Lansdowne, who succeeded Salisbury at the Foreign Office after being a failure at the War Office, but he was another renegade Whig. The lifelong Conservatives inherited by Balfour were so unimpressive as to suggest a correlation between Conservatism and dimness. Only the fact that St John Brodrick was as close to a friend as Balfour's temperament would permit can explain his appointment to the War Office, and even this can scarcely explain how he was kept on as India Secretary after 1903. As for the rest, the presence of Lords Cranborne and Selborne is explained by their belonging to the Cecil clan, while Ritchie at the Exchequer and Arnold-Foster at the Home Office were the sort of heavy furniture which encumbers most Cabinets. Balfour, like all Prime Ministers who inherit Cabinets rather than winning a parliamentary majority at an election, was in a weak position – the careers of Alec Douglas-Home and James Callaghan show the problems this can present – However, in his case things were made worse by the presence of a supremely capable alternative in the shape of Joe Chamberlain.

Of course, as a Liberal Unionist, a Unitarian, a former Radical and an *arriviste*, Chamberlain was not even considered for the succession to Salisbury, and 'AJB' stepped effortlessly into his uncle's place; but he could never fill it. Salisbury's intellect, experience and political common sense had won for him a unique authority, but even this had not stopped questions being asked about his conduct of affairs; Balfour had none of his uncle's common sense, nor yet his authority. As Colonial Secretary, Chamberlain had given Salisbury a good deal of trouble, and if even the Marquess, with his massive prestige, had found him impossible to control, it was unlikely that Balfour would be able to do so. He lacked the stature, the political courage, and perhaps the will so to do. Following Salisbury was never going to be easy. His massive imperturbability had established itself as a style which emanated from the man but which went down well with the electorate. If his authority had not, of late, been unquestioned, his position was unquestionable. He could hand his nephew his crown – but not his charisma. Balfour was a clever man – but like many of his kind he was unsuited for political leadership. Salisbury had been an even cleverer man, but he had never been as remote a figure as Balfour:

> Through all his literary and scientific culture there ran a vein as distinct as an outcrop in geological strata. He always knew beforehand what would be the 'squire's' view of any proposed legislation, and … he always sympathised with it.[1]

With Balfour this instinctive *rapport* was replaced by an intellectual remoteness. It was not that Balfour lacked feelings, it was just that he could not see that they mattered. This left him unable to comprehend the place which passion played in politics. There might be worse defects in the armoury of a politician, but it is not easy to think of them.

Historians have been kinder to the Balfour government than were contemporaries, praising its achievements in foreign, defence and educational matters; but this just goes to show why historians make poor politicians. The first two of these achievements, the Anglo-French *entente* of 1904, and the setting up of the Committee of Imperial Defence in 1902, made little impact electorally, and it could be argued that the *entente* inaugurated what was to be a disastrous change of direction in British foreign policy. The last achievement, the 1902 Education Act, could be said to have played a notable part in bringing the pillars of the temple down on Balfour's head. To the delight of good Conservatives this had provided State aid for Church of England Schools, but 'its political implications were momentous, not least for Chamberlain. It would foster the reunion of the Liberal Party and would estrange a powerful section of the Unionist following in the constituencies.'[2] 'An optimist by profession', Chamberlain told Balfour in September 1902 that the 'political future seems ... most gloomy':

> I told you that your Education Bill would destroy your own Party. It has done so. Our best friends are leaving us by scores and hundreds and they will not come back ... We are so deep in the mire that I do not see how we can get out.[3]

But, as Chamberlain once said, the difference between himself and Balfour was that where the latter 'hates difficulties: I love 'em'.[4] It was, at least in part, the furore created by the Education Act amongst his own followers which pushed Chamberlain in the direction he was to announce so dramatically in 1903 – Tariff Reform.

In retrospect, the appeal of Tariff Reform is difficult to explain. The Conservatives never won a single General Election with it as an active part of their manifesto. But if this suggests that the policy was unpopular with the wider electorate, then such persistence implies that it enjoyed the support of the party activists; there can be no doubt that it was as popular inside the party as it was unpopular elsewhere. As one long-time supporter of tariffs, the future High Commissioner of Egypt and Colonial Secretary, Lord Lloyd, put it: 'I should never have come into politics at all had it not been for Mr Chamberlain's personality and politics';[5] he was not alone in this view. What Chamberlain offered young men like George Lloyd and another future Cabinet Minister, Leopold Amery, was not just a political campaign, but a crusade – a means of regenerating both Britain and her Empire. For those worried about both – and this included all Unionist activists – the appeal of Tariff Reform was irresistible. Young men like Amery and Lloyd flocked to the banner. What Chamberlain had done was to initiate 'the first great debate on Britain's economic future after the passing of her mid-Victorian supremacy'.[6]

It is often supposed that Chamberlain's policy split the Conservative and Unionist Party, but it would be more correct to say that it took it captive. Chamberlain had played a major role in the realignment of British politics after 1886 which had helped create the Unionist ascendancy; now he was to play an even greater part in destabilizing the Coalition and destroying that ascendancy. Tariff Reform became *the* political issue, and it is some measure of Balfour's intellectual remoteness that he imagined that it could be fudged. Chamberlain left the Cabinet in 1903 and initiated what became, in effect, a civil war in two stages: the first, from 1903 to 1905, saw the soul of the party captured and the leading opponents of tariffs extruded; the second, from 1906 to 1910, was a slower guerrilla war; but the final result was that by 1910 the Conservatives were a high-tariff party. The routes by which Chamberlain arrived at his policy serve to explain its appeal.

Tariff Reform, as presented by Chamberlain, offered the Unionist alliance a way out of an impasse. The triumphs of the Salisbury era had been based upon a peculiar set of historical circumstances. Gladstone's espousal of Home Rule for Ireland and the capture of the Liberal Party by the adherents of the Newcastle Programme had allowed the Unionists to present themselves as the party of stability – without Salisbury having to do very much in the way of positively wooing votes. He was able to present the Conservative and Unionist alliance as the party of Imperialism. The Empire, it was argued, was essential if Britain was to maintain its power and prosperity. Since the Liberals could be presented as hostile to Empire, they could also be accused of threatening that power and prosperity.[7] By 1903 this exercise was more difficult to accomplish given the decline in prominence of Home Rule and the cost of paying for Empire, as exemplified by the Boer War. For Chamberlain, Tariff Reform offered an answer to the awkward question of how the Empire was to develop and how the costs of Imperialism were to be met; the foreigner would pay.

Tariff Reform also offered a way out of another dilemma. During the Salisbury period the Unionists had presented themselves as the champions of the rights of 'property' in the widest sense. Whilst Gladstone seemed to be threatening these rights, it was enough to 'defend' them. But the interests of the aristocracy, farmers and industrialists were not so easy to reconcile when the immediate threat from the Liberals was removed. Social legislation to improve the lot of those without property could only come from the taxes of those who possessed it – which was not quite what the Conservative and Unionist Party was supposed to stand for. Here again tariffs provided a way of squaring the circle; the foreigner, through taxes on imported goods, would pay.

Tariffs also provided a way of revitalizing the Salisburian coalition. Salisbury, as we have seen, had been fortunate enough to operate in a political environment which had conduced to the negative role he preferred to play; but by 1902 this was no longer enough – something more positive was needed to pull the alliance together. We shall never grasp why the Conservatives embraced tariffs with such fervour unless we appreciate their multi-faceted appeal. Disraeli had presented the Conservatives as the party of social reform and Imperialism; Tariff Reform provided a means of reasserting these credentials. If 'Joe's War' had stymied 'Joe's pensions', then 'Joe's taxes' would provide a way of squaring the circle; old folk would have their pensions, but it would be the foreigner and not the domestic taxpayer who would cough up the money. An increase in government expenditure was necessary – indeed the Education Act alone would make that necessary – but if pensions and a strong navy were also desired, then the prospect of raising the money required through direct taxation was one with little appeal to any Conservative. Tariffs provided the answer – with the added bonus that, by creating an Imperial trading area, they might strengthen the bonds of Empire. It is little wonder that the policy, expounded as it was by the most charismatic figure in British politics, swept the Conservative Party behind it. But to the Liberals it was an uncovenanted blessing. What the Education Act had begun in the way of Liberal reunion, the threat to Free Trade completed.

There were two main arguments against tariffs, the one more immediately apparent than the other. The first, and electorally most devastating riposte was that the price of food would be raised by taxing foreign imported foodstuffs – the so-called 'dear loaf'. As one historian has recently put it with succinct and devastating accuracy: 'In an electoral system dominated by low earners the Conservatives appeared to be threatening to raise the cost of living, and three general election defeats provide strong prima facie evidence that the Conservatives paid a heavy price for their advocacy of "food taxes".'[8] This was sufficient to deny the Conservatives their chance to implement the policy. But even had they been in a position to do so, they would have found another obstacle – the reluctance of the colonies of white settlement to be locked into an economic system which would have condemned them to be producers of primary products in perpetuity. Beyond that lay the centrifugal forces which would militate against Chamberlain's dreams of Imperial federation.

Thus it was that Chamberlain's successful capture of the soul of the Conservative and Unionist Party locked it into a policy which was destined to blast the political careers of a generation of Conservative leaders. After 1905 it would be ten long and tumultuous years before a Conservative would again sit on the Treasury bench; it would be seven more before there would again be a Conservative Prime Minister. If, as Harold Wilson reminded us, 'a week is a long time in politics', then 17 years is an eternity – as some of Wilson's successors will bear out.

Balfour's attempts to deal with the irruption of passion into politics were the most inept in the annals of modern Conservatism – with the possible exception of Major's equally maladroit efforts to deal with the problem of 'Europe'. His exquisite manner concealed a ruthlessness in personal and political matters which few suspected until the stiletto went in between the second and third ribs, and he imagined that a little Machiavellianism would serve him well in the crisis which arose in May 1903. By dint of not letting the leading 'free-fooders' know that Chamberlain intended to quit the Cabinet to campaign for his policy, the Prime Minister secured their resignations – but since Devonshire, whose retirement was not desired, also went, this tactic was a little too successful. There was a farcical interlude when Devonshire was prevailed upon to return – it transpired that the increasingly absent-minded peer had forgotten the key to his ministerial red box and had thus been unable to read Balfour's note telling him of Chamberlain's intention. But in the end, the old Whig left office – and left the government somewhat weaker for his departure. When he had assumed the leadership, Balfour had commented that there were only two men whose introduction to the Cabinet would 'add to its distinction and efficiency' – Austen Chamberlain and George Wyndham.[9] They had duly been added, but they hardly made up for the weight lost when 'Joe' and Devonshire went – and, as Balfour had feared, there was no talent capable of doing so. Where, in 1900, the government had had Salisbury at the Foreign Office and 10 Downing Street, and the triumvirate of Chamberlain, Devonshire and Balfour to steady the Cabinet, only the latter now remained; an increasingly isolated figure in a government which lacked both executive competence or unity. It has been argued that during Balfour's time 'the Conservatives continued to set a high standard in constructive legislation',[10] but this is to miss the point.

Successful Conservatism is not necessarily about adding to the Statute Book. As one of Balfour's junior whips, Lord Balcarres, commented in 1902, 'we have more to fear from legislation than we have to gain from it.'[11] As Gladstone had discovered between 1868 and 1874, governments that spend a good deal of their time legislating usually stir up trouble for themselves. The Education Act may, in the eyes of historians, be a piece of 'constructive legislation', but for the Conservative and Unionist alliance it was, as we have seen, destructive. Beset by the aftershocks from the Education Act, riven by their internal disputes and under effective fire from a suddenly united opposition, the government looked to Balfour for leadership – and got nimble political footwork instead. It is true that there were achievements in the last two years of the Balfour Government, but the chief of these was the Anglo-French entente, which made little impact on the electorate. The *Dreadnought* was developed, as were new naval guns, but again these had little utility when it came to gathering votes. Unable either to squash or square Chamberlain, Balfour attempted to manoeuvre into a middle position between Free Trade and tariffs. In so doing he demonstrated the limitations of the philosophic mind as applied to politics. Intellectually it was possible to conceive of a position midway between Chamberlain and Winston Churchill – but politically no one was interested in it. Balfour's fastidious mind shrank in horror from the sort of intellectual roughhouse in which Chamberlain and Churchill gloried; but that was why they were more successful in capturing the imagination of the electorate.

Balfour's intellectual dexterity has been more appreciated by posterity than by contemporaries; but with neither was it particularly effective. It may be that Balfour hoped that his sudden resignation in December 1905 would embarrass the Liberal leader, Sir Henry Campbell-Bannerman. There were well-founded rumours that some of the leading Liberals had decided that they would only enter a Cabinet under conditions which Sir Henry could accept only with humiliation, but if Balfour had calculated that his departure would provide the Liberals with a chance to display their own divisions, he had miscalculated badly; the prospect of office concentrated Liberal minds wonderfully.

As with the Liberals in 1895, and Labour in 1951, the antechamber of opposition was reached with almost indecent haste by those about to enter it. In constitutional theory there need not have been an election before 1907, but by the end of 1905 a battered and demoralized government had had enough. Balfour's attempts to hold the Cabinet together by ingenious intellectual compromises failed in 1903, and he enjoyed little more success when it came to his party. His Chancellor,

Joe's son Austen, summed things up only too accurately writing in August 1904 when he described 'the Party viewed as a whole' as 'timid, undecided, vacillating. It has no constructive policy. It does not know what is to be its future.'[12] The strain told on Balfour's health, and by early 1905 a close friend was sure that another 12 months in office would kill him.[13] Fresh assaults from Chamberlain in 1905, bringing as they did the threat of further disruption, seem to have convinced the tired Balfour that it was time to quit.[14] The leader in the Lords, Lansdowne, argued that they could postpone an election until late 1906, but admitted that, as everyone was expecting one in 1905, he could see no reason for prolonging the party's agony for another year; neither he nor Balfour expected to win.[15] For once Balfour had divined the wishes of the electorate successfully.

Because the defeat of 1906 was the greatest in the history of the modern Conservative Party it is only natural, as with that of 1945, that attempts should have been made to provide some profound explanation. Certainly there were candidates enough, according to choice. The 'free-fooders' blamed Tariff Reform, although as most of them lost their seats, this was a little perverse of them. The Chamberlainites thought that 'Chinese Labour' may have had 'an enormous influence', with trades unionists everywhere anxious about allegations that the Unionists intended to import more coolies into the Transvaal to undertake the work of reconstruction. Mrs Chamberlain found that 'Joe' had been met everywhere by cries of 'Chinese slavery' and drew the conclusion that what the ordinary working man really cared about was 'cheap labour'.[16] For Chamberlain and his followers the message of defeat was plain – what was needed was a whole-hearted commitment to tariffs.

All these causes, and a myriad local ones, no doubt had their effect, but the fact was that the Conservative vote was not dramatically less than it had been in 1900, and there had been many signs that they would lose the next election. Since 1900 they had been steadily losing by-elections: one in 1901, three the following year (including North Leeds which had always returned a Conservative), and four in 1903. By the time of the election the Conservatives had lost 20 seats – a record at that time.[17] In 1900 just over 3.5 million votes had been cast, with 35.1 per cent of the electorate not being troubled by a contest. The Unionists picked up 50.3 per cent of the vote on this occasion. But when the Liberals had won in 1892, more than 4.5 million votes had been cast. In 1906 more than 5 million men voted, and there were fewer uncontested seats.[18] The message is plain. The Conservatives benefited from a low turn out, which, in turn, seemed to be both a consequence and a cause of Liberal disunion. When, as on this occasion and again in 1910, the Liberal vote had a cause to rally around, it could expect to return a Liberal administration. What the elections of 1906 and 1910 showed were the limitations of the Salisburian ascendancy. Faced, as they were in 1906, with a Liberal revival, an anti-Conservative swing and the intervention of the Labour Representation Committee in strongholds of working-class Toryism like Lancashire (where the heir to the Derby earldom, Lord Stanley, went down to defeat in a traditional family seat to a working carpenter),[19] it was little wonder that the party was decimated.

There were only 157 Conservative MPs left, chief amongst the casualties at this political Agincourt being 'Prince Arthur' himself. Of those who had towered above the political scene in Salisbury's last government, only Joe Chamberlain survived the deluge – with his Birmingham fiefdom dented, but with all seven seats remaining in Unionist hands – almost a twentieth of the combined Conservative and Unionist strength. About 109 of the surviving Unionists were Chamberlainites. Thus, despite the heavy defeat, the Tariff Reformers were able to claim, like the Socialists after their defeat in 1983, that what was needed to bring electoral success was more of the policy which others claimed had lost the election.

With Balfour out of the House it was inevitable that Chamberlain would deputise for him – which was bound to mean that the Tariff Reformers would have their way. Lansdowne, shaken by the scale of the Unionist defeat, did not think he would 'approve' of the line which Chamberlain would take in the Commons. He told Balfour that he was sure that 'Joe' would 'nail *his* colours to the mast, and invite us to set to work at once to convert the country to his fiscal proposals'. The problem with this was that many Unionists had accepted tariffs with great intellectual reservations and these men were unlikely to 'go any further. If Joe insists on pushing his views, the schism will become deeper & the Unionist party will degenerate into two feeble and mutually suspicious groups.'[20] There were those, like the bucolic squire, Walter Long, who declared vigorously that the Conservatives would 'not be led by a bloody radical';[21] but the failure of the squirearchy and the House of Cecil to provide leadership had led to just that possibility.

But Chamberlain, at 69, had driven himself too hard. As early as 1904 Balcarres had observed that 'anxiety or overwork is beginning to tell on his physique: his colour, a luminous sallow hue, does not connote good health.'[22] In mid-1905 there had been several occasions upon which the great orator had been at a loss for words, and his magnificent memory appeared to be less than it used to be;[23] but Chamberlain's will provided the sinew which drove the strong arm of the Tariff Reform crusade. Despite debilitating attacks of gout and high blood pressure, Chamberlain fought the election campaign with fervour. Lansdowne gloomily agreed that the Chamberlainites were in the ascendant, and he could not see how 'we [can] save the unity of the party upon terms which would not be disastrous to it, and damaging to our reputations'. He told Balfour that any 'compromise' which Chamberlain would accept would 'inevitably be regarded as a surrender on your part'.[24] On St Valentine's Day 1906, Balfour agreed that the party must move towards Chamberlain's position. It was 'Joe's' finest hour. With the party captured and its machine more or less in his hands, Chamberlain's position was becoming formidable. Not only was he the only Unionist with a large claim on public opinion, he was also the only one who seemed to have a positive policy and, as the most formidable debater on the Unionist side, his reputation was bound to be further enhanced by the leading role he would play in harassing the new government. Chamberlain was looking beyond this election to the next one in 1911 or 1912; by then, with Liberal failure and economic troubles, the Tariff Reform message would be irresistible.[25]

On 7 July Birmingham gave a great celebration for its most famous adopted son: MP for the city for 30 years, its former Lord Mayor and the Chancellor of its university; it was the apotheosis of Joseph Chamberlain. On 11 July, resting from the exertions of the previous few days, Chamberlain suffered a massive paralytic stroke. Uncertain at first of the extent of his infirmities, and not wishing to jeopardise the cause for which he had given so much, Chamberlain's family kept the matter quiet, issuing bulletins saying that he was suffering from unusually severe attacks of gout. In early January 1907 Balfour had a physician examine a photograph of Chamberlain to determine what was wrong with him and whether he was likely to recover; the diagnosis was that he would not; nor did he. For seven years the stricken colossus watched helplessly from the side-lines whilst his oldest son, Austen, attempted to bend the bow of Ulysses.[26]

Chamberlain's body might no longer respond to his gigantic will – but the Conservative Party could be made to do so. The first stage of Chamberlain's campaign had seen the final political extinction of the Whigs. Devonshire, Lord Goschen and those who had followed them from Gladstone to Salisbury, went into the wilderness over tariffs and never emerged. Younger 'free-fooders', like Churchill, had also been extruded. The final victim of Chamberlain's will was the 'Hotel Cecil' itself. If the party which disappeared into opposition as the Conservative Party emerged from it as the Unionist Party, that owed much to the victory of Chamberlain – which in turn owed much to Balfour's defects as a leader.

Even in the Commons, where his effectiveness had been undoubted, Balfour was the despair of his Whips, who regretted the fact that he 'does not make up his mind what he is going to say till he actually gets up'.[27] He conveyed neither vision, nor hope, nor even passion to his demoralized troops. He knew few of his followers and seemed to care little about them or their opinions – which he quite obviously regarded as unworthy of his attention. His own intimates, politicians like George Wyndham and St John Broderick, had been failures in office and were not improved by the experience of opposition. Nor were Balfour's forensic talents best displayed in the new parliamentary environment. Re-elected for a London seat, Balfour soon found that his old undisputed mastery in debate was gone; as the journalist, J. L. Garvin, put it to Walter Long: 'They laugh and jeer at him as if he was something let down from the skylight.'[28] The Liberal majority were impatient with his philosophical disquisitions, and his own backbenchers, their morale low, found no inspiration in him; he would, in time, recover some of his old mastery, but not until it was too late to save his leadership. Indeed, the one bright spark in the gloom for the Unionists was the parliamentary debut of the MP for Liverpool, Walton, F. E. Smith. In the most famous maiden speech of the age, 'F. E.' (as he quickly became ubiquitously known) excoriated the Liberals, taking particular pleasure in raking both Lloyd George and the renegade Churchill with his rapid fire. Balfour quickly discovered what others in his position have – deprived of the quasi-divinity that doth hedge the Premiership, the wind was not tempered to the shorn lamb.

Lloyd George once said of Herbert Gladstone that he was living proof of the fact that talent is not inheritable. It would be both unfair and unkind to make such a comment about the sons of the third Marquess of Salisbury; they had plenty of talent – it was judgement and warm red blood which they lacked. But their presence in the first rank of the 'freefooders' was evidence of more than their position on tariffs. It was not only on the 'Fiscal Question' that the Cecils and the Chamberlainites parted company, they disagreed on the 'whole way of looking at politics'. To Lord Robert Cecil, the Chamberlainite view appeared 'to be utterly sordid and materialistic, not yet corrupt but on the high road to corruption'.[29] To Chamberlain, the Cecils and their aristocratic supporters appeared to be anachronistic and effete survivals of a feudal system which had had its day. Salisbury's electoral ascendancy had been precariously based upon a chance concatenation of circumstances. His own disregard for the outrage which organized labour felt over the Taff

Vale Case of 1901, which had made trades unions liable at law for the actions of their members, and Conservative disdain for the feelings of nonconformists over the Education Act seemed, like their blindness to the need to widen the tax base in order to pay for necessary social reform, signs that they, and their class, were not fit leaders for the new age. They viewed with distaste the mass electioneering tactics pioneered by Chamberlain, and they held their aristocratic noses aloof from the 'caucus' style of local party organization. Balfour himself was blind to the passions and politics which had brought his party so low, telling Lady Salisbury that defeat had 'nothing whatever to do with any of the things we have been squabbling over the last few years', but was, rather, 'a faint echo of the same movement which has produced massacres in St. Petersburg, riots in Vienna, and Socialist processions in Berlin'.[30] Even if this was so, it did not appear that Balfour had any answer to it, except to use the House of Lords to despoil the Liberals of their gains – a strategy not calculated to reduce the risk of revolution.

It would, however, be misleading to see the division in the party entirely as one between 'old Conservatism' and 'new Unionism', or between landed and commercial wealth – there were long-established landed Conservatives like the Earl of Derby and the Duke of Portland who lined up alongside Chamberlain; although it would be true to say that there were fewer 'commercial' men who took their stand with the 'free-fooders'. The real line of division was between those Unionists who saw the need for social reform, and those who did not.[31] It is no accident that the Unionist Social Reform Committee was dominated by tariff reformers. As we have seen, for this group Chamberlain was offering both a way of paying for social reform and an Imperial ideology. The 1906 election decimated Chamberlain's opponents. Forty-eight 'free-fooders' stood, only 16 of them were returned. With over 109 seats out of a total of about 157, the tariff reformers were kept from total victory in the party only by the sudden removal of their leader from the scene.

Chamberlain's incapacity, combined with an upturn in the economy between 1905 and 1907, took some of the steam out of the great crusade, but as tariffs still offered the only alternative to the Liberal plans to increase taxation on the wealthy, it was natural that their proponents would play them against the government's policy initiatives. The Tariff Reform League in the country, and a group of 50 MPs known as the 'Confederacy' in the House, formed the spearhead of the continuing campaign, even as they composed the mainstay of the Unionist opposition to the government. Balfour, who was rich in obstructionist tactics but void of any constructive strategy, became increasingly an object of scorn to the Chamberlainites. By 1907 a majority of constituency organizations had come out in favour of tariffs, and even the languid Balfour had to agree that the issue was one which ought to be pressed on the government. To the Confederates this was too little and too late. With Campbell-Bannerman's administration foiled in many of its plans by the House of Lords, and losing seats in by-elections (including, to every Conservative's delight, Churchill's in 1908), Unionist Party managers began to indulge in daydreams of a healthy majority in the next election. If this came about, there could be no doubt that the next Conservative and Unionist government would be a very different creature to its predecessor.

But the arrival in Downing Street of Chamberlain's most formidable opponent, H. H. Asquith, saw the beginning of a process which allowed the Liberals to seize the initiative. Campbell-Bannerman had threatened to 'amend' the Lords if they kept throwing out his legislation, but he had never done anything more than talk. By 1909 the government was facing a dilemma of its own making. On the one hand they were committed to pay for the old age pensions which the Chancellor, Lloyd George, advocated; but so too were they pledged to build more *Dreadnoughts*, to which the said Chancellor objected most strongly. Lloyd George and Churchill, representing the radical wing of the party, both made it clear that they would accept no reduction in spending on social reform; the imperialist wing of the Liberal Party, on the other hand, insisted on more battleships. Out of this difficulty emerged the celebrated 'People's Budget'.

David Lloyd George was already an object of peculiar aversion to the Unionists – his proposal to increase taxes on land and to tack them onto the budget made him the most loathed man whenever Unionists gathered together. In a political era that was to see the rise of the outsider to political prominence (whether in the form of Bonar Law, the Canadian-born businessman, or Ramsay MacDonald, the deracinated would-be intellectual), Lloyd George still stood out as 'not one of us'. His background was, in fact, little different in terms of class and comfort than that of his leader, Asquith, but where the latter had gone to Oxford, shed his Yorkshire accent and eventually acquired a wife who would encourage him to lose his nonconformist roots, Lloyd George remained an outsider. The fact that he grew up in an environment in which English was the second language and the badge of the oppressor, had something to do with this phenomenon. The young Lloyd George had something of the 'chippiness' often felt by talented young men from humble backgrounds who feel themselves unduly disadvantaged compared to less bright contemporaries. Lloyd George was a provincial solicitor, not a Chancery barrister, and he championed the cause of Welsh nonconformity before he breathed the radical fires of Limehouse. Personally he was nonconformist in a variety of ways, not all of them compatible with the purely religious connotation of the word. It was not that Lloyd George was unaware of the truth, but he often found it inconvenient, and inconveniences were something which he tried to avoid. His private life was of the kind which in the early 1990s was to lead to 19 ministers resigning in two years. If Liberals occupy a half-way house between Conservative and Labour, then it is fitting that Lloyd George should have combined the sexual peccadilloes of the former with the financial vices which often characterize the latter. Yet he was the greatest platform orator of the age, and its most formidable demagogue – as his scathing attacks on the Unionists in the aftermath of the defeat of the 'People's Budget' showed.

The omens for the Unionists had been favourable before the first of the 1910 elections The economy took a turn for the worse in 1907–8, with an increase in unemployment seeming to give fresh life to the Tariff Reform campaign. The failure of Campbell-Bannerman to implement his programme had also led to disillusionment amongst Liberals, and the Unionists had won control of Sheffield, Nottingham and Leicester in the local elections in 1908.[32] From a Unionist point of view the highlight of the year had been the defeat of the renegade Winston Churchill in Manchester. The following year had seen bitter disputes inside the Liberal Cabinet over 'guns and butter', with Lloyd George and Churchill both threatening to resign because of proposals to spend more money on the navy. From Asquith's point of view the election and its cause provided a welcome diversion from trying to control his own party.

The result of the two elections of 1910 paved the way for the most turbulent period in British politics this century. Despite the Whiggish tendency in historical writing which portrays the failure of the Conservatives to win as the inevitable result of fighting a campaign based on actions by the Peers, the fact was that the Unionists did as well as could be expected, and they certainly won a majority of English seats.

Whatever they had campaigned on, the Unionists faced a number of structural problems which Salisbury had never had to deal with. One of these was the shrinking of the working-class Tory vote, visible in 1906 and again in 1910. The reasons for this are complex, but broadly speaking are connected with the way in which 'secular issues, especially those relating to the workplace, displaced confessional differences as a focus of political debate'.[33] It might be noted that the 'naval scare' seems to have helped the Tories regain votes in their old naval dockyard constituencies such as Plymouth. The change in the structure of the ownership of firms, in which 'family businesses' gave way increasingly to public corporations, removed one important link between employer and employees, and as the Conservatives increasingly looked like the party of remote 'bosses', their appeal to workers declined accordingly. Of course these phenomena were not universal. In the Midlands, which retained the old family-run firms (like Baldwin's ironworks) for longer, or on Merseyside, where the old anti-Irish, anti-Catholic and anti-Temperance cries still rang out with assurance,[34] working-class Toryism survived, but there is no doubt that nationally the decline of that vote in areas where the Labour Party and the trades unions were strong damaged the Conservative Party.[35]

The second structural problem was one which magnified the effect of the first: the united front presented by the forces of radicalism. The emergence of a Labour Party was not necessarily damaging only to the Conservatives; it might, after all, be expected to pick up at least as many votes from the Liberals. But the 1903 'Lib-Lab' pact concluded by Herbert Gladstone and Ramsay MacDonald meant that the two left-of-centre parties would not compete against each other. By 1910 there were those in the Labour Party who wondered whether this was not hindering their development, but since this is something upon which historians cannot agree even 70 years later, it is hardly surprising that the pact held.[36] As Austen Chamberlain told Balfour in October 1907: 'if the struggle were now, as in former times, merely a contest between Government and Opposition, I should have no misgiving ... But the advent of the Labour and Socialist Party has changed all this.'[37] From this point of view the Liberals could not have had a better cry upon which to campaign in 1910: 'peers versus people' hardly provided the Unionists with an opportunity to split the progressive alliance.

Ironically, despite these difficulties, the Conservatives performed very strongly, winning back much of the ground they had lost in 1906. But their preferred electoral weapon, Tariff Reform, was not well-calculated to disrupt the alliance facing them, since it was easily presented to the poor as a device which would raise the price of their basic foodstuffs. The result was that even when, as in January 1910, the Unionists did well, it was not enough to give them a parliamentary majority. They may have had 272 seats to the Liberals' 274, but the 84 Irish Nationalists and 42 Labour MPs now held the balance of parliamentary power. This, of course, was nothing new. Salisbury had faced similar, if less favourable arithmetic in 1885, but this time there was no chance of the Liberal Party splitting. Representing, as they did, the majority of English seats, and conscious of having taken 116 seats from the Liberals, it was galling in the extreme for the Unionists to find themselves still in opposition because of Irish votes; it was a position they found nearly intolerable, not least because of its implications.

Immediately following the election in January, it was clear that Asquith would call for the veto of the House of Lords to be amended. This, in itself, was bad enough, but what made it worse was the fact that this was bound to be followed by a new Home Rule measure for Ireland; and with the Lords emasculated, there would be no constitutional way of preventing it. It was little wonder that many Unionists found themselves veering towards unconstitutional methods of achieving their objective.

Attempts by the party leaders to find a compromise following the death of Edward VII ended in failure, and before the new monarch, George V, would agree to Asquith's demand that he should create enough peerages to ensure the passage through the Lords of a bill designed to amend that House's power, he insisted upon another election. When the second election of 1910 produced the same stalemate, the heat and the noise of party conflict rose to new levels. The argument focused upon the House of Lords, and the intra-party dispute inside the Unionist coalition was almost as severe as that between Liberals and Unionists.

Despite efforts to portray the opponents of the Parliament Act as 'backwoodsmen' coming down from their ancestral country-seats for a day-trip to the capital in order to impede the forces of progress, the fact is that it was the most active and the most radical parts of the party which fought the hardest.[38] The journalist Leo Maxse, one of a number of 'radical right' polemicists who played a leading part in organising those Unionists known as the 'ditchers' (because of their readiness to 'die in the last ditch' rather than surrender), stigmatised the leaders of the 'hedgers', Lansdowne and Balfour, as 'a timid Whig and a cynical philosopher', and his line, that the party's 'Mandarins' were an effete, out-of-touch elite, was shared by many who also shared his general views.[39] It may, therefore, have been ironic, given his radical past, that Joseph Chamberlain should have acted as a focus for the 'ditchers', but it was hardly accidental. The 'Mandarins' took the view that they were facing a political problem which must be susceptible to a compromise solution; keen tariff reformers believed that they were facing a fundamental assault on the Constitution from Socialists and Irishmen.

Chamberlain's official biographer captured the importance of Tariff Reform for his hero when he wrote of it as 'a way to hold the working classes to their Tory allegiance'.[40] Chamberlain, although unable to play a part in either of the election campaigns, had wanted to fight on the 'issue of Tariff Reform against Socialism'.[41] What Lloyd George's budget, with its land taxes, involved was not simply an attack on the landed interest, but something which Conservatives could interpret as full-scale Socialism; it was also a formidable attack on Tariff Reform. Asquith's government, facing the dilemma which had confronted every British government since the 1880s, that of providing social services and Imperialism on a narrowly defined tax base, had taken the simple but effective option of increasing the tax rate for landowners. Where Chamberlain had been proposing to make the foreigner pay, Lloyd George wanted to 'squeeze the rich'. The result of the Liberal failure to convince a majority of the English vote of the wisdom of their policies was that the most populous part of the electoral map, England, would have them imposed by Irish, Scottish and Welsh votes – and, for good measure, would also be subject to the disruption of the United Kingdom. To add to the sense of injury, the party of the Union would be unable to prevent Home Rule for Ireland because the Liberals were bent on changing the constitutional rules by amending the powers of the Lords. The result of this situation was to create a deep chasm between 'hedgers' and 'ditchers', with the latter coming to see the former as little better than traitors; the former Viceroy of India, Curzon, became an object of particular detestation because he changed sides.

The constitutional crisis was the severest test yet of Balfour's leadership, but it drew forth from him no hitherto unsuspected qualities; he sought to handle it, as he had the Tariff Reform question, by a series of adroit tactical devices – once more revealing how little he appreciated the passion which drove other politicians. Before the second election Balfour, without consulting Austen Chamberlain, or anyone much except Lansdowne, promised that Tariff Reform would be subject to a referendum before it would be introduced. As we have seen, it had little effect on the outcome of the election, but it irritated the Chamberlainites enormously.[42] Austen Chamberlain described it as 'a slap in the face',[43] and the experience helped convince even that mild-mannered man that Balfour's leadership had not long to run.

When the Unionist frontbenchers met on 21 July to consider their reaction to the news that Asquith now possessed guarantees from the King that sufficient peerages would be created to pass the Parliament Bill, Balfour recommended acquiescence; 14 of his colleagues went along with him, but eight dissented. This was bad enough, but when the quality of the eight 'rebels' was considered, it was clear that there would be problems: Lords Selborne and Salisbury were connected by ties of family, Lord Balcarres was the new Chief Whip, whilst George Wyndham was another personal intimate. Austen Chamberlain's presence in the 'rebel' ranks symbolised great danger to party unity. This group was supported by some of the keenest and most active young MPs including Leo Amery, George Lloyd, Lord Wolmer and F. E. Smith. More senior figures like the eminent King's Counsel, Sir Edward Carson, and great Imperial proconsul, Lord Milner, also adhered to the 'ditcher' cause, joined in the Lords by the Dukes of Bedford, Marlborough and Westminster. Their nominal leader was the former Unionist Lord Chancellor, the octogenarian Lord Halsbury, and the 'Halsbury Club' became the focus not simply for opposition to the Parliament Bill, but also for discontent with the 'Mandarins'.[44]

Balfour, having begun by backing Lansdowne, failed to take a hard line with the rebels. To the astonishment of some of the whips he did nothing to try to prevent MPs attending a meeting in honour of Halsbury in late July, nor did he protest when Austen Chamberlain issued a letter in support of the 'diehard' cause. In the end, thanks to a failure of nerve or an access of judgement (depending upon one's point of view) the Parliament Bill was passed. But the episode had created a party within a party. After three election defeats in a row, Balfour's position would have been vulnerable anyway; after the fiasco over the Parliament Bill it was untenable. With the *National Review* running on its masthead the initials 'BMG', standing for 'Balfour must go', and with the 'Halsburyites' calling for a more energetic opposition, Balfour's position became a matter of intense speculation. On 8 November 1911 Balfour retired from the leadership, ostensibly on grounds of 'health', but in reality because his nerveless leadership had brought nothing but disaster. The long reign of the House of Cecil had come to an undistinguished end.

6 The Unknown Bonar Law

It quickly becomes tiresome for the reader to be presented continually with the statement that 'of all leaders of the Conservative Party, Box-Bender was the most surprising'; one might almost come to the conclusion that all leaders of the Conservative Party are surprising – which is certainly not the case. Bonar Law possessed many qualities, but an ability to surprise was hardly one of them. Still, a greater contrast to Balfour could not have been found. If Balfour almost fitted the description of the heir in Kipling's *The 'Mary Gloster'*, whose rooms at Cambridge were 'beastly – more like whore's than a man's', then Andrew Bonar Law, who was a friend of the poet's, nearly matched that of Sir Antony Gloster himself: 'I didn't begin with askings. I took my job and I stuck: I took the chances they wouldn't, an' now they're calling it luck.' There was certainly a large element of that in Law's rise to the leadership.

Balfour's sudden retirement presented the party with a dilemma. As we have seen, the last Conservative Cabinet had not been notable for its talent, and none of its surviving members had enhanced their reputation in opposition. Of the senior figures, Curzon's support for the 'hedgers' put him out of the running, which left only two realistic candidates: Austen Chamberlain and Walter Long. But both had their disadvantages: Chamberlain was a Liberal Unionist and Long was a bucolic country squire. Neither promised to command the unity of the party; indeed, neither of them seemed able to command anything at all. Long resented Chamberlain as a jumped-up Radical, whilst Austen, ever mindful of his father's reputation for 'pushiness', hardly liked to put himself forward. As in 1963, when a similar situation obtained, the circumstances were ideal for a compromise candidate to step in – in this case it was Andrew Bonar Law, a 53-year-old iron master, who had been born in Canada. The contrast with Balfour could hardly have been more exaggerated.

Bonar Law, like Sir Antony Gloster, was no aesthete. A teetotal widower whose favourite tipples were ginger beer or lime juice, he 'scarcely noticed what he ate, and, when he could, he left the table as soon as he could'; he was an inveterate pipe and cigar smoker – which may explain his lack of palate and appetite.[1] His leisure pursuits consisted of chess and bridge, and he not only possessed no great country houses, but was positively indifferent to the style of life which they represented. As a fellow Conservative, Arthur Lee, put it: 'he was the most congenital Philistine whom I had ever met or imagined; to him Art, Music, fair women and all the beautiful things of life were definitely repugnant.[2] None of this, of course, made him any less effective as a politician; indeed, as Mrs Thatcher and Gordon Brown both showed, a little Philistinism could be very effective. Some historians have seen him as representing the new type of Conservative politician, but what he really represented were the two main causes which galvanized Conservatives in 1911: Tariff Reform and Ireland. From the start he had been intellectually convinced by Chamberlain's case, and as one of the few members of the Unionist front bench who sounded at home with economics, his views carried great weight; no one could accuse him of intellectual frivolity – indeed, no one ever accused him of being either intellectual or frivolous. But he did what Balfour had conspicuously failed to do, he channelled 'the enthusiasms and frustrations of his party into a coherent Unionist strategy'.[3] There were three aspects to this strategy: Ireland; Tariff Reform; and social reform.

The visceral nature of Law's politics were best seen in his views on Ireland, where he fully agreed with Kipling's verdict that 'the dark eleventh hour/ Draws on and sees us sold/ to every evil power we fought against of old.' His father was an Ulsterman of Scottish descent, as well as a minister of the Presbyterian Church, and thus Unionism was bred in Law's very bones. Like the other two champions of Ulster's cause, the Southern Irish barrister, Sir Edward Carson, and the Birkenhead barrister, F. E. Smith, Law's attachment to Ulster was more than an intellectual fancy.

The 1910 parliamentary stalemate had left Asquith's government at the mercy of the Irish Party in the House of Commons. John Redmond, the Irish leader, had little enough sympathy with the radicalism of Lloyd George's budget, but no Nationalist could turn down the opportunity to remind the Liberals of the need to complete Gladstone's work. It was certainly true that under Campbell-Bannerman and Asquith the Liberals had shown little remembrance of their mission in Ireland – something which had helped account for their electoral success. But for all his later reputation as 'the last of the Romans', Asquith was not a fastidious politician. A man of acute perception and executive action (when he deemed it was necessary), Henry Herbert Asquith was quite willing to pay the price the Irish wanted; or, rather, he was ready to make Ulster pay it.

The cause of Ulster Unionism has inspired little in the way of sympathy, empathy of even understanding from outsiders; that this has hardly worried the Unionists is just another reason their cause has been so little celebrated. Whilst the caricature of the 'blarney' Irish 'Celt' has attracted sympathy as well as condescension from the inhabitants of the Mainland, the 'Orangeman', with the 'sash his father wore' and his bowler hat, had provoked only exasperated incomprehension; like so many of those who supported the Imperial ambitions of the British, the Ulstermen found the truth of the jibe that it was better to be the enemy of the Empire because that ensured you were bought off; they just discovered it earlier than most. Yet it is not difficult to understand why Bonar Law seized on it as the unifying issue for his party – it did indeed draw together the various strands of Conservative policy. It was not just the old Protestant struggle with the Catholics which was at stake, or even the rights of the landlord as against the tenant – although both of these causes would have found ready support on the Conservative side of the House; it was the very unity of the Empire.

One of the attractions of Tariff Reform was that it spoke to the Edwardian sense of insecurity about the Empire. The causes of the insecurity were not far to seek. The economic depression which had begun in the 1880s had cast a shadow over the high noon of mid-Victorian prosperity, and the inexorable rise of America and Germany as economic powers made it apparent that Britain needed to look to her laurels. The set-backs of the Boer War and the rising costs of Empire all contributed to this sense of insecurity which manifested itself not just in calls for Tariff Reform, but in the foundation of the Navy League and the campaign for compulsory military service; Edwardian Britain knew itself to be a society facing severe challenges: the problem was how best to meet them? The Anglo-French entente was, by origin, a deal to remove colonial differences, but under German pressure it moved, insensibly, into a diplomatic understanding, the only problem being that the French and Germans understood there to be more in it than did the British. Conscious as they were of the enemy without, Conservatives were now faced with the enemy within – and they reacted accordingly.

Parliamentary government is based upon general acceptance of the fiction that what a majority of MPs in the House of Commons decide is the law of the land; this requires a willingness first to reach consensus on that law. The failure of the political class to reach a consensus before legislation was passed, called into question the very basis of parliamentary rule. The Unionists certainly thought they had good reason to question it. The distinguished jurist, Sir William Anson, argued that since it was the Liberals who had done violence to the Constitution in the form of the Parliament Act, Unionists were justified in using any means to prevent their doing further violence upon it in the form of granting Home Rule to Ireland. Speaking at Blenheim on 29 July 1912, with more fervour than grammatical accuracy, Law declared that if the Government went ahead with Irish Home Rule he could 'imagine no length of resistance to which Ulster can go in which I should not be prepared to support them'.[4] Nor were there lacking voices to point out that the Liberals were only in office as a result of votes from the 'Celtic fringe' and that a clear majority of the largest part of the United Kingdom, England, wished for a continuation of the Union. Of course such arguments were as bogus in their way as those used by the government, but Asquith had what Disraeli once called the 'best repartee' – majority in the House. But then, as Bonar Law reminded the government in one of his first major speeches as leader, there were things more powerful than parliamentary majorities.

The real weakness of the Gladstonian case on Home Rule was that it ignored the existence of the Protestants in Ireland. These last were scattered throughout the island, particularly in Dublin, but also, more formidably, in the nine north-eastern counties. Gladstone had never had any answer to their obstinate refusal to accept what they regarded (rightly, as the existence of the Free State was to prove) as 'Rome Rule', and although subsequent Land Acts and Local Government reforms had weakened the position of Unionism in the south of Ireland, in the North and North-West it had been consolidated and strengthened. Moreover, in 1911 the Ulstermen had what they had never had before – a charismatic leader in the form of Sir Edward Carson.

A tall figure with an aquiline nose and a commanding presence, Carson was one of the most eminent KCs in an era when such men were the heroes of the popular press. Most notable for his persistent questioning and eventual conviction of Oscar Wilde, Carson brought the same single-minded determination to political life. He had one cause, the Empire, and he saw in the Home Rule debate the thin end of the wedge of Imperial dissolution. A Southern Irish Protestant himself, he made the cause of Ulster his own – and he made the Imperial Parliament listen to it. It was a mark of his success that to this day historians are unable to decide whether Carson's oblique threats of paramilitary action in the event of a Home Rule bill being passed were part of an elaborate bluff; no one was meant to be able to decide whether he meant it or not – that was the essence of his tactics. What was more dangerous for the continued existence of parliamentary government was Law's willingness to align the Unionist Party with Carson's inflammatory rhetoric. But for both men, as for many Unionists, what was at stake was so important that it commanded a higher loyalty than the parliamentary system. The bitterness evinced towards Asquith – 'old squiffy', as he was derisively nicknamed – was extraordinary, and the shadow of civil war was lifted only by the prospect of a wider Armageddon.

If Ireland strengthened Law's leadership of the party and offered the chance of electoral success, the second of the Unionist causes, Tariff Reform, did neither. In late 1912 Law announced that the party was abandoning the Balfour pledge to hold a referendum before introducing tariffs – indeed, with the Unionists promoting the idea of a referendum on Ireland, it might have seemed to some that they were proposing to take a dubious constitutional innovation as their way out of every difficulty. Law was, however, taken aback by the vehemence of the opposition to his speech – not least from the area in which his seat was situated, Lancashire. His leadership style always owed something to that of the Duke of Plaza Toro – 'I am their leader, I must follow them' – and his reaction on this occasion brought him to the edge of resignation. In an attempt to mollify Lord Derby and the Free Trade contingent, Law appeared to back-track from a commitment to a full tariff programme, which, of course, would have enraged Austen Chamberlain – had he been capable of such an emotion; Amery, Lloyd and company, who were certainly capable of it, responded on his behalf. By early January 1913 there was a fully-fledged leadership crisis when, as the Chief Whip put it: 'we are not only in danger of losing our leaders, but equally of losing the Union, the Welsh Church and Tariff Reform into the bargain.'[5] Carson, however, saved the day by persuading even some of the keenest tariff reformers to sign a memorial asking Law to stay on and to postpone food duties until after another election. Law accepted this for the same reason that most of his opponents did – none of them believed that another leader could command party unity in the same way as he could – especially over Ulster.[6] But the memorial did mark the point at which the Conservative and Unionist Party pledged itself to Imperial Preference, and henceforth this commitment would haunt Bonar Law and his successors.

If the Unionists had, to an extent, had to eat their own words, they were at least served up with an appetising sauce – electoral success. By the end of 1912 they had, thanks to five successive by-election victories, overtaken the Liberals as the largest single party in the Commons; but would they have won the election due in 1915? If Tariff Reform was linked, at least on its Imperial Preference side, with a commitment to Imperial unity which found expression both in Unionism itself and in a belief in a strong defence policy, then it also possessed a link to demands for more social reform. In this sense the policy represented a break with the Salisburian policy of throwing sops to the electorate when necessary and posited the sort of approach to domestic legislation which Gladstone had condemned as 'constructionist'; Chamberlain had not ceased to be a radical when he became a Unionist – something many Conservatives noted. One reason why younger tariff reformers, like F. E. Smith, Leo Amery and George Lloyd had, like Chamberlain himself, supported the 'diehards' was the fear that Lloyd George's confiscatory taxation would both remove one of the reasons for Tariff Reform, and, at the same time, pay for the sort of reforms, such as pensions, which had always been a plank in Chamberlain's platform. With Lloyd George successfully making 'land' a political issue after 1912, the Unionists found themselves being out-flanked. But this should not blind us to the fact that there was a significant number of Unionists, led by the Social Reform Committee, who saw their party as having a significant contribution to make in this sphere. The appeal to 'Tory Democracy' was explicit in the mouths of those like F. E. Smith (although there was no one quite like him), who proclaimed their admiration for Disraeli and Lord Randolph Churchill.

Smith came from Birkenhead and represented the Liverpool constituency of Walton, so he was well aware of the reality of working-class toryism. He saw the party as representing the many thousands of workers who were not in unions and who had no wish to be patronised and dragooned by well-meaning Liberals and their civil servants; this appeal to the 'manly' virtues was accompanied by ones to anti-Irishness and anti-temperance. Indeed, it would hardly be going too far to claim that it was the fact that the Liberals embodied government interference, temperance and support for Irish Home Rule, which constituted the bed-rock of support for Merseyside and Lancashire working-class toryism. But the party leadership proved immune to the blandishments of the Social Reform Committee, and by the eve of the war there was little sign that the Unionists would develop policies which could win working-class support which could not be garnered by appeals to patriotism and disillusionment with the Liberals; and the question remained whether this would be enough to win an election.

If Law brought what he called a 'new style' to the leadership, he also infused the party machinery and hierarchy with new life. One of the common consequences of political failure is that it reminds leaders of the existence of the party organisation; before his demise Balfour had commissioned a report into what was wrong with the Conservatives. Bonar Law inherited this commission and implemented its report, which reorganised and revitalized Conservative Central Office, as well as bringing order into the party's finances. Thanks to systematic fund-raising in the City and from Peers, the Party had £671,000 invested by 1914 – twice the figure for 1911.[7] Law also presided over the fusion of the two parts of the old Salisburian coalition in 1912, with the party formally becoming what it was to remain until the 1970s, the National Unionist Association of Conservative and Unionist Associations. But the question of whether this would have been enough to win an election was never answered. The war which so many Unionists had been expecting for so long finally broke out in August 1914 and it brought with it fresh opportunities for the party.

If Unionism, Tariff Reform and Imperial federation all fitted well with a policy which called for a strong defence policy, then this left the Conservative Party relatively well placed to benefit from the advent of the First World War. The whole ethos of Unionism was better suited to the war than its Liberal counterpart. In the Liberal scheme of things wars should not occur, and if they did, then they should be run on a 'business as usual' basis; well the Great War did break out, and despite years of pretence on Asquith's part, it could not be run on a laissez faire policy. Conservatism had no basic problem with the existence of war – that was the sort of thing which history suggested happened when Great Powers could not agree among themselves; moreover, whatever scruples Conservatives had about using the power of the state, they dissolved in the face of a great national emergency. They certainly had fewer problems about conscription than the Liberals did. Indeed, from the very outbreak of the war, the Unionists were more united than their opponents.

Whilst Asquith and Churchill struggled to persuade Lloyd George to back the war, Bonar Law was able to tell the Prime Minister that if he could not lead a united Cabinet into war, he could rely upon the Unionists for support; indeed, unless he led the country into war, he could not rely upon the Unionists at all. Asquith, who shared the general belief that the war would be over by Christmas, elected to rely upon the Unionists to provide a broad-based national consensus in favour of action. The only problem with this was that by the spring of 1915 the Unionists were far from favouring the course of action which the Liberals adopted.

The Liberals paid dearly for their unreadiness in war. Grey's diplomacy had failed to avert it, and Asquith had little idea how to prosecute it. No satisfactory machinery existed to run the grand strategy of the war, and beyond victory the Liberals had trouble formulating war aims. Asquith's tactical skills had not deserted him, and he made that great recruiting poster, Lord Kitchener, Secretary of State for War; he sought to further burnish his war-making credentials by bringing back Admiral

Fisher at the Admiralty under Churchill. But the partnership between impetuous youth and even more impetuous age was a failure – as were Kitchener's attempts to run the war; having chosen to shelter behind the 'twin colossi', Asquith found his administration having to take the blame for their failures. As it became clear that there would be no quick victory in the West, the government sought one elsewhere, only to find itself embroiled in the Dardanelles. After the failure of the sea-borne assault in March, Fisher rumbled menacingly for a while before resigning; this coincided with newspaper reports blaming a shortage of shells for the failure of the last offensive on the Western front; the result was a full-scale political crisis of the sort which was not supposed to happen during the war. But the truce which had been agreed with the Unionists was already fraying badly – and nothing could protect the government from internal dissention.

At the outbreak of the war the Conservatives had agreed, in an excess of patriotic fervour, that the normal functions of Opposition would be suspended.[8] The experience was a frustrating one. As Curzon, who was coming to play a leading role for the Unionists in the Lords, put it, they were 'expected to give a mute and almost unquestioning support to anything done by the Government', which meant that 'the Government are to have all the advantages, while we are to have the drawbacks of a coalition'.[9] Asquith's insistence on passing the Home Rule and Welsh Church Disestablishment Bills – with only the concession that they would not come into operation until the end of the war – had angered Unionists. His less than firm grasp of grand strategy, or indeed any strategy at all, had done nothing to improve his standing in Unionist eyes – but as he proved on this occasion, his mastery of tactics was second to none. In the face of the crisis he turned to the Unionist leadership and suggested a coalition. The resulting negotiations were Asquith's last political triumph.

Although, in the initial agreement reached on 19 May, Bonar Law had insisted upon parity of representation in the Cabinet for his party, and despite Asquith's conceding this in principle, nothing of the sort occurred. Law himself was fobbed off with the Colonies – an office which Joseph Chamberlain had made great but which was hardly in the first rank. Austen Chamberlain found himself at the India Office, whilst poor Curzon, who at the age of 39 had been thought fit to rule 360 million people, found himself at 55 trying to make something of the Lord Privy Seal's office. It was hardly accidental that the only Unionist who received a rich reward from Asquith was the ex-leader, Balfour, who went to Churchill's old place at the Admiralty. In a Cabinet of 22 there were 12 Liberals, eight Unionists, one non-party figure (Kitchener) and one Labour member (Arthur Henderson at the Board of Education). This was hardly 'parity' of treatment, but as Austen Chamberlain put it: 'There are no two ways about it! If our help is asked by the Govt. we must give it!'[10] They did so, but it was, as the new Minister of Agriculture Lord Selborne put it, 'purgatory to almost all of us.'[11]

It was not just that the prospect of working with old antagonists was in itself distasteful, it quickly became apparent that a great gulf was fixed between some Liberals and the Unionists about how to carry on the war, and the focus of this difference became the controversy over conscription. It is easy to see why this should have been so, for the matter went to the heart of the philosophical difference between the two creeds. For classic Liberals individual liberty was sacrosanct, and there was something more than distasteful about compelling a man to lay down his life for his country; this was a problem which did not bother most Unionists who saw the individual as owing a higher duty to the state. What made the problem particularly acute for Asquith was that as lack of success on the Western front demanded an ever-increasing sacrifice of men to the Moloch of destruction, some of his old colleagues, most particularly Lloyd George, found themselves on the same side of the dispute as the Unionists – not least because they shared the view of the latter that Asquith himself was becoming an obstacle to the winning of the war. In short, the long argument over whether to introduce conscription during late 1915 and 1916 helped form the political alignments which would appear with Asquith's resignation in December 1916.

That the Conservatives would, in the long term, do better out of the war than the Liberals was not surprising. The failures of British arms during the first few years of the war seemed to show that the Unionists had been right to condemn the Liberals for neglecting national defence. The Liberal repugnance for war seemed to militate against its efficient prosecution. Unlike the Unionists, whose benches were at times overflowing with former army officers (by 1915 more than 140 Unionist MPs were under arms), the Liberals were a profoundly civilian party. Of the Cabinet as it stood at the outbreak of the war, only Churchill had military experience – and it did not seem to do him or the war effort much good. Not the least of the ironies of the war was that it was a man who had been within an inch of resigning from the Cabinet in July 1914, Lloyd George, who emerged as the one Liberal minister of 'push and go'.

From Asquith's point of view, Bonar Law was an ideal partner. He was not without ambition, but bore it 'meekly', and he genuinely thought it unpatriotic to intrigue against the Prime Minister – which by 1916 made him something of a rarity. It was only when he had become convinced that Asquith was an impediment to victory that Law decided to join in trying to press upon him a scheme designed to secure greater central direction of the military effort; it was Asquith's contemptuous rejection of the plan and his attempt to scupper it by subsequently refusing to serve under Lloyd George and resigning which finished him off. The resulting split in the Liberal Party helped create the essential condition for what historians would see as a period of Unionist predominance. During the long nineteenth-century exile, and in the period after 1910, the Conservatives were the largest party in England and the largest homogeneous party in the Commons, but whilst the Liberals were united, they could not quite break through to become the natural Party of Government; their belief in the Union was so sincere that it quite transcended electoral self-interest. But once the anti-Conservative vote was divided, the Conservative strength in England and the weakness of their opponents did the rest.

In retrospect the lineaments of the Conservative dominance of British politics for the next 50 years can be discerned by the time Bonar Law became Lloyd George's deputy Prime Minister in December 1916. The old Disraelian card of being the 'patriotic party' was reinforced by Liberal failures to either avoid or prosecute the war; the pre-war calls for a stronger Navy and for compulsory military service, vindicated Unionist rather than Liberal rhetoric. The 'imperial' card also proved something of a trump. Again it was the Unionists rather than the Liberals who were associated with the Imperial cause, and it received a boost from the war: Australian and New Zealand troops fought at Gallipoli; Indian troops fought on the Western front and in the Middle East, whilst South African troops mopped up much of the German Empire on the borders of their own country; and even the Catholic Irish had responded to the call to defend freedom. It was true that Republicans had tried to take advantage of the war by staging an uprising at Easter 1916, but the seizure of the Post Office had been a tragedy tinged with farce, and there seemed little reason to believe that the Irish would not respond positively to the success of the British Empire in war. Indeed, the advent of Milner brought into the War Cabinet a strain of Imperial aggrandisement which added a new dimension to British war aims. The Liberals, as was their wont, had been apt to define British war aims in rhetorical terms; Milner brought a harder edge to the task, and the rhetoric, whilst still there, was accompanied by schemes for a great Middle Eastern Empire.

This claim to be the Party of Empire, and, by implication, of military success, would be one of the pillars upon which the Conservative ascendancy would rest; the impulses behind Tariff Reform, if not the actual

policy, seemed to have been justified. Those Unionists who had promoted social reform as part of the tariff programme would, like the
imperialists (and the two groups overlapped to a great extent), also
come into their own over the next few years as the challenge of how to
cope with the political changes caused by the war became acute.

The war would also, over time, provide the Unionists with the much-
needed chance to refurbish their administrative credentials. The last
Unionist Cabinet had been noticeably incompetent, and the long
period in the wilderness meant that the new men who replaced the
likes of St John Brodrick and Arnold-Foster had, perforce, little experience; compared with the massed ranks of the government Front
Bench, the Unionists had looked rather lightweight; but during the two
coalitions a whole generation of Unionists received an education in
administration which would stand them in good stead.

But clear though these things might be in retrospect, it was not just
time which concealed them from contemporaries. Politicians, whilst
claiming to see into the future, generally act upon assumptions formed
from their view of the past – and this is perhaps particularly so for
Conservatives. For Law, as for most of his Unionist colleagues in the
Cabinet, the recent past was a foreign country they had no desire to
revisit. They had spent a frustrating decade in Opposition, during
which time they seemed more disposed to fight among themselves than
engage with the political enemy. Their old Imperial and defence cards
had been played to no effect, and they seemed unable to combat the
'new Liberalism' which Asquith had fostered. This sense of weakness
was further increased by the decision taken at the end of the war to
allow a massive increase in the franchise. By the time Lloyd George
called a General Election in opportunistic fashion on the morrow of
victory (a trick learnt – if it did not come naturally, from the Unionists
in 1900), all males over the age of 21 who were not in prison, the House
of Lords or a lunatic asylum (which disqualified some people several
times over) could vote, as could all women over the age of 30 (by which
time they would, it was assumed, have acquired both a husband and the
serious outlook upon life which this entailed). The old electorate had
been increased from about seven to twenty-one million; if they had
been unable to garner enough votes from the relatively restricted electorate of 1910, how would Unionists win when the working classes now
swamped the electoral register? There was, fortunately for Unionist
peace of mind, a ready answer to this question – Lloyd George.

On the surface the elevation of the author of the 'Peoples' Budget' to
the rank of Unionist icon was surprising, but it is easily explained. As
the 'man who won the war', Lloyd George would have been a potent

electoral force in any event, but when this was combined with what was taken to be his appeal to working-class voters, Unionists had few hesitations in going into the election under his banner. The Liberal split of December 1916 had left them as by far the largest party in the Second Coalition – but the election results of 1918 made even the most optimistic Unionist catch his breath. The Asquithean Liberals were all but wiped out – only 28 kept their seats and their leader went down to defeat. The Lloyd George Liberals came in with 133 MPs, but the Unionists had 335; this was less than in 1892 or 1895, but given that the 73 Irish MPs refused to take their seats, and that Labour, despite their best showing ever, came in with 63 MPs, it was enough to put the Unionists in a commanding position.

It took the Unionists three years to take advantage of their new position. In the glory days of 1919 and 1920 few gave any thought as to whether the Coalition was a matter of convenience or whether it represented something new in British politics, and by they time men like the newly ennobled Lord Birkenhead (as F. E. Smith became in 1918) began to argue in favour of 'fusion' in 1920 and 1921, the majority of the party had lost faith in the idea that they needed Lloyd George to win elections. In part this was due to a recovery of Unionist nerve. Conservatives have weak political nerves, but with the political opposition all but annihilated, and the failure (whatever Churchill said) of the Red Revolution to migrate from the USSR to London, there was a growing sense of confidence that Conservatism had a political future; that it was not going to include Lloyd George was very largely his own doing. It was in part those things which he did which sealed his fate, but those things he did not do also contributed to the end of Conservative hopes in him.

In the first category – things done – the greatest domestic success of his administration, the solution of the Irish question, bulked large. Failing to solve the Irish rebellion by force, Lloyd George ended up agreeing to a partition of the island which gave the Ulstermen control over the north, and left Sinn Fein in control of an Irish Free State. This removed Ireland as an issue in British politics for half a century, but mortally offended many Unionists, not least Carson, whose maiden speech in the Lords in 1921 excoriated not only Lloyd George, but those Conservatives such as Birkenhead and Chamberlain who had backed partition; both men were damaged politically in their own party by their association with Lloyd George's policy. The proposals to give India and Egypt greater measures of self-government also offended imperialists who felt that the end of the war should have been accompanied by a reassertion of the Imperial will. The problem with doing this, however, as the attempt to coerce Southern Ireland showed, was that it exacted a heavy price in unfavourable publicity; the British image of their Empire did not include para-military forces murdering civilians.

Nor were these Imperial failures mitigated by foreign policy successes elsewhere. The Versailles and associated settlements may have brought an uneasy peace to Europe, but they had not brought stability, and by 1922 it had begun to seem as though they never would. Indeed, in that year the first successful revolt against the peace-makers took place as Kemal Ataturk disregarded the Treaty of Lausanne and set about driving the Greeks from Turkey. This precipitated a crisis in London as the more bellicose members of the Cabinet pressed for military action; it proved to be the final straw for most Unionists.

Fuel was added to the discontent by the feeling that Lloyd George was not playing fair. It was not just that the Unionists had only 14 Cabinet Ministers, despite their numerical predominance, there was also the fact that Lloyd George was enriching himself by selling peerages to people whom the Unionists might have expected money from.[12] The scandal caused by Lloyd George's abuse of the Honours system seemed symptomatic of a general atmosphere of corruption at the top. Those 'in the know' were well aware that Lloyd George lived openly with his mistress in London, and that Birkenhead, despite his brilliance as Lord Chancellor, was too often the worse for drink. He may have taunted his opponents with the charge that he and his colleagues were 'first class intellects', but it was a little-known junior minister, Stanley Baldwin, who provided the riposte which summed up the feelings of many of his fellows: 'England prefers second-class intellects with first-class characters to first-class intellects with second-class characters.' As it turned out this was true – but hardly boded well for the governance of England.

Matters were not helped by the retirement of Bonar Law in early 1921. For all his dourness, Law had come to be widely respected and trusted within the party; it was felt that he could act as an anchor on the flightiness of Lloyd George. His successor, Austen Chamberlain, could not serve this function. When he told his family that he accepted the leadership as 'an obvious duty but without pleasure or any great expectation except of trouble and hard labour',[13] he was exposing one of the reasons why this would be his political epitaph. He lacked the dynamism of his father, and proved incapable of giving a lead to his party. This was particularly unfortunate since his own views about the Coalition and those of his followers were coming increasingly to differ. Chamberlain, who had begun by being sceptical about the need to continue the Coalition, had become convinced by 1921 that it was essential to keep Labour at bay. But the reaction of the party to the suggestion that Law's retirement was the occasion 'for the official birth of the new party', had shown him 'how much hostility & prejudice, how many old habits & rivalries' had first 'to be softened or removed before Unionists are ready for such an open declaration'.[14] Chamberlain's only mistake here was to imagine that it would be possible to 'soften' the party up: Ireland; the scandal over honours; failure in economic and foreign policy; none of these did anything except convince an already sceptical party that Lloyd George had become a liability. Chamberlain's identification with the Coalition simply widened the gulf between him and his rank and file.

Austen was well aware of the problem he faced in arguing for 'fusion', as we have seen; indeed in January 1922 he successfully argued against those like Birkenhead who wanted to go for an early election as a means of gaining their object. But his position became increasingly difficult. He took the view that 'No Gov[ernmen]t is possible without coalition' and that no coalition was possible 'without Lloyd George and his Liberals',[15] whilst his own backbenchers were increasingly sceptical of such a line. Chamberlain was unwilling to bend to the prevailing wind and decided, instead, to rally his troops. He called a meeting at the Carlton Club on 19 October, timed to come the morning after a by-election at Newport, which was expected to show how vital to Conservative success the Coalition was; it did the opposite as the Conservative won easily, beating the Coalitionist into third place. At the meeting Chamberlain, Balfour and Birkenhead all hectored their colleagues, giving the clear impression that they regarded them as next door to imbeciles.[16] Chamberlain, at his most unbending, made the issue one of loyalty to the Coalition or to the Conservative Party without its current leadership; this was to nail your trousers to the mast with a vengeance. For one thing it forced his opponents to go further than they wanted – there had been no great desire to overthrow him; for another there was an alternative to his leadership in the form of Bonar Law, who had been persuaded to attend the meeting to try to ensure party unity, and who spoke against the continuation of the Coalition. But the surprise of the meeting was the impassioned plea of Baldwin. Calling Lloyd George a 'dynamic force' – a 'most terrible thing' – he reminded Conservatives that the Welshman had already broken one party and that it was time to stop him before he repeated the trick. When the vote came in it was decisive: 185 in favour of rejecting it, 85 in favour of its continuation. Chamberlain resigned the party leadership, which went to Bonar Law, and the same afternoon Lloyd George went to Buckingham Palace to offer his resignation. In the ensuing General Election the Unionists won 345 seats to the Liberals' 116; but the big surprise was Labour's 142 seats. Still, it was with a comfortable majority that Bonar Law became Prime Minister. It had been 11 years since he had become party leader, and no Conservative has ever waited so long – but the job was finally his.

7   Scalped by Baldwin

It was ironic that having waited so long for the Premiership, Bonar Law should have occupied the office for less time than any other twentieth-century Prime Minister; such a fate almost justified, retrospectively, his dour pessimism. The same ironic fatalism also ensured that a man who had put most of his energies into keeping the party united should have attained the highest office only as the result of a party split. Law remains, however, the only Conservative to have returned to the party leadership having once relinquished it.

One of the penalties of political defeat is historical denigration; few have testified to this more than the man Law replaced, Austen Chamberlain. Whether it is Beaverbrook's cruel lines: 'Nothing in my head I bring, only to my name I cling'; or Birkenhead's unkind comment 'Austen always played the game – and always lost it', the massive condescension of history has settled over Chamberlain's reputation like a shroud. This can lead us to misread the politics of the next two years, which were, in truth, the most confused and crucial of the early twentieth century, and where almost anyone – including Austen – could have come out on top. As Professor Williamson has recently reminded us: 'Not simply Conservative Party interests but the very structures and values which sustained those interests seemed under threat';[1] all the Carlton Club schism had shown was that there was no Conservative consensus about how to react to the threat. The notion that an administration of the 'second eleven' led by Law was the answer, seemed perfectly risible to the ousted Conservative leaders, and the fact that Law himself looked towards a Conservative reunion in short order, hardly suggests he was any more convinced than his old colleagues. Nor is the reason far to seek.

The great victory of 1918 could be written down to the effects of Lloyd George and the 'khaki election' atmosphere of the time. By 1922 the electoral landscape had about it a strange and unfamiliar look to men who had grown to political maturity in the Edwardian period. It was not just that the 1918 Representation of the People Act had handed over power to what contemporary Conservatives were apt to call 'the Democracy' – so many of the landmarks of pre-war politics had gone: women's suffrage, Welsh disestablishment, fear of Germany and even Ireland, had all either vanished or receded into the background by 1922. That unorganized, un-unionized working class to which the youthful F. E. Smith had looked for 'Tory democracy' had shrunk dramatically. Before the war the Trades Union Congress (TUC) had had about three million members; by 1920 its membership had risen to six and a half million, and thanks to the compulsory political levy, all these men were funding the Labour Party – whether they wished to or not. Thus, on paper, Labour had more than four million members, and even if this is a gratuitously inflated figure because of the trades unions, the 24 per cent of the vote garnered by Labour at the 1918 election was a better indication of support for the party than its derisory number of seats.[2] Indeed, the mismatch between Labour's support in the Commons and the country actually gave the more militant trades unionists a greater say in the affairs of the Labour movement than would be the case again until the 1970s. This all took place against the backcloth of economic and social dislocation caused by the war, whilst abroad four great empires (the Hohenzollern, Habsburg, Ottoman and Romanov) had collapsed. It was Lloyd George's evident failure to find remedies for either the domestic or the international problems besetting the country which had undermined his prestige and position. But those Conservatives who stuck with him could not see how Law could hope to succeed where the 'Welsh Wizard' had failed.

Opposition to the Coalition from within the Conservative Party had come from three main directions: the 'diehards', the Cecils and the old Tariff/Social Reform element.[3] The far Right of the party had never been happy about following Lloyd George, and his activities in Ireland (partition), India (the Montagu-Chelmsford reforms promising greater local participation in government) and Egypt (the Milner Report) made him appear as little better than a traitor; to men like the Earl of Northumberland and Sir Henry Page-Croft, the Coalition represented a continuation of the 'Mandarin rule' which had been the ruination of Great Britain since Balfour's hey-day. Their position was 'an indictment of the ruling regime ... by those who had been excluded from it.'[4]

Less shrill, but no less bitter in their criticism, were members and followers of the House of Cecil. If the younger Chamberlains and Gladstones had not proven that talent was not hereditary, the fourth Marquess of Salisbury, 'Jem', would have proved the point all by himself; but he would also have proved another point that needs no labouring – that talent is one of the lesser gifts required to attain standing in the Conservative Party; great wealth and a steady character are usually sufficient – and did it for Salisbury every time. 'Jem' represented the besieged forces of aristocratic Conservatism. It was not the style to denigrate the lower orders in the way that Churchill and Birkenhead's anti-socialist rhetoric seemed to do with such ease – and offence; a tone of decency and restraint was sought, along with terms upon which the new political class would allow the old to hold onto its spoils. Salisbury had, as he told Baldwin in 1924, 'no sympathy whatever with the hard-shelled defence of the Haves against the Have-Nots'.[5] Indeed, until the number of 'Haves' exceeded the number of 'Have Nots', this tone of Cecilian caution would be heard with respect in Conservative circles, and the complaints of the aged Earl of Stockton against the policies of the Thatcher governments were, perhaps, a long and fading echo of arguments which the young Macmillan had first heard in the distant past. The Cecils and their followers represented a 'tone' rather than an ideological position – which was why they needed an alliance with the old Tariff/Social Reformers – one which was epitomized by a book published in 1918 called *The Great Opportunity*, written by Edward Wood and George Lloyd.

Edward Wood, later Lord Halifax, was the grandson of one of Palmerston's Chancellors and the son of a High Church Anglican who devoted his life to the cause of reunion between the Church of England and the Catholic Church; he represented a Whiggish and religious version of Cecilian Conservatism; he was its natural ally against the *loucheness* of the Lloyd George regime. Despite being born with a withered left arm, Wood had chosen to fight for his country in the Great War, where he had been decorated for his bravery. Morally upright, physically brave, a prize-fellow of All Souls and a great landowner, it was hardly surprising that he was generally agreed to be a representative of 'the highest kind of Englishman now in politics'.[6] Such men found Baldwin as sympathetic as he found them, and they 'brought to politics a Gladstonian admiration for the judgement and cultural values of the Common Man' as well as a 'strong belief in the politician's duty to propagate moral rectitude'.[7]

Lloyd, whose background lay in Midland steel-making and Quakerism, was an ardent tariff reformer, but like Wood, he was a man of deep religious conviction, and he shared with him the view that the Conservative Party needed to come alongside democracy. What he hated was 'the Radical method of giving expression to Democracy – for example, Whiggery trying to keep up with the times – fraudulent, feeble and as dangerous as it is futile'.[8] Given that at base this was not a bad summary of what the Cecils, Baldwin and Wood were about, the seeds of Lloyd's future estrangement from their brand of Conservatism were there from the start, but back in 1918 he was 'genuinely stirred by the vast and crying needs of the time, and anxious to evolve something practical and progressive that is not destructive to satisfy them'.[9] In this,

Lloyd's roots in West Midlands Unionism showed through clearly, and whilst Imperial service would take him to India and prevent his following through the proposals in his book, the torch would be taken up by someone whose roots were planted even deeper in the same soil, Austen's half-brother, Neville Chamberlain, who first entered the Commons in 1918.

Thus, despite the taunts of Birkenhead, and appearances notwithstanding, the Bonar Law government contained within itself those elements which would establish the Conservative domination of British politics for the next half-century. Its tone would be one of 'English decency', its policy one of constructive, pragmatic social reform. These things were obscured in 1922, partly by Bonar Law's Scottish dourness, partly by the unresolved issue of Tariff Reform and partly by Birkenhead harping on about a government of 'under-secretaries' and doddering peers. There were certainly a great number of peers, seven in all, of whom only Curzon (who remained at the Foreign Office, hopeful of the succession to Law) had served in the previous government and could reasonably be described as more than competent. Of the other six, Salisbury, Devonshire, Derby and Peel served to demonstrate how prominent the 'diehards' and Cecils had been in the revolt against Lloyd George. But they all represented the party's past, and none of them would play much of a role in constructing the Conservative future. In this sense Birkenhead was right to go on about the 'under-secretaries', but not for the reasons he imagined. Far from representing a scraping of the barrel (and Law would hardly have been the first Conservative leader to have adopted this method when constituting his Cabinet), the recruitment into the government of men like Wood and Amery (in the Cabinet at Education and the Admiralty, respectively), Sir Douglas Hogg, Sir Samuel Hoare and Neville Chamberlain (outside the Cabinet as Attorney-General, Air Minister and Postmaster General respectively), marked the breakthrough to power of men who had been held back by the need to ensure that the Liberals had their fair share of loaves and fishes in the Coalition.

Law's immediate hope, having won the election, was to work for the reunification of his party, but he was denied the chance to do this, or anything else, by the recurrence, in fatal form, of the cancer which had persuaded him to retire earlier. With the former leader, Austen Chamberlain, still estranged from the party by the events of 18 October 1922, there were only two choices to succeed him. In his own mind, as well as that of many others, the hour for which George Nathaniel Curzon had waited since 1905 had finally come. He was incomparably the most experienced and distinguished member of the Cabinet – and not only knew it, but liked to make sure that everyone else did.[10] Law, stricken and ailing, did not see how Curzon's claims could be passed over, but was relieved when told that he did not have to recommend a successor. Still, when Curzon received a summons from the King's Private Secretary, Lord Stamfordham, to return to London from his Somerset fastness amidst the architectural splendours of Montacute, he was confident that he would soon be appointing his Cabinet. He was mortified to discover that it was the alternative candidate, the Chancellor of the Exchequer, Stanley Baldwin, who had received the King's commission.

Curzon's comment, that Baldwin was a man of the 'utmost insignificance', is well-known, true, and beside the point. Baldwin, as we have seen, had affinities to the main sections of the party who had rebelled against Lloyd George, whilst those elements, in turn, respected him for his courage in taking his political life in his hands by speaking out against the Welshman at the Carlton Club. He personified the kind of ordinary English decency which he came to represent, and which became the 'mood music' of Conservatism under him. The newly elected MP Cuthbert Headlam expressed the feelings of many at the unexpected turn of events when he wrote: 'Baldwin's advance has really been amazing … of course he had had luck … but he is an able man – and what is far better in the long run – a modest and honest man.'[11]

Appearances can be deceptive. Lucy Baldwin called her husband 'Tiger', but few people resembled one less than Stanley Baldwin – until, that is, he was cornered; but appearances were so deceptive that even after experience, few of his opponents quite believed how effective he could be. Like Balfour he was a Cambridge graduate – indeed, he was also a Trinity man – but apart from the fact that they both became leader of the Conservative Party and Prime Minister, they resembled each other not at all. Where Balfour was one of a handful of twentieth-century Conservative leaders never to win an election (the Chamberlain brothers Lord Home and William Hague being the others), Baldwin was on the winning side three times; where Balfour was a failure as leader but redeemed himself with a career which was longer and more distinguished after 1911, Baldwin was an undoubted success who came to power late in his career after a decade of undistinguished service on the backbenches. His reputation, by contrast, never stood so high as when he retired in 1937, and it went into a tail-spin in 1940 from which it has still not recovered, despite recent attempts to portray him as an underestimated political genius.

Arguments can be made on both sides: his dominance of British politics can be seen by the fact he was Prime Minister three times and was able to retire, at a time of his own choosing, in 1937, with popular plaudits ringing in his ears; the political scalps on his belt included Lloyd George, Winston Churchill, Sir Oswald Mosley, and anyone else who had tried to cross him; he had seen the country through the General Strike; the Economic Crisis of 1931, the Great Depression and the Abdication Crisis of 1936; he had maintained national unity, economic stability and encouraged a political consensus which allowed the political integration of the Labour Party. On the other hand, Baldwin lost two of the three elections he fought as Prime Minister, and led the party into another coalition in 1931 which meant the dilution of its policies, especially on Tariff Reform; he signally failed to realise the dangers posed by Hitler; and if he left office popular, he was soon the most unpopular politician in the country.

Both sides of the coin are true. Baldwin is often held to have inaugurated a period of 'new' Conservatism, but the very frequency with which this oxymoron is employed by historians gives pause for thought. As one American commentator has recently put it:

> Any time you see the adjective 'new' employed – be it in politics, religion, or commerce – assume the label is mere smoke and mirrors, calculated to obscure the fact that there is nothing 'new' about what is being described. Rather, it is the same old stuff simply repackaged.[12]

There is much in this. Baldwin was not an innovator. He made homely speeches about 'Englishness', of which (according to his publishers) he was an 'interpreter', but he said nothing new, and very seldom anything that was even striking; but in an age of turmoil and upheaval this, in itself, was a virtue. Law had appealed to the country in October 1922 on a platform of 'tranquillity'; Baldwin almost appeared to embody that quality in his own person. His rhetoric was Disraelian in that it stressed 'One Nation' Conservatism, but unless the Conservatives wished to be in perpetual opposition they were right not to play Birkenhead's class-war cards – they were, after all, outnumbered.

It might well be asked whether it really mattered that Baldwinian 'new' Conservatism was largely a matter of image; after all, in democratic politics, image, if not everything (as some appear to hold), is a great deal; and here, Baldwin was a master. No great orator, he was adept at using the new electronic amplifiers at public meetings, where he was able to come across to his audience as a regular sort of chap; he achieved the same feat through the new medium of BBC radio, where his conversational style made him a 'natural' in a way that men like Churchill and Lloyd George never were. Although he got off to a poor start as Conservative leader, Baldwin showed himself like Gladstone in one respect – he too could be terrible on the rebound.

Conservatives often talk about 'One Nation', but they tend to do best when they can identify an internal enemy whom they could depict as in some way 'Un-English'; and in the form of the Labour Party they now had such an object. Difficult though it was to depict MacDonald, Philip Snowden and Arthur Henderson as the British equivalents of Lenin, Trotsky and Zinoviev, Labour's adoption of 'socialism', and the rhetorical excesses of some of its more intellectual supporters, allowed the necessary smoke and mirrors to be deployed. Against this alien ideology, simple, honest British decency was the first, and Baldwin's only, line of defence. Once Labour was firmly established as the main party of opposition, this tune would be played, usually very loudly and with success, at every election; Churchill's untuneful rendition of it in 1945, in his 'Gestapo' blunder, was proof that old habits die hard.

But anti-Socialism and support for the social order, whilst impeccably and undoubtedly Conservative were hardly an answer to the economic distress which had helped wreck Lloyd George's Premiership. As a good Conservative Baldwin fell back upon what was, by now, the party's traditional answer to economic problems – Protection. This not only differentiated the Tories from the Liberals, it provided an answer to the Socialists who claimed that they alone had constructive answers to the country's problems. Moreover, with Amery at the Admiralty and Neville Chamberlain at the Exchequer, the influence within the government of the enthusiasts for Tariff Reform was greater than it had ever been in any Cabinet since Neville's father had first raised the issue; indeed, with hindsight, critics should have seen in Chamberlain's appointment a sign of the way Baldwin's mind was moving.[13]

Baldwin was by temperament and instinct something of a loner; for all his public *persona* as a regular chap, Baldwin had something about him of the moody introspection which the English associate with the Celts. He tended to brood upon matters, sitting, silently sucking on his pipe for long periods before coming, sometimes suddenly, to important decisions; the first sign of this tendency to his colleagues came in the autumn of 1923. Although he was reputed to be close to the Prime Minister, William Bridgeman, the Home Secretary, was amazed to be informed by Baldwin in October that he had decided to have an election on the issue of Protection. Since the Conservatives still had another four years before needing to face the electorate, even the loyal Bridgeman was somewhat surprised when Baldwin announced in

Plymouth on 25 October that he intended to call a General Election.[14] Curzon called the decision 'idiotic', and many MPs wondered what on earth the Prime Minister was thinking of – or if he was thinking at all. Historians have been asking the same question ever since – without coming to a firm answer.

It was Neville Chamberlain, as much in the dark as anyone, who provided the best rationale behind Baldwin's decision:

> He is not so simple as he makes out ... Here he has sprung a protectionist policy on the country almost at a moment's notice, with a Cabinet a substantial proportion of which consists of Free-Traders. Not one of them has resigned ... .[15]

The Chancellor also suspected that rumours that Lloyd George was about to declare for Empire Free Trade had played their part in Baldwin's decision – although it must be said that there is no evidence for this.[16] The impulsive action certainly saved Baldwin from having to try to persuade his Free Trade colleagues of the virtues of the only policy he could think of, and it had the added bonus of cutting through what were becoming protracted and bothersome negotiations to bring Austen Chamberlain and company back into the party fold; indeed, at one fell swoop Baldwin separated the ex-Coalitionists from their former leader. But he paid a heavy price for these dubious gains.

If the Conservatives could pull together, so too could the Liberals, and nothing less than such a fundamental assault upon one of the articles of their crumbling tabernacle could have persuaded Lloyd George and Asquith to cooperate; as in 1905, the Liberals reunited. Indeed, even Winston Churchill, whose hardening political arteries were beginning to reveal the 'aboriginal Tory' in him, felt that he had to rally to the tattered old standard. As for Labour, well they welcomed the prospect of a stand-up fight, confident that they would continue to improve their electoral position. Everyone except Baldwin was correct.

Bonar Law had bequeathed Baldwin 345 seats in the House of Commons; after the election of 6 December 1923 this was reduced to 258 – the lowest showing since the last Tariff Reform election in 1905. The reluctantly reunited Liberals saw their position improve, with 159 as opposed to 116 seats, whilst Labour was jubilant: with 191 seats in the House they stood poised to take office since the Liberals could hardly put Baldwin back in.

The wailing, whining and gnashing of teeth in the Conservative ranks was something to behold. Not only had the 'idiotic' leader thrown away four more years of power; he had set up a position in which the

Socialists could come to power. There were voices (such as Birkenhead's) raised in favour of a coalition with the Liberals, but Baldwin showed a real touch of political genius in declining such a solution. Baldwin did not share the Birkenhead-Churchill view of the Labour Party as a bunch of red revolutionaries in flat caps and mufflers. Unlike either of his two more intellectually able colleagues, Baldwin had long practical experience of dealing with trades unionists and working men, and his view was that whatever its constitution might say, the Labour Party was no more Socialist than he was himself. He also saw that the only circumstances in which Labour might resort to unconstitutional action were those in which it appeared that the older parties would 'gang up' on them to deprive them of the fruits of their parliamentary success; Labour had, after all, been a good deal less 'revolutionary' in tone since the parliamentary party had become more important in its counsels than the trades unionists. Moreover, if the experiment of a Socialist government was going to be undertaken, the circumstances were ideal: if Baldwin was wrong about MacDonald, then the Conservatives and Liberals could eject them from office.

In contemplation of the Liberal position, another advantage to the Conservatives became clear. Just as Salisbury had believed that the Whigs were a dangerous irrelevance in class-based politics, so did Baldwin regard the Liberals. He saw the Conservatives as the main bulwark against Socialism and he wished to attract as many Liberals to vote for them as possible – with Asquith's decision to support the advent of the country's first Labour government, Baldwin achieved his wish. Disgruntled and disgusted Liberals like Churchill looked towards Baldwin for the country's salvation, and seeing that another election could not be long distant, he entered into talks with the Tories about the prospect of a political pact between himself and any followers he might collect.

Thus it was that after a rocky few days, Baldwin survived the consequences of his own failure and was even able to unite the Conservative Party. Nor was the election long in coming, and when it arrived, the circumstances could hardly have been more favourable – although art did try to improve on nature.

Whatever Baldwin believed about the Labour leaders, it was necessary for electoral purposes to go along with the right-wing paranoia about their being virtually in the pay of Moscow, and so it was an uncovenanted blessing when MacDonald found himself being accused of allowing his government to interfere for political motives in the case of a journalist called Campbell who was said to have incited soldiers to mutiny. MacDonald, already frustrated by his position, and confident that he had already done as much as could be expected to establish Labour's position for the future, was not unwilling to inflict yet another election on the country. During the course of the election the Conservative Central Office produced the text of a letter purporting to be from the Communist leader Zinoviev which appeared to confirm that there were close contacts between Labour and Moscow. Although there weren't, the allegations damaged Labour – whilst the election itself destroyed the Liberals, whose share of the vote fell from 37.8 per cent to 30.9 per cent, and whose number of seats dropped from 159 to 40. Both MacDonald and Baldwin could therefore find one cause for mutual satisfaction; henceforth the Liberals were finished as a party of government – and the adjurations of successive Liberal leaders to their followers to the contrary represents hope triumphing over bitter experience.

It was the Conservatives who had the best reason to be hopeful. Their vote had risen from 5.5 million to nearly 8 million, whilst they had secured 419 seats – the largest number in the party's history. Indeed, so overwhelming was the victory that young candidates who had been found the usual hopeless or marginal seats were elected: included in this number were Harold Macmillan at Stockton and Duff Cooper at Oldham. Other young men with promising futures and safer seats, such as Anthony Eden at Leamington and R. A. Butler at Saffron Walden, found themselves with comfortable majorities which would last them for a political lifetime.

Young blood could wait its turn. The first item on Baldwin's agenda was the return of the prodigal sons. Austen Chamberlain was offered the post which most suited his dignity as the former leader of the party – the Foreign Office – whilst Birkenhead, who was almost as reluctant to return to the Woolsack as Baldwin was to put him there, took his reactionary views with him to the India Office. There was no real surprise about these appointments, but that could not have been said about Baldwin's choice of Winston Churchill for the Exchequer. Historians have usually contented themselves with the statement that this is a mystery, with the underlying implication that a figure as eminent as Churchill was always going to get something, but Baldwin's reasoning was shrewder than this. Churchill had already shown himself willing to lead a 'cave' of right-wing Liberals in support of Baldwin in the event of another 'hung' parliament, and the fact that this had not happened did not invalidate the assumptions behind the talks – Baldwin wanted Liberal votes, and the fact that he had obtained them directly and not via Churchill in no way lessened his need for them. There could be no better guarantee that he would not flirt with tariffs than Churchill, a convinced Free Trader, at the Exchequer. He could also be expected to act as something of a rallying point for Liberals who shared his views; moreover, with Churchill back in the Conservative fold (once he rejoined the party, which he did in 1925), Lloyd George, that 'dynamic force', was well and truly stymied.

The elements of the Conservative dominance of British politics were now falling into place. The results of the election diminished the influence of the tariff reformers such as Amery and Neville Chamberlain, and the latter turned his attention away from Protectionism to the other aspect of the tariff programme – social reform. As Minister of Health, Chamberlain presided over a programme of pragmatic social reform which not only made his name and career, but which also offered a practical alternative to Socialism. Chamberlain also provided an alternative to Protection which could win the support of Liberals like Churchill, who collaborated with him in reforming the rating and local government system in 1927 and 1928. This was the 'beef' behind the Baldwinian rhetoric: Stanley soothed the customers and Neville provided them with the goods, whilst Austen brought peace in Europe; it was a good combination. If it is correct to conclude that there was nothing 'new' about Baldwinian conservatism except presentation and timing, that is no small praise, for in politics presentation and timing are vital. Baldwin's rhetoric and Chamberlain's programme allowed the Conservatives to escape the imputation of their opponents that they were a party whose sole aim was to prevent the rich paying more income tax; the latter lent verisimilitude to the claim of the former that they led a 'National' party with policies and sympathies as broad as those of their opponents – but shorn of the ideological element.

There were those, like Birkenhead, who thought that the government would be one of 'reaction', particularly in the field of foreign and Imperial matters, but despite his best efforts, this did not quite come to pass.[17] Birkenhead expected the former coalitionists to act in a bloc to oppose Baldwin's more liberal instincts should they show themselves, but Austen Chamberlain surrendered happily to the embrace of the Foreign Office and set about pacifying Europe,[18] whilst Churchill was too busy at the Exchequer to lend more than sporadic support to those who felt that Baldwin was not firm enough on Imperial matters. Even so, Imperial matters revealed, more than anything else, a potential fault-line in the Baldwin Cabinet.

At home most MPs were content to be diverted and entertained by Churchill's brilliant budget speeches and to leave Chamberlain to get on with the necessary reforms – Baldwin certainly was. After all, the presence of Labour as the main opposition allowed the Conservatives to maintain their position as the 'patriotic party' without too much effort; indeed, there were those Conservatives who thought that the party was devoting all too little effort to justifying this claim; but it was not as easy to combine imperialism with democracy.

Staunch Imperialists like Milner, Amery and Lloyd may have hoped that the working classes would 'value the Empire more' having 'paid something for it' during the war,[19] but there was little sign of it. Perhaps the crucial incident for Conservatives like Baldwin was Lloyd George's Irish campaign, although there were other episodes, such as the Amritsar massacre, which pointed the same moral to adorn a similar tale. In the first, public opinion reacted badly to the government's brutal efforts to subdue the Southern Irish, whilst in the second, the actions of General Dyer in firing upon Indian civilians who were protesting raised a storm of protest. Of course those Conservatives who drew their sustenance from the *Morning Post* subscribed both to the fiery views of Lord Carson and the fund in support of Dyer, but as the demise of that paper in 1937 showed, these were a dwindling band. The Conservatives had forborne the pursuit of a 'forward' Imperial policy under Salisbury because they did not want to pay for it – this attitude now received reinforcement from an electorate which showed more concern with domestic politics than with events in far-away countries about which they knew little and cared less. Those Conservatives like Lloyd who, from his position as High Commissioner in Egypt, preached the necessity of taking a firmer line, could look to Birkenhead, Churchill and Amery for support, but they could never command a majority in the Cabinet. The decision to send Edward Wood (now Baron Irwin) to India as Viceroy was some indication of Baldwin's own preferences, since his liberal tendencies would balance out Birkenhead's diehard views.

In his preference for appeasement of nationalist opinion abroad and concentration upon domestic politics, Baldwin seems accurately to have reflected the mood of the nation; and in this last sphere too, Baldwin favoured appeasement. He had never accepted the views of men like Birkenhead and Churchill that the only way to deal with trades unions was to adopt a confrontational attitude – and his views continued to be the norm for Conservatives until the days of Mrs Thatcher. Of course he found himself unable to avoid a confrontation when one was thrust upon him by the General Strike in 1926 but, having done his best to do so, he was unwilling to take the alarmist measures against it that some of his ministers wanted. With a policy of economic retrenchment at home and abroad, Baldwin, Chamberlain and Churchill concentrated on purveying the message that the

Conservatives were the 'safe' party – why, in 1928 they even surprised themselves by allowing women between 21 and 30 to have the vote – no 'reaction' here then. Indeed, so tempting was their self-image that Baldwin adopted it as his 1929 election slogan – 'Safety First'. Indeed, it says much about the government that the election only took place in May 1929 because the Parliament was coming to the end of its natural life.

At their last meeting before the election, ministers voted themselves a good Cabinet and set off for the polls. It had certainly been an unusually settled ministerial team. Baldwin disliked change and, despite the claims of junior members of the party, he only disturbed the even tenor of his Cabinet when necessity demanded. The resignation of Lord Robert Cecil in 1927 caused hardly a ripple and, as he was only Chancellor of the Duchy of Lancaster, Baldwin did not see fit to replace him. The death of Lord Cave in 1928 could not be dealt with so neatly, if only because it was usually held that the country needed a Lord Chancellor. Birkenhead was quite out of the question – the idea of the head of the country's judiciary being taken into custody because he was drunk and disorderly was not an appealing one, and despite Neville Chamberlain's advice to the contrary, Sir Douglas Hogg, one of the real successes of the administration, was 'kicked upstairs' as Lord Hailsham. When F. E. himself retired later in 1928, in an effort to make enough money to keep up with his reckless expenditure, Baldwin not only declined to promote 'new blood', he went back to Earl Peel, who had held office under Balfour, to provide a Secretary of State for India. The bright young men had to be content with minor places. Anthony Eden, whose liberal views on the League of Nations and everything else made him almost the epitome of a Baldwinian Conservative, was generally regarded as having stolen a march on his rivals by becoming the junior minister at the Foreign Office, whilst Duff Cooper, whose oratorical talents bade fit to rival Churchill's, was rewarded with a junior post at the War Office; but other colleagues, like Walter Elliot and Oliver Stanley, could also look forward to promotion once the election was over.

Not even Baldwin could ignore the feeling that the 'old gang' needed clearing out. Although Austen Chamberlain had done well at the Foreign Office, he had little support in the Commons or the party. Now in his seventies and in indifferent health after a bad illness in 1928, Austen's career was thought to be over. The same was generally held to be the case with Bridgeman and with the Home Secretary, Joynson-Hicks, an ebullient solicitor from Essex whose energy exceeded his judgement. Neville Chamberlain had clearly established himself as a major figure, but he was something of a 'politician's politician'. He had come into national politics in 1918 at the age of 49, and his corvine appearance and reserved manner were against him: 'It is not any lack of ability in which he fails: it is in the spark of humanity';[20] this militated against his establishing a great popular reputation. The same could not be said of his greatest rival for the post which would have become vacant had Baldwin fallen underneath a tram – Winston Churchill.

Churchill, as a turn-coat who had turned his coat again, was distrusted by many in the party, and his political judgement was held to be poor,[21] but the further away from the Cabinet table you got, the more alluring he appeared; in this he was the opposite of Chamberlain. His long career at the top had made him the best-known figure in the government, whilst his energy, industry and volubility made him impossible to ignore; the problem for Baldwin was where to place him. On the eve of the election the betting was that he would go to the India Office – where, no doubt, after his fashion, he would have adopted the views of the officials as his own and pursued a programme of Home Rule for India with the vehemence he had once brought to doing the same thing for Ireland. Posterity was spared this alluring spectacle by the verdict of the electorate, which ungratefully declined to endorse the Cabinet's view of itself. From India, Irwin had warned of the dangers of leaving the electorate 'to judge between doing nothing and accepting an extreme policy such as Socialism', adding that although they might dislike the latter, they might 'think that even that is better than just going on as we are';[22] so it proved. When the votes were counted, the Conservatives were left with 260 seats to Labour's 288. The Liberals, with 59 seats, ought to have held the balance of power, but unfortunately no one was interested in cooperating with them,[23] so MacDonald became Prime Minister whilst open season was declared on Baldwin.

Anti-Socialism was a theme which could be played more than one way, and with his defeat, those who had not liked Baldwin's tune felt free to try to change it.[24] There were two main alternative themes which suggested themselves: Imperial matters and Tariff Reform. In fact, as we have seen, the two themes were part of a much bigger one, but it was Baldwin's good fortune that their proponents did not see matters this way.

The first assault came as early as June, when Churchill tried to take advantage of Labour's dismissal of Lord Lloyd to rally diehard support in the Commons. But Chamberlain and Baldwin had got wind of what he was up to, and when Churchill rose to speak he found himself without any support on his own side of the House. Churchill ended up looking 'exceedingly foolish' – much to the satisfaction of his main rival, Neville Chamberlain.[25] The former Chancellor dimly realised that he had been set up, and he bemoaned the fact that Britain 'alone among modern states chooses to cast away her [imperial] rights, her interests and her strength'; it was a theme which was to become monotonously familiar in the years to come. The stakes were raised even higher in October when Baldwin appeared to commit the party to the declaration sponsored by Irwin and the Labour government that the eventual aim of British rule in India was Dominion Status for the country. Birkenhead fulminated from the Lords, and after his early death in 1930, Churchill raised the stricken flag and carried it about the battlefield bellowing mightily. In early 1931 he resigned from the 'Business Committee' (the precursor of the modern Shadow Cabinet) in order to get a better shot at Baldwin.

By this time the leader was well under siege.[26] The Protectionists, freed from the incubus of Churchill at the Exchequer, took their opportunity to agitate for tariffs, the lead being taken by the press magnate, Beaverbrook, who, with the true genius of the publicist, came up with the slogan 'Empire Free Trade' to describe Protection. The two campaigns, tariffs and Indian, kept up a steady fire, with Beaverbrook and his fellow press lord, Rothermere, actually running candidates against the party at by-elections. As ever, in opposition, the party became more right-wing. Those young MPs sitting for marginal seats had lost them, and the Page-Crofts, Churchills and Lord Lloyds all made hay whilst the sun shone. By early 1931 the situation was so serious that *The Times* set up a leader with the heading 'Mr Baldwin withdraws'; but they had underestimated 'Tiger' Baldwin.

Baldwin's spiritual home was in the last ditch, and this had been reached by March 1931. Despite the mass of young ex-MPs looking for seats, there were no takers for one of the safest constituencies in the country – St George's Westminster – when it became vacant in February 1931; no one seemed to want to fight Beaverbrook's candidate, an engineer and businessman called Sir Ernest Petter. Baldwin even thought of resigning his own seat to do the job himself, but he was saved from this tiresome necessity by Duff Cooper.[27]

If Baldwin would not describe the press barons as 'swine', it was only because he did not want to 'libel' a 'very decent, clean animal';[28] to him they represented everything that was loathsome about British public life. The fact that they were so reminiscent of the bad old days of the Coalition gave Baldwin the chance to play his 'decency' card, and he did so to devastating effect. Speaking in the Queen's Hall before the by-election, he accused the press barons of wanting 'power without responsibility – the prerogative of the harlot down the ages'; apart from Cooper's agent who lamented: 'there goes the harlot vote', most other

Conservatives were delighted to fall in behind the old flag. A few days earlier he had rallied the troops with a fighting speech on India and, with Cooper winning by 6000 votes, Baldwin had saved himself by his own endeavours; but it remained to be seen whether he could keep this up. He had obtained a breathing-space, not a reprieve. If the Conservatives won the next election, men like Churchill and Lloyd could not be ignored, and poor old Baldwin could expect the sort of trouble which he had had between 1924 and 1929 over Imperial matters – added to which would be a renewed cry for Protection as the only way to deal with the country's growing economic problems.

It was quite certain that, their claims to the contrary notwithstanding, the Socialists had not the slightest idea of how to solve the economic difficulties facing them; even Baldwin, who believed in being nice to them, could not restrain himself from commenting upon the failure of the promised miracle cures for unemployment. This was not quite fair. The former Conservative MP, now Labour minister, Sir Oswald Mosley, did have some original ideas, but the Chancellor, Philip Snowden, distrusted any economic thinking which had not received the imprimatur of Gladstone, so Mosley resigned and a few months later, in August, the government, by now clueless, encountered a set of circumstances which demanded action. With a severe economic crisis afflicting Western Europe, the May Committee, which had been set up earlier in the year to consider public spending, chose this moment to report – with recommendations of severe cuts. Ministers agreed this was necessary, but with that peculiar logic that Socialists employ on such occasions, many could not bring themselves to make the necessary cuts, and by late August the Cabinet was on the verge of resignation. It was time for all men of goodwill to rally round the flag.

It was with the greatest reluctance that Baldwin returned from his yearly holiday in Aix-les-Bains, and he stayed only one day before leaving everything to Chamberlain. From one point of view this was a mistake. Baldwin himself was not very keen on the idea of an emergency coalition, but Chamberlain, although no more in favour of a 'national government', had begun to think that it might be the only way to ditch Lloyd George and to get Labour to face up to its responsibilities.[29] Baldwin's indolence left Chamberlain to negotiate with MacDonald and the Liberals, so he had only himself to blame if the final result was not what he really wanted. By September a National Government had been formed, with MacDonald as Prime Minister, Baldwin Lord President of the Council and the Labour Party split; the one bonus for Baldwin was that Lloyd George was too ill to take part in the negotiations; his prostate was playing up.

The government was a temporary expedient designed to meet a national emergency and keep the country on the gold standard; its first act was to devalue sterling and its second was to call a General Election. The Opposition was massacred. The new government had 554 seats, of which 473 were Conservative, whilst Labour was left with 52 and the Liberals were all but wiped out. The National Government had polled 14.5 million votes to Labour's 6.6 million, and the man who had risen to power by destroying one Coalition had now scalped his enemies by forming another one. Perhaps Mrs Baldwin was right to call him 'Tiger' after all.

8 Chamberlain in Charge

The original National Government was 'a collection of people collected together to save the situation', and no one expected it to last; but having failed to 'save the situation', its members proved more adept at saving themselves.[1] The decision by the mass of the Labour Party to oppose the government's economic programme, and its promises to restore the cuts and soak the rich, had helped ensure that August's expedient became November's permanency. The task which had fallen to the Conservatives – of acting as the bulwark against Socialism and fostering moderate Labour – had now fallen to the 'National' government which incorporated what was left of that last ravaged entity. This, along with the economic crisis and the rhetoric upon which the election had been fought, would have precluded any crude schemes to drop MacDonald and company, even had Baldwin not felt in honour bound to the former Labour leader.[2] But the Conservative dominance does not mean that we can accept Labour's claims that 'National' was a label signifying the same as Conservative.

The next Conservative government would have been more 'Imperial' and Protectionist, and places would have had to be found for the likes of Churchill, Amery and Lloyd, who could all now be left out. Baldwin would certainly not have been able to pursue the major item in the government's programme, the India Bill, at the head of a Conservative Cabinet. It would have been argued that as the Conservatives were the 'national' party, such measures were necessary in the national interest; now Baldwin could turn the tables and claim that it was in the interests of the unity of the 'National' government that imperialism and Protection should be down-played. This would be done in tones of regret, but the tears were those of the crocodile. The demons, which had plagued him since 1923, could be banished with this talisman. Baldwin appreciated the 'National' label, and he was willing to let his party pay the price. Despite their overwhelming majority, the Conservatives received nothing like a proportionate share of government posts in the new National Administration; 'National' Labour, by contrast, received jobs for most of its 'boys'. Baldwin could point out that in a Cabinet of 20, his party held 11 posts, but that was to ignore their distribution. Macdonald remained Prime Minister whilst his fellow 'National' Labourites, Snowden, Sankey and J. H. Thomas received the Privy Seal, the Lord Chancellorship and the Colonial Office, respectively. From the tiny Liberal contingent, Sir John Simon got the Foreign Office and Herbert Samuel went to the Home Office. Only Neville Chamberlain, who insisted on the Exchequer despite MacDonald not wanting to put a tariff reformer there, received a weighty office. It had come to be expected that the Conservative leader in a coalition should take the post of Lord President of the Council; since its duties were largely honorific and far from onerous, this arrangement suited Baldwin well enough. It was true that the Conservatives had a monopoly of the Service departments, but since they were all in line for heavy cuts, this was a mixed blessing; the only other Conservative to occupy a prominent position was Hoare at the India Office, which soon became the hottest seat in the Government. Whatever its opponents may have claimed in the heady atmosphere of the hustings, there were not lacking Conservatives who charged the government with being less Conservative than it should have been.

In general, the government's line was close to what Baldwin would have liked to have pursued between 1924 and 1929 had he not had the Protectionists and the 'diehards' on his back. Although they were still there, and in some numbers, he had a massive majority to play against them – as well as the excuse that the alternative to the sort of compromise he was asking for was a Socialist administration; he played both cards effectively.

There was one area where MacDonald and company were asked to compromise; given the circumstances of the economy the Conservatives could hardly fail to press for Protection, particularly with Chamberlain at the Treasury. MacDonald had feared before the election that it might be a Conservative device for obtaining 'a majority for Tariff reform', and he saw the retention of a significant Liberal element in the government as a guarantee against becoming a 'Tory slave'.[3] Before the 1983 Election, Francis Pym was incautious enough to hope for a small majority, and after Mrs Thatcher was delivered of a large one he was consigned to the outer darkness, but this is the nearest one can get to MacDonald's position in 1931; after the event he saw that 'the size of the victory has weakened me.'[4] The delegation which Baldwin and Chamberlain led to the Imperial Conference at Ottawa in August 1932 was dominated by Protectionists, and if the pure gospel as desired by Amery was not delivered, then the meeting did at least agree to the introduction of tariffs on non-Imperial goods and upon the setting up of a monetary sterling area. But what was small beer for Amery was too strong for Samuel and his band of Liberal pilgrims – who departed into eternal night, along with Snowden, leaving MacDonald an increasingly lonely and forlorn figure. Neville Chamberlain could reflect that something of his father's dream had come to pass, whilst Baldwin could thankfully let the issue rest – the first Conservative leader in the twentieth century to have been able to do so. It even helped compensate the 'Imperial' wing of the Conservative Party, which found little comfort elsewhere.

The outward and visible sign of what Lord Lloyd called 'that devilish MacBaldwinism' was the government's India policy. It is not always easy to differentiate between the 'diehard' and the man of principle; Lloyd's view that it was 'far better to wreck the Conservative Party and let the Socialists rule indefinitely than acquiesce in Baldwin's attitude'; [5] placed him firmly in both camps; the same can be said of Churchill, who soon emerged as the biggest thorn in the side of Hoare and the rest of the government. He saw the world in the early 1930s in Hobbesian terms, as the struggle of all against all, one in which the 'mild and vague Liberalism of the early twentieth century' had no place. No longer sanguine in his old Whiggish belief in progress, Churchill found history too full of 'unexpected turns and retrogressions' to share the views of those like Baldwin and Irwin, whom he saw as 'mouthing the bland platitudes of an easy safe triumphant age which has passed away'.[6] Only by hanging on to her Empire could Britain survive in an age of 'aggressive nationalism', and he would apply this insight to Europe as well as to India – as indeed would Lloyd, who shared his world view.

But to Hoare, Irwin and Baldwin, Churchill was mouthing the prejudices of the subaltern of 1896, albeit in the grand oratorical style. The fact was that the line taken on India by the National Government reflected that adopted by Baldwin after 1922. Unlike Churchill, Baldwin and company did not believe that a mere assertion of Imperial 'will' would solve the problems confronting them in India, if only because the problems were too complex for such simplicity to work. The period of Churchill's youth, when the British had acquired large tracts of Africa and practised formal Imperialism, is, in retrospect, an aberration in British Imperial history. Before that the British had preferred to practice 'informal' – that is economic – Imperialism; in the aftermath of the First World War successive governments began to revert to this model. Here the events of 1921 and 1922 were of vital importance: Ireland showed that dominion by the gun and the armoured car, although feasible, was not practical politics, either from the financial or the moral point of view, whilst the Milner Report pointed the way to the future. It isolated Britain's main interests in Egypt, the Canal, foreign and economic policy, and proposed to hang on to them whilst conceding self-rule elsewhere to the native politicians whose collaboration was, in any case, essential to the continuation of

Imperial rule. It was this same impulse which lay behind the government's India policy. Nationalism was a fact of life and it had to be lived with. If the native elites could be persuaded to carry on their cooperation with the British by tactical concessions, the purposes of Imperial rule could be carried out; if they did not cooperate, then no amount of force could carry through that purpose.

At this level the fight between Churchill, Lloyd, the India Defence League and the government was so bitter because it was a civil war between two conceptions of what Conservatism was about; it was the age-old struggle between those who argued that accommodation with change was necessary to preserve what could be preserved, and those who argued that tactical concessions always led to strategic ones. Baldwin was right to argue that Churchill had no constructive alternative to propose to all-India federation and greater self-government in home affairs, but Churchill and Lloyd were right to think that events would not stop where Hoare and company wanted them to. Of course, Hoare and Baldwin did not expect things to stop anywhere short of independence for India – but it was hardly expedient to say so. Successive party conferences in 1932 and 1933 saw the government under heavy attack from the diehards, but even in these Conservative-dominated assemblies, Churchill could never secure a majority. He gave Hoare some nasty moments, and in early 1933 the latter feared that they were about to witness 'the break away of three-quarters of the Conservative Party',[7] but this said more for the level of panic Churchill had managed to engender in Hoare than it did about political reality. The fact was that most Conservative MPs were prepared to back the government's India policy, however reluctantly, if that was the price to be paid for keeping themselves in and the Socialists out. Since the government had managed to restore a measure of economic stability as well as dealing with the tariff and India problems, its record was not, after all, a bad one.

It was little wonder that Baldwin was content – the government allowed him a quieter life than he had had before and was, in many ways, the epitome of Baldwinian Conservatism. It pushed extremists of the left and the right to the political margins. Mosley, who in 1931 had gambled that the existing political parties would not be able to deal with the immediate crisis, now increased the stake by betting that the system as a whole would not be able to cope, and set himself up as the English-speaking version of Mussolini by establishing his British Union of Fascists. His activism led him into a wilderness from which there would be no return. Lloyd George, Churchill and the India Defence League were all effectively marginalised. It was, of course, unfortunate that the Labour Party also seemed to have been pushed further left – but that was a convincing argument for the continuation of the 'National' government; at least it convinced Baldwin and others who also wished to be convinced. There were, of course, those who regarded both Baldwin and MacDonald as 'second-rate men whom chance had made our leaders',[8] but even Neville Chamberlain, whose orderly mind and imperious spirit chafed increasingly at the muddled antics of MacDonald, and whose patience was strained by having to put up with Simon and the Liberal Nationals, had to acknowledge that for all his being able to supply 'the policy and the drive', Baldwin managed something even more valuable – to retain 'the floating vote';[9] this was the *raison d'être* of the Coalition. There were, of course, good reasons for never referring to the government as the 'Coalition', but it was one, all the same, and in embracing it Baldwin was accepting the logic of Austen Chamberlain's argument back in 1922 that the Conservative Party was better off not standing by itself. The difference was that this time it was the Conservatives who were firmly in command.

One of the most beneficial results of the events of 1931 from the Conservative point of view was that it marked the extinction of the Liberals as a force in British politics. The 'National' label and the presence of the Simonites allowed Baldwin to garner votes from those Liberals who could not quite bring themselves to vote Conservative, whilst Samuel and the Lloyd George family faction disposed of too little power and territorial presence to mount a nationwide campaign. This allowed more Conservatives a straight fight against Labour; in 1931 some 400 Labour candidates had faced straight contests compared with only 82 in 1929. This was a valuable bonus to Conservatives for, despite the electoral catastrophe, Labour had polled 30.9 per cent of the vote, and its 6.6 million voters compared well with the number which had brought office in 1923; but without the Liberals to help split the anti-Conservative vote, it was clear that, although there were many people who would vote Labour, they were concentrated in too few areas. But Labour had been pushed back to its bed-rock in 1931, and both its leaders and those of the Coalition expected it to do better next time; this suited Baldwin since it helped keep the diehards at bay.

The Coalition had the disadvantage for the Conservatives which had attended upon its successor – that the number of loaves and fishes doled out to the smaller parties deprived deserving Conservatives, and given the stability of the Cabinet personnel after the departure of the Samuelites, this helped create a situation not unlike the one which had developed towards the end of the last Baldwin government. In 1933 Chamberlain was successful in getting one of his acolytes, Sir Kingsley

Wood, into the Cabinet, but for the younger men promotion was painfully slow in coming – however, the reshuffle of 1934 finally saw a breakthrough of sorts. Although it was a Scotsman, Walter Elliot, who was first to find his place in the Cabinet at Health, perhaps the most promising of the younger members was Anthony Eden who, having been Simon's deputy at the Foreign Office, was brought into the Cabinet in 1934 as Lord Privy Seal and Minister for League of Nations Affairs. This put him ahead of contemporaries like Duff Cooper, who remained at the War Office under Hailsham until 1934 when he reached the ante-chamber to the Cabinet by becoming Financial Secretary to the Treasury. Just to show that the old Tory grandees were not being totally ignored, Baldwin persuaded MacDonald to bring Oliver Stanley, Derby's second son, into the Cabinet in 1934 as Minister of Labour. There was no promotion for 'Rab' Butler, but his sterling work at the India Office in tackling Churchill won him golden opinions and the promise of better things to come. There was no place, however, for the 'bookish and unprepossessing' MP for Stockton, Harold Macmillan – but this was hardly surprising since he played a prominent part in criticising the government for its lack of initiative in industrial and employment policy. The 'left' of the party received preferment from Baldwin – but only those MPs who behaved themselves could expect a reward. As Baldwin told Butler in 1935, leading the Conservative Party meant steering a course mid-way between Macmillan and Page-Croft.[10]

The promotions were a sign of growing Conservative predominance. In part this was the natural result of their numerical majority, but it also reflected the declining powers and prestige of the Prime Minister. Although many Conservatives had had doubts about serving under MacDonald in 1931, the part he played in the election campaign and his obvious popularity in the country and prestige abroad had to some extent reconciled them to what necessity demanded; by 1934 prestige and popularity had dwindled to vanishing point. MacDonald's oratory had always had a tendency to become prolix and over-rhetorical, but by 1933 it had become plain embarrassing. In part this was the result of exhaustion and premature ageing, but the weight of the past lay heavily upon the emotional Scotsman. His entire life had been devoted to building up the Labour Party, and the rupture of 1931 had been traumatic. MacDonald lacked the thick epidermis possessed by most senior politicians, and he winced at the shafts directed against him by former colleagues; neither did he find any solace in his new ones. By 1935 two things were clear: there would have to be another election within 18 months; and it was inconceivable that 'Ramshackle Mac' could lead the Coalition into it.[11] It was, however, a mark of the Coalition's main success – the 1931 election result – that there were few senior Conservatives who questioned whether it should continue. There were, as Baldwin once put it, only two parties – 'Socialist' and 'anti-Socialist' – so he could not imagine why some thought it 'hypocritical' of him to claim that there should be another 'non-party' election.

By the end of 1934 the prestige of the government was low enough for rumours to be circulating that Lloyd George might be invited to join it – but, although MacDonald would not have minded this, Chamberlain did and the idea was knocked firmly on the head. After George V's Silver Jubilee in May 1935, the long-expected reshuffle took place, with MacDonald and Baldwin swapping offices and an attempt being made to clear out some of the other detritus. The main 'victim' was Simon, whose tenure of the Foreign Office had been, to put it kindly, undistinguished, and Hoare – whose tenure would be shorter and even less distinguished, replaced him. With Hoare at the Foreign Office and Hailsham going to the Woolsack, and with Baldwin as Prime Minister and Chamberlain remaining at the Exchequer, it was becoming difficult for outsiders to see where the government differed from a Conservative one. For Baldwin, who knew quite well where it differed, it remained essential to wear the 'National' label into the election.

The election took place in November. No one expected the 1931 result to be repeated, but neither was there a repeat of the Liberal experience of 1910 when most of the vast majority won in 1906 had been lost; the Coalition romped home with 429 seats, of which 388 were Conservative (down from 473 in 1931), 33 National Liberal (down from 35 in 1931) and only eight were National Labour (down from 13) – with MacDonald losing his seat at Seaham. The Lord President fell victim not only to his own shortcomings, but to Labour's revival in the North-East, Scotland and Wales. The party saw its number of MPs rise from 52 to 154. Labour garnered 38 per cent of the vote – more than it had in 1929, but the demise of the Liberal challenge to the Conservatives once more hit the party badly; the 'National' label had, as Baldwin had always contended, helped his party's fortunes. The election results serve as a reminder of how biased the portrait of 'Depression Britain' is. In the old industrial heartlands of the North and North-East, and, of course, in Scotland and Wales, Labour's revival did, indeed, feed off widespread unemployment and social deprivation; but in the Midlands, the South and the South-East, where the motor car industry and other new businesses were creating employment and prosperity, there was every reason to vote for Baldwin.

1935 was the high-water mark of Baldwin's strategy, and it is easy to forget how successful it had been, and would continue to be. Because the Churchillian account of the 1930s as the 'years which the locusts have eaten' has been so influential, it has been assumed that Baldwin was a failure and that there was some sort of caesura between him and the Conservatism of the Churchillian era; neither of these things stand up to examination.

The 1930s was a decade of global instability, and international disorder was reflected in and caused by domestic upheavals: Japan became more militaristic; the fascist dictatorship installed by Mussolini in 1922 became more adventurous and provided a model for other European nations, most notably Germany in 1933, to copy. If France did not succumb to the fashion, her politics became even more unstable, whilst from 1936 onwards Spain dissolved into a bloody civil war in which both fascists and communists sought to gain the upper hand; even in America the economic and political crisis led to extreme measures in the form of Roosevelt's 'New Deal' – and Britain had Oswald Mosley.

Men like Lord Lloyd, who feared that the party was drifting too far 'to the left' under Baldwin, were anxious lest this should lead 'the young and middle-aged men' towards 'Fascism', and there were, indeed, rumours in 1933 that Lloyd himself intended to lead such a movement. Yet it never happened. Mosley was a man of undoubted talent and charisma, yet he got nowhere. Lloyd and other right-wingers stayed in the party and Britain came nowhere near revolution. When this record is compared with that of other parts of the world, it gives some indication of the success enjoyed by Baldwin; if the main task of Conservatism is to preserve the social and constitutional order against the forces of change and decay, then it was achieved here under the most adverse circumstances.

Two lines of argument may be advanced against the contention that the Coalition was a success; its failure to deal with unemployment; and its ultimately much more serious failure to deal with international disorder. Since Neville Chamberlain was intimately associated with both failures, his reputation has suffered correspondingly.

In the more comfortable circumstances of the 1950s and 1960s, when it appeared that Keynesian economics had provided the 'philosopher's stone' which would deliver full employment and ever-increasing standards of living, it was quite the fashion to slate the National Government for not doing more about unemployment, not least because some of its severest critics on this issue, including Harold Macmillan, seemed to be about to deliver what Baldwin and Chamberlain had not; but from the vantage point of later experience, when the unemployment figures were so high that they were subject to constant massage, such complacency is less natural. There were, it was true, contemporary politicians who dealt with the problem, but few would have wanted to follow the nostrums of Mussolini, Hitler and Stalin. Roosevelt's much-vaunted efforts actually achieved little in the way of creating real jobs, and it was not until the outbreak of the war in Europe that the American economy really began to recover from the slump. The British economy itself benefited, after 1935, from the growth in the armaments industry, but again, no one actively advocated this as a solution to the problem. Within the context of a stable international order, and with agreements on fixed-exchange rates and an International Monetary Fund, it might be that Keynesian solutions bring short-term benefits, but Baldwin and Chamberlain did not operate in such a context. With autarchic Nationalist regimes in Germany and Italy, and with the Americans imposing tariffs, circumstances could hardly have been more different to those in which Keynesian experiments were tried. Indeed, it might be argued that by promoting a climate in which money was 'cheap' and labour costs low, the government did as much as it could to promote the right climate for economic recovery.

But the most conspicuous failure of Baldwin's Conservatism lay else-where – in its failure to meet the challenges of an age of aggressive nationalism; nor is this surprising. Baldwin's was a Conservatism tinged throughout with liberalism, and it quite lacked that vein of pessimism which arises on the right from a conviction (religious or secular) of 'original sin'. Part of Baldwin's consensus was an acceptance of the League of Nations and the assumptions that went with it – after all, both were based upon a fundamental premise of human reasonable-ness; there was, surely, nothing that men of goodwill could not settle between themselves? This assumption had worked well enough with the Labour Party and the trades unions, it had brought peace and tran-quillity at home – so why not abroad? The same ideas permeated British Imperial policy; some ground could be found for cooperation with nationalism, if only the right set of Indian or Egyptian politicians could be found. The League of Nations was a popular concept with the new democracy at home; it embodied all their woolly minded assump-tions that foreigners were really Englishmen who spoke with odd accents for reasons of their own. If there were fairies at the bottom of the garden of international relations, they were heavily armed ones with designs on their neighbour's vegetable patch. If the will to international cooperation that the League presupposed had actually existed, there would have been no need for it, and if that will was lacking, there was no use for it. But such views were as unpopular then as they are now: 'our intellectuals are mad on the League of Nations and anyone who points out the truth about that absurd body, and suggested that we had better depend on ourselves, is looked upon as mad or bad.'[12] Such allegations came only from the political right – who also advocated rearmament.

These calls should be seen not simply as a reaction to Hitler, but rather as part of a general reaction to the 'sloppy internationalism' which Lloyd thought had come to dominate the Conservative Party.[13] But as the despairing comments of Churchill, Lloyd, Headlam and others suggest, the Conservative Party under Baldwin was firmly wedded to a belief in the League as part of their belief in consensus. Whereas, before the Great War, the Conservative Party had believed in rearmament and Imperial defence and had thus been well-placed to deal with the consequences of Liberal illusions and failure, in the late 1930s it partook of those delusions itself, and was thus badly placed to deal with the rise of Hitler. But this is not to accept the old Churchillian argument that the government was composed of a bunch of simpletons and knaves who failed to see the reality that lay before them. It was certainly true that both MacDonald and Baldwin were horrified by the events of the early 1930s – the rise of militant Japanese nationalism in the Far East, the adventurism of Mussolini nearer home, and the intervention of fascists and communists in the Spanish Civil War – and they had good reason to be so: these things undermined the fundamental assumptions upon which they had based their foreign policy, but this did not mean that they failed to recognise a need to rearm the country. From 1934 onwards a series of rearmament policies were implemented, but things were not as easy as the rhetoric of the critics suggested.

Rearmament posed a series of problems for the government. In the first place, whatever people pretended after 1939, it was not a policy which commanded, or could expect to command, widespread support. Although its significance can be exaggerated, the loss of the East Fulham by-election in October 1933, to a Labour candidate who campaigned on a 'peace' platform, indicated the political dangers in a programme of rearmament. There were also economic difficulties; the country was slowly recovering from the great slump, and it would not take much push to damage the fragile recovery. Then there were what might be called the problems of definition: what sort of rearmament was being aimed for and against whom should it be directed? Different answers to these questions gave different types of rearmament, and the government which put its money on Germany being the main problem could, and in 1935 did, find itself in trouble.

In 1934, in one of his last significant acts as Prime Minister, MacDonald came to an agreement with Mussolini and the French – the Stresa Front – designed to frustrate any designs Hitler had upon

Austria; it was not the 'new' diplomacy of the League, but it appeared to be effective all the same. However, when Italy attacked Abyssinia in 1935 and outraged League opinion, the argument that it was not worth losing Italy to Germany over such an issue was submerged in the tide of sentimentalism from British public opinion. The government, during the election, had calmed the fears raised at East Fulham by committing itself to support the League. Afterwards, the new Foreign Secretary, Hoare, won golden opinions by his rhetoric at Geneva. This, of course, helped neither the Abyssinians nor yet contributed to the diplomatic effort which was needed to restrain Hitler – but outraged idealism does not consider such matters. However, it transpired that Hoare and his French opposite number, Pierre Laval, had come to an agreement which would give Mussolini most of what he wanted, whilst allowing the Abyssinians a token state. This might just have prevented Italy falling into the ranks of Britain's potential enemies, but it was all too much like *Realpolitik* to be acceptable to those brought up on the Baldwinian consensus. Hoare was swept from office by public outcry, and in an effort to prove that he really was a 'League' man, Baldwin hastily promoted Eden to the Foreign Office. This sent the political problem away – but made the underlying international one worse. The Defence Requirements Committee now had to consider Italy as a possible enemy. It was quite clear that Britain could not take on Italy, Germany and Japan at the same time, but Baldwin appeared to be unclear just how diplomacy was going to keep the three apart; he was equally uncertain about how to order the rearmament programme.

But if Baldwin's skills failed him when it came to dealing with foreigners, he still enjoyed one last chance to show how effective they could be at home. When George V died in early 1936, Edward VIII became king. Edward was, like all George V's sons, an unstable and neurotic character who needed a strong partner; unfortunately for him, unlike his brother Albert, who found it in a Scottish peer's daughter, his chosen help-meet was an American divorcée who was still married to her second husband. The monarchy had come to play a pivotal role in the Baldwinian consensus, if only as a national lynch-pin. As the head of the Church and of the State, as the repository of a thousand years of tradition, and as the head of the Empire, the monarchy was well-placed to take on the role which it assumed under Baldwin; all that was needed was for it to become somehow 'democratic' – or at least less obviously aristocratic. George V had been ideally suited to fulfil this function. An ordinary little man with the philistine tastes of most of his subjects, he could be presented as the archetypal English paterfamilias getting on with his duties without fuss or more ostentation than must necessarily surround a king-emperor. He and Baldwin had made a formidable conservative team, with their ordinary, honest, English decency proving the first (and most effective) bulwark against revolution. The monarchy took on during this time the attributes which it would maintain until the 1990s, and which even then the ageing and greatly respected Queen Mother would still personify. It would have been unfortunate if all this had been lost because Edward wished to marry Mrs Simpson; it was hardly to be expected that the British people would identify with 'Queen Wally' in quite the way they had with Queen Mary. Baldwin's last service to the state was to smooth the way for Edward to abdicate, leaving the throne to the Duke of York who, in the capable hands of his consort, carried on in the style of his father – an intention signified in his adoption of the title of George VI. Their young daughter, Elizabeth, would prove to be another out of the Baldwinian mould.

This last service also allowed Baldwin to become the first Prime Minister since Salisbury to lay down his task at a time of his own choosing and of his own free will. After a brief spell under the unfamiliar title of Sir Stanley Baldwin, he duly became Earl Baldwin of Bewdley and retired to his Worcestershire home under a hail of plaudits such as few Prime Ministers ever receive. He had done much to deserve them – but democracies are fickle entities, and it would not be many years before he found himself more reviled than any living politician.

With his going, the 'last but not least' of Joe Chamberlain's sons, Neville, finally became Prime Minister. He was proposed for the leadership by Lord Derby, who was ably seconded in this task by none other than Winston Churchill (something one would hardly guess from his memoirs). Historians are agreed upon the irony of the fact that a man who had made his name as a social reformer and who intended to devote his Premiership to that task should instead have spent all his time dealing with foreign affairs; this is the last, indeed it is the only thing, upon which historians are agreed. It was not always so. For three decades after 1940 Chamberlain was generally agreed to have been a weak and ineffectual character, but since then his achievements at home have been given greater recognition.[14] With the opening of the Cabinet papers in 1967 a more informed appreciation of both his policies and the difficulties he faced became possible; but two decades later, although historians can agree about the fact that Chamberlain faced almost insuperable problems, there is still no consensus about the tactics he used to solve them.[15]

Politically, the change from Baldwin to Chamberlain had two main effects: it sharpened the divide between the parties within the

government and made it feel somehow less 'National'. The first phenomenon derived from Chamberlain's manner towards the Labour
Party, which was cold and sarcastic; he never suffered fools gladly, or
even at all, and he made it plain that the entire Labour Party fell into
this category.[16] This was a grave shortcoming in the head of a coalition administration, and even before foreign affairs began to dominate the agenda, there was, in some quarters, a nostalgia for good old
Baldwin with his vague but soothing rhetoric; it was not long before
there was talk of the need for a 'broader Government with more
idealism and less brutal clarity'.[17] It is usual to dwell on the resignations of Eden and Duff Cooper in February and October 1938,
respectively, from the view point of the debate about appeasement;
whilst not denying that angle, it might also be useful to point out that
both of them were Baldwinians with doubts about Chamberlain's style
of government, and their departure made the government more
Chamberlainite.

Chamberlain was himself an executive man of action, and as Eden
and Cooper discovered, he could be ruthless in getting his own way; a
wimp in a wing collar he was not. Unfortunately for him, he was also
unsuccessful in his attempt to find a solution to the international instability caused by the ambitions of Hitler. In politics, success excuses most
things, and Chamberlain's lack of political emollience would not have
grated so much had it been attended with it; but as things transpired,
his policies served to fracture the Baldwinian coalition and polarised
British politics. It is noteworthy that Halifax, who replaced Eden at the
Foreign Office, and who saw himself as Baldwin's residuary legatee,
argued that Chamberlain should take the opportunity afforded by his
success at Munich in September 1938 to broaden the base of his government, in particular by inviting back the paladin of the Baldwinites,
Eden – but the Prime Minister would have none of it. He knew his own
mind, and he prided himself upon having brought order where
Baldwin had left vacillation and chaos; and if the weaker brethren were
frightened off, then real Conservatives would, Chamberlain thought,
be heartened. No doubt, had he succeeded, he would have been
proved right; but he failed.

Chamberlain had answers to the various questions posed by the problem of rearmament. He assumed that Germany would be the main
enemy in case of war, so his diplomacy first set out to detach Mussolini
from the 'axis' with Hitler – which was why Eden had to go in February
1938 when he could not seem to see the need to recognise the Italian
conquest of Abyssinia. Priority would be given to fighter aircraft, the
defensive system which became known as 'radar', and to a mechanised

army; the programme was due to reach a peak in 1939, and it was not entirely coincidental that Chamberlain felt able to take a tougher line with Hitler that year. For the rest, Chamberlain set out in business-like fashion to remedy Hitler's grievances – if necessary before he had announced them himself. The intervention in Czechoslovakia in 1938 had this aim in mind. There were those in the government, particularly Halifax's junior, Rab Butler, who thought that it would have been wiser to have left Central Europe alone altogether, but Chamberlain could not shake the habit of acting as the leader of a Great Power and trying to broker a settlement. One was finally reached at Munich. This, Chamberlain hoped, would provide the acid test of Hitler's intentions and show that he really was just a German Nationalist. He came back to Heston airport waving an additional piece of paper, proclaiming 'peace in our time', and was tempted to call a quick election. It was Chamberlain's apotheosis; Hitler was, after all, amenable to compromise – one simply had to know how to deal with the 'common-looking' little fellow.

The problem was that whilst Chamberlain had averted war over the future of Czechoslovakia, he had not converted Hitler to the cause of peace; nor could he have done since war was the very essence of Hitler's political creed – the survival of the fittest. The country had expressed its relief after Munich, but as Hitler failed to stick to the terms of the settlement and stories percolated through about his treatment of the Jews, Halifax led the way in advocating a more cautious approach – hence the call to bring back Eden. Halifax's instincts were, as usual, accurate. The political left had been horrified by the immorality of sacrificing democratic Czechoslovakia to the Fascists; Churchill, and those Conservatives who shared his views such as Lloyd and Cooper, thought it rank folly to upset the balance of power by letting Germany expand her power and influence. In the absence of a diplomatic breakthrough, it would have made sense to have sown division in the ranks of the opposition by poaching some of the more ambitious of the critics. This was an appeal Halifax renewed after the Germans occupied Prague in March 1939; but again, Chamberlain refused to pay heed. This was political foolishness of a high order. At some point in the next year a General Election would have to be held, and the government's 'National' credentials were certainly in need of refurbishment; Eden or Cooper could have been won over with the right offer, and even Churchill could be kept on side by a little flattery. But Chamberlain's stubbornness paid no heed to such matters.

Politics, no less than nature, abhors a vacuum, and into that left by the failure of the Baldwinian approach to foreign affairs there was obtruding a new one, made up of old-fashioned Conservative Realpolitik and

Socialist abhorrence of fascism. From one side came Churchill, Lloyd and Amery, who all agreed that Britain had to stop Germany because she was a threat to the balance of power in Europe and to the British Empire; behind them, but not quite with them, came those younger Conservatives with League credentials like Eden, his former junior Lord Cranborne and Duff Cooper, who in their hearts shared something of Churchill's approach but couched it in Baldwinian language about 'collective security'. This concept provided the bridge between these Conservative dissidents and those in the Labour Party who had abandoned their attachment to pacifism under the impact of Hitler. Here one of the key figures was Hugh Dalton, who kept open links with Churchill, but others such as the trade union leader Ernest Bevin and the former leader of London County Council, Herbert Morrison, along with the Labour leader, Clement Attlee, were moving in a similar direction. Mistrust of Hitler – and dislike of Chamberlain and his domineering manner – provided the foundations of a new consensus.

Facing the gradual breakdown of the 'National' consensus because of the failure of his foreign policy, Chamberlain decided to push ahead with the policies which were already proving so divisive. He gave territorial guarantees to Poland and to Greece and Romania, hoping that these would act as deterrents, showing Hitler where he must stop; this would have been fine, had Hitler had any intention of stopping. In September Hitler attacked Poland. After a short delay, during which Chamberlain frantically hoped that peace could be saved, he announced, on 3 September 1939, that a 'state of war now exists' between Britain and Germany. Finally, long after it would have been seen as an act of political shrewdness, Chamberlain decided to bring Churchill into the Cabinet; those with long memories wondered if Asquith had just promoted his Lloyd George.

9 Churchill's Consensus

Writing to President Roosevelt in 1942, Beaverbrook commented that where the old Liberal Party had been the main casualty of the last war, this time it was the Conservatives who were the victims.[1] At the same time, one of the leading Conservative backbenchers, Lord William Scott, was writing that the party had 'ceased to exist' as an 'effective body either in the House or in the country'.[2] Nor can such opinions be dismissed as unduly pessimistic. The Conservatives did consistently badly in contested by-elections from 1942 to 1945, and in the election they went down to a defeat which was more shattering than anything since 1905–6; and all of this despite being led by the man who had become the national hero – Winston Churchill. Unsurprisingly the event had a traumatic effect on those members of the party who experienced it, and it had an effect upon the direction in which they pushed it after the war. Two questions arise, one obvious, the other not so frequently asked: what had gone wrong?; and was the disaster quite as total as has been claimed?

As the last chapter showed, the most obvious failure of the Chamberlain style was in foreign affairs. Chamberlain's claims to leadership depended upon his being able to prove that he could solve the problem of Hitler, and the clearer it became that he could not do this, the more his position weakened. He was no war leader, and he knew it. Until April 1940 his strategy was based upon the assumption that Hitler would make an unsuccessful assault upon the Maginot Line, after which he would be deposed by the Nazi satraps who would then conclude a negotiated peace. This did not happen. The Maginot Line was by-passed and the Anglo-French forces were routed; but by this time Chamberlain had ceased to be Prime Minister.

Halifax's fear that the 'National' character of the government had been dangerously eroded by Chamberlain's abrasive and combative style proved correct. Ironically it was Churchill's pet project which once more brought a Prime Minister face to face with a ministerial crisis – this time it was Narvik in Norway rather than the Dardanelles – and this time it was the Prime Minister and not Churchill who suffered. During a debate upon the Norwegian fiasco Chamberlain tried to rally the troops by calling upon his 'friends' to support him, whilst behind the scenes the Chief Whip, David Margesson, promised that there would be changes in the government. But the effect of these measures was diluted by Amery making the speech of his life. Although he had been out of office during the 1930s, he was not generally regarded as a malcontent; as a fellow Birmingham MP and a devoted follower of Joe Chamberlain's, he was generally held to be friendly towards the Prime Minister. This gave the final words of his oration even more force, as he called up the memory of Cromwell, telling the Front Bench: 'You have sat too long for any good you have been doing. Depart, I say, and let us have done with you. In the name of God, go!' It was devastating stuff. Still, we must not be too carried away; the Conservative Party held more or less solid and the government won by 281 to 200 votes. In peace-time that would have been enough, but in war it was not – it showed that the government had failed to maintain its 'National' character. Liberals and Labour had voted solidly against Chamberlain, whilst within the party itself the offended Baldwinians and the other malcontents had had their day, with 33 voting against the Prime Minister and another 60 Conservatives abstaining.

The Prime Minister had three choices: to resign; to soldier on relying upon the Conservative Party; or to reconstruct his government. In view of the promises made by Margesson, as well as the national emergency, the second of these options was never on the cards, whilst it went against every instinct Chamberlain possessed to do the first. But when he consulted the Labour leaders on 9 May they refused to serve under him and they demanded the removal of at least Sir John Simon and Sir Samuel Hoare. It was clearly time to consult with Churchill and Halifax about the succession.

Myths abound about this crucial episode, with everyone from Brendan Bracken to Beaverbrook claiming to have advised Churchill, and with everyone equally claiming at a later date that Churchill was the only man for the job. It was not like that in 1940. The King would have preferred Halifax, as would the Conservative Party, and Labour would have been happy to have served under the good Viscount; the one person who was unhappy with this choice was Halifax himself; the idea gave him, he recorded in his diary, a 'stomach ache', which is why he told Chamberlain that it would have to be Churchill. It is a good job he did not take it – he would have had an ulcer by July. The fact was, as Churchill later reminded the House, there were no other takers for the job of Prime Minister in May 1940. The German invasion of the Low Countries on 10 May did give Chamberlain an opportunity to say that perhaps he should stay on – but nobody was interested.

Writing to Chamberlain's widow in December 1940, Rab Butler commented: 'I do not think the Party will ever be the same again. I looked upon him as the last leader of the organization in the State which I joined very late in its life, but which had the responsibility for so much of England's greatness.'[3] He spoke for many Conservatives who never forgave Churchill for displacing the man who remained leader of the party.[4] Indeed, Churchill himself acknowledged the importance of Chamberlain by keeping him on as Lord President of the Council; he had no choice, whatever Labour would have liked. As one loyalist wrote to Chamberlain on the morrow of his resignation from the premiership: 'the fact that you are prepared to serve under the new Prime Minister resolves the doubts of a good many of us who had been doubtful of whether we would take the Whip under these circumstances. If he is good enough for you he must be good enough for us.'[5] Patrick Donner, who had served alongside Churchill in the campaign over India, told Chamberlain that he thought that it was 'only by the negation of democracy' that 'the Ministry forced its temporary will'.[6] This may now seem an odd point of view, as no doubt it is, but it was one held by many, perhaps by most, Conservative MPs. The tremendous cheer which greeted Chamberlain when he entered the Chamber of the House on 13 May bore witness to the way the Conservative Party felt about him. Margesson was obliged to tell his chaps that they ought to imitate Labour and give the new Premier a big cheer; they did so – but half-heartedly. This feeling in the majority party in the new Coalition explains much about its make-up.

Churchill may have been Prime Minister, but he was not a party leader; indeed, this might have been a suitable epitaph – and given Churchill's opinion of the Conservative Party it is by no means certain that he would have disdained it. Had Chamberlain elected to play the role which Asquith had in 1916, there would have been a split in the Conservative Party and it might well have met the fate which the Liberals suffered thereafter; but Chamberlain elected to do what he thought his patriotic duty demanded, and stayed on as Lord President. He was a great source of strength to the new Prime Minister during some of his most vulnerable moments; but he was also the buckler behind which the Conservative Party sheltered. Thus, despite the acrimonious attitude of Labour, there was no wholesale massacre of the men of Munich. Only Sam Hoare was sacked – and he went off to be Ambassador to Franco, a position for which some Labour members thought he was only too well qualified. Hoare had, in any case, no following in the party and had offended Churchill over India. But for the rest, Halifax stayed at the Foreign Office, and even old 'Soapy' Simon stayed on, elevated to the Upper House as Lord Chancellor. Loaves and fishes were in short supply for the 'anti-appeasers', all of whom now remembered themselves as being a good deal bolder in the past than had actually been the case. Eden remained outside the War Cabinet at the War Office, Duff Cooper came into the government in the thankless post of Minister of Information (the job of governments in war is to withhold that commodity – a fact rarely appreciated by journalists), whilst even Amery was fobbed off with India; only the faithful Lloyd was happy – sitting in the Colonial Office where his great hero had presided. The younger men like Bob Boothby and Harold Macmillan received only junior posts. Amery concluded that 'Winston has not been nearly bold enough – too much afraid of the Party which he feels has never quite admitted him to the fold';[7] there was much in this.

There were two reactions to this state of affairs. As Britain staggered from disaster to disaster in France in June and July, Labour publicists adopted Roman names and produced vitriolic polemics against what 'Cato' called 'the Guilty Men'; enough mud was thrown for some of it to stick. The Labour leadership, now safely ensconced in office, disowned such diatribes – but benefited from them all the same. From the discontented Churchillians came what was called the 'undersecretaries' revolt'. Macmillan, who had spent long years out of office, seems to have been unsettled by the experience of finally getting a job, and by mid-June, assuming that Britain was about to be defeated, got 'rather excited and convinced that we ought to have an immediate revolution from below to sweep away the old governing powers.'[8] Churchill, who was quite content with the present 'governing power', told Amery, Macmillan and Boothby to resign if they were unhappy, but advised that otherwise they should keep quiet and get on with their jobs.

Had the war not gone badly, and had not Chamberlain sickened and died in late 1940, then the Churchill premiership might have left little impact upon the Conservative Party. But the swift and crushing defeat of June 1940 was taken not as a sign that Churchill's earlier advocacy of war against Hitler was a policy which had been doomed to failure because Britain and France were not up to the job, but rather as an indictment of Chamberlain's policy. As Britain was as ready for war in 1939 as she was ever going to be, this was perverse. The only thing which Chamberlain could have done which would have had an effect in 1940 would have been to have imitated Stalin and to have purged his own General Staff in the late 1930s; a good idea, but not one advocated at the time. Still, history's long-term verdict was no good to Halifax and company. They may have remained, even after Dunkirk, essential to Churchill, but their reputations were undermined. Chamberlain's sudden death in November marked, as Butler realised, an epoch in the party's history.

In the first place, this allowed Churchill (against the wishes of his wife) to become leader of the Conservative Party. If this seemed to have no long-term implications at the time, it was because the longer term is not normally associated with men in their sixties: Churchill was clearly the man to lead the country during the war, but few expected him to go on after that. The second effect of Chamberlain's death was that it deprived the Conservatives of the one remaining senior figure who had a firm grasp of the home front. As Lord President of the Council, Chamberlain had presided over those Cabinet committees which dealt with the home front, and he had kept his eye on Conservative Party interests and organisation; with his death there was no one left to do this. Gradually Labour took over the running of the domestic side of the war. Churchill had little interest in this area and was quite happy to see Attlee and Labour deal with it; it was a mistake Chamberlain would not have made. The effect of Chamberlain's death in weakening the position of the Conservative Party in the Coalition was compounded in December 1940 when Halifax was packed off to Washington as ambassador, to be replaced by Eden. Neither Eden nor Churchill had much time or respect for the Conservative Party, both agreeing 'how little we liked it and how little it liked us'.[9] It was small wonder that faithful Chamberlainites felt that their party's interests were suffering.

There were other ways in which traditional Conservative interests suffered. One of the fundamental tenets of Conservatism under Baldwin, reflecting the infusion of Liberalism which had been one of his main achievements, had been the defence of individual liberty; Socialism and state control had been objects of scorn, and the Soviet Union had been a useful example of what happened to the nation which succumbed to them. These old certainties were removed by the war. Britain became the most heavily mobilised of any of the states at war, with the possible exception of the Soviet Union. The state controlled everything, including the decision over whether individuals should go to war or not; even married women were conscripted into factories. The result was that Britain won the war. If this was not enough of a recommendation for increasing the powers of government, there was always the example of the Soviet Union which, unlike Tsarist Russia, failed to collapse under German hammerblows and rallied to play the major part in the Allied victory; what price the Communist menace now?

The very atmosphere in which the war was fought on the home front also eroded another pillar of Conservatism – class differentiation. The party claimed to be in favour of 'One Nation', but its vision was very much one of the traditional ruling classes governing the country in the interest of all. It was not impossible for a poor man to become a

Conservative MP – but it was unheard of for such to receive high office. Indeed, many constituencies demanded that their MP should fund the local association. The assumption, in a deferential society, was that the ruling classes existed to do just that – rule. But their claim to competence had been badly dented by the events of 1938 to 1941, when they had not only failed to avoid a war, but also to prosecute it successfully. At home the exhortation was 'equality of sacrifice', and the prevailing mood (if not reality) was one of egalitarianism; whatever the Conservative Party is, it has never been egalitarian. Baldwinian Conservatism had existed on a diet of 'national' rhetoric and piecemeal Chamberlainite reform, but whilst Churchill had more than taken over the former, its content would need beefing up if the new Coalition was to survive.

If the war had gone well, it might have been possible to ignore the question of post-war planning, but until late 1942 the British had little to celebrate except surviving. Churchill's proclaimed war aim, 'victory, victory at all costs', seemed to be costing just that – everything, and the failure to achieve it created a vacuum into which others rushed with their more complicated versions of what the war was being fought for; nor was Churchill in a strong position by 1942 to reject other options.

He had built up an enormous credit with the British people in 1940, and in his great speeches of that summer he had successfully appealed over the heads of Halifax and other Conservatives who had doubts about a quick British victory. Churchill had firmly identified himself with the continuation of the war, but he had produced little in the way of success. His Conservative critics may have been defeated, but they muttered mutinously. At the end of January 1942, after the humiliating defeat at Singapore, Churchill was forced to ask for a vote of confidence in the Commons. He won by 464 votes to 1, but this belied the widespread feeling that Churchill ought not to continue to combine his position as Prime Minister with that of Minister of Defence. The Labour Party, the Tory backbench 1922 Committee and the junior members of the government all wanted a revitalized War Cabinet, and Churchill moved swiftly to contain the discontent by inviting the new popular hero, the former Ambassador to the Soviet Union, Sir Stafford Cripps, into the administration. It may have been an astute move politically, but it marked a tactical willingness to make concessions to those on the left who were calling for radical reform at home. Amery summed up the reaction of the average Conservative when he commented that the party 'will not like ... an extreme left-winger leading the House and a War Cabinet containing not a single real Conservative, for they certainly do not class Winston or Anthony [Eden] as such'.[10] Churchill's own fears for his position were assuaged by the victories in

North Africa in October and November, but those of the Conservative Party were not. As one MP put it to the new Chief Whip, James Stuart: 'Throughout the country the Conservative Party has become a cheap joke';[11] the situation was not to improve.

At the end of November 1942 a major contender arrived to plug the gap left by the failure to achieve Churchill's war aim, with the publication of Sir William Beveridge's plans to create what became known as the 'Welfare State' (although this was not a phrase used by Beveridge himself). Amery's view of it as a 'bold and comprehensive plan' may have reflected the views of old-style Chamberlainites, but it was not representative of the party's general opinion. When the Chancellor, Sir Kingsley Wood, presented the report to Conservative ministers on 30 November, he was 'definitely unfriendly'.[12] He spoke the language of fiscal orthodoxy when he said that he doubted whether the country would be able to afford such largesse after its sacrifices in the war, asking Churchill on 6 January: 'Is this the time to assume that the general taxpayer has a bottomless purse?';[13] the nation clearly thought so.

Not all Conservatives showed themselves as blind to their party's tradition of pragmatic opportunism as Sir Kingsley. Rab Butler, who had admired Baldwin for the way in which he had defused class conflict, came from a background which emphasised the Disraelian 'One Nation' tradition and saw no reason why the Conservative Party should be hostile to Beveridge. He was anxious, as he told Eden, to demonstrate that the Tories were capable of 'carrying out a great and unprecedented programme of social reforms'.[14] Support for such a line also came from some younger Conservatives, including the son of Lord Hailsham, Quintin Hogg. More impetuous than Butler, Hogg warned the House that 'if you do not give the people social reform, they are going to give you social revolution.'[15] On 17 March Hogg and 35 other Conservatives set up the Tory Reform Group, whose main aim was to challenge the 'laissez-faire' economics which they felt had come to dominate the party's thinking. His own personal formula was: 'Publicly organised social services, privately owned industry.'[16] The Group fused the 'old Tory tradition of state interventionism with the more recent ideas of Harold Macmillan and other radical Conservatives of the 1930s'.[17] This line of thinking would provide an important element of continuity between the Baldwinian period and the 1940s – but it received as little support from Churchill at the time as it did appreciation from Mrs Thatcher at a much later date.

If the Tory Reform Group represented one strand of Conservative thinking, then another was symbolised by the leader himself. Although Churchill had paid little detailed attention to social policy since his days as a Liberal reformer, his instincts remained liberal.[18] He was not keen to initiate post-war planning, at home or abroad, and his attitude towards Beveridge was much what it was to Eden's attempts to interest him in post-war planning: 'first catch your hare!'.[19] But his efforts to stifle discussion of 'reconstruction policy' in early 1943 simply provoked a split within his government. The Labour Party insisted that 'Beveridge' should be discussed, and in the end the Home Secretary, Sir John Anderson, duly promised that the proposals would be implemented. But his manner of so doing was so unsympathetic that, according to one Labour minister, the House was 'deadened' and scarcely able to grasp that 'something was to be done'.[20] This was a paradigm of the political situation: whatever the Conservatives said, no one really believed that their hearts were in 'Beveridge', and those Tories who did want to do something found themselves marooned between Churchillian indifference and the hostility of the right. The result was exactly what Butler had feared – the Conservatives came across as having nothing constructive to offer the country in the post-war period: 'blood, toils, tears and sweat' were all very well in their place – but as a permanent diet they were unappetising.

Nor did Churchill's reconstructions of his Cabinet do anything to counteract this impression. It was Butler's own initiative once he had been shifted to the Board of Education which led to the Education Act which bore his name – and he received little if any help from the Prime Minister.[21] Eden, as deputy leader of the party and Churchill's heir-apparent, lacked the 'constructive imagination' as well as the 'understanding of social and economic problems' to make up for his leader's defect.[22] It is indicative of Eden's semi-detached position as well as of his view of the Conservative Party that the death of Kingsley Wood in September 1943 should have drawn from him the comment that: 'the little man was no doubt a loss in a certain sphere, particularly to Tory party politics … but in the larger sphere of statesmanship' he was 'no loss'.[23] To those like Amery, who were not so ready to distance 'Conservative party politics' from 'statesmanship', Wood's death was a further blow to the party's position. Back in February 1942 Butler had commented that the Cabinet was remarkably short of proper Conservatives: 'Churchill was not orthodox; Eden was not liked; [Sir John] Anderson had never called himself a Tory; [Oliver] Lyttelton [Minister of Production] nobody knew & he was regarded as a City shark!'[24] With Wood's death the matter had become even worse. Amery regarded him as the last 'real constructive Conservative in the Cabinet'.[25]

Churchill's absorption with the war, and the indifference which he and Eden felt for the Conservative Party, all redounded to Labour's advantage in a situation which by 1943 had developed very firmly in their favour; Churchill's allowing them to seize most of the credit for Beveridge made a bad situation worse. As early as 1941, members of the 1922 Committee were complaining to Eden about the amount of 'socialistic legislation ... passed under the guise of war needs',[26] but this was the necessary consequence of Churchill's decision to commit the Empire to 'total war'. The whole of the economy and society had to be mobilised by the state to support the war effort: food rationing; conscription; direction of Labour; nationalisation of the railways and of the mines; all these measures were passed by a government headed by a Conservative. It was not unreasonable of the public to conclude that if such measures could win the war, they might also be able to avoid a return to the unemployment of the 1930s; at the time Chamberlain had said that little could be done except to encourage the economy to recover, but now men and women accepted the Keynesian view that there was plenty the government could do. Those Tories, like Churchill's friend Bracken, who believed in unrestricted capitalism and wished to see state controls abolished at the end of the war, were living in a fantasy world; the people were being promised a better future – and this time, in contrast to 1918, they wanted to ensure it was delivered. If it was, as government propaganda stated, a 'people's war', then it had to be followed by a 'people's peace', and the Beveridge Report became 'a symbol and a test. It was the symbol of post-war Britain and a test of the Government's sincerity.'[27] The Conservatives, under Churchill's benign neglect, had failed the test as early as 1943.

The electoral truce which was declared in 1940 should have created a situation in which as MPs died or retired they were simply replaced by others of the same party. In the early days of the war this happened, with one of the first beneficiaries being the Prime Minister's son, Randolph, at Preston; since he had never won, and never would win, a contested election, this was the only way he would ever get a seat. But dissatisfaction with the government's performance created space for a party of protest, which led to the rise of the Common Wealth Party led by the radically-minded Sir Richard Acland. Of the 28 Conservative seats which fell vacant during the war, 19 were contested and three were lost: 'the by-election independent knew his trade – blame the Tories' – and the voters responded.[28] The fact that the Conservatives managed to hold onto most of the seats concealed the fact that large numbers of people were prepared to vote against Churchill's party, even though opinion polls were showing a vast measure of support for the Prime Minister himself. There were, however, some spectacular failures which showed the way the wind was blowing – at least to those who had eyes in that direction.

The seat vacated by the former Chief Whip, Margesson, in early 1942 was contested by an Independent – W. J. Brown (who had stood for Mosley's New Party in 1931) – who converted a Tory majority of over 7000 into a narrow victory; he hung onto the seat in 1945. If the old Tory wire-pullers could not produce the required results at by-elections, there were signs too that the deference vote might also be difficult to garner. The ducal interest just held out in Central Bristol, where the widow of the heir to the Duke of Wellington, Lady Apsley, narrowly managed to defeat the radical Jennie Lee; but her husband had died in action whilst Miss Lee's was Aneurin Bevan, whom Churchill had described as a 'squalid nuisance'.[29] However, the ancient Cavendish interest in West Derbyshire suffered a crushing blow when the heir to the Duke of Devonshire lost to a local Alderman called White.[30] To those who asked what on earth the country was coming to when a Cavendish could lose to a radical in the old family stronghold, the answer was 'troubled times for the Tories'. Of course, at the time it was possible to write these things off and to assume, as most Conservatives did, that Churchill would do for them at the next election what Lloyd George had in 1918.

Nor were the Conservatives the only ones to assume this. As victory came nearer the question of whether to continue the Coalition occupied the minds of Labour ministers. The Coalition had worked well enough, and although Labour had learned to overcome, or at least to swallow, its instinctive distrust of Churchill, this feeling was not transferred to his acolytes like Bracken and Lord Cherwell; indeed, the more Churchill approached the sacrosanct position of a medieval monarch, the more did his friends assume the guise of those 'evil counsellors' so deplored by reforming barons. Suspicions that men like Kingsley Wood intended to keep Labour in the government 'just as long as it suited the Tory party' and would then 'push them out with as much discredit as possible',[31] were only natural in Labour men who had witnessed the cataclysm of 1931. Assumptions that a 'snap' election would result in their being 'scrubbed out as completely as in 1931', helped the Labour leaders keep their followers in check,[32] but by late 1944 the future had to be faced. In December the Labour Party Conference decided that there should be an election within a year of the defeat of Germany. It was a crucial decision, and meant that there would be no continuation of a 'National' government.

There had been many Conservatives who had reciprocated this Labour distrust. Beaverbrook, who was regarded with loathing by

Labour, was convinced as early as 1940 that Labour intended to 'unhorse' the government as soon as Churchill's energies flagged.[33] Churchill, who liked the idea of being a national rather than a party leader, spoke to Conservative ministers in April 1943 about the 'need for keeping the coalition going as long as possible' – but warned them that it was necessary to keep 'the Conservative powder dry and the Party together'.[34] The problem was that Churchill had little to offer in the way of electioneering other than himself. He thought that if the party selected 'young warriors' as candidates in the post-war election, this would be quite enough; but as Eden reminded him, it was not always easy to put pressure on local associations – something for which men had been grateful enough in the 1930s. Eden's view was that 'this is a stale Parliament and the Tory Party as a whole is discredited'.[35] It was no wonder that with set-backs like the West Derbyshire result, Churchill resisted the temptation to go to the country; but Labour's decision undermined his political strategy and meant that whatever he called his administration, he would go to the country as the head of a Conservative government. The prospect of dwindling back to leader of a faction depressed him: 'in '40 one could put up with anything because one felt one had the country behind one. Now the people were not united.'[36]

The 'Khaki election' syndrome dominated men's calculations: in 1900 and again in 1918 the Conservatives had benefited from being able to shelter under cover of the Union flag. It was in the expectation of being able to repeat this that Churchill put pressure on the Labour leaders to commit themselves to remaining in the government until Japan was defeated; since this was not expected to be until 1946 at the earliest, it meant that Labour would be tied to Churchill's apron-strings for even longer. Still fearful of a defeat of 1931 dimensions, Attlee, Bevin and Dalton advised their party to stick with the old man – and were told in turn to stick their advice. It was appropriate that the Coalition should end as it had begun, with a decision by the Labour Conference.[37]

It was a sign of how important the Conservatives considered the 'National' label that Churchill retained it for what has become known to history as his 'Caretaker' government; others were uncertain whether the presence of Sir John Anderson and the inclusion of the Liberal Hore-Belisha, quite warranted such a cognomen – it made the 1935 administration seem quite heterogeneous by comparison. But there were some interesting appointments. Butler's appointment as Minister of Labour marked his breakthrough to high office, as did Macmillan's arrival at the Air Ministry. The assumption was that after a resounding victory there would be a general clearing-out of dead wood – perhaps even that most glorious piece of all, Churchill himself, would retire, laden with glory and honours. Meanwhile it was electioneering as usual.

There is a David Low cartoon from this period which describes the Churchill campaign better than any words. It shows Beaverbrook and Bracken in a naval dockyard. By their side is a gigantic figurehead for a ship, carved in the shape of Churchill's head; the caption reads: 'we have an admiral [Bracken was First Lord of the Admiralty] and a figurehead, with any luck no one will notice that we haven't got a ship'; but the electorate did notice.

Although the substance of the two manifestos was not vastly different, 'Mr Churchill's address to the electors' breathed as old-fashioned an air as did his attempts to run the old Tory 'scare-tactics' by claiming that Labour would need a 'Gestapo' to implement their Socialist programme; it just did not wash. If the election was about who the people wanted to buy a brand spanking 'New Jerusalem' from, then the Conservatives stood no chance.

The Conservatives suffered from a number of disadvantages in the election. Afterwards it was commonly held that the decrepitude of the party's organisation was responsible for what happened, but it was no worse than Labour's; of course it was usually much better than Labour's, but it is to be doubted whether even had the Archangel Gabriel appeared to take charge of the campaign, the Tories could have won; so many of their old trump cards were no longer of use. The charge, so potent after 1931, that the Socialists were unfit to govern rang hollow in the ears of an electorate who had become used to Bevin, Attlee, Dalton, Morrison and Cripps. Indeed, as one wag commented when the left-wing Archbishop of York, William Temple, was appointed to Canterbury in 1942: 'You socialists are getting in everywhere.'[38] If Labour was now respectable, the Tories had also lost the 'red scare' card; the Soviets were, after all, our gallant allies – and Churchill's attempt to try a 'fascist smear' instead backfired. Moreover, throughout Europe the left had benefited from two things: the association of the right with fascism and the part the Soviets had played in winning the victory in Europe. In France, Italy and the Low Countries, it was the Communists who benefited from this phenomenon – in Britain it was the Labour Party.

Lords Beaverbrook and Woolton asked Churchill what issues they should play at the election, but they received little by way of an answer.[39] As the presence of Churchill's picture on every Tory candidate's husting showed, the Tories intended to shelter behind his formidable reputation. Woolton, formerly a Liverpool businessman who was not yet a member of the Conservative Party, recognised that even playing the 'Good old Winnie, let him finish the job!' line would probably not work. His canvassers told him that the question 'most people were asking' was 'whether the great war leader will be a good peace leader – "is he really interested in reconstruction and social reform?" ' Woolton was not convinced that Churchill would pass muster here, and he thought it essential for the Party to play up the questions of housing and the Welfare State. The sort of 'propaganda' Churchill liked was, he thought, best directed at the 'unstable vote' – that is 'the politically ignorant' and the 'highly intelligent'.[40]

Even had the Prime Minister taken Woolton's highly sensible advice, it is hard too see how the Conservatives could have won with so much running against them; memories of the 1930s, with its images of mass unemployment and the Jarrow hunger marchers, were hard to shake off. Instead, of course, Churchill plunged into a robust partisan campaign of the old type. As Amery put it, he 'jumped straight off his pedestal' and tore into poor old Attlee with a 'fantastical exaggerated onslaught'.[41] Other robust Tories like James Stuart, the Chief Whip, rather liked this sort of thing, but there is no sign that the electorate did – and its verdict was the one that mattered. Eden, who was kept out of the campaign by an ulcer, doubted whether the 'sordid medium of Party politics' was the best way to construct that 'better England' which the electorate wanted, but he was enough of a realist to know that there was no other medium available. He thought that he might be able to 'make something of the Tory Party if I had it';[42] but he was not to get hold of it for a good long while. He left with Churchill for Potsdam and the reordering of the world – but the election result revealed that it would be Attlee and Bevin, not Churchill and Eden, who would be returning to the ruins of Berlin.

10 The New Model Tory Party?

On the morrow of defeat when, like all good wives, Mrs Churchill tried to cheer up her downcast husband, she remarked that 'Perhaps it was a blessing in disguise', to which she received the reply: 'At the moment it seems quite effectively disguised.' But there was something in her comment, all the same.

Upon sober reflection, the Conservatives had not done as badly as it looked; indeed, to some extent, the facts outlined in the previous chapter explain something that did not really happen – a Conservative massacre. It was true that, at 213 seats, the Conservatives had fewer seats than at any time since 1906, but, when one considers the way the cards were stacked against them, the only surprise is that they did not do worse. Moreover, if the total number of votes is taken into account, at 11 million, the Conservatives polled nearly as many votes as they had done in 1935, and only 3 million fewer than Labour; this time the peculiarities of the British electoral system had favoured Labour. In the 1930s there had been a 'soft' anti-Socialist vote which had ended up being distributed unequally between the Conservatives and the Liberals; now there was an anti-Conservative vote which had divided in similar fashion between Labour and the Liberals. At the time, and later, Conservative mythology made much of the effect of the 'service vote', but it would be more accurate to say that it was the younger generation as a whole which was more likely to have voted Labour in 1945; nor was this surprising. It had been ten years since the last general election, and there were many of electors who had never voted before. Their formative experiences had included the slump, appeasement and the war, and they were the ones who were most susceptible to the appeal of the 'New Jerusalem' promised by Labour. They had no experience of a Labour government; young and eager to believe, they lacked the cynicism engendered in their elders by such promises. This generation of Labour voters was to stick with the party for two decades to come, and its gradual disintegration through death and disillusion would play its part in the decline in Labour's fortunes.

Defeat also saved Churchill and the Conservatives from having to tackle the onerous job of reconstructing a Britain which had lost a quarter of its national wealth and which had seen its cities and its trade devastated by the war. All the members of the Coalition were tired after their exertions, but Churchill was more exhausted than most – and neither he nor the party as a whole were brimming with ideas. Free from the toils of office for the first time in 15 years, the Conservatives were free to think about what their party stood for and where it thought Britain was going. These things may be apparent to historians, but they were not available to comfort contemporaries who shared the view expressed by James Stuart: 'my present feeling is not so much one of depression as of waking up bewildered in a world completely strange to me.'[1]

It was not much use anyone in such a mood looking to Churchill for a lead. Although he made it plain that he had no intention of retiring, it soon became clear that he had equally little intention of actively leading any opposition. At one level this was sensible enough. Labour had a massive majority and could get any legislation they liked through the House, so opposition would be a thankless task. Churchill had his lucrative memoirs to write – and had little, save his reputation and views on foreign affairs, to contribute to contemporary political debate. There were, in any case, other and younger men, still with their careers to make, to whom such tasks could be safely left – chief amongst whom was the newly appointed head of the Conservative Research Department, Rab Butler.

In retrospect, a golden glow can be discerned hovering about this period of the party's history, as heroic modernizers dragged the party into the twentieth century and inaugurated a period of 'new' Conservatism; the fact that much of this emanates from the writings of Butler and those who helped him would, by itself, make one sceptical, but the presence of that one word – 'new' – automatically raises doubts. No doubt Butler did feel, as he later claimed, that 'as in the days of Peel, the Conservatives must be seen to have accommodated themselves to a social revolution',[2] and he certainly irritated some of his elders by commenting, when they hankered for 'old Toryism', that he did not 'know what that is';[3] but that is not quite the same as reinventing Conservatism.[4] Indeed, what Butler's throw-away remark showed was that he stood firmly in the Baldwinian tradition of adapting oneself to the demands of 'the democracy'. Nor should this surprise us. Butler was, after all, a protégé of Baldwin's, and Conservatism is, by its very nature, hardly susceptible to 'being made new'. Still, it was a pretty conceit, and it certainly sustained Butler through his battles with those who thought they knew only too well what 'old Toryism' was.

It has been customary to label Butler and the 'young warriors' who thronged to the Research Department (having, most of them, failed to get seats) as 'progressives' or as 'left-wing', but the utility of such labels is open to question. The heir to the Marquess of Salisbury, and the future leader of the Imperialist wing of the party, Lord Cranborne, who was hardly a 'progressive', told Eden in 1946 that 'people don't want to go back to the old days',[5] whilst a self-made man like Bracken, who regarded the squirearchy as 'troglodytes', called for a return to red-blooded, unrestrained capitalism.[6] The real distinction was between those Conservatives like Butler who looked back to that part of their tradition which saw nothing illegitimate in using the powers of the state to look after the interests of the many,[7] and so were able to adapt themselves without too many problems to the corporate state which the war had ushered into existence, and those more Hayekian Tories, like Beaverbrook and Bracken, who saw the party as the instrument of unrestricted 'free enterprise'.[8] The old paternalist tradition, which Baldwin had accepted and, at least rhetorically, embodied, could accommodate the Welfare State and even nationalisation; the newer, libertarian Conservatism, which actually owed much to old-fashioned Liberalism, was sharply out of kilter with the mood of post-war Britain, which had turned sharply against free enterprise after 1945. That future idol of Thatcherism, Professor Hayek was just not being read or listened to. His ideas were simply 'out of touch' with the mood of the period; it would take a political generation before they became anything like respectable.

Although the idea of a war-time consensus has been questioned by some historians, this seems largely to be a matter of quibbling over the meaning of the word. No one has actually argued that there were no differences between the two main parties, but it would be fruitless to deny that these were fewer and less acrimonious than they had been in the 1930s or would be again in the 1980s. This has usually been presented as a matter of the Conservatives adapting themselves to the new era – to Keynesian economics, the Welfare State, and a high taxation economy. It is certainly true that some Conservatives had a good deal of adapting to do, but one of their reasons for so adapting is often overlooked – and that is the element in the consensus which marked a shift in Labour's position. If there seemed something strange in the Tories accepting a high level of taxation, there was something equally odd about the Labour Party accepting a higher level of spending on defence than had existed before the war; for perhaps the most important element in 'Churchill's consensus' was the new agreement over the conduct of British foreign policy.

As we have seen, the incipient coalition between Churchill and the Labour leaders had, as its central point, the need to oppose Hitler and, by extension, other dictators. This assumed the requirement of a larger tax base to pay for increased defence spending. If Labour could accept the last part of this syllogism, the Tories were prepared to accept the first part. In the first volume of his *History of the Second World War*, published in 1948, Churchill pushed home the fundamental tenet of the new consensus – that Britain must be well-armed and able to pursue an active diplomacy – her 'will' must be able to be exercised, and she must seek close contacts with America, in particular, so that the world could be made safe for democracy. There were no Conservatives who found this difficult to accept – after all, Chamberlain, so it was commonly held, had tried the alternative policy, and look where that had brought the nation. The fact that the Labour Party now accepted this version of events reconciled many Conservatives to the need for higher taxation and the Welfare State; some *quid pro quo* was necessary – and the taxes were needed to keep the nation safe. As Labour committed Britain to the atom bomb, NATO and the Cold War, Conservatives found themselves in agreement that Bevin was not a bad fellow after all; it was thought to be sour grapes when some Socialists commented that 'Eden has grown fat'.

Moreover, for some Conservatives, like Butler and Eden, the distance to be travelled to reach the 'middle ground' on domestic politics was not that far. Commentators generally accept that Eden had little interest in domestic policy, but his speeches in 1945 and 1946 were festooned with liberal adornments and Woolton was correct to comment that Eden had 'never wavered in his Conservatism, but had propounded Liberal principles'.[9] His fears about 'the lack of an industrial policy, or indeed of any creed with regard to the domestic future of this country which can be presented to the Party and the electorate as a practical alternative to socialism', were shared by many leading Conservatives of his generation. Baldwin had managed to keep Socialism at bay by making a bogey of it; now that that strategy was no longer feasible, an alternative had to be found. As Cranborne, who found Churchill's supine attitude infuriating, commented, in an 'unrestricted political democracy' it was no longer enough to expect the voters to accord due deference to the supposedly superior wisdom of the traditional ruling elite; the old ties of social hierarchy, geographical immobility and economic dependence were weakened, if not gone, whilst the Church was no longer a rallying point for the Conservative voter; in a secular and egalitarian age, waiting upon events was likely to prove costly. In what the former American Vice President, Henry Wallace, had called the 'age of the common man', the sensible thing for Conservatives to do was to give him 'a stake in the country ... something that he himself knows he will lose if, as an elector, he acts irresponsibly'. Cranborne,

like Eden, Butler, Macmillan and others, thought that an encouragement of the wider ownership of shares and housing – a 'property-
owning democracy' – was the best hope for the future of the party.
Simply 'sitting down and waiting for the Government to become
unpopular', as Churchill seemed to want, was not enough to win the
next election.[10]

Churchill's line might not have been enough, but it was not that bad
a strategy. As a very old political hand Churchill knew well the problem
of trying to put forward a detailed policy when in opposition, and he
rather deprecated the idea. He knew that all reforming governments
make enemies; those whose repose is disturbed will vote against the
government, whilst those upon whose behalf reforms are enacted are
rarely fully satisfied. If this was true as a general rule of politics, how
much more so would it be of a radical government facing the problems
besetting Labour? But of course, young men would not listen; and of
course problems arose from this refusal to heed the wise world of the
tribal elder – not least from other elders of the tribe.

Whenever the Conservative Party loses an election (an experience,
admittedly, hardly common enough in its history to allow of the for-
mulation of such generalisations), it is thrown back onto its bed-rock;
the more seats it loses, the closer to the base it gets. The bright young
men in marginal seats go down to defeat, whilst those safe seats which
survived the tidal wave tended to be held by old loyalists. In the normal
course of events in Parliament this did not matter that much, and it
mattered even less at the centre of the party, where the old guard were
either silent or without effective representation (their most effective
speaker was, after all, leader of the party); but it was a different matter
at party conferences, where, by definition, the loyalists and activists
from the constituencies gathered. The first post-war Conference, at
Blackpool in 1946, saw a revolt from the right, as proposals for
modernising the party were condemned as 'creeping pink socialism'.[11]
As early as 1942 disgruntled Conservatives and businessmen had
combined to form a pressure group called 'Aims of Industry' to
fight against over-regulation of the economy by the government. In
April 1943 another group, 'The National League for Freedom', was
founded to 'fight the strong movement now on foot to continue unnecessary official control of trade, industry, business and private lives after
the war'.[12] The existence of such pressure groups, and the cult status
enjoyed in these quarters by a book called *The Road to Serfdom* by an
Austrian refugee, Professor Hayek, provided the atmosphere in which
a younger generation of Conservatives, including the young Margaret
Roberts, came to political awareness. At the time their effect was

limited, but with old-style Chamberlainites like Sir Douglas Hacking and Sir Waldron Smithers as leading lights, they provided a link between the past and the future of Conservatism.

The cries from such quarters at the 1946 Conference were evidence that Churchill's tactics were not quite as bad as some would have it. But although Cranborne may have been a little severe in saying that no lead could be expected from a leader who 'never had any principles',[13] it was certainly the case that Churchill's attempts to define the Conservative faith lacked both originality and penetration. Speaking in Edinburgh in April 1946 he outlined the party's aims as: 'liberty with security; stability combined with progress; the maintenance of religion, the Crown and Parliamentary Government',[14] this could have been said by any Conservative leader since Peel; indeed, it had been said by most of them. It reflected Churchill's strategy of waiting for the government to become unpopular; but the wisdom of the old is always called into question by those with the energy of the young. At Blackpool the Young Conservatives and the Tory Reform Group tried to elicit something a little less vague from the leadership, with the ever-hyperactive Quintin Hogg warning that the party needed something more positive to combat Labour's charges that it had no policies at all. This gave Eden the opportunity to press the 'Great Man' for a policy statement, but he was too wily an old bird to be caught so easily, and his eight-point definition of Tory principles came close to matching a comment he once made about one of Eden's speeches: 'It contained every cliché apart from "God is love" and "kindly adjust your dress before leaving".'[15] He did, however, agree to set up an Industrial Committee to look at Conservative policy in that area.

By their nature, Conservative conferences are a rallying of the most faithful; to anyone who has ever attended one without being a true believer, they can be a frightening occasion, and the 1946 affair came close to hearing what Evelyn Waugh once described as the most frightening sound in the world – 'the English upper-classes baying for broken glass'. It was with some glee that Bracken, who combined an unreconstructed liberal view on economics with reactionary tendencies on everything else, watched angry delegates demand 'a real Conservative policy instead of a synthetic Socialist one so dear to the heart of the Macmillans and the Butlers'; the 'neo-Socialists', as he called them, were 'lucky to escape with their scalps'.[16]

But away from Blackpool's bracing air, Bracken and those who thought like him did nothing to further their vision of Conservatism. Perhaps they felt that nothing needed to be done. 'Real Conservative policy', by their definition, abhorred activism and was essentially unconstructive in its approach; it was happy to criticise. That, after all, had been almost enough in the 1930s, and given the food and fuel shortages which made the post-war years the 'age of austerity', it might yet prove enough again. Labour may not have needed a 'Gestapo', but they had presided over the continuing bureaucratisation of Britain; the man in Whitehall, it was held, really did know best. Benign socialist central planning was not particularly popular with the trades union movement, which then, as later, was expected to restrain the demands of its members for better pay and conditions as the price to be paid for a Labour government; rashes of unofficial strikes provided an indication of what some union members thought of such an arrangement. Nor were the middle classes happy with a situation which saw their standards of living fall. Servants became a thing of the past for middle-class households, allowing Socialist academics like A. J. P. Taylor to sneer that the middle-class definition of 'decline' was dons having to do their own washing-up. But rationing, endemic bureaucracy and the rest had to be set against the creation of a National Health Service and, after 1947, a slow but sure economic recovery. This last, directed as it was by an export drive by industry, failed to deliver consumer goods or other comforts to the long-suffering people, which led to later charges that whilst the Labour Chancellor, Hugh Gaitskell, may have been a good economist, he was a poor politician.

There were, then, both chances and risks in a policy of doing nothing very much, but the Conservatives did not suffer much from it because they followed another policy. The Research Department laboured away to produce the polices which would be put before the electorate, whilst Woolton, who became Chairman of the party on the morrow of defeat (when, incidentally, he also joined it), worked to improve its organisation.[17] Here there was at least as much work to be done as there was on policy – and there were the same sorts of problems of inertia and vested interests to be tackled. In the eyes of self-styled 'progressives' like Eden, the party was still too much in the hands of the 'old guard'. Other 'progressives' such as Richard Law, Peter Thorneycroft and Harold Macmillan, who had lost their seats in 1945, ought, Eden thought, to be found seats with despatch. He told the soon-to-be former Party Chairman, Ralph Assheton, in front of Churchill, that 'if he and his friends continued to regard our Party as a close corporation for the extreme Right, it had no future.'[18] When one ex-minister put forward the idea that they might care to invite Sir Samuel Hoare, now Lord Templewood, to attend the deliberations of the Shadow Cabinet, Eden once more had occasion to express his exasperation: 'There is no hope

for the Tory Party unless we can clear these disastrous old men out –
and some of the middle-aged ones too!'[19]

One problem the party faced in doing this was the fact that it had
long been the case that, as Cuthbert Headlam had put it before the war,
'money in your pocket is really a *sine qua non* if one is to get on as a
politician on the Conservative side.'[20] Local associations often, if not
usually, expected MPs or candidates to bear a considerable cost of their
upkeep, as well as shelling out for elections. Men like Headlam, who
contested marginal seats in County Durham and elsewhere, faced the
prospect of spending large sums of money only to find that they lost
their seats in any swing against the party, and it was always men like him,
who found it difficult to afford these costs, who ended up in such seats;
rich men could afford to buy their way into safer seats. Of course there
were always seats available for young men with talent and/or good
connections, and if, like Rab Butler, one had both of these and considerable wealth, then life in the party was plain sailing. But it was clear
that this system was standing in the way of attracting as candidates the
sort of bright young men – the 'warriors' of whom Churchill had
spoken with such longing – who might lead the Conservative recovery.
A committee headed by the leading KC, David Maxwell-Fyfe, reported
in 1948, recommending that the contribution of MPs to local associations should be limited to a token amount, and that election expenses
should be borne by the party centrally to a much greater extent. This
did not clear out the augean stables overnight, indeed it could be
argued that it did not clear them out to any great extent, but it did
make it possible for more men like Edward Heath, Enoch Powell and
Reginald Maudling to find winnable seats; to this extent the reform did
its job in providing an entry into politics on the Conservative side for
young meritocrats who, through the accident of birth, fate had
neglected to provide with sufficient funding.

The fact that the three individuals mentioned had, however, already
found seats before the committee reported, suggests that Maxwell-Fyfe
was responding to a mood that was already prevailing in the party.[21]
The 'old men', however, would continue to sit for their safe seats, and
they would continue to pose problems for 'the Young Turks'. One old
man, in particular, posed great problems – and that was the member
for Woodford, the Rt Hon. Winston S. Churchill. Despite the election
defeat, Churchill remained quite simply the best-known and most popular politician in the country – at least outside South Wales and other
parts of Labour's heartland. Whatever he chose to write or to say was
instantly news, and his prestige was obviously a massive asset to the
party. Some of those closest to the old hero had urged him to retire

after the election defeat. It would be at least another five years before
another General Election, and, given the size of Labour's majority, it
might take yet another election five years on from that; indeed, given
the size of the majority there might never be another Conservative government: ten years in opposition was an eternity to a man of 71. But
Churchill ignored such advice, telling his old friend, Field Marshall
Smuts: 'I must have a platform.' Smuts' reply that 'he had only to get up
on a chair in Hyde Park', rather missed the point.[22] The press magnate,
Lord Camrose, had it right when he told Eden in late 1946 that
'Winston had maintained leadership of the Party meant power and he
didn't mean to give up power';[23] nor did he. His presence did not, however, prevent Butler and his bright young men refurbishing the image
of the party.[24] The story is told that when Churchill was shown an early
draft of what became *The Industrial Charter*, he chuckled and said, 'Ah!
Now we have the Socialists!', and was most disappointed to be told that
it was not a Labour Party production.[25]

One of the problems with post-Second World War history is that our
perspective on it is still, in many ways, too short. Much of the argument
between historians concerns their diagnoses of our contemporary ills
as much as it does genuine historical disagreement. During the long
hey-day of what came to be called 'Attlee's consensus' (although it had
as much to do with Churchill and Bevin as anyone else), historians of a
liberal frame of mind found much in it to praise, and even in the (for
such historians) dark days of Mrs Thatcher, they could write approv-
ingly of 'a hegemony of enlightened opinion' which 'succeeded in preserving the post-war settlement from its enemies until the mid-1970s'.[26]
Those rare historians who took up their positions on the right found in
the said consensus a prime cause of Britain's decline.[27] Meanwhile
politicians of all persuasions plundered the arguments of the historians
for support for their own preconceived positions. From our point of
view these debates affected the politics of the Conservative Party in
such a way that writing about the party's post-war history was to become
part of the contemporary political debate.

Those Conservatives who were described during the 1980s as 'wets' –
people such as Sir Ian Gilmour – looked with longing to the tradition
symbolised by Butler, seeing in him the epitome of their type of
Conservatism.[28] The Thatcherites agreed with the conclusion, but
nothing else. They came to regard Butler and Macmillan with something approaching contempt – as men who sold out true Conservatism
in the cause of political expediency.[29] Butler, Macmillan and Heath all
came to be seen as men who failed to advance the Conservative cause
and arrest the decline of Britain. It was only when the high-tide of

Thatcherism receded that questions began to be asked again inside the party as to whether the blanket, almost Stalinist, condemnation of the former leaders as 'non-persons' had quite so much to be said for it.[30] Of course it can be, and is, still argued that it is too soon to reach a verdict upon Mrs Thatcher's period of power and, judging by the way our view of the 1940s and 1950s has changed in the past decade, there would seem to be much wisdom in this. Historians should be mindful of the advice of Sir Walter Raleigh, who warned that those who followed too closely upon the heel of history were apt to find themselves being kicked in the teeth.

The internal squabbles over one set of myths rather distracts from the need to deconstruct an older set – namely that 1945 marks a break with the past so far as the Conservative Party was concerned. Woolton, who had taken no part in Conservative Party politics, was happily ignorant of what his predecessors had done, and Churchill and Eden, who did not have this excuse, had even better reasons for wishing to emphasise the break with what had gone before. Those who had no particular personal reason to peddle the notion of a break with the past, like Butler, did so nevertheless – if only for political reasons. The fact that the old pre-war Conservative leaders were all absent from the highest counsels of the party reinforced the idea that Churchill and Eden were presiding over something very different than Baldwin and Chamberlain; they were doing no such thing. A change of personnel did not absolve the party from its perennial challenge of how to come to terms with what was happening in the society around it. Between 1906 and 1916, the Conservatives had lost the ability to try to set the terms of the political debate, and they had been forced to react to the agenda of their opponents. During the inter-war years a combination of luck, the decline and fall of the Liberal Party and the incapacity of Labour had all created conditions in which a policy of resistance to Socialism and piecemeal social reform had allowed them to set the terms of the political debate. After 1940 they had increasingly been losing this capacity; by 1945 they were back to having to respond to the agenda of their opponents.

Yet, as we have seen, not all parts of the so-called consensus were inimical to the Conservatives. Labour's staunchly anti-Soviet and pro-American foreign policy commanded more unanimity within the Conservative Party than it did in Attlee's own ranks, whilst there was general applause for the decision to join the Americans in 1950 in resisting Communist aggression in Korea. The other elements of the consensus may have commanded less universal support in the party, but few of its elements were hostile to the Conservative tradition, and none of them were inimical to the exercise of that principled opportunism which Disraeli had exhibited.

At the heart of the post-war order was the notion of a 'mixed economy', in which private enterprise and public ownership co-existed; here the terms of the political debate, even in Mrs Thatcher's early years, were over the areas which the state should control and the amount of regulation to which private enterprise should be subjected. It could hardly be contended that undiluted private enterprise had brought prosperity to all before the war, and Chamberlain's government had certainly considered whether the mines might not have to be taken into public ownership. The method adopted by Labour to secure this was not the setting up of workers' collectives, but rather boards dominated by bureaucrats and answerable to ministers. The *Industrial Charter*, which was accepted by the 1947 Conference, committed the party to 'central direction of the economy' with a view to securing full employment; it also promised cooperation between government, industry and the trades unions. From one point of view this was certainly compromising with the 'corporate state', but from another it was simply an extension of the old Conservative survival technique. Butler presented it as a compromise between 'Manchester and Moscow', stressing that the Conservatives had never shrunk from using the power of the state in the national interest. After all, Butler and company were not saying that collectivism was a good thing – they were merely proposing to use its resources in a Conservative fashion. It was, after all, a good Conservative tradition – the eschewing of dogma. There was also an equally long tradition, dating back to Disraeli and Salisbury, of crying 'treason' at such moments.

The main purpose behind the *Charter* was to show that the Conservatives were as committed as Labour to the objective which had been set forth by the Churchill coalition itself – full employment. This was the *quid pro quo* which was to persuade the trades unions to cooperate with the government. From the point of view of the party, which had gone down to defeat in 1945 at least partly because of the shadow of Jarrow, it was an earnest of intentions for the future. The party could, of course, have continued to proclaim the orthodox line of the 1930s, but to have done so would have been to have rejected the latest economic thinking – which was electoral suicide.

As for the third element in the consensus, state provision of education to provide equality of opportunity, the Conservatives were also associated with that, thanks to Butler's Education Act of 1944. Since the system was based upon equality of opportunity rather than outcome, not even the Brackens and the Beaverbrooks could find that much to criticise. They could, of course, be snobbish about 'grammar school boys and girls', but since the future of the party lay in the hands of such, it was best to be so in private.

The fourth element in the consensus was the Welfare State, which formally came into effect in 1948, but this, again, was the product of the Churchill Coalition, and whilst there were objections to the way in which Bevan carried out the policy, no Conservative leader would ever publicly say that they wanted to abolish the thing; it was too popular.

It was Butler's genius as a publicist which presented this extension of the Baldwinian tradition of adaptation to the legitimate demands of the democracy as a reconstruction of the Conservative Party, and it was probably necessary to do so in order to divert attacks from the Opposition; but it would be wise at this distance of time not to overestimate the break with the past represented by the 1950 Conservative Manifesto, *This is the Road*. It would have been inhuman of Butler not to have claimed the credit for the reversal in the fortunes of the party. The election produced a House with 298 Conservatives and 315 Labour MPs, with the Liberals holding nine seats and 'Others', three. This left Labour with a slender majority of five, and ensured that Churchill would stay on as leader – with 'one more push' the Socialists would be gone.

But Labour's plight had at least as much to do with its own shortcomings as it did with any refurbishment of the Conservative image. No doubt the increase in the membership of the Conservative Party, the reforms in its organisation and the manifesto played their part, but Churchill had not been wrong in his instinct that Labour would do for itself. In part the sheer size of the problems confronting the government, and the great expectations they had raised at the 1945 election, were bound to lead to voters being disillusioned. Victory in the war was all very well, but when the population of Great Britain was being asked to eat 'snoek' (a kind of whale meat with a vile smell and an oily consistency) three years afterwards, and bread was rationed, it was too much to expect the voters not to begin to have their doubts. The Conservatives were able to poke fun at a government which, situated on an island surrounded by fish and built on coal, managed to engineer a shortage of both at the same time; that was Socialist planning for you. The Labour Ministers of Fuel and Food were dragged into a new Tory slogan – 'Shiver with Shinwell and starve with Strachey' – all very unfair, no doubt, but good for party morale and great fun all round. The greatest failure of the Attlee administration was in not fulfilling its promises to provide enough homes for the returning heroes and the bombed-out population; as late as 1951 many people in places like Norwich and Glasgow were still living in temporary, 'pre-fabricated' accommodation. Indeed, this last was so durable that some of the 'new universities' of the 1960s were to find themselves setting up home there.

Labour had run out of ideas – or at least it had failed to find a consensus within its own ranks as to which way it should go in the future. More cautious ministers like Herbert Morrison wanted to 'consolidate' the position, younger, more radical figures, like Bevan, wanted to push on with further measures of nationalisation and implement a 'real Socialist' policy. This last attitude was the first sign that Labour, like the Conservatives after 1903, were afflicted by that strange political disease carried by ideological zealots; this has the effect of helping to intensify the propensity to lose elections through propagating the delusion that if a policy is unpopular with the electorate, what you need to do is to make it the centrepiece of your programme and thrust it down their throats. It did not work for the Tories between 1903 and 1923 with Tariff Reform, and it did not work for Labour in the 1950s, nor yet in the 1980s; but it does help one's political opponents. The resignation of Bevan, along with Harold Wilson and John Freeman, in April 1951 over Gaitskell's plans to introduce charges for prescriptions, was the outward and visible sign of this inward malaise, and it prefigured an early election. The Labour leadership was literally dying off. Cripps resigned in October 1950, as did Bevin in March 1951, and both men died within months of leaving office, exhausted by the strain of a decade's toil. When Bevan resigned, Attlee was ill in hospital, and Morrison's health was showing signs of giving way. It was a government exhausted in mind, body and manifesto commitments. Attlee went to the country on 25 October, and the following day, with an overall majority of 17, Churchill was once more asked to form an administration. It was time to see how the 'new model Toryism' would perform in action.

11 A Conservative Consensus?

Despite Labour's propaganda – and the disappointment of later Conservatives – the Churchill years marked no great change in, but rather a reinforcement of, the prevailing consensus. Butler's strategy in opposition had been aimed at trying to convince the electorate that the Conservatives could preside over a Welfare State with high public spending, and that there would be no return to the austerity of the 1930s. The Conservatives had fought a campaign which emphasised this theme; as Churchill put it: the nation needed a rest 'if only to allow for Socialist legislation to reach its full fruition'.[1] Nor did the election result suggest that the nation was anxious for any change. More votes had been cast for Labour than for the Conservatives (13,948,605 as opposed to 13,717,538),[2] and the Conservatives had a slender majority of 17 seats. If the campaign and the result suggested that a period of consolidation was in order, Churchill was only too happy to oblige.

From the very start, Churchill strove to be a national rather than a party leader. Had the Liberal leader, Clement Davies, not been forced by his own party to turn down Churchill's offer of the Ministry of Education, then the government would have been a 'Conservative-Liberal' one, and as it was it contained in its ranks many who were not, in political origin, Conservatives. There were the old 'National Liberals', who had been formally integrated into the party on 1947 under the Woolton-Teviot agreement, and these included the Lord Chancellor, Lord Simonds, as well as the Minister of Fuel and Power, Gwilym Lloyd-George; other members of the 18-strong Liberal contingent received minor office. In addition to this group, there was another intake who might be characterised as Churchill's cronies: these included Lords Cherwell, Ismay, Alexander and Leathers; the first three all initially refused the offer of a post in the government, but acceded to Churchill's pressure. The number in this group would have been even greater had not Lords Asquith, Waverley and Portal not all managed to resist the Prime Minister's blandishments. One recent commentator has called the government 'the least recognizably Conservative in history'.[3]

If the make-up of the government indicated its non-partisan nature, then so too did some of the key appointments. It had been widely expected that Oliver Lyttelton would go to the Exchequer, but Churchill appointed Rab Butler instead, telling him: 'Oliver ... is absolutely tainted with the City. We couldn't have a Chancellor in the House of Commons who was a City Man.'[4] Butler struck the head of the Economic Sector of the Cabinet Office as 'almost pathetically anxious to stand in well with his officials', but expected that he would show 'enough firmness when it was necessary' and 'enough ability to follow most of the arguments'.[5] If Butler's appointment was a sop to Labour, then the decision to place another of Churchill's cronies, Sir Walter Monckton, at the Ministry of Labour, was an act of outright appeasement. Monckton was professionally and personally oleaginous, totally out of sympathy with the Conservative Party, and his view was that if anything was done to 'rock the boat in our relations with the Trades Unions I will resign';[6] there was no need for that. Indeed, so conciliatory was Monckton that there were those who wondered if he was the Minister *for* Labour.

The same Baldwinian emphasis upon maintaining social harmony and industrial peace at almost any cost was visible in the emphasis given to the housing programme, where another characteristic of the government was also visible – its faith in planning and central control. The failure of the Attlee governments to build enough houses had been one of the items in the Conservative indictment against Labour, but party leaders were wary of setting a target for the next Conservative government. At the 1950 Conservative Party Conference a pressure group which included some prominent backbenchers pressed for and secured a commitment to build 300,000 houses a year. Churchill made it 'our first priority', and repeated the promise in the 1951 manifesto. It was a task which would 'make or mar' the career of the minister whose responsibility it was – or at least that was what Churchill told a rather disappointed Harold Macmillan when appointing him Minister of Housing. Macmillan was, however, able to utilise the political sensitivity of his post to secure his objective. He was able to insist upon the import of timber and bricks, and was even able to divert scarce supplies of steel in his direction. Much of the building was done under the aegis of the local authorities, although Macmillan did his best to encourage private housebuilding. By the end of 1953 he was able to announce that the target of 300,000 houses had been achieved. Both at the time and later, the scale and pace of the housing drive were criticised; it was said that materials which could have been put to better use elsewhere in the economy had been sacrificed to political expediency, and that repairs to the existing housing stock as well as the building of factories and schools were put off in order to boost Macmillan's political stock.

There was much in these criticisms, but it is rather pointless not to expect politicians to make concessions to the business of electioneering – and both the government and Macmillan benefited from the achievement.[7]

If the housing programme exhibited some of the main characteristics of consensus Conservatism, then perhaps an addiction to the short-term objective should be added to the list which includes support for central planning, government intervention and the maintenance of social harmony. The fact that the Conservatives maintained the consensus led *The Economist* to write about the rise of 'Butskellism'. Nor was a reason hard to find. The Conservatives made no real move to denationalise those industries taken into State ownership by Labour, with only iron and steel and road haulage being handed back to the private sector. Their devotion to the Health Service was made plain by the Minister of Health after 1952. Iain Macleod, who ensured that adequate resources were devoted to Labour's showpiece. On the industrial relations front, the unions could not have asked for a more complaisant government. Abroad the Conservatives remained devoted to the structures provided by the Anglo-American relationship and NATO, whilst proving as resistant as Labour to the Schuman Plan and schemes for European union. They even showed themselves flexible enough, despite Churchill's reactionary mutterings, to finally negotiate Britain out of Egypt, thus fulfilling a promise first made by Gladstone in 1882. Eden would continue the line which Bevin had followed – not least because, in doing so, Bevin had been following a path set by Eden. But ironically, in coupling the names of the last Labour Chancellor, Gaitskell, with that of Butler, 'Butskellism' actually highlighted the one area – economic management – where there was a difference between the two parties. Labour had been wedded to physical controls over the economy in the form of planning targets and active state intervention, the Conservatives favoured the use of credit restrictions and other monetary instruments; their emphasis, as with the housebuilding programme, was upon the consumer rather than the exporter.

The Conservative Party had used a lot of rhetoric about 'setting the people' free in its manifesto, and there were those in the party who thought that this should go further than simply abolishing some of the remaining wartime restrictions. The 'free marketeers', such as Bracken, Lord Hichinbrooke and Richard Law, as well as the Chairman of the Party's Finance Committee, Ralph Assheton, wanted the Chancellor to encourage the development of a more 'laissez-faire' economy, and there was, right at the start of Butler's period of office, a chance to break decisively with Labour's economic policy which might well have gone some way to satisfying this strand of opinion in the party.

In early 1952, some of the officials at the Treasury came up with a possible answer to the balance of payments crisis facing the government which would involve removing the pound from its fixed exchange rate. The balance of payments crisis was leading to calls for cuts in public expenditure and in imports and consumer spending, all three of which were vital areas in which the government was trying to establish a record for being able to outdo Labour. One obvious way of ameliorating the situation was to devalue sterling, as Labour had done in 1949, but that would have been to lose face. An alternative was to let sterling find its own level on the markets and thus 'take the strain off the reserves and put it on the rate of exchange'. The main line of objection was that this would mean a rise in the cost of living and a growth in unemployment. That it might actually help prevent a constant balance of payments crisis was, to Churchill, Eden and company, a secondary consideration to maintaining the social fabric as woven by the post-war consensus.[8] It was, as one commentator has concluded, 'an historic moment in post-war Conservative history. A party devoted to decontrol and encouraging the private market decided in favour of control and management.'[9]

Some commentators have gone much further than this, arguing in dramatic language that the 1945 defeat had 'broken' the Conservative Party's political 'nerve' and 'emasculated' 'an entire generation of Tory politicians' who 'ceded the intellectual high-ground to the collectivists for a quarter of a century and settled down to manage Imperial and commercial decline'.[10] Others, however, less addicted to tough rhetoric, have preferred to see it as the flowering of a liberal Toryism with its roots in the 'Tory democracy' of Disraeli and Lord Randolph Churchill.[11] Recalling the admonition that much of the writing about the Conservative Party is, itself, a tool in the contemporary political battle, it might be convenient here to note how two myths overlap at this point. On the one hand there is the 'liberal Tory' line, expounded by Butler, Quintin Hogg, Ian Gilmour and other self-styled Liberal Conservatives, who see in their avoidance of ideology a positive virtue. As Hogg put it in a classic statement of *The Case for Conservatism* published in 1947:

Unlike their opponents, the last thing Conservatives believe is that they have a monopoly of the truth. They do not even claim a monopoly of Conservatism. Modern Conservatives believe in the Liberal democratic state as it has gradually developed according to the Liberal tradition.[12]

As a creed, Conservatism is rooted in the past, and this rhetoric is, in fact, an attempt to provide a pedigree and thus legitimacy for the Conservatism of the consensus.[13] A claim that Conservatism has always eschewed ideology can only be maintained by disregarding the Tariff Reform controversy and the later espousal of monetarism. If this is done, then it does indeed leave the Conservatism of the consensus period as the only 'real' Conservatism – which is, of course, the object of the whole line of argument. Those who repudiate this position, such as Enoch Powell and Mrs Thatcher, are accused of being economic liberals, rather than Conservatives. As the economist Milton Friedman said of Mrs Thatcher in 1982, 'She is a nineteenth-century Liberal.'[14]

But for all its claims to historical pedigree, the 'liberal Tory' line is as much an instrument in the contemporary struggle for the soul of the Conservative Party as the line of argument which it seeks to attack. Those who looked back with nostalgia to the days when their party was led by gentlemen rather than a grocer's daughter from Grantham, were in turn assailed as 'wets' by those who argue that the Churchill-Macmillan-Heath years simply saw the Conservatives yield to the 'ratchet' effect of Labour. Mrs Thatcher, it is argued, turned back the collectivist tide, and thus restored 'true' Conservative values after the compromises, muddle and defeatism of the consensus years.[15]

The attempts at mutual anathema, which have grown even more bitter since Mrs Thatcher's extrusion in 1990, cannot disguise two things: namely that for most of the period up to 1974 most Conservative MPs, including Margaret Thatcher and Sir Keith Joseph, accepted high government spending and the other planks of the consensus without too much in the way of complaint; and that, after 1979, there was either a convenient lapse of memory or else a conscious renunciation of past sins. In this sense, Conservatism has been defined as being what Conservative leaders do according to the circumstances confronting them. In the 1950s this dictated an acceptance of a political philosophy which gave government credit for high economic growth and sustained levels of 'full' employment; by the late 1970s it equally suggested a repudiation of a political philosophy which appeared to be delivering 'stagflation' and unemployment. Thus the period from Churchill to Heath can be seen as a continuation of the Baldwin theme of adjustment and adaptation to the needs and desires of the 'Democracy', whilst the Thatcher years might well appear, in retrospect, like a return to the (Joe) Chamberlainite spirit of seeking radical solutions to a perceived state of national decline.[16]

Conservative attachment to the consensus endured for so long for four reasons: in the first place there was a succession of leaders – Churchill, Eden, Macmillan, Home and Heath – who accepted its premises and believed that Britain was best governed from 'the centre'; in the second place, for a very long period the consensus actually seemed to be delivering unprecedented levels of prosperity and Conservative electoral success; in the third place the consensus was cemented into place very firmly through the collectivist nature of the post-war settlement – and in particular the powerful place occupied by the trades unions; and finally, for many years it seemed as though there was no alternative to following the received wisdom which was accepted not only by politicians and trade unionists but also by intellectuals, the press and, through their instrumentality, the general public.[17]

There were, however, one or two contemporary voices raised in criticism of the prevailing wisdom. In May 1954 the 'One Nation' group published a booklet called *Change is Our Ally*. The chief author was the new MP for Wolverhampton South-West, Enoch Powell. Powell was one of those 'young warriors' whom Churchill had wanted to attract into the party after the war and, like others of his kind, including Edward Heath, his first port of call had been to work in the Conservative Research Department under Butler. Powell was a brilliant classical scholar whose intellect made him a disturbing colleague for those who wished to muddle along with the status quo. He was an Imperialist of a romantic bent, and originally supported the Suez Group, but applying his logical mind to an analysis of Britain's position in the world he began to come to the conclusion that with the loss of India, the Empire no longer existed. One of Powell's 'distinctive convictions is that it is impossible to go on behaving sensibly while constantly talking nonsense',[18] and he thought that the Conservatives should admit that the Empire was gone and acknowledge that Britain's future lay in its own hands, not that of an American or European alliance designed to maintain the illusion of power. Few Conservatives could follow Powell in his rejection of some of the main planks of the consensus as it related to external affairs, and his impatience with slower minds was to have profound consequences for his own career; but the critique of the domestic planks of the consensus was to prove more congenial – at least to some Conservatives.

Change is Our Ally set out to analyse the argument that government interference in the economy was both necessary and beneficial, and in some of its findings it anticipated the work of historians such as Correlli Barnett. Powell acknowledged that the war could not have been won without centralised direction of the economy, but he argued that that success was only relative and that it was due to government direction of labour. He did not think that planning had made the best use of national resources, and when he came to analyse the forecasts of the planners about the shape of the post-war world, he concluded that most of their work had been in vain. If the plans of 1944 had been wrong, what guarantee was there that those of 1952 would be any better guides for the future?[19] Sceptical of the efforts of the planners, Powell's solution was to move back towards a situation in which market forces were allowed greater play. More competition, more risk-taking and investment by individual firms, not governments – that was what was needed in Powell's view. But it was not what Churchill's Conservative Party intended to provide; and with Eden as the obvious successor, there seemed little likelihood that the odd ideas propounded by Powell and a few others would get much of a hearing.

Despite the proto-Thatcherite arguments advanced by Powell in the early 1950s, arguments within the Conservative Party at that time centred around personalities rather than policies. From the very start of the Churchill administration attention focused upon the position of the aged leader. At 77, he was the oldest Prime Minister since Gladstone, and he lacked the energy and purpose of the latter; he did, however, like being Prime Minister and proved remarkably durable in office. Churchill's benign presence had prevented Butler's opponents from making headway against his 'modernisation' of the party whilst it had been in Opposition, and back in power, with Butler himself as Chancellor of the Exchequer, junior ranks were filled with his protégés, with Iain Macleod becoming the first to break through to ministerial rank when he became Health Secretary in 1952: but with Heath, Powell, Reginald Maudling and Angus Maude all receiving junior posts, there could be little doubt as to the future political shape of the party. But for their seniors the question was more one of when would Churchill go, and what would happen then. Here too, the broad shape of the future seemed fixed: Churchill would be succeeded by Eden, who would lead the Conservatives into the next election and beyond. This duly happened, but not quite in the way that had been expected.

Despite the impression conveyed in the diaries of Churchill's doctor, Lord Moran, the Prime Minister seems to have been perfectly *compos mentis* at least until he suffered a massive stroke in 1953; and even after that he was able to soldier on, albeit with decreasing competence.[20] In part Churchill held on because he liked being in office and feared being left with nothing to do in retirement; his entire life had been devoted to politics and he was not anxious to go. He seized upon whatever excuse was to hand to prolong his stay at No. 10: first there was the death of George VI in 1952; then he had to wait for the coronation of Elizabeth II; then the death of Stalin transformed things, and it became a question of 'one more summit conference'. Of his sincerity on the last point there can be no doubt; he genuinely felt that his personal influence might be able to produce a thaw in the Cold War. But the main victim of this campaign of limpet-like persistence was Eden. Churchill used the promise of his retirement (and the threat that he would stay on) quite ruthlessly with Eden.[21]

Eden, who had not come to love the Conservative Party any more after 1945, was nevertheless acknowledged to be Churchill's successor, and for all his protestations of unwillingness, he did not want anyone else to take that position; but Eden would not fight for it himself.[22] Like his mentor, Austen Chamberlain, he was too decent a man to use underhand tactics to get his way, and Churchill had already seen how, between 1938 and 1940, he had done nothing to try to undermine Neville Chamberlain. In private Eden fretted and fumed about the way he was treated, but he was unable to stand up to the great man, and this brought out the bullying streak in Churchill's nature.[23] Other ministers were also anxious for Churchill to go, but if the man who would benefit most from this event was unwilling to make a move, no one else would do so. There were periodic meetings of ministers and suggestions as to how to get the old man to go, but when he had his stroke in 1953 and the golden opportunity arose, it could not be taken because Eden was in hospital in Boston having his bile duct operated on. It is some testimony to the strength of the sentiment that 'Anthony should have his chance', that plans were made for Salisbury to take over as caretaker premier in case Churchill died.[24] These precautions were unnecessary. Somewhat to Eden's disappointment, the Prime Minister proved able to address the party faithful in Bournemouth in October, and having done this, the old man saw no reason to hand over the leadership.

Between 1953 and 1955, power fell increasingly into the hands of the triumvirate of Eden, Butler and Macmillan – an experience that did nothing to convince the latter two that the former was their political or intellectual superior. There was much talk, and even correspondence, about replacing 'Winston' and 'forcing his hand', but Churchill's prestige in the country was such that it was difficult to shift him at all, and impossible to do so without damaging the party in the process. The difficulties Eden faced can be gauged from Churchill's reaction on 15 December 1954 to the suggestion that he should go before June in order to give time for Eden to prepare for a General Election: 'I know you are trying to get rid of me and it is up to me to go to the Queen and hand her my resignation and yours – but I won't do it.' He told Eden that he and his colleagues could 'force my hand' by resigning en masse, but that if they did so he would tell the country that he was not going willingly.[25] The effect of such a move on the party's fortunes at the next election would have been devastating, and for a time Eden was in despair and talked of resigning himself.[26] It seems to have been the realisation that he would not get his precious summit before an election, and the knowledge that he could not lead the party at that election, which finally prompted Churchill to go – but even then he did not make his decision until February 1955, and no one was sure that he was really going until he went in April.

This all created problems for Eden. His prestige rose momentarily as he led the party straight into an election and became the first Prime Minister since Palmerston in 1865 to increase his majority. In fact the Conservatives won their largest percentage of the vote this century, with 49.7 per cent of the electorate opting for them, whilst Labour's share slipped from 48.8 to 46.4 per cent. With Labour divided, and entering a difficult leadership election, where Gaitskell succeeded Attlee, but only at the price of further alienating Bevan and the Labour left, Eden's prospects seemed set fair. But as with Bonar Law, who had also waited years for the Premiership, Eden's experience of it was to be cruelly brief.

Although it was the Suez crisis which led to Eden's resignation, both of these events stemmed from the same basic cause: Eden's inadequacy for the job of Prime Minister. As party leader he was popular in the country with Conservatives and non-Conservatives alike; his good looks, his reputation as an anti-appeaser, and his gentlemanly air all appealed to the electorate; but the nearer one got to him the more the doubts arose. Eden had never cultivated a wide range of support inside the party, and he was to pay dearly for his neglect of the 'black arts' of politics. If he had no vociferous supporters, he did have vocal critics, including the former Prime Minister's son, Randolph, and the Imperialist right, as represented by the Suez Group, which included Macmillan's son-in-law, Julian Amery.

Eden was quite unable to mobilise the resources of his position to deal with his critics, and his 'thin skin' made him far too sensitive to their jibes. Eden was used to the admiration which his record as Foreign Secretary had earned him, but as Prime Minister he found himself in a more exposed position. The criticisms began to be heard that he had no experience of domestic political office, and that he was particularly unable to handle economic questions; this would not have mattered very much had he been able to scotch the critics by his actions, but he could not do so. His febrile style of management, telephoning ministers incessantly, may have been meant to demonstrate that he was in control, but it seemed to do the opposite. Nor were his relations with his two senior colleagues entirely happy.

Butler found it hard to take Eden seriously.[27] 'Rab' was renowned for his lugubrious comments on events, and his declaration of support for Eden as 'the best Prime Minister we have' was felt by most people to be a less than resounding vote of confidence.[28] But the most damaging contribution Butler made to political instability was his 'give away' budget before the election, which had to be followed by one taking back the tax cuts afterwards; it did neither his career nor Eden's much good.

Macmillan posed an even more severe problem. It was a sign of the lack of confidence which was eventually to undermine him that Eden did not feel able to appoint his old friend and supporter Lord Salisbury to the post of Foreign Secretary; and it was a symptom of his fidgetiness that, having appointed Macmillan to it, he wanted to move him as soon as the election was over. Eden had been Foreign Secretary for so long that he could not tolerate another strong political personality in the job. Macmillan resented Eden's interference and let him know it, and the appointment of Selwyn Lloyd to the post in October was taken by everyone as a sign that Eden wished to be his own Foreign Secretary. It was a further manifestation of Eden's weakness that he let Macmillan press him into issuing a statement that his move to the Exchequer was not a demotion.

With even the Conservative *Daily Telegraph* calling for 'the smack of firm Government', the eruption of the Suez crisis in July 1956 gave the Prime Minister a chance to assert himself. The 'nationalisation' of the Suez Canal by the Egyptian leader, Colonel Nasser, was seen by many as a direct challenge to British power; for Churchill's successor not to have responded firmly would have smacked of 'appeasement'. The nation expected the Prime Minister to act.

Eden's position was difficult – if not impossible. His backbenchers – and his Chancellor – were pressing for firm action which the Chiefs of Staff told him was militarily impossible and which the Foreign Office thought was diplomatically unfeasible; force could not be used at once, and even if it could have been, an immediate resort to it would have offended both the United States (where it was an election year) and that great body of domestic opinion which supported the United Nations. But the diplomatic efforts sponsored by the Americans to solve the crisis moved with agonising slowness for a Prime Minister under pressure. By the end of October there was still no solution in sight. It was in these circumstances that Eden resorted to 'collusion' with the French and the Israelis, but the Americans were able to use their financial muscle to scupper the military operation.

Eisenhower made it clear that he would not support Eden's actions, and that he resented having been deceived by the Prime Minister; he also allowed the Treasury to block Britain's request for a loan from the International Monetary Fund to cover a run on sterling. Eden now discovered what happened to a British Prime Minister who lost American support. Macmillan, who had been quite the keenest advocate of intervention at Suez, now backed away with the same enthusiasm. His claims for the amount of money Britain was losing in the financial crisis were greatly exaggerated, and this, combined with his behind the scenes contacts with the American Embassy, have led some to suspect that there was a conspiracy to remove Eden.[29] The evidence can certainly be read that way, but it is too exiguous to cover the whole story or to be thoroughly convincing. There can, however, be little doubt that Macmillan was willing to give the stricken Prime Minster a helping hand into political oblivion.

With his health breaking down, and with the Americans in effect refusing to deal with him, Eden was persuaded to go to Jamaica to recuperate. He stayed at the house of Ian Fleming, who later became famous as the author of the 'James Bond' thrillers. Eden could have done with James Bond at this time, but there was no *deus ex machina* to be found. Whilst he was away Butler chaired the Cabinet and took responsibility for agreeing to withdraw British troops from the Canal area, whilst Macmillan assiduously courted backbench opinion; if the difference between his anti-appeasement stance in the 1930s, and that of Butler was mentioned and their contemporary resonances were noted, it was, no doubt, purely in the course of making conversation. Butler, who had been moved from the Exchequer by Eden, had already slipped back in the political betting; without a great department of state behind him a minister is always a lesser figure. This disadvantage was increased by the sadness which had befallen Butler with his wife's death. He felt unable to entertain even old friends, let alone cultivate strangers; Macmillan suffered from no such disadvantage. At one meeting of backbenchers in December, Enoch Powell noticed the 'almost devilish' skill with which Macmillan played on the prejudices and fears of the party. The fact was that the whole episode amounted to a national humiliation and, bereft of Churchill's comforting hand at the helm, the Conservatives looked to someone to fill the same role. As Macmillan had been mounting a decent impersonation of some of Churchill's traits for some time, it was not surprising that the party preferred his up-beat mood to Butler's lugubrious one.

There was, of course, the little problem of Eden to solve, but his doctor's verdict that his health would not hold up saved anyone having to tell him that he would have to go because the Americans had lost confidence in him. In the feverish political atmosphere of early January 1957, speculation about who his successor would be centred on the rival claims of Butler and Macmillan. Butler was undoubtedly the senior figure, but his Baldwinian associations were now remembered – to his disadvantage. Macmillan, by contrast, was an old personal friend of Eisenhower's, had something of the Churchillian style about him, and, if that was not enough to endear him to Washington, it could always be mentioned that he was half-American. It was true that being 'hot for certainty' he had been, in Harold Wilson's inelegant phrase, 'first in, first out' over Suez, but at least he had been decisive; unlike Butler. To the outsider this may seem an odd argument, but it was one which appealed to contemporary Conservatives. When Maxwell-Fyfe and Salisbury questioned Cabinet members, with the latter asking 'Will it be Wab or Hawold?', all but one minister plumped for 'Hawold'.

Because of his longevity (he did not die until 1987 at the age of 92), there are, as it were, two Macmillans in the public memory. One is the frail nonagenarian who spoke out against Mrs Thatcher 'selling the family silver', and who captured the headlines and public sympathy largely because he seemed an exotic survival from an almost unimaginably remote past; a sort of political version of the Queen Mother. The other, however, can still be glimpsed in the satires of the early 1960s. This is the man stigmatised by Malcolm Muggeridge as a 'faded, attitudinizing Turf Club bummarree', and derided by the young Bernard Levin as an 'actor manager' in the same vein as John Osborne's 'Archie Rice' – a down-at-heel vaudevillian who knew the importance of 'keeping them smiling'.[30] This last mood certainly caught the air he exuded to some of being an 'actor', but like all satire it ignored the man behind the mask; although it might in fairness be riposted that since Macmillan put so much emphasis upon appearances, it was not unfair to judge him by them. However, attempts at satire have been known to backfire, and the attempt by the *Evening Standard* cartoonist, 'Vicky', to depict him as 'Super Mac', complete with padded chest and shoulder-pads, boomeranged badly; such was the air which he exuded in the early days of his Premiership that the sobriquet, bereft of satirical undertones, attached itself effortlessly to him.

Perhaps because of Mrs Thatcher's own admiration for 'Winston', it has been Macmillan who has been subject to the fiercest fire from commentators who regard the consensus period as one in which the Conservatives ceded ground to the collectivists. He has been seen as a 'double crosser', and even – a deadly epithet in the Thatcherite vocabulary – 'a Whig'.[31] In describing Macmillan as 'a Whig', Enoch Powell has attributed to him 'the Whig's true vocation of detecting trends in events and riding them skilfully so as to preserve the privileges, property and interests of his class';[32] leaving aside the question as to whether the 'true vocation' of the Tory is to do the opposite and die in the last ditch, there is something in this. When he was at the Exchequer under Eden it is said that his officials kept a tally of the number of times he mentioned Stockton in conversation,[33] and there can be no doubt of the effect which his years as MP for that depressed area of the North-East had upon his thinking. It had made him a devotee of planning and economic expansionism in the 1930s, and it confirmed him in these opinions in the 1950s. He would not question the consumer-orientated policies of his predecessors; if anything his predisposition was to intensify them.

With the possible exception of Baldwin, there has been no Conservative leader who has presented such a gap between his private and public faces. As an upper-middle-class publisher with a pushy American mother, Macmillan had grown used to being patronised by the Cavendish relatives of his wife, Lady Dorothy. He had endured the pain and the humiliation of Lady Dorothy's long affair with his back-bench colleague, the roguish Bob Boothby, even as he had had to accept the setbacks and lack of progress in his political career. A man with less steel in him would have broken under these pressures, but Macmillan sublimated his disappointments and anguish in the career which revived under Churchill. His public face became one of bon-homie and optimism, and the impression he tried to create with his Guards' tie and Whites' Club mannerisms struck some as contrived, but it all served to allow a deeply sensitive, not to say shy, man to operate in a bruising political arena. It was said of him that he had spent years concealing his intelligence after realising in the 1930s how much the party distrusted intellect, and there was about him something of the insincerity of the professional actor. He liked to cultivate an air of calm detachment, putting up the notice 'Quiet calm deliberation untangles every knot', on the door between the Cabinet Room and the Private Office,[34] and he took pride in being able to pick up a novel by Jane Austen or Trollope during a political crisis; but in reality he was a nervous, even diffident man. However, he understood, earlier than many, that in an era when radio and even television were becoming important political tools, image can be more important than substance. Indeed, in the eyes of his critics, this was Macmillan's besetting sin.

For all the air of optimism he liked to exude, Macmillan's cast of mind was essentially pessimistic. His 'perceived duty [was] to defend the social order by participating in the safe management of inevitable decline.'[35] He did not believe that it was possible for a Conservative government to resist the trades unions, and he saw no harm in allowing a little inflation to hit the economy if that was the price necessary to maintain social harmony. His defenders perceive 'two constant purposes' beneath the histrionics: 'the improvement of the condition of the people; the security and influence of Britain'.[36] Both critics and defenders admit that the tone of his administration was set from the very start; but they disagree on how to assess it.

On the evening after he was appointed Prime Minister, Macmillan took the Chief Whip, Edward Heath, off to the Turf Club for a supper of champagne and oysters; a splendid gesture designed to instil a sense of confidence into a badly shaken party, according to some; others see it as accurately presaging what was to come – 'an excess of style over substance'.[37] A similar dichotomy of opinion can be observed in reactions to his famous speech at Bedford on 20 July 1957. His critics see the misquoted 'You've never had it so good' as the cry of the wastrel who never understood economics and was determined to buy social peace even at the expense of economic ruin; his defenders are more apt to quote the phrase 'most of our people have never had it so good' correctly and to remember that he went on to say 'Is it too good to last?' and to warn about the dangers of inflation.[38] He made the right noises about refusing to print more money to fund excessive wage demands, but when it came to the crunch he did just that. For the Thatcherites the defining moment came in January 1958 when Macmillan's entire Treasury team resigned over proposals to increase public spending by another £50 million, despite pledges to the contrary. His admirers tend to dwell on Macmillan's splendidly insouciant dismissal of the event as one of his 'little local difficulties' before embarking upon a tour of Africa, whilst those of a more censorious frame of mind see it as almost unbelievably frivolous and a sign that he was incurably addicted to public spending, even at the risk of inflation. Friendly commentators point out that inflation was not a serious menace by the end of Macmillan's time in office, whilst those less inclined to find excuses for the old boy point out that this was largely due to a favourable turn in world trade in 1958 and 1959 and that the real trouble lay in the future.[39]

If the two main strands of late twentieth-century Conservatism can arrive at no consensus as to Macmillan's merits on the home front, there is a similar, if less fierce, debate over his achievements abroad. Again, from the very start of the government, Macmillan sought to strike an optimistic note in order to rally his party and the country. In his first broadcast as Prime Minister he declared: 'We are a great world power and intend to remain so.' To some this was 'a fantastic display of his cynicism',[40] but others saw it as a genuine expression of his beliefs.[41] Much of the bitterness here derives from two sources, one contemporary, the other retrospective. Macmillan's contemporary critics came from the imperialist right of the party, led by Lord Salisbury after his resignation in 1958. To this section of the party the speed of the decolonisation programme upon which Macmillan embarked after 1957 was a cynical 'scuttle', a betrayal of Britain's responsibilities in Africa. The retrospective strand of criticism (although there was plenty of it at the time, too) comes from those Conservatives who opposed his moves towards the Common Market after 1959. His defenders see both moves as a necessary part of the 'modernisation' of the Conservative Party. Suez had shown, it is said, that Britain was no longer a great Imperial power, so it was necessary to liquidate commitments she could no longer fulfil; if Macmillan went about this speedily and in a way which left some sections of his party bewildered, that was because it was necessary to do so. Similar arguments are advanced about the Common Market. If Britain was to remain a Great Power, it is argued, then it was essential for her to join a larger grouping of nations. To critics like Enoch Powell this was simply another one of Macmillan's pessimistic and false 'axioms':

> since Britain had once been 'great' by reason of its Empire, it was doomed henceforward to be 'small' unless it could belong to some new large entity, be that cloudy and unreal like the Commonwealth or foreign and uncongenial like a politically unified Europe.[42]

There is no doubt that Macmillan believed his own 'axioms', but sincerity is no guarantee of sense.

Macmillan belonged firmly to what might be called the 'Peelite' wing of the party and, for all his disagreements with Baldwin in the 1930s, his Conservatism was closer to Baldwin's than it was to Salisbury's. Macmillan's brand of Conservatism saw itself as the only viable one for the party in modern conditions; adapt or die was its motto. It lacked the rigid logic of the Powellite position, and it suffered from memories of the 1920s and 1930s in a way that Thatcherism would despise as sentimentalism engendered by a bad conscience and a failure of nerve. That there was a failure of nerve can hardly be doubted. Macmillan did not think that it was possible to stand up to the unions, and towards the middle classes, from which he was sprung but affected to know little about. His attitude can be summed up in a comment to Michael Fraser, head of the Conservative Research Department, in 1957: 'I am always hearing about the Middle Classes. What is it they really want? Can you put it down on a sheet of notepaper, and I will see if we can give it to them?'[43] Giving them and the working classes what 'they really want', became the leitmotif of his Conservatism, and thanks to the economic conditions of the late 1950s he was able to deliver prosperity on a scale which seemed unimaginable to those who had lived through the 1930s; food rationing ended, consumer goods such as refrigerators, vacuum cleaners and modern cookers became widely available, even, thanks to the hire purchase system, to the working classes, as did televisions and foreign holidays. Macmillan was in fact speaking no more than the plain truth when he said that most people had 'never had it so good', and the question of 'Will it last?' was not one to mention at the 1959 election.

It was not just Macmillan's adroit handling of public affairs and the economy which ensured that his initial fears that the government would not last for six weeks were dissipated. Certainly his upbeat style, his ability to mend fences with the Americans, and the confidence which he managed to instil into his party rallied the Conservatives, but he was greatly helped in his task by the opposition – or rather the lack of one. The divisions between Gaitskell and the Bevanites not only gave the correct impression to the electorate that Labour did not know its own mind, it also provided an opening for the Conservatives to claim that it was Labour which was more likely to disrupt one of the main planks of the consensus – the bi-partisan foreign policy. The Labour left opposed both the American alliance and the commitment to nuclear weapons upon which it rested;[44] this all contrasted with Macmillan's good relations with his old friend 'Ike' Eisenhower, who happened to pay a visit to London on the eve of the 1959 Election.

The combination of a weak Opposition, economic prosperity and a confident Prime Minister made the outcome of the 1959 election pre-dictable. Even had Gaitskell not made tactical errors, the slogan 'Conservative prosperity works, don't let Labour ruin it!' was a difficult one to match. On a slightly higher turn-out than in 1955 (78.7 per cent compared with 76.8 per cent) the Conservatives polled more votes (13,749,830) but, thanks to an increase in support for the Liberals, they received a slightly smaller percentage (49.4 per cent compared with 49.7 per cent). But with Labour's share of the vote dropping from 46.4 per cent to 43.8 per cent, the Conservatives increased their major-ity in the Commons. Before the election they had had 345 seats, they now had 365 – a clear majority of 100 seats over the other parties.[45]

With the exception of the 1924 election, it was the largest number of seats the Conservatives had ever won standing alone (they had done better in 1918 and 1931, but on both occasions under a Coalition label), and it was the first time since the early nineteenth century that a political party had won three General Elections in a row, increasing its majority every time. As intellectuals rushed to speculate 'Must Labour lose?' and went on to produce a rash of arguments as to why the country was doomed to Conservative ascendancy, it would have seemed both churlish and extraordinary to contemporaries to question the wisdom of Macmillan's tactics, let alone his strategy. Certainly the newly elected MP for Finchley, Mrs Margaret Thatcher, had no reason to feel anything but pleasure with the results of Macmillan's leadership. But 'would it last?'

12 Decline and Fall

To use the sort of vernacular phrase of which Macmillan was fond, his premiership was 'a game of two halves'. His Chief Whip, Martin Redmayne, thought that the turning point came in the autumn of 1960; before that little went wrong, after that almost everything that could go wrong did so.[1] To some extent this was the result of complacency. With three election victories in a row and Labour thoroughly trounced, Rab Butler thought it quite in order to tell the new Tory MPs that 'if the Party played its cards well, we would be in power for the next twenty-five years'.[2] The economics of the consensus, with their Keynesian demand management and government intervention to ensure high employment, had delivered affluence, and even some Labour theorists were beginning to argue that the old 'class-based' politics had had their day; the problems of the future, Anthony Crosland claimed, would be about how to distribute affluence more evenly, not about how to make enough money. With a Prime Minister whose pose as a world statesman helped obscure some of the uncomfortable reality of Britain's decline, and a united party behind him at home, it did indeed seem that only some bad handling of the cards could bring the Conservatives down; but as a lover of classical literature, Macmillan might have remembered the fate that the gods have in store for those who suffer from such *hubris*.

The *hubris* and the style of Macmillan's Conservatism were both evident in the first major reshuffle after the election in July 1960. The main object of the exercise was to replace the Chancellor, Heathcote Amory, whose performance at the Exchequer had been lacklustre and who was beginning to tire Macmillan by his warnings of economic difficulties ahead. Macmillan moved Selwyn Lloyd from the Foreign Office to the Treasury, which signalled his determination to pursue his own economic policy quite as much as Lloyd's arrival at the Foreign Office in 1955 had shown that Eden would be his own Foreign Secretary. It was a sign of the Prime Minister's self-confidence that he appointed a peer, Lord Home, to succeed Lloyd at the Foreign Office, ignoring jibes about it being the most astonishing appointment since the Roman Emperor Caligula had made his horse a consul. The chance for a wholesale promotion of the 'class of 1950' was not taken, however. Macmillan thought that 'some of the younger ones were not ready yet'.[3] Ted Heath, whose talents as Chief Whip had had much to do with the government's successes in the Commons, did however receive his reward, becoming Home's number two at the Foreign Office as Lord Privy Seal with special responsibility for dealing with the Common Market. There was one other move which signalled Macmillan's determination to retain the political initiative, and that was Iain Macleod's at the Colonial Office. Both appointments marked a quickening of the liberal Tory spirit.

It seemed that under Macmillan, the Conservative Party had successfully adapted itself to the new age of affluence. The very model of a modern Tory candidate was someone like the young MP for Leeds North-East, Sir Keith Joseph, who 'simply arrived in Parliament full of goodwill, with a passionate concern about poverty'; coming, like Macmillan, from a well-to-do upper middle-class family, he was 'shocked' by the poverty he saw around him, and he gravitated naturally to the 'Statism' espoused by Macmillan.[4] The 'natural path to promotion and success' in the Tory Party at this time lay, as Margaret Thatcher later commented, 'on the left', and, 'above all, the up-and-coming Tory politician had to avoid being "reactionary"'.[5] The aspirant to high office who hoped for success had to be non-ideological, without admitting that this was, in itself, an ideological position. It might seem to the untutored eye that there was little difference between the Conservative and Labour parties but the latter came fully-equipped with an ideological left which got hot under the collar about 'The Bomb' and went on rather pointless marches to Aldermaston. Yet even the highly tutored eye of Iain Macleod had to admit that the 'feeling' of most people was that 'all three parties have the same aims'; in this situation: 'the party to vote for is obviously that which appears to be the most competent and efficient in execution'.[6] It was on precisely this point that the Conservatives ceased to seem to have the edge in the three years following the reshuffle.

If Macleod was correct in thinking the electorate wanted to vote for the party which seemed the most efficiently managerial, and the signs are that he was, the Conservatives had a number of problems in presenting themselves as a thoroughly 'modern' party. It was ironic that the 'satire boom' of the early 1960s should have fixed on the ageing Macmillan as a symbol of how outdated the Tories were becoming after more than a decade in office because, for all the deliberate air he projected of Edwardian aristocratic languor, he was determined that the party should not stand still in an age of rapid change. It was Macmillan, and the young men he encouraged, who wanted to make the Conservatives a truly 'modern party', and in doing so he aroused bitter opposition from those who saw themselves as 'more Conservative than thou'. When the new Colonial Secretary, Iain Macleod, moved rapidly ahead with the decolonisation programme, responding to what Macmillan had called 'the winds of change' which were sweeping through the African continent, he drew growls of disapproval from Salisbury, who called him 'too clever by half'. To those on the old Imperial right of the party there was something infinitely distasteful about the striving to set the sails of the party to be filled by 'winds of change'. As Salisbury commented to Eden, 'sailors who make it a rule to run before the wind generally end up on the rocks.'[7] But such was the hold of Macmillan on the party and such was the faith in his line of 'modernisation', that apart from protests in the Lords and at party conferences, there was nothing the right could do but watch what they took to be the 'scuttling' of the British Empire.

Macleod's abrasive style and obvious impatience with what he took to be the antediluvian Toryism of the Cecils made him Macmillan's lightning conductor, but the policy he presided over was part of Macmillan's 'Grand Design' for the future of Britain's external policy. This included another item which was to arouse the wrath of the Salisburian wing of the party and which was destined to disrupt the party for the next half-century – the decision to apply for membership of the Common Market. It was typical of Macmillan, at least in the eyes of his critics, that he could not simply come out after the Cabinet decision on 22 July 1961 and say that Britain was going to apply to join the Common Market, but that he should, instead, have announced that he was going to enter into talks to see whether the right conditions might exist upon which Britain might negotiate to see if she would enter the Market. Given the opposition within his own party, and from Labour, not to mention the indifference and hostility of the electorate to the idea, there was no other way Macmillan could have gone about an enterprise which was at the very heart of his 'modernising' policy. As one senior party official put it, one of the main motives for the policy 'was to create a new, contemporary political argument with insular socialism; dish the Liberals by stealing their clothes; give us something *new* after 12–13 years; act as the catalyst of modernization; [and] give us a new place in the international sun'.[8] Europe would at once align the Conservative Party with the most 'modern' cause in contemporary politics, offer the chance of economic prosperity, and promise a continuation of international peace; it would also allow Britain to maintain her old position in the world by other means. There was also another dimension to the policy:

Beyond all pragmatic considerations, it was however also clear that Macmillan felt that full entry into Europe would provide a great psychological boost to the British people, and would have an energising impulse – impossible to quantify – on the economy … .[9]

The oblique approach to 'Europe' helped defuse the arguments within the party, but the central pillar of Macmillan's strategy for the future lay in the 'talks about talks' conducted by Heath in Brussels.

At the same time, Macmillan's devotion to appearing up to date could also be seen in his cultivation of the 'Special Relationship' with America. This had been easy enough with his old friend 'Ike', but might have been more difficult to do with the new American President after November 1960, John F. Kennedy. The election of a youthful, vibrant American leader was to provide the satirists and critics with another opportunity to point out just how old the Prime Minister was, but for Macmillan himself it provided yet another opportunity to use his personal charm and style to help obscure just how far Britain had fallen from her position as a Great Power. After Suez it was clear enough to Macmillan that a purely British foreign policy of the sort attempted by Eden was no longer possible in the modern world, and with his move towards 'Europe' on the one hand, and his cultivation of the Americans on the other, his 'Grand Design' for the future was set in place.

If Macmillan's progressive Conservatism allowed him to envisage a new world role for Britain, then it also pointed the way to fresh initiatives at home. After 1959 the Conservative Research Department worked away at producing 'five-year' plans for developments in social, industrial and educational policy, and these fed through into initiatives such as the setting up of the Robbins Committee to investigate the future of higher education in Britain. Conscious that Britain was beginning to fall behind the pace set by the economies of Western Europe, Macmillan looked for ways of remedying this. Joining the 'Six' was one of them, but providing a larger and more open system of higher education was another. The solutions were, in accordance with the prevailing consensus, all 'Statist': the government would provide the money for more universities, or it would help improve the central direction of the economy through setting up the National Economic Development Council (or 'Neddy' as it became known), which provided a forum at which ministers, trades unions leaders and management from industry could meet.

Macmillan was thus determined to adapt Conservatism to meet the demands of the 'new Britain' which was emerging in the early 1960s; the problem was that an age increasingly devoted to 'youth culture' and avid for novelty was not one which was disposed to respond positively to an ageing aristocrat. To the youthful satirists who had the ear (and, through television, the eyes) of the young generation of prosperous 'baby-boomers', Macmillan and his party represented a social and sexual conservatism which was stifling, and which playwrights and television satirists delighted in lampooning. It was, of course, ironic that the man who set so much (too much, his critics said) store by style should have been hoist by his own petard. He may have been a moderniser, but he looked like an ageing aristocrat who was out of touch with the vitality of 'sixties' Britain. From this point of view, the sudden death of Hugh Gaitskell in 1962 was a great blow to Macmillan, since his replacement, Harold Wilson, was to prove highly adept at pursuing the line set out by the satirists. Always something of a fantasist, Wilson, who was a similar age to Kennedy, liked to portray himself as 'a Kennedy' – a dynamic, thrusting technocrat who would, through the 'white heat of the technological revolution', bring Britain into the 1960s.

If Macmillan could not be expected to join in the laughter, he might have been able to laugh off such attacks had it not been for a combination of circumstances which rendered the Conservatives peculiarly vulnerable to them. In the first place, the early 1960s saw the first signs of the economic malaise which was to dominate British politics thereafter. Even Macmillan's naturally expansionist tendencies were held in check by 1962 as continuing balance of payments problems, and a rate of growth which was less than the rate of pay rises, all cast clouds across the economic sun. Attempts in 1961 and 1962 to 'persuade' trades unions to moderate their pay demands by first a 'pay pause' and then a 'guiding light' for pay rises, proved not only unsuccessful but also unpopular. In a phenomenon which would become depressingly familiar, it was usually groups in the public sector such as the nurses, who commanded popular sympathy, who were hit first by such tactics, whilst those workers in the private sector with powerful unions behind them could usually drive an articulated lorry through the policy. It was hoped that talks on 'Neddy' would produce a concordat between unions, management and government, but with rising inflation, most union leaders faced demands from the employees for pay rises 'in line' with inflation. Not until the late 1970s would a Labour Prime Minister admit that there might be a connection between these two phenomena, but even then Jim Callaghan had no answer to the problem other than to hope that the union leaders would cooperate. For all the excuses offered by Macmillan's defenders that both inflation and unemployment were low during his last administration, he was travelling, albeit more slowly, down the road which would lead to this impasse.

If economic slow-down was one of the reasons why Macmillan was vulnerable to the charges of his opponents that he was unable to manage a modern economy, his response to the crises created by this and other developments added weight to the allegation that he was incompetent and out of touch.

For two decades Britain had run a two-party system, but dissatisfaction with the performance of the Conservatives began a revival in the fortunes of the Liberal Party, the most dramatic sign of which was the gain of the previously safe Conservative seat of Orpington in Kent in early 1962. To a generation accustomed to a Conservative government losing every by-election it has to fight, there is nothing dramatic in the recital of such a bare statistic, but to Macmillan it was a shattering blow. It seemed to crystallise the feeling that things were beginning to go wrong. The opposition to his colonial and European policies had been ventilated at the party conference in October 1961 and again at the by-election, with Salisbury arguing (much to Macmillan's annoyance) that opinion was slipping towards the Liberals because 'real' Conservatives felt betrayed. Macmillan felt that this was a somewhat cock-eyed argument – but it was one he was to hear more of. There were also quarrels within the Cabinet, and with the economy refusing to respond to the management of Lloyd as much as the major unions were ignoring his 'guiding light' on pay policy, Macmillan decided upon dramatic action to restore the party's fortunes.

In the eyes of his critics, the reshuffle of July 1962 – 'the night of the long knives' – was a sign that the old vaudevillian had lost his nerve, and he laid himself open to the charge from the Liberal MP Jeremy Thorpe (who later turned out to know whereof he spoke) that 'Greater love hath no man than that he should lay down his friends for his life.' Macmillan himself saw it as the necessary prelude to fresh initiatives in economic and social policy, and the main aim, as in 1960, was to divest himself of an unpopular and tiring Chancellor, but this time his touch deserted him. He decided to remove Lloyd and to take the opportunity to promote some of the younger men whom he had signally failed to reward in 1960. Combining the two things meant that he sacked almost half his Cabinet – with Wilson jibing that it was 'the wrong half'.[10] The manner in which the 'massacre' took place, following soon on newspaper revelations of what was afoot, and the fact that poor Lloyd was given no warning, imparted an air of panic to the proceedings which gravely damaged Macmillan's personal authority. The moves themselves were mostly sensible ones which worked out well. Maudling at the Exchequer and the progressive figure of Sir Edward Boyle at Education both presided over new initiatives of the sort Macmillan had wanted, whilst Sir Keith Joseph at Housing showed himself such a capable and energetic spender of public money that he would later have cause to regret his success. But if the new Cabinet looked younger and more vital, then this simply emphasised how old the Prime Minister was. Authority is something men can command but not demand, and after the events of July 1962 Macmillan's was never the same; over the next year he was to sustain a series of blows which would leave him a damaged and diminished figure.

The setbacks were of two kinds: political and personal. On the first front General de Gaulle's veto of Britain's entry into the Common Market came as by far the greatest disaster. It was the trumping of the Prime Minister's ace and left his 'grand design' in ruins. Those Conservatives who had never liked the policy were relieved, but it left the Prime Minister bereft: 'the central plank of the government's policy had ... broken and Macmillan had nothing to put in its place in order to fight a viable and victorious election campaign'.[11] On the more 'personal' front, a series of scandals rocked the government, starting with allegations of spying at the Admiralty and ending in the revelation that the Minister of War, John Profumo, had been sharing the same mistress as a Soviet naval attaché. By the summer of 1963 the government seemed to be sinking beneath a sea of allegations of further sexual improprieties. Macmillan's handling of the Profumo affair was inept to put it mildly (and not many did put it that way). His admission in the Commons that he did not 'live among young people much myself', seemed to confirm the charges of his enemies that he was an outdated old 'fuddy-duddy' who should be relegated to the dustbin of history as soon as possible. Nigel Birch, one of the Treasury team which had resigned in 1958, who had criticised Macmillan at the time of Lloyd's removal, spoke the most devastating words addressed to a Conservative Prime Minister since Leo Amery had quoted Cromwell when he repeated some lines from Browning's 'The Lost Leader':

let him never come back to us!
There would be doubt, hesitation and pain,
Forced praise on our part – the glimmer of twilight,
Never glad confident morning again!

Nor was it. A distinction must be drawn between the damage done to Macmillan by the scandals of 1963 and that done to the Conservative Party. If Birch was right about the future relationship between Macmillan and the party, perspective is foreshortened by the fact that Macmillan chose to retire in October 1963 and the subsequent loss of

the 1964 election; this makes it look as though after 1963 a fatally
wounded party meandered, exhausted, towards its preordained defeat –
but it was not quite like that.

In the first place, the resources of liberal Conservatism were far from
played out. With fresh initiatives in housebuilding, education and economic policy, the new ministers showed that there was still plenty of life
left in the Conservative consensus, whilst Macmillan managed to add
some lustre to his reputation abroad by playing a leading part in the
Test Ban Treaty which controlled the spread of nuclear weapons. This
enabled the Prime Minister to face down his backbench critics and to
get a rousing cheer from the 1922 Committee when he addressed its
members in July before the summer recess. By August his press
secretary was writing that Macmillan was 'jauntily and firmly back in
the saddle',[12] and with the opinion polls finally showing that the
Conservatives were catching up on Labour, there seemed every reason
for optimism. But what really wrecked the chances of Macmillan's strategy of modernisation more than anything except de Gaulle's veto was his
own resignation in October 1963 and the events which surrounded it.

Macmillan found himself in a position not dissimilar to that occupied
by Churchill in 1954. Although he was only 69, in the new climate created by Kennedy, Wilson and the 'youth culture', he seemed a survival
from the Edwardian age, and the Labour leader had already shown a
talent for playing on this weakness during the Profumo business. But
despite his own increasing tiredness and his lamentations about the
burdens he carried, Macmillan, like almost everyone else in his position, had succumbed to the two weaknesses of a long-serving Prime
Minister: the illusion that he was indispensable and the feeling that the
young men were 'not ready' to take over from him.[13] But no sooner had
he made up his mind to stay on that he was taken ill with prostate
trouble and rushed to hospital.

The timing of the illness could hardly have been worse. Although he
later came bitterly to regret the decision, Macmillan, in pessimistic
mood, decided that he ought to resign the leadership of the party –
which meant that the Conference would become, in effect, a leadership convention. The struggle that followed has continued to fascinate
historians as much as it did contemporaries, but in terms of the outcome it had no effect on the direction which the party would follow.
The obvious candidate to succeed Macmillan was Butler, who had
missed out in 1957 and was widely acknowledged to be the most experienced as well as the best candidate for the post; but the fact that
Macmillan dissented from this view proved to be decisive. Macmillan
had not actually resigned as Prime Minister or party leader, and after

he came round from his operation on 17 October, he energetically pulled every possible string to prevent Butler from being his successor. The reasons for Macmillan's attitude and actions are largely a matter of speculation: to some it was the memory of the different attitudes the two men had taken to appeasement which determined these things, to others it was because he did not feel that Rab was the right man for the job; the motives may be unclear, but the determination was not; yet Macmillan's actions set off a civil war in the party which may well have helped cost it the next election.

The first candidate to show his hand (and much else besides) was the ebullient former Party Chairman, Lord Hailsham, then Minister for the North-East. He made a barnstorming speech at the opening of the Conference, declaring his intention to take advantage of recently passed legislation to renounce his peerage so that he could be a candidate for the leadership; neither the speed of his announcement, nor yet the manner of it, helped his cause, indeed quite the opposite, since the episode reinforced doubts about his stability and temperament. Lord Home, who had supported him until that moment, changed his mind after the speech,[14] whilst Macmillan's Press Secretary noted the 'curled lip' of the 'Establishment' at Hailsham's 'Nuremberg rally'.[15]

If Hailsham went into speedy eclipse because of the nakedness of his ambition, then Butler went a similar way for quite a different reason. The prize was now in his grasp, but he could not bring himself to seize it. Perhaps, as his official biographer has speculated, he had already conceded defeat in advance, and having convinced himself that it would not be the end of the world if he failed to gain the top prize, he almost willed himself into defeat.[16] Nor was the Party Conference the arena where Butler's talents were most likely to be shown to their best effect. He did not much like the party faithful, and many of them did not care for him. In Macmillan's absence it fell to him as the senior minister to give the leader's speech, but his delivery was 'flat and uninspiring', and he did himself nothing but harm.[17] He may have hoped that, with the Conference over, he could rely upon the 'usual processes' to ensure he became leader – but since there was no established method of selecting a Conservative leader, this was, in effect, to leave himself in Macmillan's hands.

In 1957, when Eden had resigned through ill-health, the job of choosing his successor lay, constitutionally, with the Queen, but then, as on this occasion, she looked to the Conservative Party for advice. The obvious figure to give that advice was the outgoing Prime Minister, although this was by no means the rule: Eden had given no advice in 1957, nor had he been asked to;[18] Bonar Law had asked to be excused from proffering advice; to set against this were the precedents of Churchill recommending Eden just as Baldwin had Neville Chamberlain, but on both these occasions there had been no doubt as to who the successor should be. With so many possible challengers it was impossible to follow the example of 1957 and have two senior ministers sound out the Cabinet; theoretically Butler, Hailsham, Macleod, Maudling and Heath could all be candidates. This left the situation open to manipulation by Macmillan.

Butler's main problem, apart from his inability to rouse the party faithful, was that he was distrusted by the right of the party, who were already disaffected with the government's policies on decolonisation and Europe and who saw Butler as the archetypal liberal Conservative. It was equally clear that Butler's supporters, and others, would not have Hailsham, which left Macmillan with a problem. If 'Rab' had been willing to exert himself and to run the risk of splitting the party he could have had the job, but the party was already suffering from the bad publicity surrounding the contest, and Butler had spent his life as a loyal servant of the party; he could not break the habit now. Since Macmillan had not formally resigned, he was able to keep the reins in his hands, and when soundings taken on his behalf established that there was a commonly accepted 'second choice' candidate, he duly recommended to the Queen that she should ask Lord Home to become Prime Minister.

The situation was slightly more complicated. Home was as surprised by his selection as most other people were to be, and he knew that unless Butler and his supporters agreed to serve under him he could not take on the post, so he asked the Queen to commission him to see whether he could form an administration. It was all very reminiscent of the nineteenth century, with fourteenth earls being asked to see if the materials existed to form an administration which might carry on the Queen's government – and Wilson did not miss the opportunity to add this to his litany of events which showed how out-of-touch and out-of-date the Conservative Party was. The key figure was Butler. Macleod and Powell, who had both been ardent supporters of Rab, urged him to refuse Home's offer. Both men disliked the manner in which Macmillan had manipulated the succession and they both regarded Home as an electorally disastrous choice; at a time when the Conservatives were being lampooned for their 'grousemoor' and 'Establishment' image, to select a Scottish earl who had not sat in the Commons since 1947 as their leader was indeed to make Labour's task easier than it already was. But despite their best efforts Butler would not take a decision which he regarded as even more damaging to the party, so he agreed to serve under Home and duly became Deputy Prime Minister and lord-high everything else. Macleod and Powell were less pliable and both refused posts in the new government.

The reverberations of the leadership battle rumbled on for years, flaring up most notably in January 1964 when Macleod published a review of Randolph Churchill's mendacious account of the contest and in effect gave weight to the line taken by Labour by accusing the party of having chosen its leader through the 'magic circle' of old Etonians; but the die had been cast and the party would go into the next election with Home as leader.

Everything that Macleod and Powell had feared came to pass, although there were those Conservatives who would find it hard to forgive either man for not putting his shoulder to the wheel and who would blame them for the election defeat. Home's advantages were easily listed – and heavily outweighed by his disadvantages. He was a decent, honest and upright figure who commanded respect even from his opponents; if an antidote to what was later to be called 'sleaze' was needed, Alec Home was your man. But he was a 'belted earl' and his selection did rather give verisimilitude to the accusations that in their time of trouble the Tories, unable to find a single member of the Commons fit to lead them, had reverted atavistically to the old ruling order. It was possible to push this line too far, and since Wilson was always apt to work a good argument to death, he did so with repeated references to the 'fourteenth earl' – until that is, Home put a stop to this piece of 1960s inverted snobbery by pointing out that when one came to think about it 'I suppose Mr Wilson is the fourteenth Mr Wilson'. But it was the only example of Home scoring off Wilson. Home renounced his ancient peerage and stood for the Commons as Sir Alec Douglas-Home, but he was not at home either on the Treasury Front Bench or on the hustings, and he could never get the measure of Wilson. His transparent honesty did not always help matters either. Facing a man with a first-class degree in economics at a time when the economy was a major political issue, it was endearing, if unwise, of Home to admit that he did his mathematics with matchsticks; for all the good Wilson's expertise did him, he might as well have imitated Home, but at the time and in the context it added fuel to Labour's charges that the Conservatives were a bunch of bumbling amateurs.

Yet, when all allowances have been made for Home's defects, what is most remarkable about his leadership is how very close the Conservatives came to winning the election in 1964. Sir Alec remained firmly behind Wilson in the opinion polls (he never exceeded a 48 per cent approval rating compared to Wilson's, which never went below 61 per cent),[19] but he quickly set about reviving party morale, touring local associations and making them feel that there was a firm hand on the tiller. His task was made no easier by Macleod's revelations in *The Spectator* and by the fury aroused amongst Conservative supporters by Ted Heath's bill to abolish Resale Price Maintenance. This last measure, which hit the owners of corner shops and small grocers in particular, 'touched off the most prolonged Conservative revolt since Suez'.[20] Allegations were also made that with Home as leader the party would veer to the right.

But, as Home showed, this last rumour was as far from the truth as it was possible to get. The work which the Conservative Research Department had been doing since 1959 now began to bear fruit,[21] and Home became the beneficiary of the counter-attack which Macmillan had been preparing since the 'night of the long knives'. Home's main weakness, his knowledge of domestic affairs, was well-covered by the activities of his two speechwriters, promising young men with a long future in the party by the names of Nigel Lawson and John Macgregor, who were given a good script to work from. For all Wilson's boasts about 'technology', the Conservative counter-attack made it clear that even under Home they were preparing for a brave new world which promised more of what they had delivered in the past. The problem with this line of approach was that it made it even more difficult to differentiate between the Conservatives and the other two parties. The question did indeed become one of asking which of the two major parties would manage a modern economy more efficiently and which of them was more in tune with contemporary social mores; if it was difficult for Home to sound convincing on the first point, it was even more so for his party to do so on the second. Then there was the Liberal revival to take into account.

When the election came in October, the result suggested that Home's counter-attack had very nearly worked, and that those who had been writing the Conservatives off had underestimated the resilience of the party. The Conservatives had been able successfully to play on fears of Labour's nationalisation plans and upon the party's inexperience, but in the end the Liberal revival scuppered Home's chances. The turnout was slightly lower than in 1959 (77.1 per cent compared to 78.7 per cent), and the Conservatives received only 200,000 fewer votes than Labour (12,001,396 to 12,205,814), but their share of the vote dropped from nearly 50 to 43.4 per cent, their poorest showing since 1950 (although as the turn-out in that year had been much higher, the comparison makes the 1964 figure look even worse); most startling of all was the Liberal performance. The Liberal share of the vote nearly doubled from 5.9 to 11.2 per cent and this was enough to put Labour in power with 317 seats compared to the Conservatives' 304; the 'thirteen wasted years' were over.[22]

The Conservatives reacted to the defeat rather more badly than the results warranted. Part of the problem was that they had been in office such a long time that it was difficult to adjust to the different conditions of Opposition. In this Sir Alec was not much help. He had been able to project a reassuring image as Prime Minister, but he was not the stuff of which leaders of the Opposition were made – or so many Conservatives felt. This mood was summed up in the comments made by one 'senior industrial manager' in a letter to Central Office in December 1963:

> We are looking for a 1963 leader. Do you remember Kennedy? We liked him. We are sick of seeing old-looking men dressed in flat caps and bedraggled tweeds strolling with a 12 bore … . The nearest approach to our man is Heath. In every task he performs, win or lose, he has the facts, figures and knowledge. We don't give a damn if he is a bachelor. He is our age, he is capable, he looks a director (of the Country) and most of all he is different from these tired old men … .[23]

By 1965, many others were of the same line of thinking. Although the Conservatives had done well in the local elections, Wilson made it clear that there would not be an election before 1966. The Conservatives now faced the possibility of two more years of Home, a prospect which brought the grumbling about his supposed deficiencies to audible level. Sir Alec, unlike most party leaders, was not prepared to hold his post if he felt that he was standing in the way of an election victory, and on 22 July 1965 he told the 1922 Committee that he was standing down.

This time, there was no repeat of the fiasco of 1963. After that episode the party had decided that it should elect its leader in future, and the first contest under the new system now took place. Of the three candidates, two represented a clear continuation of Macmillanite Conservatism. Since it was generally felt that the new leader ought to come from the same generation as Wilson, senior figures like Selwyn Lloyd, Julian Amery and Peter Thorneycroft all stood aside (some of them rather reluctantly, hoping to come in on a second ballot);[24] Butler was quite out of the running, having accepted the Mastership at Trinity College, Cambridge. It was the ex-Chancellor, Reginald Maudling, who was the favourite to win the contest, but he had a reputation for laziness and had not struck as good a patch in Opposition as his main challenger, Edward Heath, whose merciless attacks on James

Callaghan's Finance Bill had rallied Tory morale. The third challenger was Enoch Powell, who was already making dissenting noises about the attitude of the party towards public spending. In the ballot held on 27 July 1965 Heath collected 150 votes compared to 133 for Maudling and 15 for Powell; under the rules Maudling could have demanded a second ballot, but he gracefully accepted defeat and Edward Heath became the leader of the Conservative Party.

The Conservatives made much of Heath's meritocratic background, which finally allowed them to escape from allegations about the Old Etonian mafia and 'magic circles', and both at the time and since, his advent has been seen as marking the arrival of a new type of Conservative leader. He was certainly the first leader of the party to have come from a working-class background and to have attended grammar school, but, accent apart, he was in fact a remarkable example of social adaptation. An organ scholar at Balliol in the late 1930s, he had had 'a good war' and had entered the Commons in 1950 as MP for Bexley. As Macmillan's Chief Whip he had entered the inner sanctum of power, if not Macleod's 'magic circle', and by 1965 he combined impeccably 'Establishment' credentials with a thrustingly technocratic image; as the 1963 correspondent had noted, he looked like a 'director' – and he certainly acted like one.

13   From Heath to Thatcher

Contemplating the rise of Thatcherism in the late 1970s Heath's former chief speech writer, Michael Wolff, commented with evident disgust: they 'want to wipe out the past'.[1] The Thatcherite response would have been that this was a worthwhile enterprise. The warning given earlier about the use to which historically minded Conservatives put their party's history is more necessary than ever when contemplating the decade after the departure of Sir Alec Douglas-Home. The period was even more traumatic than the party's previous prolonged period in the 'wilderness'. Although in electoral terms the Conservatives did better than in the years 1906 to 1915 in so far as they actually managed to win an election, the experience of government between 1970 and 1974 was to prove a shattering one for most Conservatives and, by 1975, with a record of having lost four out of the last five elections, the party seemed bereft of direction. For the Thatcherites the story of the early 1970s is less important than what came next, whilst the liberal Conservative grandees who dominated the party then have their own reasons for glossing over the period. It is a shame that this should be so, since a look at the policy developments of the late 1960s and early 1970s shows how much Thatcherism owes to what preceded the arrival of the woman herself; but naturally neither she, nor her later opponents, would care to dwell on this phenomenon: it makes her look less unique and it makes Edward Heath seem something of a failed proto-Thatcher.

Although, as a protégé of Macmillan's, Heath was expected to lead the party from the same left-of-centre position, in practice the ideas adumbrated under his leadership marked a break with consensual politics. We have already witnessed the schizophrenia between Conservative rhetoric about 'setting the people free' and the corporatism of the 1950s; the experience of office, particularly sensitivities towards the unions and the need to maintain full employment, had all widened the gap; in opposition it could be narrowed. Freed of the trammels of having to govern the country and thus to utilise the tools of the consensus, the Conservatives were free to contemplate once more what their role should be.

Heath was a strange figure. His close friends proclaimed him a convivial man; but they were few, and to most observers he came across as cold and somewhat aloof. He had risen further up the social scale than

190

any previous Conservative leader, his father having been a jobbing builder, and this may have accounted, in part, for the rather peculiar accent he acquired on his ascent to the top; but his slightly strangulated vowel sounds and his version of 'received pronunciation', marked him out as one who had assimilated to the old order of things; Wilson, who had had a not dissimilar accent earlier in his career, had adapted to the times by reacquiring a northern burr. Something of an unclubbable figure, Heath's bachelor status and long period in the Whips office all contributed to his personal remoteness. As leader he was determined to be 'modern', and in his mind that seemed to involve behaving as an autocratic Chief Executive. Shadow portfolios were allotted with a rigidity previously unknown in the history of the party, and 'Shadows' were expected to stick to their briefs, with Heath and Central Office delineating the broad lines of strategy. Heath disliked woolly thinking, and in the aftermath of 1964 his 'Full Steam Ahead and Damn the Torpedoes' approach was congenial to many in the party;[2] whatever anyone could say of 'Ted', no one could accuse him of not giving a lead; had anyone behaved to him as he did to his successor, he would have given them short shrift.

The leading exponent of the liberal Conservative version of the party's history, Lord Blake, has called the 1965 Conservative policy document, *Putting Britain Right Ahead*, 'a clear departure from the paternalistic progressivism of 1959–63'.[3] The need to put what a later generation would call 'clear blue water' between the Conservatives and Labour ensured that there was no mention of grandiose national economic plans nor yet of incomes policies; both these items figured prominently in Wilson's programme and it was rather pointless for the Conservatives to challenge Labour when it came to paying danegeld to the unions. In their places were calls for reductions in public spending, more selectivity in social security spending, lower direct taxation and legislation to restrain the powers of the unions. There was not much here that Thatcherites would cavil at. The problem was that whilst Heath was good at espousing proto-Thatcherism, he was a good deal less adept at implementing it.

Heath's main objective when he became leader was to win the next election, but there were a number of obstacles in his way. The Conservatives suffered at this time and later from the delusion that the key to electoral success was in capturing the 'younger management types, men who believed in a meritocratic, efficiency-orientated approach and who found Wilson's newly-acquired technology attractive'.[4] Even had it been possible to target such a group, its numbers would hardly have been statistically significant, and what Heath was never to come up with was a strategy for attracting the members of the skilled manual working classes who in 1966 and on subsequent occasions saw Labour as their natural home. This was not a mistake which Heath's successor would make, nor was it one made by that shrewd electioneer Harold Wilson. It was Wilson who presented Heath with his most formidable problems. After '13 wasted years' it was an obvious gambit for Wilson to claim that Labour deserved a proper sustained period in office to carry out the 'modernisation' of the country. Wilson benefited from having a tiny majority which was eventually to dwindle to a bare one; there could be no question of implementing a Socialist policy – even had Wilson had one. He was also the beneficiary of one of the failures of Macleod's colonial policy with regard to the Central African Federation. In November 1964 after a victory for the Rhodesian Front Party its leader, Ian Smith, made a unilateral declaration of independence. The Tory Party split three ways, with the Salisburian contingent sympathising with 'our kith and kin', the progressives wanting to support firm UN sanctions, and the majority of the party, who favoured neither solution and just hoped that the situation would resolve itself. Heath found it impossible to maintain any semblance of unity on the issue, and Wilson was able to exploit the divisions which Rhodesia created. It quickly became apparent that for all his 'abrasive' style, Heath was even less capable than Home of dealing with the mercurial Labour leader. It was some small indication of the difference between the two men that whereas Heath tended to have hecklers escorted from his meetings, Wilson positively relished interruptions. Wilson could be a brilliant performer on the floor of the Commons, whilst poor Heath appeared stiff and lacking in humour: it was Macmillan and Gaitskell all over again, but this time with the boot on Labour's foot. A similar verdict could be delivered on the 1966 election which was held on 31 March.

It was the worst performance by the Conservatives since 1945, with their share of the poll declining to 41.9 per cent. No doubt the party was again hit by the Liberals, who polled 8.5 per cent, but with Labour getting 47.9 per cent there could be no doubt that there had been a massive vote of confidence in Wilson, who captured 363 seats compared to 253 for the Conservatives, 12 Liberals and two 'others'. Heath escaped the fate often doled out to defeated Conservative leaders. No one had really expected him to win, and the legacy of 1961 to 1964 provided a convenient and plausible scapegoat.

This enabled Heath to continue with the initiative he had begun soon after becoming leader, when he had set up 'study groups' to look at the party's policies across the whole political spectrum; the election seemed to prove that a thorough-going revision of party policy was necessary. With five years before an election, Heath had the time to carry out the thorough refurbishment of the party for which he already had the inclination. The break with the past which had begun in 1965 with Butler's retirement continued apace, as men like Selwyn Lloyd, Henry Brooke and other stalwarts of the Macmillan years gave way finally to the 'class of 1950'; only Home, as Shadow Foreign Secretary, remained from the upper echelons of the older generation. Macleod became Shadow Chancellor, Lord Hailsham, now once more known as Quintin Hogg, became the Home Affairs spokesman, whilst Enoch Powell shadowed Defence. Such changes were the outward and most visible sign of Heath's determination to modernise the party.

Heath wanted to find 'new practical ways in which to apply our principles to current problems': 'action, not words' was his slogan (and the title of the 1966 manifesto).[5] Not for Heath the Churchillian dislike of 'setting forth detailed projects whilst in Opposition'; indeed this was what he liked doing best. 'Action not words' was a good slogan for the times, but it was one of Heath's major defects as leader that he was unable to give any impression of having a vision of where he wanted to lead the country.

In rethinking the party's position, conscious parallels with the period 1945–50 were made. Then, at least according to the party's own mythology, the Conservatives had come to terms with the world created by Labour. As we have seen, the reality had been at once more and less complex: more in so far as the 'consensus' was the product of the Churchill Coalition; less because this meant that the process of 'adaptation' became largely a matter of presentation. This time, however, there could be no question of the party adapting itself to what Labour was doing. This was partly because no one in his right mind would have chosen to imitate the disastrous performance of Labour's much-vaunted 'National Plan', but it was also due to a feeling reinforced by the failures of Labour in office that the corporatist experiment was running out of steam. As Mrs Thatcher put it later: 'Anyone seriously thinking about the way forward for Conservatism would have to start by examining whether the established tendency to fight on socialist ground with corporatist weapons had not something to do with the Party's predicament.'[6] If by that she meant to imply that this was her achievement, she was wrong; that line of thinking began under Heath.

On trades unions, on the Welfare State and on incomes policy, the position evolved under Heath was not dissimilar to some of the basics of Thatcherism: there would be legislation to curb union powers; there would be greater selectivity in the targeting of benefits and there would be an end to incomes policies. Business would be 'freed' to create the wealth which the nation needed. As one young Conservative, Timothy Raison, put it at the time, the party's problem was that it had tried to operate a 'largely capitalist economy without a capitalist ideology'.[7] These themes had, as we have seen, always remained a part of Conservative rhetoric, but in office under Churchill and his successors little had been done to translate rhetoric into practice; Heath's decisive manner made it seem as though the moment was coming when this would all change.

But at best Heath was only a proto-Thatcherite. The main difference between him and his successor was in the different view they held of the role of the state. In the mid-1960s, it was still possible to believe that action by the state held the key to economic recovery. If the state could only target investment in the way it was going to do with social security benefits, then the future of the economy might yet be bright. This was very much in tune with the song that Macmillan had sung since the 1930s, as well as with the 'managerial' ethos espoused by Heath himself; it was institutional rather than philosophical change which was needed, and it was that which Heath would deliver. However, with the State committed to policies of full-employment and subsidies for the nationalised industries, and with the Trades Unions as strong as they were, Heath's rhetoric would, at some point, come into conflict with harsh political reality.

If Heath was content to try to get the agenda of the next Conservative government sorted out, at least one of his colleagues saw the period of opposition as one for a fundamental rethinking of the Conservative mission – and that was Enoch Powell. Powell was a truly 'radical' thinker in a way few Conservatives are; he was not afraid to go to the roots of a problem in order to find an answer. This made him a disturbing presence in the Shadow Cabinet but firmly established him in Thatcherite retrospect as Mrs Thatcher's John the Baptist.

Powell wanted to draw a clear distinction between what Conservatism and Socialism had to offer Britain. He knew that, in practice, with the Socialists failing to carry through the rigours of their ideology and the Conservatives forsaking their electioneering rhetoric when in power, there seemed little difference between the two parties, and he wanted to end this situation by calling the Conservatives back to their mission to 'free the people'. Powell thought that indicative planning, 'Neddy' and all the regional planning boards and other apparatus of the corporate state were a logical nonsense. Governments were not equipped to decide where business and industry should invest; they should leave that to the operation of the 'free market'. He found 'the habit of looking automatically to government for the solution whenever confronted by any kind of problem' deeply worrying. It was attitudes such as this which obliged 'even Tory Governments to operate within the framework of an implicitly socialist public opinion'.[8] For Powell 'the essence of the Tory faith' was 'in the conviction that salvation lies within the grasp of the people themselves.'[9] On a practical level it was possible for Powell's philosophy to coexist with Heath's addiction to detail, but on a personal level it was not possible for Powell and Heath to remain in the same Shadow Cabinet.

Heath expected his colleagues to confine themselves to their shadow portfolios, something of which Powell was incapable. Even on his own topic, Defence, Powell's ideas struck many Conservatives as radical and unsettling. Following the light of his own logic, Powell saw no problem with Labour's withdrawal from 'east of Suez' after 1967; the Empire was over and the bases which had sprung up to protect the routes to India were no longer necessary; this was as far from the sentimentality with which many Conservatives viewed the Empire as it was possible to get without being a Socialist. But it was another aspect of the Imperial legacy which led to the breach between Powell and Heath – immigration. As Minister of Health under Macmillan, Powell had helped preside over the steady flow of immigrants from the Commonwealth to Britain which shortages in the labour market encouraged. Since the immigrants tended to congregate only in certain parts of the country it was relatively easy to ignore the immense social changes which they brought in their wake. There had been attempts by the *revenant* Sir Oswald Mosley to play the 'race card' in the late 1950s, but these had come to nothing. There had also been obscure Conservative backbenchers who had been accused of racialism in West Midlands seats in 1964, but no senior member of the party had spoken up on the question of immigration; Powell broke this taboo. Since the West Midlands had one of the largest concentration of immigrants it was natural for Powell, as a Wolverhampton MP, to have views on the issue; and with Labour due to bring in a Race Relations Bill in April 1968, it was equally natural for him to speak on it to his constituents.

Both front benches were well aware of the problems beginning to be posed by the 'race' issue, which was why Labour was trying to restrict immigration at the same time as trying to rule against discrimination, but the issue was such a sensitive one that on the rare occasions it was discussed politicians took great care over their language. Powell was probably the greatest orator on the Conservative Front Bench, and his love of striking classical metaphor was to land him in a major public row which was to rumble on within and without the Conservative Party until after the next election. Read nearly 30 years later, 'the speech' strikes one much as it struck the audience to whom it was addressed; it is a forceful and perhaps at times melodramatic argument for government to address the problems which race was beginning to create in the inner city areas. In the light of later events, such as (perhaps) the riots on the Broadwater Farm Estate in the 1980s, even Powell's controversial peroration seems ominously accurate:

> As I look ahead, I am filled with foreboding. Like the Roman I seem to see 'the River Tiber foaming with much blood'. That tragic and intractable phenomenon which we watch with horror on the other side of the Atlantic but which there is interwoven with history and the existence of the States itself, is coming upon us here by our own volition and our own neglect.

He thought that 'to see, and not to speak, would be the great betrayal'; but to speak in such a manner was to bring down upon him a storm whose effects shaped the rest of his political career.[10]

Powell was immediately branded a 'racialist' by those on the political left – but he was reflecting both the experiences of his constituents and the views of many voters; within his own party a fierce argument broke forth. The question of legislating over racial discrimination, like the whole question of immigration, showed up fault-lines within the Conservative Party. So deep were the divisions that Quintin Hogg had proposed that the issue should be the subject of a 'free vote', but the Shadow Cabinet had come up with the compromise of voting against Labour's bill on practical grounds whilst expressing sympathy with its general aim. Even this went too far for some of the more liberal members of the party. Humphrey Berkeley resigned the Whip whilst Sir Edward Boyle, who was a senior member of the Shadow Cabinet, made it clear that he would vote with Labour. Thanks to the storm raised by Powell's speech, attention switched from what Heath would do about Boyle (in the event the answer was nothing) to how he would handle Powell. The answer came immediately, as Heath sacked him from the Shadow Cabinet.

The weeks following Powell's speech revealed the extent to which the immigration issue was capable of attracting working-class support, with dockers, Billingsgate porters and other members of the manual working classes demonstrating in support of 'good old Enoch'. But at the same time it revealed how determinedly liberal the Conservative Party hierarchy was on the issue. The identification of Powell with 'race' also helped obscure his ideas on economics and industrial policy – but it did not stop them affecting Conservative thinking.

Henceforth Powell's ministerial career was over, but he was to have a greater influence upon the future direction of the party than most ministers have ever dreamed of. Over the next few years Powell would be one of the most popular (as well as the most controversial) speakers at Conservative gatherings, and his influence on the next election was incalculable.

Conservative hopes, pinned as they were on that election, were certainly high through 1968 and 1969 as Labour staggered from one disaster to another, and public and private opinion polls showed a consistent Conservative lead. Wilson would now have to campaign on his record, such as it was, rather than that of the Conservatives. But it was here that the Heath approach proved less than helpful. A Churchillian line of leaving the government to discredit itself would have left the Tories with the not frightfully difficult job of attacking Labour's shortcomings, but Heath's addiction to detailed policy statements gave that old master of repartee, Harold Wilson, a whole series of 'one-liners' with which to attack the Conservatives; Heath even provided a convenient label for him to use – 'Selsdon Man'.

By March 1970, the ferment of activity within the Conservative Party had produced a programme for the next government, but it was not thought to be 'the sort of manifesto with which we can win a General Election'.[11] It was decided to 'launch' it, and to capture the political initiative by holding a weekend conference for the Shadow Cabinet at the Selsdon Park Hotel – where the 'new' Conservatism would be give the highest possible profile. In the early months of 1970 the Conservatives had begun to slip behind in the opinion polls as Labour, with the safe hands of Roy Jenkins at the Treasury, began to emerge from its travails, so the launch of 'Selsdon Man' was a calculated attempt to reverse the tide. Wilson himself seems to have thought that the conscious abandonment of so many parts of the consensus made the Conservatives even more unelectable than Heath's lacklustre performances, and when he called the election in June everyone apart from Heath and a few leading Conservatives expected the old wizard to be returned, albeit with a reduced majority. Heath's private polls had been predicting a Conservative majority of about 30 seats – and so it turned out.

The election was the biggest upset to the pollsters before 1992, and even today opinions differ as to why nearly all of them got things so consistently wrong. The usual stand-by at such times is to say that Labour 'won the campaign', but it is rather difficult to know, either in 1970 or in 1987 and 1992, what such language actually means beyond saying that 'Labour impressed the media'. The only opinion poll which really counts is that on Election Day, and in the untrained eyes of the electorate, the Conservatives had won the campaign; so Heath, as with his two successors, could afford a condescending smile towards the prejudices of the chattering classes. In any event, Wilson's over-confident approach to the election may well have backfired; he was accused by one of Heath's lieutenants, Willie Whitelaw, of 'going about stirring up apathy'. There were those who argued that it was the votes of the non-chattering but rather more numerous 'C2s' who swung the election, and that this group – the semi-skilled working-class voters – had in turn been influenced by Enoch Powell's call on the eve of the election for those who agreed with him to vote for Heath and the Conservatives. The very idea was anathema to Heath and his supporters, but the Conservatives had been targeting this group carefully in a number of highly marginal constituencies. There can be no doubt that they were susceptible to Powell's views, particularly on immigration, and that it was the switch to the Conservatives in these marginal seats which clinched the result, but it would be to go beyond the evidence to say that Powell was the decisive factor.[12]

The make-up of Heath's Cabinet firmly reflected the Prime Minister's intentions. He had made it clear before the election that there would be no place for Powell, and there was equally no place for those who might dissent from his own views. With 18 members, it was the smallest Cabinet since the early days of Macmillan; its job was not to discuss policy, that had already been done, its job was to implement the manifesto in the most efficient manner possible.[13] The appointments of Macleod, Maudling, Hogg and Home were all expected, with the last two (rather comically some thought) being given life peerages so that they could serve as respectively Lord Chancellor and Foreign Secretary; Quintin Hogg had completed his exercises in name-changing to become once more Lord Hailsham – his old seat at St Marylebone went to a bright young man in the Heathite mould called Kenneth Baker. But when Macleod died only a month after being appointed to the Exchequer and Heath appointed his protégé, Anthony Barber, to the post, it was as clear a sign as one could wish that Heath intended to be the main voice in his own administration. Macleod's loss not only removed a formidable political operator, it also deprived the party of a Front Bench figure of real weight. The appointments of Peter Walker (Housing), Peter Thomas (Wales), James Prior (Agriculture) and Robert Carr (Employment) all demonstrated how useful it was to have worked with the new Prime Minister before; Margaret Thatcher at Education had also worked with Heath, but she was one of the few members of the Shadow Cabinet who had the reputation of being prepared to argue with him.[14] Still, Heath needed a token woman, and as a junior member of the Cabinet she would be expected, like everyone else, to stick to her own department and let the Prime Minister, who was well-known for his musical skills, both conduct the orchestra and play the piano.

The intention was to implement the manifesto, and in one important respect this was done. Heath had made a firm commitment to take Britain into the Common Market and he carried it out, despite dissent from within the ranks – most notably from Powell. But it was a different tale elsewhere – one of good intentions frustrated. As Walker later commented on the early efforts of the Thatcher Government: 'We tried all that stuff and it just didn't do.'[15] Heath's defenders point to an unpredictable concatenation of circumstances such as the 1973 oil crisis in mitigation of his 'U-turn' and argue that what took place was a 'turn away on timing and method rather than a shift of intentions';[16] but to a party which had been told, 'We were returned to office to change the course and the history of this nation, nothing less', to have to settle for so much less was galling; instead of the government changing history, history changed the government.

The key to Heath's success would be his Industrial Relations Act. Heath had taken great care to consult the Union leaders before coming into office, and his programme of legislation, which would put an end to wild-cat strikes and make arbitration compulsory, was designed to create mechanisms by which the old corporatism could be renewed; that the Unions had rejected a not dissimilar set of ideas from Barbara Castle and Harold Wilson suggested that the way ahead would not be plain sailing. Heath, however, ever the technocrat, made two crucial, but mistaken assumptions: the first was that the unions would welcome incorporation into his vision of a statist Britain; the second was that the union leaders would be able to control their followers; both of these were wrong.

From the start, Heath failed to secure the sort of cooperation he wanted: the local government manual workers gained a pay rise of 14.5 per cent, whilst the electricity workers, having imposed a work-to-rule which led Heath to declare a state of emergency, ended up getting between 15 and 18 per cent; this proved a contested backdrop to the passing of the Industrial Relations Act. With 163 clauses, and running to 160 pages, the Act was scarcely understood by its own advocates, and whilst parts of it were corporatist and allowed employers and unions to reach legally binding collective agreements, other parts were libertarian, in that such agreements could not be legally enforced unless both sides agreed that it should be so. What the unions disliked was its attempt to define (and thus limit) their powers and privileges; what proved politically disastrous was its legalism. Although there was no intention that it should be used to jail striking workers, it contained provisions that did just that – if workers did not obey the law. In 1972 a dockers' strike led to picketing the Midland Cold Storage terminal in East London; the local dockers' leaders refused to abide by the terms of the new Act, and, after a series of surprising legal judgements, it was ruled that the employers could seek financial redress from them; as they refused to pay up, it seemed inevitable that all five of them would end up in Pentonville jail for contempt of Court. However, no sooner had they been imprisoned than an hithertofore obscure functionary called the Official Solicitor appeared to release them, pending an appeal in the Lords which set aside the previous court rulings. It was a fiasco, and marked the point at which the larger unions decided not to cooperate any further with the Act.

If the well-intentioned Industrial Relations Act ended up ruining the government's relations with the unions, its Prices and Incomes policy had much the same effect on its economic policy. In opposition Heath had made great play out of the failure of Wilson's attempts to implement a prices and incomes policy; relying as he was on the Industrial Relations Act to curb the rate of wage rises, Heath decided that his government would be able to do without a policy to control prices and wages; nor, he declared, would his government bail out bankrupt British industries. It was, indeed, proto-Thatcherism – but it failed totally.

The failure of the Industrial Relations Act to provide a mechanism for controlling wages rises was driven home by the Miners' Strike of the winter of 1971–72. Unprepared for such action, the government had insufficient stockpiles of coal, and, anxious to avoid unrest, Heath conceded a massive pay rise (although less than the 47 per cent being demanded) in February 1972. Heath's answer to these failures was to invite unions and industrialists to cooperate in a partnership with government to run the economy. His search for a 'solemn and binding agreement' (or, as the journalist Bernard Levin called it 'Solomon Binding') failed to produce an agreement, and so, despite his earlier boasts about not needing one, Heath was forced back towards a Prices and Incomes policy.

The need for such a policy by 1973 was all too apparent. In the period 1967 to 1969 hourly wage-rates had risen by an average of 6 per cent; by 1973 that had risen to 12.9 per cent, and by the end of the Heath Government it would rise to 15 per cent; at the same time consumer prices rose from 4.2 per cent in the last years of Wilson to 9.2 per cent in 1973, and 16 per cent by 1974. Unemployment, that spectre from the 1930s, was also on the rise: in March 1971 it topped 800,000 for the first time since the war, and by December it was nearing the politically damaging figure of one million. Keynes had not envisaged a situation in which inflation would rise at the same time as unemployment and economic stagnation; 'stagflation' as it became known, was economic proof that something was not working; but the government, correctly, was more worried about people not working. In March 1972 it announced what became known as the 'Barber boom', named after the Chancellor, Anthony Barber. His budget cut taxes and increased public expenditure; there would be a 'dash for growth' as a way out of the government's problems. Combined with the relaxation of credit restrictions which the government had brought in during 1971, this led to a surge in the money supply, with a rise in house prices, bank lending and private indebtedness; it also encouraged the unions to demand pay rises which outstripped the rising inflation. Far from helping the government out of its difficulties, the Barber boom seemed to compound them. The announcement by Heath in the Commons in November 1972 that he was proposing to implement a Prices and Incomes policy was, in the circumstances, inevitable; but it was a 'u-turn' and a politically damaging one to a Prime Minister who was already in a difficult position politically.

In one area, however, the Prime Minister stuck firmly to his beliefs, and enjoyed a great measure of success – and that was the issue of Britain's entry into the Common Market. Heath was, in a manner of speaking, an hereditary 'European': his experiences during the war had left him with an abiding view that Europe should join together in cooperation; and as a minister in Macmillan's government, he had headed up the negotiations; he was firmly convinced that for political, economic and diplomatic reasons, Britain should be part of Europe. He was, however, in a minority in this view. The Labour Party, which in government had espoused the cause of the Common Market had, out of office, reverted to hostility to the idea. This, in itself was significant, given Wilson's shrewd eye for the main chance. Nor could Heath rely on wholehearted support from within his own ranks; in 1970, 44 Conservatives had signed an early day motion opposing Britain's entry into the Common Market.

Heath proved himself an able and ruthless exponent of his own policy. Always inclined to follow a clear lead, many Conservatives were happy to follow the one their new Prime Minister gave. Heath allowed a free vote on the issue, and 284 Conservatives voted for Britain's entry into the Common Market, with only 39 opposing it; among the opponents, only Enoch Powell had any public following or resonance. It would have taken a gift for prophecy to have seen that this one great area of success for Heath would become the battleground for Conservative civil war over the next three decades.

'Europe' was, however, a sole exception to the growing sense that the government had lost its way. Nor was it just on the economy and industrial relations that the government seemed to be creating crises with which it was unable to deal. It was bad luck that Heath's period in office coincided with the deterioration of the situation in Northern Ireland, but the introduction of internment without trial made a bad situation worse. The 'suspension' of Stormont, the Northern Ireland parliament, in 1972, ended the Lloyd George experiment begun 50 years earlier. The attempt by Heath and Whitelaw to find a solution through secret negotiations with the IRA and then a 'power-sharing' Executive in the 1973 Sunningdale agreement alienated Protestant opinion without conciliating the Catholics. The Ulster Unionist Party, riven by internal divisions, severed its long alliance with the Conservative Party. By early 1974 the government seemed deeply embroiled in an Irish crisis which was beyond its powers to solve.

In the retrospective provided by the Thatcher years, the Heath 'u-turns' of 1972 were a seminal disaster from which that government never recovered, as well as something to be avoided at all costs; for this verdict, Heath himself must take some of the blame. If it seems a little paradoxical to blame him for the critique of his successors, the explanation for that lies in the fact that it was his own decision to go to the country in early 1974 which foreshortened the perspective on his achievements, just as it created the aura of failure which attended it.

What stood out at the time was the fact that for all the later beating of breasts, most Conservatives accepted the government's decision to go for a Prices and Incomes policy. It is true that Mrs Thatcher expressed doubts at the time, but she did not press them to the point of resignation, and as for the other Ministers, they were quite prepared to accept anything that kept them in office and offered a chance of success; it was the want of this latter quality which, as with appeasement, doomed it to the massive condescension which history written by the victors always offers. The industrial relations 'crisis' of early 1974 became a political one only because Heath chose to treat it as such; he chose to do so because he thought there were political dividends to be had by so doing; he was wrong, and massively so. If, as he spent the rest of his life arguing, his government had been more successful than many acknowledged, he had only himself to thank for its inglorious ending and the shadow that cast over the whole administration; as Heath found admitting error more difficult than the average Pope, it was little wonder that he gave the impression of going off into a mega-sulk.

Heath's government had been running behind Labour in the opinion polls since February 1971; its economic policies had had to be completely reversed; its wages and prices policy, like its Industrial Relations Act, was not working; inflation and unemployment were rising; the way to entry into the Common Market was now clear, so the Miners' Strike called in November 1973 offered a political opportunity. Heath had an opportunity to reassert himself as a man of action. The National Union of Mineworkers began its overtime ban on 12 November 1973; the following day a 'state of emergency' was declared, with restrictions put on the use of heat and lighting. The NUM's timing was excellent. The Yom Kippur War between Israel and the Arab states had broken out on 6 October, and had led to an immediate shortage of oil, with a consequent hike in prices, as well as inculcating a general atmosphere of gloom; the country needed more coal, and only the miners could provide it. Heath warned the Miners on 22 November that he would not allow the country to be held hostage to their demands; on 13 December he announced that from 31 December the country would be on a 'three day week'. An atmosphere of impending crisis having thus been created, so had an excuse for an early general election.

That is not to say, as James Callaghan is reputed to have said a little later, 'crisis, what crisis?' There clearly was an industrial relations crisis and an economic one; by linking them and claiming that there was a political one, Heath, and those who advised him, were able to gamble that an early election would renew the Conservative mandate and face down the unions; from December 1973 the Conservatives began to prepare for an election, and by January 1974 many of those around Heath were said to be converted to the idea; Heath himself remained uncertain. But the continued failure to find a resolution to the Miners' Strike, and the fact that a lack of coal stocks made a defeat for the government highly likely, helped tip the balance. On 7 February Heath announced there would be a General Election on 28 February.

The truncated period of time allowed for campaigning enabled Heath to underline his sense of urgency and increased the atmosphere of crisis, allowing him to ask 'Who governs the country?' His own answer was, of course, clear; unfortunately for him, too many people felt that any Prime Minister who had to ask that question had forfeited the right to their vote; not the least of Heath's achievements was that he managed to lose an election to the quarrelsome shambles that was Harold Wilson's Labour Party.

Powell, who had bitterly opposed the entry into the Common Market, denounced the decision to hold an election as a fraud on the electorate, declined to stand in the Conservative interest and on the eve of the election told his supporters to vote Labour because of its commitment to withdraw from Europe.[17] The electorate, which was also rather puzzled by the right answer to Heath's question, returned an answer which reflected their uncertainty; for the first time since the 1920s the electoral system failed in its one justification – there was no clear-cut winner.

At first it was not clear that Heath's gamble had failed. Labour had 301 seats compared to 297 for the Conservatives, but the latter had a slight majority of the popular vote, and with an astounding (for this period) 14 Liberals finding their way to the Commons, Heath could (and did) legitimately argue that he should stay on to see if a deal could be cut with the triumphant Liberal leader, Jeremy Thorpe. This was the best chance the Liberals would ever receive to revive their fortunes, but Thorpe's actions in refusing to support the Conservatives proved an earlier Conservative spokesman right when he had called the Liberal Party a 'gigantic wish-fulfilment machine'. If Heath had not lost the support of the Ulster Unionists over his Irish policy, then the Conservatives would have been home and dry, but he had, and he was unable to win the support of the Liberals, so he resigned on 4 March 1974 to be succeeded in Downing Street by Mr Wilson, who solved the problem of the miners by the simple expedient of giving them what they wanted. Wilson hoped for a repeat of 1964 to 1966, when for the second time in the century Britain had another General Election in the same year, but although he gained 18 seats whilst the Conservatives lost 20, it hardly amounted to a ringing endorsement. The fact that Heath went into the second election of 1974 promising to form a 'Government of National Unity' if he won, suggested that even the leader of the Conservatives had lost confidence in his party's ability to govern the country.[18]

If Wilson could not claim any great popular enthusiasm for himself and his policies, Heath was now the proud possessor of the worst record of any Conservative leader since Balfour, who had once commented that although it was not Conservative theory to knife unsuccessful leaders in the back, in practice that was what usually happened; naturally there was speculation on his future. But he possessed great advantages in the support of the party machine and the great majority of the Shadow Cabinet; nothing in his leadership suggested either that he would give it up easily, or that anyone who challenged him for it and failed would have a future in politics. These two considerations, added to fears about the effect which a period of civil war might have in what might prove to be a pre-election period, meant that there was no immediate challenge to Heath.

This did not mean that there was not considerable discontent with Heath. Both his manner and his style remained as abrasive and aloof as ever. These things might have been borne more easily had he delivered the electoral success which would have made them worth bearing, but he did not seem to see things in this way. Moreover, there was the question of just what it was the party now stood for; the gap between rhetoric and practice was now so great that it might be said to have swallowed the government whole. After the failure of February 1974 two of Heath's colleagues, Margaret Thatcher and Sir Keith Joseph, founded the Centre for Policy Studies, a 'think tank' designed to construct – or on the argument offered here, reconstruct – a Conservative policy which would match its rhetoric. The fact that its first director, Alfred Sherman, was an avowed and forceful exponent of economic neo-liberalism was some indication of the direction it would follow. But it was all very well coming up with ideas (although the CPS was designed to supplement rather than to replace the Conservative Research Department),[19] the problem lay where it always had – how were they to be implemented?

Sir Keith Joseph, who was persuaded by Sherman and two other economists, Alan Walters and Peter Bauer, that the Conservatives needed to re-examine their economic policy, argued with Heath in the Shadow Cabinet and, getting nowhere there, he made a series of speeches in which, as well as calling for greater devotion to free market economics, he also criticised the record of the government of which he had been a member. Always a man of intellectual honesty, Sir Keith now admitted that he had been wrong before.[20] Many of the ideas which Joseph espoused had been coming from Powell and from other radical thinkers such as Arthur Seldon and Ralph Harris of the Institute for Economic Affairs, so there was nothing new about them; but what was new was that they were being propounded by a leading member of the Shadow Cabinet along with a critique of the Heath years: the peculiar ingredients that went to make up 'Thatcherism' were being mixed.

The one missing, yet vital ingredient was Mrs Thatcher herself. Because her period in office is still so recent and all the sources for writing about her are touched by the controversies which surround her leadership, it would be difficult to adopt a tone of suitably scholarly objectivity, even if it were not for the fact that the one emotion which Mrs Thatcher never aroused was indifference. Since the present author has been labelled a 'Thatcherite historian',[21] it would be unwise to pretend to rise above the limitations of evidence and circumstances and pronounce in a suitably grand and impartial manner on her claim to be the greatest British Prime Minister of the past half-century; but fortunately, in the context of this study, it is only necessary to assess her contribution to the history of the Conservative Party – and not even her bitterest critics could deny that it has been immense – for good, as well as for ill.

In many ways, Margaret Thatcher was an accidental leader. If a challenge to Heath was needed Joseph was the obvious man to mount it, but Sir Keith lacked both the temperament and the tact necessary to lead the Conservatives; a speech in late 1974 in which he decanted upon the genetic inadequacies produced in the British race by the pro-liferation of babies amongst the lower social orders whose women-folk appeared not to have heard of the contraceptive devices which pre-vented their socially superior sisters from breeding like rabbits, was a little tactlessly phrased, even if it did not warrant the increasingly eccentric Tony Benn's comment that Sir Keith was raising the flag which had flown over Auschwitz. As a Jew himself, Sir Keith was entitled to take this as badly as the 'left' had his own speech, but the whole episode showed how useless he would be as leader; and, unlike most politicians, he was prepared to admit as much to himself and to others. The problem for the anti-Heath lobby was that there seemed to be no alternative. Only someone from the Shadow Cabinet would have suffi-cient weight to make a credible challenge, and they were all well aware that, in the event of Heath winning, they would suffer Powell's fate. It was an opportunity which would be taken only by someone of excep-tional courage – who did not mind risking the consignment of his (or her) career to the scrap-heap. Afterwards it would be easy to under-estimate the risk – but at the time Margaret Thatcher's decision to force a leadership contest was extremely courageous.

Although Mrs Thatcher had been uncomfortable with the infamous 'u-turn', she had not, as she later acknowledged, taken her views to the point of resignation or open opposition; but in a sense that made her all the more representative of the main body of Conservative opinion, for she, like others, had come to feel that Sir Keith was right to have con-cluded that the government had made massive mistakes, and that, what-ever justification Heath had claimed for his actions, they had none the less done 'huge harm to the Conservative Party and to the country'.[22] For all the later claims to radicalism, Thatcherism began as a reac-tionary movement. It was a reaction against the lessons of 1970 to 1974, and against the defeats of the latter year; it was a reaction *back* to the spirit which had inspired 'Selsdon Man' and against the drift back towards the so-called 'middle way'; it was also a reaction against the humiliation which the Conservatives, and the nation, were suffering under the Wilson administration. Within the party her candidature represented a chance to protest against Heath's policy of 'more of the same'.

Because it was easy to underestimate her, and her opponents were used to taking the line of least resistance, the Heath camp did not take her challenge very seriously – something her advisers were quite happy to see continue. For all her commitment to the economic theories of monetarism, it was the fact that she was not 'Ted' and offered an alternative to his increasingly petulant manner which attracted votes to her. It must be concluded that in 1975, as on so many later occasions, people voted for her because of her opponents as much as they did because of the content of her policy; but they did so in part because of the manner in which she propagated her views. To her opponents, particularly those in Heath's camp, she seemed a rather strident middle-class housewife whose cocksure views smacked of the simplistic; but to a party suffering from indecision and lack of direction, she was a morale-booster – even as she would be later for a nation suffering from the same symptoms.

Despite some rather underhand tactics on the part of her opponents, and the fact of her sex, the Conservative Party once again proved capable of surprising itself and the nation by making a radical choice. On 4 February 1975 the first ballot was held. Mrs Thatcher, to her own amazement, had come top of the poll, with 130 votes to Heath's 119; Hugh Fraser, who had decided to stand to offer a choice of the middle ground, suffered the fate of armadillos all over the world who occupy the middle of the road – he was firmly squashed, receiving only 16 votes. Under the leadership election rules this meant that there would have to be a second ballot since she was 31 votes away from the majority needed to win outright; but it was the end of Heath's leadership. With his resignation, other Shadow Cabinet colleagues felt free to enter the fray, including the former chief Whip, Willie Whitelaw, who was the quintessential 'Establishment' figure. Many commentators expected the immensely experienced and conciliatory Whitelaw to win the contest, but Mrs Thatcher had behind her the momentum from the first round – and the feeling that since she had had the guts (although another anatomical metaphor was more often employed) to challenge 'Ted' she should reap her reward. Her campaign manager, Airey Neave, had already proved an assiduous cultivator of backbench opinion, more than making up for the fact that her sex effectively debarred her from the smoking room and bars of the Commons. In the final ballot 146 MPs voted for Mrs Thatcher, 76 for Whitelaw, whilst the other three candidates obtained 50 votes between them. For the first time in British history a woman had become the leader of one of the major British political parties – and as usual it was the Conservatives who had broken the mould.

14 The Iron Lady

A distinction should be drawn between the philosophical and political roots of what became known as Thatcherism. Mrs Thatcher is the only British politician of the twentieth century to have had her name enshrined in an ideology, and because of this and her combative character it was easy for her critics to call her an ideologue; this is to miss the main point of naming a creed after the woman – which was that it was closely bound up with her personality. Hayek, Friedman and the Institute of Economic Affairs simply gave 'substance and intellectual respectability to her beliefs and instincts, but most of these derive from her own experience and her idea of what is commonsense.'[1] When she told the Party Conference in 1975 that 'the economy had gone wrong because something had gone wrong spiritually and philosophically', she was expressing her deepest feelings and those of millions who could identify with what she was saying; if Sir Keith told her that monetarism could help deal with this situation, all well and good. The personal nature of Thatcherism helps explain some of its contradictions. She passionately believed in getting the state off peoples' backs, just as she disdained statist solutions to political problems – she loathed the 'nanny state', yet she was one of nature's 'nannies', passionately believing that she knew how to save the country she loved; not surprisingly this created tension between instinct and action. This would have existed in any case – the frontiers of the state cannot be rolled back except by action from the centre – but it was made more acute by Mrs Thatcher's personality. At the time of her selection as leader and during the ensuing years of opposition, as during the election campaign of 1979, her personality was an issue; it was one her opponents hoped to exploit, and one which many of her colleagues feared might yet hand Labour a victory: but without Margaret Thatcher there would have been no 'Thatcherism'.

To her many enemies, Mrs. Thatcher was 'that woman', and even decades after her retirement to praise her is to raise the hackles of liberals of a certain age; for such folk she was a corrosive force in public life, presiding over the de-industrialisation of Britain, mass unemployment, and cuts in public expenditure, whilst encouraging a 'greed is good' mentality which led to massive disparities in wealth. To her admirers, she inherited a country which was drifting to the rocks, riven by crises and in terminal decline, and she 'made Britain great' again.

Neither verdict is totally inaccurate; both are partisan to the point at which they simply muddy the water.

Her leadership passed through three phases. The morning, which was overcast and clouded; she made a bad leader of the Opposition, and most expected her to fail; these doubts persisted until at least the Falklands War in 1983. The second phase – high noon – saw her at the height of her power. She was the 'Warrior Queen' of the Falklands, the woman who finally outfaced the militants in the National Union of Miners, and the leader who invented 'privatisation'. It was during this period, 1983–87 that she acquired that 'aura of indomitable resolution' which will be forever associated with her. She was 'brilliant at badgering, twisting and cajoling' her party into supporting her government.[2] There were problems and scandals, but somehow she survived them – sometimes only just; but at the height of her power it could be written that 'she has gone blithely on her way, rewriting the conventions of British government and inventing as she goes – by opportunity out of instinct crossed with dogma.'[3] But after 1987 the shadows began to gather, and when the night came, it was with a swiftness no one could predict, and her fall, like her rise, was dramatic and the result of a chance concatenation of circumstance; but it was to be marked by a sunset which none who witnessed it would ever forget.

During the clouded morning of her leadership, no one could have predicted such a dénouement. Heath's refusal to serve under her, which was followed by a few of his lieutenants, gave Mrs Thatcher some room for manoeuvre when she constructed her team, but she was still hardly able to imitate him and create a Shadow Cabinet in her own image. The loyalty shown to her by Whitelaw was of inestimable value, and when she later unwittingly gave rise to some ribald hilarity by remarking that 'every Cabinet should have a Willie', she was actually only expressing her appreciation of the part he played in her success. By acting as her faithful lieutenant he not only warded off the possibility of any immediate assault on her position, but he also offered a line of communication with the party's grandees; he had not been Chief Whip for nothing. Joseph was left in charge of policy development, but for the rest her appointments show what Patrick Cosgrave has described as her sense of lacking 'legitimacy' – 'the feeling that she was not wholly in control of events.'[4] A description which Angus Maude used of the party as a whole certainly applied both to this team and her first administration; it contained

within itself, perfectly preserved and visible like the contents of archaeological strata, specimens from all its historical stages and of all its acquisitions from the Liberals.[5]

There were the 'Whigs' (Carrington and Soames), the 'Disraelians' (Gilmour, Prior and Maudling), the state collectivists (Heseltine and Prior) and even some economic neo-liberals (Thatcher, Joseph and Howe). As Maude noted of the party, 'the juxtaposition of seeming incompatibles generates tension'.

Mrs Thatcher was even less willing than most politicians to acknowledge her mistakes (she could always rely upon a host of critics to point them out, so why bother herself?), but even she could hardly not admit that appointing Maudling as Shadow Foreign Secretary was a bad move. His views, especially on the Soviet Union and the need for détente, were very different from her own. The appointment of Sir Ian Gilmour as Shadow Home Secretary was another sop to her opponents. It would take her some time to discover that the appetite of the liberal Conservatives for sops was limitless; and even longer to realise that her tact in appointing them was taken as a sign that she could not dispense with their help. Other 'Heathmen' such as Michael Heseltine (Industry) and Lord Carrington (leader in the Lords) were also kept on, as was Jim Prior (one of the defeated leadership candidates) at Employment. These were, on the whole, men seared by the experience of the Heath government, and of most of them it could be said that 'once bitten is twice shy'. The only member of the Shadow team other than Joseph who actually took her line on economic policy was Geoffrey Howe but, as he was another of the defeated opponents for the leadership, relations were not particularly close at this time. It was an uneasy amalgam. If Mrs Thatcher sounded shrill at times it was hardly surprising: she did not even command a majority in her own Shadow Cabinet. She had intended to embark upon a 'crusade'; instead, she found herself having endless debates with members of her own team.

This helps underline the point that Thatcherism must be understood as having political as well as intellectual roots. The animus which was later shown towards those Conservatives who had upheld the consensus derives from the fight with representatives of this tradition between 1975 and 1981 as much as it does from the intellectual disagreement with the components of the consensus. The wariness in action which contrasted with the boldness of the rhetoric also owed its origin to this period, when she was not even mistress in her own house and had to tread with caution. She was an 'outsider' in a way none of her predecessors, with the possible exception of Disraeli, had been. Nigel Lawson wrote of her that 'more than any other Prime Minister [she] was unafraid of controversy, and generally devoid of the instincts and thought processes of the establishment'.[6] Mrs Thatcher had no inside knowledge of what she called 'machine politics' and few enough supporters amongst the party's grandees. As a woman she did not have the easy bonhomie which comes to some from time spent at the bar or in the smoking room of the Commons. (Heath, of course, did not have this either, but it was his own personality, not his sex, which precluded him from it.) It was a shrewd move on her part to resurrect the career of Peter Thorneycroft by making him Party Chairman, not least because it provided her with access to the legendary resignations of 1958 as a reference point for her own desire to curb public expenditure. She knew that, unlike Heath, she would get just one chance at becoming Prime Minister and that her first General Election as leader would be her last in that position – if she failed, the 'Heathmen' would be back, made more complacent than ever by her failure. She did not intend to fail.

She was often accused of arrogance, but there was nothing of that about her decision to work on her own public image. She was aware that her voice, like that of many women who struggle to make themselves heard over the rowdiness in the Commons, had a tendency to shrillness, and despite the taunts she would receive, she took elocution lessons to teach her how to lower her voice and project it without strain – something that was of vital importance to someone who would have to put across her message in hundreds of speeches over the next few years. Unlike her male colleagues, she also had to worry about her clothing. Macmillan could appear to own only two ties, Old Etonian and Guards', and he could turn up in slightly shabby pin-stripe suits, and Heath could appear for ever in the same grey suit, but women are judged by different standards. Labour's Barbara Castle had shown how important it could be for a female minister to be well turned-out, and Mrs Thatcher followed suit. As Minister for Education she had gone in for the usual costume of 'Tory women with hats', but gradually, as leader, she modified her hairstyle, adopting a softer look which went down well on television; she also took infinite care with her clothes, wearing colours which would look good on the public platform and on television. But not all the PR man's wiles could prevent the combative Margaret Thatcher from showing through – to the delight of her opponents.

This made her particularly vulnerable to the experienced Labour leaders she faced. It was true that in response to Wilson's attempts to patronise her she was able to respond: 'What the Prime Minister means is that he has been around a long time – and is beginning to show it', but as with Home's 'fourteenth Mr Wilson', this was an isolated success. Callaghan's avuncular cynicism she found particularly infuriating; here was a man who was presiding over the IMF dictating his economic policies and who, after 1976, survived only by virtue of a pact with the Liberals, yet he carried on as though nothing was wrong. Callaghan 'got to' her, and she consistently lagged behind him in public popularity. Nor was her position helped by interventions from Heath and Prior which revealed dissension over something as fundamental as whether the next Conservative government would have an incomes policy. Like Churchill in 1945, Margaret Thatcher was hampered by the legacy of predecessors whom she sought to disavow. The problem was that she lacked experience – and it showed.

This was a defect which only time could rectify, and Mrs Thatcher could only keep pounding away with the message that Labour rule was not something anyone would want to experience for longer than possible. But it proved difficult for her to make much of a dent in Callaghan's complacency. She made more of a mark with her pronouncements on foreign policy. Mrs Thatcher was deeply disturbed by the decline in Britain's reputation abroad, particularly in America, whose help she continued to regard as essential if the 'free world' was to win the struggle against Communism. This last conviction made her something of an oddity in an era of détente when America, traumatised by Vietnam and Watergate, seemed to lack the self-confidence to contain Communism. Her views on Communism, as on so much else, were not those held by 'men of experience' at the top of British politics. Her uncompromising language about the Communist menace caused a breach between her and Maudling, whom she sacked in November 1976. The Soviet propaganda machine labelled her 'the Iron Lady', a sobriquet she revelled in – again to the unease of some of her own colleagues.[7]

Commentators tend to agree that she was not a successful leader of the Opposition; on the other hand she won the 1979 General Election, so it would be perverse to call her a failure. The fact is, as every Conservative leader since John Major has rediscovered, being in Opposition is a miserable business; whatever you do, you have to rely on the government of the day to lose the election; fortunately for her, that was the one thing she could rely on. The anti-Thatcher press did its best to portray her as far too right-wing and to appeal to the electorate to stick with good old 'Uncle Jim'; as the *Sunday Mirror's* cartoonist put it under a picture of Callaghan: 'if you must have a Conservative Prime Minister, I'm your man.'[8] As so often, the cartoonist caught an important truth about the election: that it was the Conservative leader who was offering a 'real change'. As she told Callaghan's constituents in her first major election speech, she was 'a conviction politician'. Nor did she shy away from language that other politicians could and would never have used:

> The Old Testament prophets didn't merely say: 'Brothers, I want a consensus.' They said: 'This is my faith and vision. This is what I passionately believe. If you believe it too, then come with me.' Tonight I say to you just that. Away with the recent bleak and dismal past.[9]

It was perhaps not surprising that Peter Thorneycroft should have suggested during the campaign that they should get Heath to make a broadcast to reassure the electorate – nor that Mrs Thatcher should have rejected the proposal with contumely.

For all Labour's hopes that 'she' would make some appalling gaffe, the fact was that Mrs Thatcher's harder line was more acceptable than it would have been a year before – something revealed by the contrast between Conservative proposals on trades unions in 1978 and 1979. In 1978, in deference to Prior's wishes and fears, the Conservatives had held back from proposing legislation which would impose strike ballots; by 1979 Mrs Thatcher was able to get this reinstated. What had changed was the public perception of the unions, and this was caused by the wave of strikes known as the 'winter of discontent'. Callaghan had refused to go the country in the autumn of 1978 and had consequently missed his best opportunity of winning. The events of the winter revealed that Callaghan could not control the unions, nor even influence them. There was no need to ask Heath's 1974 question – it was obvious who ruled the country. Callaghan's own carefully cultivated image of unflappability *à la* Macmillan failed him when, on returning from a conference in Guadeloupe, he was reported to have said 'Crisis, what crisis?' He may never have uttered the immortal words, but they seemed to sum up his mood. Thus, when Mrs Thatcher was able to force an election after the government lost a vote of confidence in March 1979, the scene was set for her to offer an alternative.

It was later to become fashionable to point out that 1979 did not mark some great turning-point in British political history. This is a highly debatable point, and will no doubt carry on being so, but what cannot be doubted was the impact of Mrs Thatcher's triumph on the Conservative Party. Those who wish to argue that the change has been exaggerated can cite the election statistics. The turn-out was slightly higher than in October 1974 (76 per cent compared with 72.8) which explains why, although Labour increased its number of votes by a few thousand, its share of the poll dropped from 39.2 to 37 per cent, its lowest since 1931. The Conservatives, by contrast, failed to scale even the far-from-dizzy heights of 1970. Where Heath had won 46.4 per cent of the electorate, Mrs Thatcher gained 43.9 per cent.[10] Even if the oft-heard cries of her critics that more than half of the electorate had not voted for her are disregarded on the ground that no Prime Minister in the post-war era has ever won 50 per cent of the vote, it could be argued that it is still hard to interpret the result as a decisive endorsement of Mrs Thatcher. On the other hand, the swing from Labour to the Conservatives was the largest in any election since 1945, and the fact that this did not show up more dramatically in the result was due to the uneven nature of that swing – it was much larger in the English South, South-West and South-East than anywhere else. In this sense, from the very start, Mrs Thatcher's Government rested principally upon English support.[11]

It is also true that her administration was, like her Shadow Cabinet, less radical than her rhetoric – something her admirers have called attention to by labelling her first 12 months in power 'the wasted year'.[12] The leader who had declared that she could not 'waste time' having arguments inside her Cabinet spent a good deal of time doing just that. She was also bound by election pledges to respect the finding of the Clegg Commission on pay levels, which meant that she presided over an immediate increase in public spending – which was not quite what she had come into power to do. Even after her great victory, with a majority of 43 seats over all other parties, she was still beset by the insecurities which had hobbled her in Opposition. Gilmour, like other members of her Cabinet, did not think that she or her policies would last, and there was some quiet betting on when she would perform her 'u-turn'. Few doubted that, like Heath and Callaghan before her, she would have to give way to the power of the unions; the only questions appeared to be 'when and how?'[13] Enoch Powell once observed of her that 'When she trusts her instincts she's almost always right. When she stops to think she's all too often wrong.'[14] She had something of the same feeling herself, but for the first year she perhaps spent too much time thinking and not enough time listening to her gut instincts. She knew 'instinctively' that 'despite the siren voices advising her to adopt less radical policies she was not elected to head a government exactly like those of her predecessors', but she frequently found herself fighting not just her own corner 'but all four corners simultaneously'. In her first major interview as Prime Minister she hotly denied that she had or would indulge in 'u-turns', proclaiming: 'I've not seen these u-turns yet. I'm going to set my face firmly into the future and that way I go.'[15]

Whoever had won the election, certain things would have remained constant. On the positive side the advent of North Sea Oil would have provided an economic cushion for any government, whilst the reaction against statism which was apparent in other European countries and in America after 1980 would probably have ensured that even a Labour administration would have continued along the path taken by Healey and Callaghan. There would also have been a problem with maintaining 'full employment' as the numbers entering the job market would have risen sharply even if more women than ever before had not entered the workforce. This would have involved an increase in social spending, as would the rise in the number of the elderly and the increasing costs of hospital treatment. Labour had already begun to react to some of these developments in the way Mrs Thatcher would, by trying to curb public spending where possible (funding for council housing and higher education received sharp cuts, and for the first time 'real' spending on the NHS went down). Even one of the most dramatic measures in Sir Geoffrey Howe's first budget, the lowering of the standard rate of income tax to 30 per cent, had been promised in Labour's manifesto.[16] So what difference did Mrs Thatcher make?

If Conservatism had always been 'what Conservative leaders do', then it is more than usually necessary to concentrate on the Prime Minister rather than the 'ism' which bears her name. It has become the fashion to accentuate the advantages just listed in explanation of Mrs Thatcher's successes, which is one way of downplaying her role, but during the years 1980 to 1981, and again in 1982, she was hit by a series of political storms which were expected to throw her off course quite as decisively as they had 'Selsdon Man'. The difference Mrs Thatcher made was that the government held to its objectives.

Some of the problems which beset her were her own fault. Howe's first budget was, as predicted, based on monetarist principles. The standard rate of tax went down to 30 per cent and exchange controls were abolished; more controversially the VAT rate was raised to 15 per cent, with a consequent effect upon the cost of living and the rate of inflation. Unfortunately, the scope for making the sort of cuts in public expenditure which would have made up for the shortfall in revenue was limited: Labour had already made commitments which could not be scrapped in the middle of the financial year; and Mrs Thatcher herself had pledged to implement in full the recommendations of the Clegg Commission on public service pay. On top of this, the end of the year saw another massive hike in oil prices. By the summer of 1980 inflation, which she had promised to bring under control, was running at 22 per cent and unemployment, over which Labour had been taunted, rose to nearly three million. Sterling was running at $2.40 to the pound, which had a devastating effect on British manufacturing industry; even the giant chemical business, ICI, returned its first ever quarterly loss – thousands of smaller firms went to the wall. To critics, the Thatcher/Howe insistence on carrying through their monetarist experiment in the face of a world recession made an already bad situation worse;[17] to which her defence was that since much of British industry was overmanned and inefficient, what occurred was a gigantic clearing out which prepared the way for the growth of newer service industries;[18] in fact there was something to be said for both explanations.

Some of the problems were ones she inherited. Rhodesia had dragged on as an embarrassment to both political parties in Britain; indeed, just before the election Mrs Thatcher had felt obliged to sack two junior members of the team, Sir John Biggs-Davison and Winston Churchill junior, for voting against the continuation of sanctions on the regime of Ian Smith. There were many who expected the most right-wing Conservative leader in living memory to soft-pedal on the issue. But persuaded by her Foreign Secretary Lord Carrington that a settlement was possible, she ended up delivering one which resulted in the creation of Zimbabwe under black majority rule, with the Marxist former rebel Robert Mugabe as Prime Minister. It was, many Conservatives thought, a 'rum do', and not what had been expected; but the problem was out of the way, and that was what seemed to matter most to British politicians.

The other inherited problem which caused her difficulties was one from which she was able, thanks to her determination, to extract rather more credit from her supporters on the right – and that was the question of Britain's contribution to the Common Market's budget. Mrs Thatcher had played a minor part in the 1975 Referendum campaign, although she had campaigned for a 'yes' vote; but she was well aware that the question of Britain's relations with Europe remained a vexed issue in the party. For the old 'Heathmen', Britain's membership was an act of almost quasi-mystical faith, and squabbling over little things like money was seen as not only rather vulgar, but as a distraction from the main point – which was to unite Western Europe. From the very start of her administration, Margaret Thatcher took a different view. In her first major interview as Prime Minister she made it plain that since 'we are having to make public expenditure economies', the European budget would have to take its share. Her tone shocked those used to the more diplomatic style of her predecessors: 'We have just got to', she declared, 'We are not supplicants to the Common Market. We are not asking them for anything. We are the Common Market's biggest benefactor.'[19] It was an approach which won her popularity in sections of her party and from newspapers such as the Sun, for whom 'Maggie's' habit of 'handbagging the Frogs' would become almost an annual celebration. There was here, and in her outspoken support for the hard anti-Soviet line pursued by the new American President, Ronald Reagan, something which Conservatives had not heard for years – the voice of British nationalism. If her pro-Americanism marked something of a return to the post-war consensual position, then it was the only one of her actions which did.

By the 1980 Budget, it was clear that two of the main planks of the consensus had been abandoned. The 'pretence that full employment and economic growth were the gift of the Government' was abandoned, and no yardsticks for either employment or output were set.[20] Another of the fundamental tenets of consensual Conservatism, the desire to appease the trades unions, was also discarded – although this was not at first attended by any great signs of success. A 13-week strike by the steel workers led to their demands being conceded, whilst similar results attended a drawn-out strike by civil servants; so much, it seemed, for Mrs Thatcher's confrontational style.

By the autumn of 1980, the Thatcher government was in serious political trouble. Inflation was rising, as was unemployment; far from being under control, the money supply was rising by 18 per cent; the appreciation of sterling was pricing British products out of overseas markets; respected economists were predicting that the recession would turn into a slump; the Prime Minister's own opinion poll ratings had already slumped. Reluctantly convinced that the monetary targets being set were worsening the situation, Mrs. Thatcher allowed them to be modified in the 1981 budget; she also agreed to a reduction in the minimum lending rate in November, which threw a much-needed lifeline to those businesses surviving the hurricane. Monetarism quietly faded away; its defenders claimed that it had dealt a death blow to the inflationary pressures in the economy; in so far as these could be identified with wages demands that was true to an extent; the unemployed did not demand pay rises. Mrs Thatcher's critics claimed that the distinction between monetarism and old-fashioned deflation was indistinguishable.

During the torrid summer of 1980, the press was filled with rumours that Mrs Thatcher was heading for a repeat of Heath's *annus horribilis* of 1972. The so-called 'wets' in her own party were openly talking of the need to get back to the 'middle ground', and the split inside the Labour Party which led to the formation of the Social Democratic Party stimulated speculation about 'breaking the mould' of British politics with a realignment which would leave the left-wing Labour faction under Callaghan's successor, Michael Foot, isolated on one margin, and Mrs Thatcher's brand of right-wing Conservatism in the same position on the other; a 'centre government' composed of the likes of Roy

Jenkins, David Owen, Shirley Williams, Sir Ian Gilmour, Jim Prior and the 'Heathmen', was mooted: a reverse version of a 'government of all the talents'. Mrs Thatcher's response to this heated frenzy in the press and the corridors of parliament was characteristic, right down to its manner of expression. She told the Party Conference on 10 October 1980:

> To those waiting with bated breath for that favourite media catch-phrase, the 'U-turn', I have only one thing to say. 'You turn if you want to. The Lady's not for turning.'[21]

The key moment for Mrs Thatcher came with Howe's third budget in 1981, which showed, decisively that there would be no 'u-turn'. What her critics always missed about Mrs Thatcher was that she was a practical politician and not (appearances notwithstanding) an ideologue. Monetarism was attractive to her because it seemed to offer a straightforward way of controlling inflation, which was part of the key to her real objective – the creation of an 'enterprise' Britain in which the government would not spend half the national income on propping up nationalised industries, handing out inflationary pay rises to over mighty unions, or trying to control prices and incomes. Howe's budget continued the deflationary policy, cutting the rate (although not the growth) of public expenditure and imposing new taxes. The 'Wets' were horrified, prophesying that it would bring about a slump; the Thatcherites proclaimed their determination to push ahead. In retrospect it can be seen as the point at which the economic recovery began. Politically, its significance lay in the fact that for all their contemporary grumbling and later criticisms, men like Gilmour and Prior signally failed to resign; for the moment at least, the Lady had survived.

But survival was not the same as succeeding, and it is some mark of the darkness of the situation for Mrs Thatcher that at the time the difference seemed immaterial. Her poll ratings remained abysmally low; indeed, no Prime Minister was to match them until John Major's ill-fated 'Black Wednesday'; salvation came from two directions: the Labour Party and Argentina.

Mrs Thatcher was always fortunate in her enemies. The election of Michael Foot as Labour leader in 1980 had provided her with an almost perfect foil. A bookish rhetoritician with a shock of uncontrollable white hair, he looked and sounded what he was – a Hampstead socialist who would only have recognised the ordinary working man if he was wearing a cloth cap and drinking a 'pint'. Mrs Thatcher, who was still developing as a Commons performer, regularly trounced him at Prime

Minister's Question Time, and he proved equally incapable of giving a lead to his own followers outside the House. Within the Labour Party an unpleasant civil war was breaking out between those, like the left-wing figurehead, Tony Benn, who argued that the moment for socialist action was dawning, and the more moderate figures such as Denis Healey, who argued that Labour had to show itself as fit to govern in order to save the country from what he called 'sado-monetarism'. At the end of March the Labour Party split, with four former Cabinet Ministers, David Owen, Shirley Williams, Roy Jenkins and William Rodgers, breaking away to form what they called the Social Democratic Party. In July Jenkins, newly returned from Brussels where he had been president of the European Commission, came within 2000 votes of taking the safe Labour seat of Warrington; for the next two general elections the left of centre vote would split three ways – to the great advantage of the Conservative Party. As though that was not enough of a political gift, Mrs Thatcher also benefited from events on the other side of the world.

Despite somewhat over-ingenious attempts to argue otherwise, it is commonly accepted that what saved Mrs Thatcher's bacon was the fact that she showed her usual resolution and courage during the crisis precipitated by the Argentinean invasion of the Falkland Islands in early 1982. It may well be the case that, with the onset of the economic recovery and the failure of the Opposition to make any headway, the reputation and popularity of the government were recovering slowly in any case, but it takes a political scientist to argue that the effect noted by all contemporaries of the Falklands episode was an illusion.[22] Plain historians tend to prefer the more usual version of events – that Mrs Thatcher's seemingly unstoppable momentum gathered pace during this period.

Once more she showed her talent for not doing what the 'Establishment' advised her – not least because it was following that advice which had helped bring about the crisis. Again one is reminded of Enoch Powell's comments about the difference in her performance when she listened to her own instincts; she certainly did on this occasion. The Foreign Office, with what she later called 'the flexibility of principle characteristic of that department',[23] pointed out the multifarious and serious obstacles in the way of her idea of sending a Task Force 7000 miles into the South Atlantic to retake a group of islands which most people in Britain had never heard of. She disregarded this as reminiscent of 'appeasement' and announced during the emergency debate in the Commons on Saturday 3 May (the first Saturday sitting since Suez) that a Task Force was being immediately despatched.

It was, once again, Enoch Powell who correctly summarised the position she was in. Referring to her sobriquet as the 'Iron Lady', he said that 'in the next week or two this House, the nation and the Rt Hon. Lady herself will learn of what metal she is made'. It was certainly an extraordinary risk, but the performance of the British armed forces more than justified it. After the war was over Powell rose in the House to announce the 'result' of the tests on 'the metal'. It was, he said, 'ferrous matter of the highest quality ... of exceptional tensile strength, is highly resistant to wear and tear and to stress, and may be used to advantage to all national purposes';[24] coming from the source it did, this was the highest possible compliment. It was also a defining moment in the Thatcher legend.

Even before the Falklands, she had begun to deal with the 'wets' in her Cabinet. In January 1981 the indiscreet Norman St John Stevas, whose witty descriptions of his 'leaderene' had failed to endear him to her, left the government, and an MP called Norman Tebbit came into a junior post under Joseph at Trade and Industry; the first was a warning to the other 'wets'; the significance of the last appointment would only become apparent later. But the dissenters did not heed the message, and after urban riots in the Toxteth area of Liverpool in Julyl,[25] they made a play for more public spending and for the introduction of an incomes policy. Francis Pym, who as Paymaster-General was in charge of the presentation of the government's policy, made gloomy noises about the slow pace of any recovery and talked about the need for 'partnership' with the unions, whilst the Party Chairman, Thorneycroft, dilated on the shortcomings of monetarism. This time she acted. The gloomier and 'wetter' members of her team, Lord Soames and Sir Ian Gilmour, were sacked outright, whilst Prior, who had been a block on union reform, had his bluff called. He had been making noises in the press about refusing to be moved, but faced with the stark alternative of Northern Ireland or nothing, he went to Belfast; in his place came the formidable figure of Norman Tebbit. The 'Chingford skinhead' as he was, not always wholly affectionately, known, symbolised the upwardly mobile upper-working-class types who were immensely attracted by Mrs Thatcher's determination and her message that individual enterprise should be rewarded. Tebbit was to become the hero of 'Essex man' (and woman), and for a while, he seemed to be a genuine possibility as a successor to the 'Iron Lady'. Equally symbolic, but in a different way, was the promotion of the neo-liberal economic journalist, Nigel Lawson, to the Department of Energy. As a 'true believer' in the economics of Thatcherism, he would be, along with Tebbit, a valuable ally in Cabinet. Thorneycroft was removed as Party Chairman, to be replaced with another Thatcherite loyalist, Cecil Parkinson, another upwardly mobile figure, although rather smoother in manner than Tebbit.

If the roots of the economic recovery lay before the Falklands, then so did those of the government's own recovery, but what the incident did was to boost Mrs Thatcher's personal rating to a level it was not to lose for many years. She had shown her ability to 'summon the troops to the battle and divert them from internal dissension', which would keep her going as party leader for long; 'she could turn a glum afternoon in the Commons into St Crispin's Day at Agincourt'.[26] For all the hatred she aroused from intellectuals and university lecturers, she became the darling of the *Sun* and its massive readership. Since 1956 Britain had been in retreat on the world stage, now she had reasserted national pride; Britain's name once more stood proud in the eyes of the world. It was a reaction which seemed to puzzle her critics, who cavilled at the cost and argued about the necessity of the enterprise; the difference between her reaction and theirs shows why she won three elections and they remained on the side-lines.

It was the Falklands which firmly established Mrs Thatcher and her lieutenants as the directing force in the Conservative Party; henceforth the 'wets' would be, on the whole, ineffectual critics marginalised within their own party. Pym, the last remaining figure of substance from the band, hoped that the 1983 election would not bring an increased majority for Mrs Thatcher, and when it did he found himself sacked from the Foreign Office. She had intended to replace him with Cecil Parkinson, whose performance as Party Chairman before and during the election had greatly enhanced his reputation, but complications in his private life prevented this and so Sir Geoffrey Howe went there instead.

Mrs Thatcher was helped, as she so often was during this and later periods, by the activities of what ought to have been the opposition. The divided ranks of Labour, SDP and Liberals appeared unsure whether they were fighting each other or the Tories, and Labour's 1983 election manifesto was crisply summarised as 'the longest suicide note in history'. With the left dominant within the party, Labour offered the electorate a large dose of socialism and old-style corporatism. With their electoral base in the old historic working-class culture already under long-term erosion from the effects of affluence, and with the country becoming used to the Thatcherite line that governments could not be expected to solve everything, Labour gambled on the old certainty that a high level of unemployment would finish off the Tories – and lost.

Mrs Thatcher was able to stigmatise Labour as being at the behest of every 'loony left' pressure group in the country, and its pacifistic anti-nuclear missile defence policy was hardly going to attract the 'floating' voter. For once no one could argue that Labour had 'won' the campaign, and its defeat was decisive. With just 27.6 per cent of the poll, Labour's share was at its lowest since 1918, and only the peculiarities of the electoral system and Labour's strength in the North of England prevented a wipe-out; the SDP-Liberal Alliance, with 26 per cent of the vote, got 23 seats compared to Labour's 209. Mrs Thatcher, with 42.9 per cent of the vote, had 397 seats – a larger number than any Conservative Prime Minister since Baldwin in 1924; she also became the first Premier since Eden to increase her majority at a general election. The trends visible in 1979 had accentuated, with the Conservatives doing badly on Merseyside and in the North of Great Britain generally; the South of England, by contrast, seemed to be a sea of almost unbroken blue on the maps of the television pundits. If 'Thatcherism' existed, the years after 1983 would allow its lineaments to become more discernible.

Back in 1980, Nigel Lawson, who now became Chancellor of the Exchequer, had said that what was 'new' about the 'new Conservatism' was that it had

> embarked on the task – it is not an easy one: nothing worthwhile in politics is; but at least it runs with rather than against the grain of human nature – of re-educating the people in some old truths. They are no less true for being old.[27]

The combination of economic liberalism with a rather strident nationalism was proving a popular one, especially when presented by a Prime Minister who wove a moral message into both strands. Mrs Thatcher had not made a 'u-turn'. She believed that her economic polices were necessary to produce the sort of society she wanted. She was equally determined not to lose momentum in dismantling what was left of the consensus after her victory.

15 High Tide and After

The Conservative manifesto for the 1983 election has been described as 'one of the thinnest on record', and it soon became the received wisdom that the want of radical proposals meant that the first and second sessions of the new parliament were partially wasted;[1] such verdicts reflect the expectation which Mrs Thatcher had created rather than an accurate verdict upon the government's performance. The legislative achievement would have astonished earlier generations of Conservatives who had thought that their creed was more to do with *not* adding to the Statute book. But the majority of the measures passed were to do with dismantling the structures of the consensus; the same might be said of the major confrontation of this period, the facing down of the miners' strike. Commentators who thought that the privatisation of British Telecom, British Gas, the British Airport Authorities, the Naval Dockyards and the Royal Ordnance Factories, plus the abolition of the Greater London and other Metropolitan Councils, along with legislation which made union ballots for leadership elections compulsory, were insufficiently radical, clearly harboured unrealistic expectations. Yet the disappointment does catch something of what may be the eventual verdict upon Mrs Thatcher's second administration – that, for all its energy and activity, it seemed to lose its way. For this there were two main reasons: the nature of some of the legislation; and problems of a more human kind.

The privatisations proved immensely popular (except with Labour), but the legislation on the unions and the abolition of the GLC were highly controversial and the latter in particular involved the government in a long and bruising campaign. The GLC leader, Ken Livingstone, was not alone in finding it odd that a Conservative government was abolishing local authorities and taking more power into its own hands. The review of the social services, from which much was expected, turned out to be a damp squib, with savings proving difficult to make. Indeed, across the range of government activities, particularly with the Defence budget being maintained, it proved far more difficult to reduce public expenditure than Mrs Thatcher and her admirers had imagined. The economic growth of these years enabled government spending to become a smaller proportion of a larger GNP, but the vaunted cuts did not happen; as some disgruntled Thatcherites complained; she really had meant it when she had said before the election that the 'Health Service is safe in our hands'. She was always less of a Thatcherite than some of her admirers.

There were also problems of a more personal kind. The public revelation on the eve of the Party Conference that the new Industry Secretary, Cecil Parkinson, had been carrying on a long-running affair and that his mistress was pregnant, not unnaturally created cries for him to resign. Thatcherism was as conservative in its social attitudes as it was liberal in its economic ones, and for a party which espoused 'family values', the 'Parkinson scandal' was a major public embarrassment. Mrs Thatcher, who actually took a more tolerant view of such matters than her critics might have expected, hardly helped matters, since her attempt to persuade her friend to stay simply ensured that the whole matter dragged on. Parkinson was replaced by Norman Tebbit at the important post of Trade and Industry, but no sooner had the new minister mastered his department than he was removed from it by an event which also came close to terminating Mrs Thatcher's life – the IRA bombing of the Grand Hotel in Brighton in October 1984. This last event, however, rallied public sympathy to the Prime Minister's side; her bravery under real fire was as impressive as her political courage.

Viewed in the longer perspective, however, these dramatic events were the foam on the crest of the Thatcherite wave. With the economy improving, inflation low and house prices rising, most people in work felt themselves to be better off than they had been before the election. Her opponents cavilled that this was only in comparison with 1981, and that it wouldn't last. They also pointed to the gulf that seemed to be opening up between those who had a job and those who did not. The appearance of the phenomenon of the 'Yuppie' (the young upwardly mobile professional) seemed to epitomise both sides of the Thatcher revolution. On the one hand was the rising prosperity made possible by the encouragement of the entrepreneurial spirit, but on the other came a vulgar materialism which more refined souls found somewhat objectionable. It was all very well for the archetypal yuppie Gordon Gekko in the film *Wall Street,* to declare 'Greed is good', but for critics of Thatcherism greed seemed to be the essence of her creed. Nigel Lawson, whose self-confidence as Chancellor made Denis Healey seem almost a shrinking violet, pursued a deliberate policy of reducing personal taxation, and he proved immune to allegations that his policies were encouraging social inequality. Inequality was, after all, part of man's natural state, and to many on the 'New Right' it seemed an inescapable part of setting people free; freedom to fail was part of what was involved in making people free to succeed; it was a response which would come to haunt the government.

If the old right as represented by Macmillan had been paternalist, and if even the 'Heathmen' had evinced traces of this in their managerialism and enthusiasm for corporatism, then the new Right was iconoclastic, radical and, at least in economic terms, committed to its own vision of modernity.[2] This affected all the bastions of British life: the Civil Service, the universities, the Arts, education, the newspaper industry and even the Church of England; all felt the effects of Thatcherism, and it may have been rude, but it was hardly surprising when the dons of Oxford declined to confer an honorary degree on her in 1985. Yet it was part of the paradox of Thatcherism that at the same time as wishing to 'make the people free', the government should have arrogated to itself more power over matters such as education and local government. For the Thatcherites the paradox was explained by the need to sweep aside barriers in the way of economic liberalisation and the march of the consumer society; but the paradox was there, all the same.

At the heart of Mrs Thatcher's vision was the drive to reduce the influence of the state in British public and private life; but she was temperamentally unsuited to such a task, and the methods she adopted achieved the opposite effect. She was, by nature, unable to resist trying to deal with problems herself, and she presided over an extension of government interference in private matters that paved the way for the Blair years. The notion of the 'professional' getting on with his job exercising suitable discretion, was replaced by a more managerial ethos with 'targets' and 'guidelines', which spawned a whole new industry of auditors who were supposed to ensure 'compliance'; the answer to the Platonic question of who was to guard the guardians was easy enough – the appointment of auditors to audit the auditors was one way of reducing unemployment. However, between that, and the payment of unemployment benefit, it was to prove difficult to actually reduce public expenditure; over the period from 1979 to 1990, that fell precisely 2 per cent from 41 to 39 per cent. The frontiers of the state were not so much rolled back as placed elsewhere.

The need to use state power to preserve freedom was, thanks to Mrs Thatcher's choice of opponents, one that could easily be made. During her first administration she had managed to avoid repeating Heath's clash with the Mineworker' Union; thanks to its new leader, the centrepiece of her second term would be facing down what she was able to plausibly present as a militant threat to the democratic process. One of the features of the decay of the Labour Party at the local level had been its infiltration by forces of the so-called 'hard' left. The Militant Tendency, a generic term which came to be applied to a set of fairly anarchistic Trotskyites, was able to gain control of local councils in places such a Liverpool, where the new leader, Derek Hatton, became a favourite hate-figure for the right-wing press. But he paled into insignificance compared to the NUM leader, Arthur Scargill.

Scargill was a genuine syndicalist; a socialist who believed in using union power to influence government policy, he took the view that having helped to destroy Heath's government, it was his duty to do the same to the Thatcher regime; that she was the head of a democratically elected government did not concern him – but it did allow her to present him as a communist subversive. Mrs Thatcher was always most comfortable when involved in a good fight; Scargill was good enough to provide her with one which allowed her, yet again, to show her mettle.

It was a widely held nostrum (especially after 1974) that no government should 'take on' the NUM. In 1981, advised by Jim Prior, Mrs. Thatcher had backed away from a confrontation with the miners over pay; but if she gave in then, she prepared the way for the future by setting up a committee to ensure that when the show-down came there would be sufficient coal reserves, enough hauliers to transport the coal, and a police force ready to ensure that it could move. For a class warrior, Scargill seems to have had a very naïve view of how the other 'side' operated; had he believed his own rhetoric about the 'boss class' he would hardly have blundered as he did. In March 1984 the new head of the National Coal Board, Sir Ian MacGregor, announced that 20 uneconomic pits would be closed over the next year or so, with the loss of more than 20,000 jobs. Without going to a national ballot, Scargill engineered a series of regional strikes designed, in the first place, to stop the closures; but it was clear that his ultimate objective was much greater – to bring down Mrs Thatcher.

Initial public sympathy for the miners was forfeited by Scargill's tactics; not only was there no national ballot to validate his policy, but the use of violent flying pickets to close down coal depots and stop all movement of coal, produced nightly scenes of violence on the television screens of the nation which allowed Mrs. Thatcher to play the law and order card. The new Labour leader, Neil Kinnock, whose own objective was to break the hold of the Militant Tendency, found himself between a rock and a very hard place; he could hardly be seen to endorse Scargill, but Labour solidarity demanded he show support for the miners; it was easy to caricature him as an ineffectual windbag. Scargill was comprehensively outgeneralled in his own class war, and Mrs Thatcher's image as a strong leader received much-needed refurbishment. In March 1985 the miners went back to work – their demands unmet; first Galtieri, now Scargill, she was indeed fortunate in her enemies.

With Scargill finished off, Mrs. Thatcher turned to another manifestation of the 'loony left' – the Greater London Council under its left-wing leader, Ken Livingstone. One of the features of the Thatcher years was the gradual but steady erosion of the powers of local government; on the surface this was an odd thing to do for a Conservative committed to the diminution of government control, but her mistrust of the left-leaning councils led her to enact measure which, whilst designed to curb the abuses of the few, limited the powers of the many. The GLC was a good example of what Mrs. Thatcher hated. Livingstone made no secret of his intention to use his local power base as a platform from which to challenge the government; the London rate-payers enjoyed the dubious privilege of funding both his political advertising campaigns and his host of special advisers. But the battle to abolish the GLC was handled badly and allowed Livingstone to pose as a democrat facing up to an over-bearing state.

The feeling that under Mrs Thatcher the state was indeed becoming overbearing was strengthened by the growing list of those who found themselves embroiled with the government; this impression was happily confirmed by the BBC itself, which found itself under intense pressure during the Miners' Strike. Mrs Thatcher's patriotism had been outraged during the Falklands War by the Corporation's stance of neutrality; she failed (as did many others) to see how the state broadcaster could be 'neutral' as between the elected British government and an Argentinian dictator; she was equally dismayed by its tone during the dispute with Scargill. She used her power over the appointment of the BBC governor and chairman to ensure that figures sympathetic to her were installed; this was fair enough as far as it went; but it was the very public warnings delivered in unmistakable tones of menace by the government's chief rotweiller, Norman Tebbit, which created public controversy. The fact was, as her treatment of the BBC, the Universities and the Civil Service showed, she regarded most of the old Establishment as riddled with a quasi-socialist mindset; after all, those who relied upon the public purse for their living were hardly likely to welcome cuts in expenditure.

If most of Mrs. Thatcher's enemies failed to defeat her, one of them, the IRA, came close to killing her in 1984. During her first term she had gained the undying hatred of the IRA by standing up to their campaign of hunger strikes; they gambled that she would be willing to concede their prisoners political status rather than see them die in prison – but they were wrong. She was, however, far from being a hard-line Unionist, and during 1983 showed a willingness to move ahead with negotiations with the Irish government. In October, during the

Conservative Party Conference, the IRA exploded a bomb in the Grand Hotel in Brighton; it was sheer good luck that she was not killed, but others were, including the MP Anthony Berry, and the wife of John Wakeham, the Chief Whip. The most dramatic pictures were of a gaunt and stricken Norman Tebbit nursing his wife as she lay helpless in the wreckage of the hotel. Perhaps only her worst enemies (and there were many competitors for that title) could withhold admiration for the fortitude she showed on that occasion; yet again, she had shown herself to be cast in the Churchillian mould.

Ironically, it was her own *hubris* rather than the machinations of enemies within or without which came closest to bringing her down: the so-called Westland affair of 1986 was almost a crisis too far. That an argument between Cabinet colleagues about the future of a West Country helicopter firm could lead the most powerful Conservative leader of the century so close to the brink will always strike historians as remarkable. It was both part of her personal style as well as one of the consequences of the way her leadership had evolved in the early days that Mrs Thatcher preferred to operate through small groups of ministers and her advisers rather than through the full Cabinet, and it was this which lay behind the dramatic resignation of the Defence Secretary, Michael Heseltine, in January 1986. When it transpired that a 'leaked' letter revealing that Heseltine had been rebuked by one of the Law Officers had come from the Department of Trade and Industry, Leon Brittan became the third minister in as many years to leave that department without having time to settle in. Rumours abounded that Mrs Thatcher herself had been involved in a 'smear' campaign against Heseltine, and had she performed badly in the Commons' debate on the affair she might well have had to go. However, she could rely upon the new and verbose Labour leader Neil Kinnock to muffle his attack in a welter of verbiage, and she survived – although her prestige was badly tarnished.

Westland had shown that the Iron Lady was vulnerable, and it had led to speculation as to her likely successor; Geoffrey Howe, Michael Heseltine, Norman Tebbit and Douglas Hurd all found their backers. But in the short term she proved remarkably resilient. For a short while something liked Cabinet government obtained, as she fought shy of creating any fresh crises. In March she made it clear that she intended to continue in power should she win a third term; she still had to finish the work of dismantling the old consensus.

The one part of Attlee's consensus which survived intact was the part with which few Conservatives had ever argued – that was the Atlantic Alliance. Underpinning the Thatcher image as the Iron Lady was her resolute opposition to the Soviet Union and her steadfast support for the United States. The Falklands had demonstrated the benefits to be reaped from maintaining defence spending at a high level (and from the American connection), and her firm support for Trident nuclear missiles being based in Britain, despite the unease this stirred in some quarters, was a sign both of her determination to maintain Britain's status as a major power and of her devotion to the Anglo-American alliance. It came as something of a surprise to her critics to find her talking about the new Soviet leader, Gorbachev, as a man 'with whom we can do business', but she had correctly spotted that the Soviet Union, on the brink of economic collapse, was willing to change some of its policies with a little encouragement from the West. With this new role almost as a mediator in the Cold War, and the credit she garnered by 'standing up for Britain' in her dealings with the Common Market, Mrs Thatcher became the first Prime Minister since Macmillan who could, with some degree of plausibility, claim to be a world leader.

Her reputation in the eyes of history as an election-winner of unparalleled virtuosity was firmly cemented by the 1987 General Election. With Labour no longer writing suicide notes to the electorate and with some of the baggage left over from previous Conservative crises, it was hardly to be expected that the majority of 1983 would remain intact, but, despite one of those campaigns which Labour 'won', she still remained in Downing Street – to the bafflement of her enemies, who had begun to wonder if they would ever see the back of her. The Conservative share of the vote remained almost constant at 42.3 per cent, whilst Labour could still only garner 30.8 per cent. The Conservatives lost some seats, but came back with 376 compared with Labour's 229 and the Alliance's 22. For Mrs Thatcher, the mandate was clear: on with the revolution.

She had presided over not just the dismantling of the apparatus of the old consensus, but also over a sustained attempt to replace the assumptions which underlay it with a free market philosophy. To a nation which had been raised to look to the state for its needs, as to an Establishment which had been used to being treated with due deference by government, it all came as a shock. 'Freedom' sounded good, until it encompassed the 'freedom' to be without a job; 'cutting public spending' sounded equally desirable, until it meant that workers in the public sector could not expect an automatic pay rise – and, even worse, that the old idea of a 'job for life' was gone. Even the universities were exposed to the strange and barbarous language of 'efficiency savings' and 'performance indicators'; it was no wonder that support for her in that quarter, which had never been great, seemed to vanish almost without trace.

The *quid pro quo* for all this turmoil was, of course, the economic prosperity which the 'Lawson boom' was bringing in its wake, and as long as this continued and people could imagine that the 'market' produced such an effect almost inevitably, then the 'free market' philosophy came with a nicely sugared coating; the question of how the public would react if the coating wore off was not long in being asked. In October stock markets around the world crashed, with the London *Financial Times* Index dropping by a massive 24 per cent. Lawson refused to panic, which was an admirable trait at such a moment, but his decision to press ahead with tax cuts helped to stoke up inflation and sucked in imports which led to a massive balance of payments deficit. With the pound under pressure on the foreign exchanges and inflation beginning to rise (it reached 8.3 per cent in January 1989), interest rates had to be raised constantly, and by 31 October they had reached 15 per cent. All this took its toll on the 'property-owning democracy', as people saw the cost of their investment go up at a time when the returns from it, in the form of house prices, were falling; for those yuppies who had thought that house prices, like the sun in the morning, always rose, it was all a ghastly revelation of how capricious capitalism could be. Unsurprisingly the newspapers began to fill with articles about the value of the need for compassion.

Even the government began to make noises designed to show how 'caring' it was, with some ministers seeming to positively revel in declaring how spending 'in real terms' on education and the Health Service had increased; the cynics thought that this may have had something to do with the problems the same ministers faced in trying to implement further measures of reform in these areas. Not only were the measures proposed controversial in themselves, but they seemed to be part of an almost Maoist state of 'permanent revolution'. Stung by the accusation that she had lost momentum after 1987, Mrs Thatcher seemed determined to press on with her 'revolution' – even if most people seemed tired of it all.

But the new measures of privatisation lacked the appeal and glamour of the first tranche, with controversy surrounding the selling off of the Electricity Supply and Water Companies. whilst the most radical of the new proposals, the reform of local government finance through the introduction of the Community Charge, created a furore, first in Scotland, where it was introduced in 1989, and then in England and Wales in 1990. The principle behind the new tax was eminently Thatcherite – that everyone should pay for the local services which they used – but finding a way of doing so which combined equity with efficiency was so difficult that it almost seemed as if the government gave up the attempt. Because rates had not been re-evaluated for years, any new tax was bound to increase the imposition on the householder, and as this would coincide with a period of financial stringency, it would inevitably make the government unpopular, but a system which seemed to mean that a duke and a dustman would pay the same amount for the same services (which was not actually the case, although it was too good an angle for the media to ignore) was too much for many people's sense of fairness. There were riots in London and elsewhere, and there was a concerted campaign to evade what became known as 'the poll tax'. The nickname had echoes of the Peasant's Revolt of 1381, which had threatened to dethrone the Monarch; there were echoes of that in the contemporary situation, too, with Mrs Thatcher now cast in the role of Richard II.

The reasons behind the challenge to Mrs Thatcher in the autumn of 1990 are complex, and some of them go back to the resignation of Michael Heseltine. In so far as Heseltine was protesting about her style of government he was voicing a concern expressed by others. What had been, back in the early 'heroic' days of the 'revolution', a necessary technique for circumventing or overriding opposition within her own Cabinet had come to seem like bossiness. Her reaction to calls for her to change her style was dismissive: 'Why should I change my style of government? I am not going to.'[3] But what was tolerable, and tolerated, when accompanied by success, became increasingly intolerable when failure seemed to loom ahead. There was a growing sense that she had been at the helm for an awfully long time; would she imitate 'Winston' and stay on after she had become a political liability? Secondly, she was becoming more remote from her original powerbase in the parliamentary party. Whitelaw's retirement after the 1987 victory did not help matters in this respect. On 'every normal assessment he was a "wet" ', but he had become the 'linchpin' of the government. On the one hand he insisted on an almost 'military loyalty' to the 'leader', and did not flinch from enforcing it: on the other he 'was possessed of almost supernatural political antennae', and knew when to warn Mrs Thatcher that 'a situation had reached breaking point'; he was sorely missed.[4] Other changes at the top intensified the trend towards 'splendid isolation'. Norman Tebbit retired from the Party Chairmanship in an atmosphere of acrimony with another Thatcher favourite, Lord Young; both men were a loss to her. Mrs Thatcher was increasingly left facing two ministers whose own seniority and experience made them less and less willing to take anything like dictation from her – Lawson and Howe.

The Conservative Party has never been blessed with strong political nerves, and the unease generated by Mrs Thatcher's evident unpopularity in the opinion polls was turned to something approaching panic by a series of lost by-elections: 'poll-tax' riots, Irish bombing campaigns, political scandals, and record Labour leads in opinion surveys all contributed to a somewhat fevered atmosphere in the party. On top of these things came continual and continuing tussles over 'Europe'. Both Sir Geoffrey Howe and Nigel Lawson were a good deal keener on further European integration than she was, and it was largely thanks to their pressure that at the Madrid summit in 1989 she agreed in principle to Britain joining the European Monetary System; it was a defeat she would not forgive.[5] Soon afterwards, in circumstances of some acrimony, Howe was removed from the Foreign Office to be Leader of the House. It was evident that the three senior figures in the party were now on the worst possible terms – the only question seemed to be over the timing of Howe's resignation.

But it was Lawson who was the first to go, in October 1989, over a dispute concerning Mrs Thatcher's economic adviser, Sir Alan Walters. There had been speculation in the press for some time about Lawson's position, and these were hardly quelled when Mrs Thatcher described his position as 'unassailable'; it sounded rather like the sort of thing the chairman of a football club would say just before sacking the manager of the team. So it proved here. It had been clear to observers that Mrs Thatcher was increasingly at odds with her self-confident Chancellor, and that Sir Alan Walters' advice was confirming her own suspicions that not even Lawson could 'buck the market'. Lawson demanded Walters' removal. The incident brought to a head the conflict between the two. To her surprise, Lawson chose to resign on an issue which did not, on the surface, appear worthy of such a dramatic move Still, she greeted it with some relief; it was a sign of how far things had gone that only a few years before she had called Lawson one of the greatest chancellors of modern times. His replacement was a former Chief Secretary to the Treasury, John Major, who had only recently been made Foreign Secretary; Major's promotions were quite unprecedented, and there were many who thought that 'the lady' was grooming him to be her successor.

Virgil wrote that the descent from the Avernian hill was easy. That autumn Mrs Thatcher faced the first formal challenge to her leadership. It came from a backbencher of almost startling obscurity, Sir Anthony Meyer, who appeared as a sort of water-logged survival from the era of the 'wets'. Although everyone knew that he would be defeated, it was significant that the challenge was made at all; rumours abounded that Meyer was a 'stalking horse' (some preferred to use the word 'donkey') for a possible bid by Heseltine the following year.

Certainly Meyer's challenge revealed the tip of the iceberg of discontent with Mrs Thatcher's style of leadership – and its longevity. As everyone had predicted, Mrs Thatcher won by a massive margin, getting 317 votes to Meyer's 33; but, with 24 spoilt ballots and three abstentions, it rather looked as though there was a sizeable minority who did not mind signalling their disaffection. In the circumstances, this was a worrying development. With the electorate disgruntled by the recession and the 'poll tax', and with the party itself split over attitudes to the forthcoming European summit at Maastricht, the nerve of Conservative MPs, never naturally robust, began to give way.

Mrs Thatcher's position was now weaker than at any time since 1981; having lost Howe and Lawson, she was hardly in any position to provoke either of their successors; this gave John Major and Douglas Hurd a powerful political position; the latter, in particular, brought an air of calm patrician confidence to an office badly in need of strong political leadership. If these were moving into pole position in any bookmaker's list of possible successors, there were others, in particular the rambunctious Health Secretary, Kenneth Clarke, who fancied their chances; and in the wings was Heseltine, waiting for the right moment to launch his challenge. Suddenly, the Iron Lady appeared very vulnerable. Observers began to notice that she was, for the first time, beginning to look her age; a decade in office was beginning to take its toll. In politics, as in other wild places, the law of the jungle dictates that the wounded leader will attract challengers; and so it proved here.

There was no doubting Mrs Thatcher's intention to carry on, at least until the next election; and there was certainly a more than full agenda – not least with the Iraqi invasion of Kuwait in August 1990; just when she needed it, it seemed that another Galtieri was offering himself as the 'enemy without'; any such calculation reckoned without the enemy within. As might have been predicted, it was the issue of Europe which set the light to the powder trail.

Both John Major and Douglas Hurd were convinced that Britain ought to join the European Monetary System, and that sterling ought to be pegged to the Exchange Rate Mechanism, designed to bring the currencies of the EU into alignment; for Mrs Thatcher this remained a bridge too far, and it is some measure of her weakened position that by October she had been persuaded to agree to it. Bitter experience would show that whatever the merits of the scheme, Britain had joined at the wrong time and the wrong rate. However, when faced as she was in October with the decision by the other European States to push ahead with further measures of integration, she recoiled. In response to jibes from Kinnock that she had lost control over events, and that

Sir Geoffrey Howe's more integrationist stance would prevail, she responded in her most haughty vein that her answer to suggestions for a democratically elected European parliament with the Commission as its Executive and the Council of Ministers as its senate was 'No. No. No.' She made it clear that sterling would retain its identity and that she, personally if necessary, would resist any further integration. The *Sun* was ecstatic, as were the *Telegraph* and the *Daily Mail* and the Euro sceptics in the party; elsewhere there was dismay, with John Major seeing all the work of the past year going up in smoke. The most dramatic reaction came from Sir Geoffrey Howe. He had accepted a decade of being shouted down, lectured and trampled over; he had even accepted his demotion and marginalisation; but this he was not prepared to swallow. He had believed that Britain's entry into the ERM gave her a chance to shape Europe's monetary policy for years to come – and now Mrs Thatcher was throwing it away; it was too much – and he handed in his letter of resignation the day after her speech in the House. Mrs Thatcher shrugged it off and reshuffled her Cabinet once again; but this time she had miscalculated.

Westminster was awash with rumours. The Minister for Defence Procurement and Thatcher admirer, Alan Clark, noted in his diary that: 'In the woodwork stir all those who have lived for the day when they could emerge and have a gloat without fear of retribution';[6] it was not an edifying spectacle. Hemmed in by the speculation, Heseltine had to decide whether (to adopt a phase) to 'put up or shut up'. Alan Clark's speculation that he would 'stand and that he will win', proved to be half right.[7] Denis Healey had once memorably quipped that being attacked by Sir Geoffrey was like being 'savaged by a dead sheep', but now it appeared that dead sheep could be pretty toxic; Howe's resignation speech on 13 November was political dynamite. In part, of course, this was because he was such an unexpected source for an attack. The epitome of the loyal grey man in the grey suit, everyone knew how much Howe had taken from his leader without complaint; that made the complaint all the more telling now it came; what made it devastating was that not even her best friend could have denied its accuracy. The previous day, at the Guildhall, Mrs Thatcher had referred to her 11 years 'at the crease' and to her hitting the bowling 'all round the ground'; Howe's speech stayed with the cricketing metaphor. He revealed that as far back as 1985 he and Lawson had wanted to join the ERM, and that they had both threatened to resign if Thatcher refused, and he warned against Britain becoming isolated in Europe. Then, turning to her public repudiation of the monetary policy favoured by Major and the Governor of the Bank of England, he said that it was 'like sending your opening batsmen to the crease, only for them to find, the moment the first balls are bowled, that their bats have been broken before the game by the team captain.' He had, he said, struggled for a long time with the competing demands of loyalty to the leader and 'the true interests of the nation'; he could do so no longer. The time had come, he concluded, 'for others to consider their own response to the tragic conflict of loyalties with which I myself have wrestled for perhaps too long.' It was, everyone conceded, a masterly exercise in political assassination; the only remaining question was whether someone would use the knife which Howe had unsheathed. The following day Heseltine announced his candidacy for the leadership of the party.

Because Heseltine was known to favour more active government intervention in industry, and because he was (at least then) a declared Europhile, there is a temptation to see in his challenge the revenge of the 'Heathmen', but if it can be interpreted as such it is only at the level of his sharing their desire for revenge on Mrs Thatcher; whatever his ideas (which were few and stale) Heseltine stood not against Thatcherism, but rather against Mrs Thatcher herself. Had she and her advisers handled the matter with her usual thoroughness, Heseltine could have been defeated on the first ballot. But what she could not have done was to have kept his vote down to double figures – there were just too many people prepared to vote against her to disguise the fact that the party was split.

In the aftermath of Howe's speech, Heseltine was batting on a good wicket. Many MPs were fearful of losing their seats at the next election, and they had begun to see their leader as a millstone. Heseltine offered a chance to get rid of her – and to reconsider the deeply unpopular 'poll tax'. The vote was not so much one for Heseltine, as one for the removal of Mrs Thatcher. The Conservative Party proved, once again, that Lloyd George was right when he said that 'there are no friendships at the top' – nor is there much gratitude. Mrs Thatcher's absence in Paris at a summit on the day of the first ballot did not help matters, nor did the lethargy of her PPS, Peter Morrison. It was at such moments that she missed the steady hand of Ian Gow, who had just been murdered by the IRA, and the loss of whose old seat at Eastbourne had been one of the precipitants of the panic which gripped many Conservative MPs.

The frightened, the vengeful and the 'wobblers' amounted to 152 votes and 16 abstentions when the result of the first ballot was announced on 19 November. Mrs Thatcher had got 204 votes – four less than she needed to avoid a second ballot. Even as the

BBC reporter was retailing this news from outside the Paris Conference, Mrs Thatcher emerged announcing she would 'fight, and fight to win'. Few doubted her resolution, but as the implications of the vote sank in many ministers began to doubt the wisdom of her fighting on. Even if she won she would inevitably look like something of a 'lame duck' leader, and Labour would have further evidence for their line that the Conservative Party was too badly split to govern the country. Then the next election would be lost – and after that? It did not bear thinking about. As the personal consequences of the probable answer to this last question were considered, the advice began to be heard that she had had 'a good innings' and should 'retire in the cause of Party unity'. It was not the parliamentary party's vote which sank Mrs Thatcher, it was the refusal of her closest Cabinet colleagues to back her wholeheartedly.

The first sign of what was to come was the refusal of a 'card-carrying Thatcherite', the Industry Minister, Peter Lilley, to help the Prime Minister in drafting her speech for the 'No Confidence' motion which Labour had tabled for 1 November; there was 'no point' he said, she was 'finished': 'coming from such a source, this upset me more than I can say', she later recorded.[8] As the penultimate act in the drama unfolded and she saw each of her Cabinet ministers individually, it was clear that the vast majority of them agreed with Lilley; loyalists like Alan Clark tried to rally her for a last Romantic gesture of defiance, but she was too experienced a hand not to know that the game was up. The following morning the country was startled by the news that she would not, after all, be standing for re-election.

Why did she go? It was clear to her that she could no longer command the support of her closest colleagues, and to have forced a second ballot would have been to have intensified the current divisions; it was better to stand aside and to let someone else defend her legacy against Heseltine. But there was still one last act to come. Alan Clark, who felt 'empty and cross' was furious at the manner in which she had gone: 'Unbeaten in three elections, never rejected by the people. Brought down by nonentities' – but the style of her going was worthy of what had come before.[9] At the Cabinet she had been subdued, even tearful, but on the floor of the Commons on that afternoon of 22 November she gave a bravura performance which no one who saw it will ever forget. Her spirit high, she routed the Opposition and put on a performance which had many asking what on earth the party had thought it was doing in getting rid of her.

Mrs Thatcher may have gone, and in the grand style, but her shadow hung heavily over the second ballot and over the new administration.

As the contenders for the second ballot went through their paces all of them, even Heseltine, claimed to able to carry on the standard of Thatcherism, but the best comment on this came from the Thatcherite loyalist Charles Moore in the *Daily Telegraph*:

> It is vain to search for a second Mrs Thatcher. Her legacy will be long-lasting, but much of the impact of Thatcherism came from the force of her personality and that cannot be replaced ... the choice is not ideological, not between differing policies, and should not be a fruitless attempt to replicate the lost leader.

It was, he said, referring to Douglas Hurd and John Major, 'a straight contest between two worthy, dependable men', neither of whom was 'a Thatcherite in any dynamic or radical sense'.[10] It was good advice, but it would prove difficult to follow because Mrs Thatcher was, as everyone acknowledged, unique.

It is too soon to reach anything like a considered verdict on her long period in office. She had spent 11 years and six months as Prime Minister, winning three successive elections – a feat unmatched since the days of Lord Liverpool in the early nineteenth century; in modern politics only Salisbury and Gladstone had spent longer at No. 10, but they had needed three and four separate Premierships to do so. On a personal level it was a towering achievement; but what had she achieved?

On the economic front, she had certainly dealt with the twin dragons of inflation and the trades unions; but the cost in unemployment had been tremendous. Britain's position in the world economic league table was much as it had been before 1979. Productivity was better than it had been in the previous decade, rising by 4.2 per cent per annum compared with 1.1 per cent for the period 1973–79; Britain even outpaced Japan here. Personal consumption rose to the highest point ever seen – 3.2 per cent annually, which actually outstripped the 2.2 per cent annual rise in earnings. Moreover, for all the fuss her opponents made about cuts in the public services, spending on health and education were at record highs by the end of her time in office.[11] But caveats had to be set against these figures. On productivity it could be argued that the result reflected fewer people engaged in manufacturing working harder with the aid of more advanced technology, whilst the consumer boom was funded by an astronomical rise in house prices and easier credit; whatever else it was built on, the 'Lawson boom' was not based on the Thatcherite injunction to spend only what you earn.

But, as the editor of the *Daily Telegraph*, Charles Moore, rightly commented:

> Thatcherism is not a technical economic doctrine: it is not really an economic doctrine at all. ... It believes that men should be free and that they should be responsible, and that freedom without responsibility is not real freedom at all. ... It is a strenuous doctrine but it is one that puts faith in individual human dignity and repudiates the schemes of political visionaries to put the world to right.[12]

She had set out to cure the British people from nearly half a century of dependence upon the state, but in so doing, she had found herself using the state in a way which had made it more intrusive than ever before. Fearing that the old institutions of the Establishment were tinged with the instincts of socialism and statism, she had weakened them, and local government – leaving the state stronger than ever. She had tried to establish a culture of enterprise and competition that would produce prosperity long after she was gone, but in so doing, she had contributed to the prevalence of a materialistic view of society that was the antithesis of her own deeply moral views. The elevation of the rights of the consumer helped to create a society in which any *raison d'être* beyond the accumulation of wealth and the consumption of its products was hard to perceive. If Oscar Wilde was correct to define a Philistine as one who knows the price of everything and the value of nothing, then British society became markedly more philistine under Mrs Thatcher. For many of those who did well out of her, that was, ironically, a price they paid gladly; for others, it was a further cause of regret.

Both at the time, and in retrospect, the question of what sort of Conservative Mrs Thatcher was – and even whether she was one at all – was a difficult one to answer. For those who saw Conservatism as being attached to institutions such as the Church of England, the Universities and the Civil Service, and as the defender of manufacturing industry, Mrs Thatcher had sawn off the branch on which the Conservative Party sat.[13] But this missed the point that she did not regard Conservatism as being immanent in any set of institutions. She was a Conservative in a way in which few of Britain's leaders have ever been, not least because she sprang from the soil in which the party has been rooted throughout the era studied here – lower-middle-class England, with its shopkeepers, its gentility, petty snobberies and deep, abiding integrity. Mrs Thatcher felt she had a unique rapport with the British people, and if opinion polls did not always support her instinct then, as three election results showed, perhaps it was time to wonder at the efficacy of opinion polls; political scientists and journalists can manufacture scenarios where parties 'win' campaigns, but Mrs Thatcher managed to create conditions in which a Prime Minister, who was hugely unpopular at times, still managed to win the only opinion poll which counted – three times running.

If Mrs Thatcher came from the traditional bastion of British Conservatism, she was able to fashion an appeal to the aspirational working classes through the attempt to create a genuinely popular capitalism. The Conservatism she was reared in had three salient characteristics: 'It is diligent, it is serious, and it is unfashionable'; she was all three.[14] Most Conservative leaders this century would have agreed with Balfour, who is said to have been of the opinion that he would as soon take the advice of his valet as he would that of the Conservative Party Conference. Mrs Thatcher and her husband Denis were the sort of people who would have been in the audience at the annual conference; this gave her a visceral understanding of the party which was beyond the old grandees. She has recorded how, when she fired Churchill's son-in-law, Christopher Soames, she got the 'distinct impression that he felt the natural order of things was being violated and that he was, in effect, being dismissed by his housemaid';[15] it is a telling vignette. The more patrician Tory came to loathe her as much for the manner of what she had done, as for what it was she did; in this many on the political left would have agreed; nearly two decades after her departure she remains a deeply divisive and controversial figure.[16] But the fact that that consummate political operator, Tony Blair, lost few opportunities to appropriate her legacy, says more about her achievement than the verdict of the chattering classes.

The depth of the emotions stirred in local Conservative associations by her departure was a testimony to how well she had kept the faith in which she had been brought up.[17] She had won an unprecedented three elections, she was a figure with a world reputation, and yet in the end the sheer funk of her party and Cabinet meant that she had to go; it was, as she told her colleagues, 'a funny old world'.[18] But it was, both for the British people and for her own party, a world which had been changed by her actions. By resigning as she did, Mrs Thatcher ensured that Heseltine would not be her successor; feeling against him ran so high in some localities that even some of the more sceptical MPs had to take account of it. For those who wished to prevent the assassin ascending the throne it was a straight choice between what the guru of the Conservative right, Maurice Cowling, called 'the mandarin and the meritocrat',[19] Douglas Hurd, despite his earlier credentials as a

'Heathman', came as close as the modern Conservative Party was able to producing a 'toff' candidate for the leadership, and it was an index of how things had changed in the party and the country that his Old Etonian background was generally felt, even by himself, to be a disadvantage; his attempt to play it down by presenting his father, Lord Hurd, as a sort of tenant farmer was singularly unconvincing.[20] Realistically then this left the man who had risen without trace – John Major, who could be, and was, represented as just the sort of meritocratic figure who symbolised the Thatcherite achievement. The *Daily Telegraph*, in its first profile of Major, emphasised that 'he represents the new Tory generation'.[21] This was so with a vengeance. It was not just that he had not been to the right sort of university, he had not been to university at all. A grammar school boy from a theatrical background, he had left school at 16 and had actually been on the dole before eventually finding a job in banking and working his way up from the cashier's desk. Whilst at Standard Chartered Bank he had become a protégé of the former Chancellor, Lord Barber. He had come into politics through local government in London, and he had not even entered the Commons until 1979. It was, from an electoral point of view, a 'dream' background, and since he was also thought to be closer to Mrs Thatcher's views as well as to her roots than Hurd, it was no wonder he received her benison.[22] However much Major said that he was not running as the 'son of Thatcher', most of her supporters backed him as the man to 'carry on her policies', in the words of a *Times*' main headline. When the ballot was counted on 27 November, John Major had 185 votes to Heseltine's 131, with Hurd trailing in last with only 56; under the rules there could have been another ballot, but Heseltine, sensing the game was up, conceded defeat, knowing that in return for his gesture, Major would have to offer him a post in his new Cabinet.[23]

When Lord Hanson described Major as looking 'like someone on the 7.15 to Waterloo', he successfully identified both the main weakness and the main strength of the new Prime Minister.[24] Part of Major's success, at the time and later, was that, as one former Labour MP put it, 'he looks like everyone's bank manager'. There was no 'side' to the 47-year-old Prime Minister who only two years before had been the most junior member of the Cabinet; he appeared to be a genuinely likeable 'bloke' of the sort one might well meet on the commuter train to London. As his wife, Norma, commented on his election: 'This doesn't happen to people like us.' But it had done, and it had done so in circumstances which would prove to be as much of a burden as they had been an opportunity. It is impossible to imagine other circumstances in which such an inexperienced and uncharismatic figure might have become Prime Minister, but he now had to carry the burden of the expectations of the Thatcherites. No one could have fulfilled these except for the deposed Prime Minister herself, and although Major never pretended that he could, this did not stop those who had expected him to carry on the Thatcherite crusade from being disappointed. Major also, of course, had to deal with the political aftermath of Mrs Thatcher's fall, and in terms of the party this meant finding a place for Heseltine and some of his supporters; it was clearly impolitic and unwise, even had it been possible, for the new Premier to have ignored the man who had brought Mrs Thatcher down.

Major faced a very different task than the one which had faced Mrs Thatcher. Her job had been to win over her colleagues to her point of view and to win the next election – or else. His job was to move the Thatcherite agenda on to the next phase and to unite the party in order to retain power; the problem here was that the personal nature of Thatcherism made it rather difficult to know what the next phase might be. A second, and related, difficulty was that the issue which had helped damage party unity under Mrs Thatcher, Europe, was going to be an even more acute problem in the near future because of the need to negotiate the Maastricht settlement; this would ensure that whatever else he was in for, the new Premier would not get a quiet life.

But John Major did have some advantages. With an election only two years away at most, he could expect to remain leader without being challenged, and he inherited a willingness on the part of his backbenchers to close ranks to keep Kinnock and the Labour Party out. His skilful handling of the Heseltine issue – offering him the post of Secretary of State for the Environment and making him responsible for revising the 'poll tax' – showed a keen political sense; it pandered to Heseltine's vanity whilst landing him with a task that would keep him busy: it would also ensure that his hands were kept away from areas such as Industry and Europe, where his views might be expected to arouse the ire of the Thatcherites. The episode revealed something which would become clear over the next two years – that the Tories had a man in the Baldwin class when it came to party management. If the 'true believers' missed the passion, the energy and the excitement, others welcomed a rest from the strenuous but heroic days of yore. The question of whether Mr Major would be a pale afterglow from those halcyon days or whether he might establish a position of his own depended upon the next election – and what would happen afterwards.

16   After the Ball was Over

John Major's premiership was marked by the two events that framed it: the defenestration of Mrs Thatcher at one end, and the greatest election defeat ever suffered by the Conservative at the other. The first of these mattered because it signalled the beginning of a pattern of disloyalty to the leader of the party which was still recognisable two decades later; the second mattered because it cast a retrospective pall over his whole premiership. But from the very start there were those who were 'getting ready to be "disillusioned" and who duly arrived at that state'.[1] Although such people tended to say that it was 'not just that Major is not Mrs Thatcher', at bottom that was exactly what it was. In style there was a return to the old days of pragmatism unseasoned by the rhetoric of the radical right, or even with the spice of 'conviction politics'. It was true that Major relaxed public spending curbs in 1991, but with an election on the horizon a little pandering to the electorate was understandable. If the pace of reform slowed down, then it could be said that it had already been doing so in the last years of the Great Lady. Major successfully followed through on her policy in the Gulf War, although there were those who wondered if 'She' would have let President Bush stop short of Baghdad – whatever the UN resolutions said. Nor could he be faulted over the 'poll tax', coming up with a sensible compromise which, if it could hardly be expected to satisfy everyone, at least took the sting out of the problem. On Europe the ride was bumpier, but not as rough as it would get in the future. All in all, Major did everything which anyone save the 'true believers' could have wished.

There was always the 'back-seat driver' problem, but even this was not as bad as some had expected. Mrs Thatcher remained an MP, and she had not, after all, gone because of fatigue or because she had lost a general election; she remained as full of energy and of ideas as ever she had been, and if she spoke out now and then, she did not serve her successor as she had been served by her predecessor. She did not give a major interview to a newspaper until June 1991, and if some of her remarks about Major could be interpreted as less than warm, it was hard to disagree with her comment that 'You can't expect a person who's not been in the heat of the fire and the teeth of the wind to have the same viewpoint as someone who has been through it all.'[2] This was

243

a widely-held view, and after the election Major himself would admit that he needed the legitimacy that only a General Election could confer to feel fully in control. For the first period of his Premiership he ran the risk of being another Douglas-Home – a short-term stop-gap who had never won an election. Indeed, if the opinion polls, the pundits and the bookmakers were to be believed, this would be his fate. But although he might appear to be a grey little man, he was one with a great sense of self-confidence; there would be times when people wondered what it was he had to be confident about – but it would carry him through an election which only he expected to win.

Major left it to almost the last minute to call the 1992 General Election. On the eve of the election day MORI polls were indicating a 7-point lead for Labour, and eminent political scientists, whilst entering the usual caveats with which they reveal how much faith they really have in their psephological wizardry, talked confidently of the Tories being 'in peril of [the] worst swing since 1945'. Neil Kinnock, it was predicted, would 'be propelled into Downing Street on a massive swing of 9 per cent with an overall majority of 38', with the poor old Tories losing 116 seats; 'the Conservative tide does appear to be ebbing fast'. The party had, it was concluded, lost the campaign and this time, finally, it would lose the election too; so much for opinion polls and punditry.[3] Major's resort to the soap-box was not, it was thought, quite the answer to the glittering array of acting 'luvvies' and other luminaries who assembled at Sheffield for a triumphal rally at which Kinnock was introduced as the 'next Prime Minister'. Of course, at the last minute, the pollsters covered their flanks by pointing out that the polls had been unusually volatile, but instead of concluding that their expensive polls were next door to useless, they decided that 'Tories' hopes still look slim'.[4]

Inevitably, much of the burden of the Conservative campaign fell on having to defend the Thatcher legacy, but Major added his own touches, talking about the need to create a 'classless society' (to the surprise of those Conservatives who imagined that their party existed to 'defend existing inequalities').[5] In good Thatcherite style he lambasted the Socialists for being stuck in the same old groove; despite the gimmickry and the razzmatazz Labour 'still wanted people to pay for the privilege of being told what to do. That is the badge of Socialism.'[6] He appealed to those who had bought their own council houses, or shares in the privatised industries, and to those who were taking responsibility for their own lives in a variety of ways not to let Labour 'ruin it'. Equally expected were the criticisms of Labour for being too ready to sacrifice Britain's interests in Europe, and the scepticism about Labour's spending and taxation plans. There had been no 'u-turn'; the

Thatcherite revolution was, after all, safe in Major's hands. Indeed, to the surprise of many, he even decided to take a firm stand on the Union itself, telling Scottish voters plainly that if they wished to remain part of the Union they only had one choice – to vote for the Conservatives. Had Major gone down to defeat, it could plausibly have been presented as the repudiation of Mrs Thatcher and all her works; it might not have saved Mr Major from the 'men in grey suits' who, it was popularly supposed, appeared like spectres of ill-omen to hand Tory leaders the black spot, but it would have been enough .to have derailed the Thatcher agenda and to have raised cries of 'whither the Tories now?' On the very morning the result was to be announced, first editions of *The Times* carried the headline 'Exit polls point to certainty of hung parliament';[7] if not quite on a par with the famous 1948 American headline 'Dewey wins!', it was certainly in the same league. It had disappeared by later editions as the truth sank in slowly – for an unprecedented fourth time in a row the Conservatives had secured a majority from the electoral system.

The results could be, and soon were, interpreted in a variety of ways, and no doubt if the following election is won by Labour it will be seen as part of a long-term erosion of support for the Conservatives which began in 1987. There could be little doubt that Neil Kinnock's assiduous attempts to play down the Socialist element in his party's programme had been successful, and his successors would continue down the same path; indeed Mr Blair would even invent something called 'the new Labour party', just to make the matter clear to those who had missed the point. But twist which way they would, it remained true that, as one headline put it, 'voters let pollsters down'.[8] The Conservatives had 336 seats, Labour 271, the Liberal Democrats 20 and 'others' 24. Despite the severest recession since the war, Mr Major had managed to secure a larger share of the vote (just) than Mrs Thatcher had at the height of the 'Lawson boom' – 43 per cent. At 35 per cent, Labour had improved its position yet again, but had still come nowhere near the peak of 1966.

With the exception of metropolitan areas in London, Manchester, West Yorkshire and the West Midlands, the electoral map of England was still largely blue, and even in Scotland the Tory vote held up better than expected. Here, as in other ways, the results looked like a continuation of trends noted in 1987. The C2s, or skilled manual workers, had swung towards Labour, but, given the level of house repossessions and the severity of the recession, the Conservatives could probably count themselves lucky only to have lost 4 per cent of the vote here since 1987. Oddly enough there was an increase in the Conservative vote among both the unemployed and in the north of England, and another encouraging sign for the party was that amongst the better-off and young men the Conservative support had held up well. It was not a great victory viewed in the perspective of the Thatcher years – but in the context of the times it was a very considerable and unexpected achievement – and no one could doubt that much of it was down to Mr Major. He had taken a risk by putting himself in the front line of the election; it remained to be seen what he would manage to do with his new-found authority.

In retrospect, the 1992 election was one to lose. For once Labour did not have to come into power just in time to deal with the economic consequences of a Conservative government; instead it had the chance to regroup in opposition. Initially, as usual, it fluffed things by choosing the likeable but deeply uncharismatic Scotsman, John Smith, to succeed the charismatic but volatile Welshman, Neil Kinnock; but Smith's unexpected and premature death in 1995 gave Labour one final chance – which it did not miss; the election of the charismatic, charming and deeply English Tony Blair marked the point at which the Labour Party became once more electable. Time was also given for the Conservatives to turn from destroying their leader to doing the same job on themselves.

If a fourth successive victory was unprecedented, then so too were 21 resignations from the government in the 19 months after the election; for a party where ministers had resigned to spend more time with their families, it seemed that some were rather fond of spending it with the wives of other people; and the welter of sexual scandal was accompanied, as it had not been in 1963, by financial ones too. At the same time the size of his majority left Major vulnerable to a determined assault from the Eurosceptics on European legislation, and he was fortunate on more than one occasion to survive by narrow margins – and then only after making it clear that he would resign if defeated; given the low position in the polls of the Tories this was enough to prompt some MPs to decide against voting for an early election. Getting tough, Major actually deprived some of his MPs of the party Whip, but when they refused to make concessions to him he took them back anyway; it did nothing to help his authority. In addition to these continuing problems there were fiascos such as Heseltine's attempt to close further coal mines in early 1992, which led to an embarrassing backbench revolt.

However much Major might have blamed irresponsible and rebellious backbenchers for his troubles, he had only himself to thank for the greatest blow suffered by his administration – the events of 'Black Wednesday' in 1992. The decision to allow sterling to enter the ERM in

1990 now returned to haunt the man who had been Chancellor at the time. As some had warned at the time, sterling had entered the Exchange Rate Mechanism at too high a value; in September 1992 the markets decided to sell it, anticipating that it could not be maintained at the level much longer. The government decided to tough things out, with the hapless Chancellor, Norman Lamont, committing some £15 billion of the country's gold reserves to a fruitless attempt to stave off the inevitable; on 16 September interests rates were hiked three times; but it was no use; as Mrs (now Lady) Thatcher commented: 'If you try to buck the market, the market will buck you.' The Conservatives' trump card – their economic competence – was also devalued; more than a decade later, Labour's electoral tacticians would think it worth their while to reprint photographs of that dark day, showing the new Conservative leader, David Cameron, who had been one of Lamont's advisers; the message was plain: 'you can't trust the Tories with the economy'. Whatever benefits a fourth election victory had brought were as nothing compared to the damage done to the Conservative Party by the events of 'Black Wednesday'.

If the Conservatives had regrouped behind their leader, perhaps something could have been retrieved from the wreckage; instead, they continued to behave with atrocious disloyalty – which simply reinforced a growing public contempt. Once again there were rumours of a leadership challenge. The main fault-line over Europe corresponded roughly to one between the holders of the Thatcherite flame and the more pragmatic figures who surrounded Major, and when the Prime Minister was accidentally (so it was said) caught on tape referring to 'three bastards' in his Cabinet, it was generally understood that these were Messrs Portillo, Lilley and Redwood. Some thought that the Home Secretary, Michael Howard, should be included, but it was not clear to some whether this was because he was a Thatcherite or on more general grounds. By the summer of 1995 the speculation had reached such a pitch that Major decided he would not wait for a leadership challenge in the autumn and, to general surprise, he announced that he was standing for re-election.

It was a shrewd, if desperate move; the doubters would have, in his words, 'to put up or shut up'. At first it looked as though Major's gamble that no real challenge would be forthcoming might pay off, but then, in a further surprise move, the Welsh Secretary, John Redwood, decided to make a real challenge. A figure of some obscurity to the general public, Mr Redwood was most notable for his reputed likeness to fictional characters from the *Star Trek* series called Vulcans – something the newly famous candidate took in good part. Redwood deliberately did not mount a great offensive against Major – indeed, it would have been odd if he had – but his candidature was understood to be a warning from the Thatcherites that the Prime Minister should not deviate too far from her legacy, a point underlined by those newspapers who chose to highlight the support which Mr Redwood enjoyed from Thatcherite academics.

With such support, it was hardly to be expected that the challenger would win a famous victory. Everything depended upon Michael Heseltine's supporters – labelled the 'Heselteenies'. Would they calculate that their man could, with one last effort, become Prime Minister if Major went, and so abstain on the first ballot, or even vote for Redwood; similarly how would the 'Portillistas' vote? Rumour had it that the flamboyant Secretary of State for Employment, famous for his extravagant hair style and his right-wing views, was secretly encouraging his supporters to prepare for the second round; but counter-rumour had it that his nose had been put thoroughly out of joint by being overtaken as Mrs Thatcher's heir by 'the Vulcan'. Whatever the truth of this, the campaign itself suggested that habits of intrigue and betrayal had now infected the bloodstream of the Conservative Party.

In the flurry of speculation before and during the contest, there were few signs of dissent from the main themes of Thatcherism, and the fact that Heath was still banging out the same tired old themes about the Conservatives always eschewing ideology went to prove not that he was correct, but how far away from the mainstream he was.[9] Heath's litany of 'traditional Tory values', such as a 'concern for reconciling different interests', was a world away from the tough-minded realism of Redwood, and even Major, who both accepted that there was some level at which some interests were simply irreconcilable, and that there were some principles which came before expediency disguising itself as compassion. Heath's tirade against 'ideology' sounded like something from the late 1970s 'wets', which, of course, it was; it was a sign of how much influence Thatcher had had that many of her ideas were now so commonplace that they no longer seemed like 'ideology'. It took someone from the antediluvian age to remember that they were part of an ideology, although Heath's own ostensibly non-ideological position was, in itself, an emanation of the formerly dominant liberal Conservative ethos. The battleground between Redwood and Major was not over whether to repudiate Mrs Thatcher's legacy, but rather how best to press forward with it – and in particular what the best tactics for dealing with the question of further European integration might be. In the end the 'Heselteenies' seem to have decided that their man would never make it, and that even if Major went it would be someone else who would succeed him, so 'Prezza Hezza' (as the *Sun* liked to call him) decided that there was more to be gained by cutting a deal with a Prime Minister who needed his support. Redwood's expected support turned out, and he received a respectable 89 votes, but the abstentions failed to materialise; only 22 MPs did not vote for either candidate (one did not vote at all). Major's 218 votes (out of 329 MPs), although in the region which the media had labelled as requiring a further ballot, saw him comfortably home. He quickly regrouped his troops, with Heseltine becoming 'Deputy Prime Minister' and lord high everything else. It was taken by the press to be a move to the 'left'; it would certainly ensure that Mr Major and Heseltine would sink or swim together.

Looking back on the leadership battle of summer 1995, Ian Lang, a member of Major's campaign team reflected: 'Apart from John Redwood, the malcontents didn't put up and they didn't shut up. Had he known how the destructive minority within the party would continue to behave after July 1995, and the debacle that would follow, John Major might well have stood down and let others fight for his job that autumn.'[10] What Major's victory did mark was a consolidation of the pragmatic tendency – that line of approach which some Thatcherites labelled the 'Whig', more because of its style than its content – although its contentlessness made it difficult to pronounce on the last point. This was certainly a more helpful description of the division within the party than the old 'left'/'right' phraseology. The 'Whigs' offered an 'attractively cynical approach to politics with a strong tradition of public service', they were 'men of the world' who knew that politics was 'the art of the possible' even if they were prepared to accept that Mrs Thatcher had altered the boundaries of what *was* possible.[11] Their pragmatism made them 'men of government', but they would be lost in Opposition. They were 'so preoccupied with *raison d'état*' that they lost sight of the party's *raison d'être* – which was where Redwood and his supporters came in. Even if the description of them as men who believed 'in a politics which is strongly moral though not intrusively moralistic … men of energy and ideas' might have been thought a little self-serving, it was none the less essentially accurate. Redwood himself had been one of the architects of privatisation and, as a free-market radical and a sceptic on the issue of European unification, his ideas put him on the cutting edge of the Thatcherite advance; it was not surprising that after the contest was over he should have set up a 'think tank'.

After so long in office, there was a danger that the party would forget what it was in power to do, that it would succumb to the idea that it was simply there to govern, as though governing is an act separate from ideology. Ministers have little time for reflection, and when their party has been in power for 17 years then it is indeed tempting to assume the mantle of the pragmatic man of action who is steering the ship of state. Redwood and his supporters held that it was important to have a map and a compass so that you knew where you were going.

Where was the party going? To the gloomy it was heading towards the 'Balfour scenario' in which a weak leader, who succeeds a strong and imposing one, fails to keep the party together and loses the next election by a landslide; to the optimists, there was the chance to win yet another period in office. Major's boldness in calling a leadership election before the summer recess gave the party a summer of peace – and offered him a chance to 'relaunch' his leadership. By September 1995 he was calling his colleagues together to formulate a programme which could win the party a fifth election victory. It was difficult to see what 'new ideas' were on offer – and after 16 years ministers were open to the jibes flung at Macmillan – 'Why had they not come up with any bright ideas earlier?' But it was another sign of Major's main quality – stubborn determination – that he should have made the attempt at all. Redwood and his supporters had argued 'no change, no chance', and this was true – although not for the reason they believed. The real threat to the Prime Minister came from Mrs Thatcher's greatest political success – the transformation of the Labour Party.

After two decades of hearing 'that woman' excoriated by Labour leaders, it was a surprise, as well as a sign of the changes she had wrought, that the new Labour leader, Tony Blair, should have publicly expressed his admiration for Mrs Thatcher (an admiration which was reciprocated). Blair, who pushed the 'desocialisation' process even further than his two predecessors, claimed that 'only a Labour Government could complete the economic and social revolution begun by Margaret Thatcher in the 1980s.' Labour had, he said, accepted the changes she had made and which were now imperilled by the revival of the 'old boy network' in the Tory Party; those who wanted some real 'radicalism' to upset the 'Establishment' should, the Labour leader claimed with considerable chutzpah, vote for him. Mrs Thatcher, he argued, was a 'radical, not a Tory'.[12] When the question could be asked: 'Is Labour the true heir to Thatcher?', it was time not only for the Conservatives to count their political spoons when Mr Blair left, but to reflect that the Labour Party needed to be added to the long list of institutions which had been changed by their encounter with Thatcherism. The spectacle of a Labour leader asking the electorate to believe that 'he can overturn almost everything his party stands for and give them a sanitised version of the Conservative government which they have had for 16 years'[13] was, in its show of nerve, worthy of Mrs Thatcher; and the fact that Mr Blair spoke as he did was testimony to the powerful appeal of the Thatcherite legend. It was also a sign of how low Mr Major was thought to have fallen in public esteem, thanks to allegations of 'sleaze' and controversies over the salaries paid to the directors of the privatised utilities, that Blair could get away with it. It may, of course, simply have been a sign of desperation for power, but the fact that so shrewd a politician as Blair should have thought that the best way to win was to imitate Mrs Thatcher was, in itself, a sign of how dead the old consensus was and how powerful the Thatcher influence had become.

Blair's 'New Labour', had adapted to the Thatcherite revolution, and offered, in the form of its charismatic leader, to soften its rough edges without destroying the benefits it had brought to many voters. Blair recognised the need for politics to be more than the business of creating conditions in which wealth could be acquired and consumed; it was a mark of Major's failure that his own administration had seemed to be full of MPs with no other aim in life. Blair had offered Thatcherism with a human face – and a manifesto from which the word 'socialism' was conspicuously absent, Blair imitated Baldwin in offering mood music rather than specific polices; the number of times Labour 'Shadow' Ministers had to argue that their policy was 'perfectly clear' was enough to show that it was not. But the public was fed up with the squabbling Tories, led by an uncharismatic man who appeared to be unable to impose discipline on his own party.

Until the advent of Mrs Thatcher, the Conservatives had dominated British politics without ever dominating the political agenda; by 1997 this position was exactly reversed. Conservative ideas were so dominant that 'New Labour' intended to work within the Thatcherite legacy, rather than abolish it. Before his first major European summit Mr Blair even asked Lady Thatcher to Downing Street to listen to her views on Europe; one or two of his more troglodyte backbenchers objected, but most people found it a sensible move; it was also a symbolic one.

The Conservative Party had been too successful for its own good. The spectres of Soviet Communism and domestic Socialism had both been exorcised. The notion of 'Big Government' with high taxes to pay for its ambitions was also dead. Everything that was worth privatising had been sold off; Major's privatisation of the rail network was widely held to be a move too far. Promises of further 'radicalism' from the Conservatives seemed to threaten the Health Service and the provision of pensions, offering Blair's Labour easy opportunities for unfounded scare stories. With no more dragons to slay, no more crusades to fight, the era of the giants was over. The Tory Party had been stale, divided and fat with the arrogance of office. With its local base severely damaged by its virtual elimination as a party of local government, with its MPs more interested in arguing over Europe than in fighting Labour, and with a leader who was no match for Blair when it came to public relations, the Conservative Party was uniquely vulnerable to a volatile electorate who thought that it was more than time for a change.

Perhaps the most symbolic result of the 1997 election came in what was the fifth safest Conservative seat, Tatton in Cheshire, where the well-heeled upper-middle-classes from Manchester predominated. For 14 years they had been represented by Neil Hamilton, a charming and urbane lawyer, who fitted into the constituency like a hand into a custom-made glove. An able and ambitious Thatcherite he rose to become Consumer Affairs Minister, before resigning in 1996 after allegations of 'sleaze'. His resignation was not an admission of guilt, but rather a recognition of the fact that he needed to clear his name against charges of improperly accepting money and other favours from Mr Al-Fayed. His legal cases collapsed in early 1997, after which the *Guardian* newspaper publicly accused him of being a liar and a cheat. The announcement of the 1997 election caught Mr Hamilton between this situation and the publication of Sir Gordon Downey's report on this and other allegations of corruption in public life. Despite some speculation to the contrary and some local opposition, Mr Hamilton decided to stand at the election and was adopted, after a struggle, by his local party association. By this stage, however, both the Labour and Liberal-Democrats had announced a willingness to consider standing down if a 'non-party' candidate could be found to oppose Mr Hamilton. A BBC war correspondent, Martin Bell, declared a willingness to stand, in the hope of forcing Mr Hamilton to withdraw. But supported by his now egregious wife Christine, Mr Hamilton went forth to battle, confident of success. Mr Bell romped home with a majority of over 11,000. It seemed not to matter that Mr Bell had few discernible political views and that Mr Hamilton had been convicted of nothing save extreme unwisdom in his choice of political associates. The latter had come to epitomise Tory arrogance and sleaze, the former, in his white suit, to symbolise a longing for purer politics. For the first time in 60 years an Independent MP had secured the seat.

It was the end, it was the flood – the worst result in the long history of the Conservative Party. It lost nearly 12 per cent of its 1992 vote, and won only 165 seats. 'New' Labour saw a swing of nearly 10 per cent, winning 418 seats; it made the Blair mantra 'things can only get better' a little dubious, since it was hard to see how, at least in electoral terms, that could ever be so. In Scotland and Wales the Tories had not a single seat; the North of England was almost a Tory-free zone; it would be tempting to say that the party was thrown back onto its South-East England heartland, but even that would have been over-optimistic. The iconic moment of the night was Michael Portillo hastily leaving the safety of a BBC studio to attend his count at Enfield, where, with a massive swing against him of 17.4 per cent, he lost his seat by 1433 votes to an unknown Labour tyro. 'Were you up for Portillo?' the chattering classes gloated. The question that Portillo had been asked by the commentator, Jeremy Paxman, just before he left seemed curiously apposite: 'Are we seeing the end of the Conservative Party as a credible force in British politics?'

17 No Direction Home?

At London's Royal Festival Hall, Tony Blair arrived from his Sedgefield Constituency to announce 'a new day has dawned, has it not?' All over Britain, Conservatives were not coming to terms with a massive electoral defeat. The result of the 1997 election had not been unexpected, but the sheer scale of the disaster was overwhelming; whatever the polls said, many Conservatives, activists and Members of Parliament had come to believe that they could not possibly be accurate. The pollsters' errors in 1992 may have encouraged this attitude, but the reaction of those canvassed (when canvassing took place) seems to have added to this. Disillusioned Conservative Europhile, Julian Critchley, spoke of a wilful self-deception 'passed up the line'.[1] As it was, for many activists the tidal wave which had hit them was totally unexpected. MPs who had confidently been looking forward to participating in the leadership contest that was sure to follow the election found themselves needing to look for alternative employment, as seats that had been Conservative for as long as anyone could remember suddenly acquired Labour or Liberal Democrat MPs.

Like a deep-sea diver suddenly yanked to the surface, the Tories were suffering from the change in pressure; a decade later it would still be unclear whether they could recover. Men who, the previous day, had had ministerial cars, private offices and the resources of the Civil Service at their disposal to answer questions now found themselves unemployed. This bewilderment was passed down the line; six months later chairmen of Conservative Associations were still offering people access to 'Downing St' before being reminded that it was unlikely that Mr. Blair would respond favourably to such requests. Possession of power had become a habit; the withdrawal symptoms were severe. John Major cut short speculation about his future by, for once, taking decisive action. After commiserating with his colleagues at Conservative Central Office, he returned to Downing Street for the last time. Outside, he announced his resignation from the leadership of the Conservative Party, with the words 'When the curtain falls it is time to get off the stage.' After tendering his resignation to the Queen, Major and his wife moved on to the Oval to watch a cricket match.[2] With the captain gone, there was feverish speculation about who would replace him; having been intriguing almost constantly since the political demise of the Iron Lady, Conservative MPs – or those who were left – could get down to some serious in-fighting. Thus it was that whilst the new, charismatic Prime Minister was proclaiming Britain to be a 'young country', the 'old gang' gave themselves up to a frenzy which would have done justice to the local branch of the Mafia; the contrast was not lost on the electorate – as the Labour spinmeister, Alistair Campbell made sure.

The scale of the Tory defeat had made the contest to succeed Major at once less and more interesting; less so because the obvious front-runner, Michael Portillo, was no longer an MP and could not stand for the post; more so because it was unclear who would win, which, in turn, raised speculation about who would stand to fever pitch; no cliché would be left unused.

As had become the norm in the party, there was a dearth of long-term thinking or planning. So ingrained were the habits of power that despite the electoral Himalayas that would have to be climbed to make it happen, there was a widespread assumption that the Conservatives would win the next election; those who argued that they should be prepared for at least a decade out of power were written off as pessimists; events would show they had been over-optimistic. Had that longer view been taken, the sensible policy would have been to have offered experience and tough pragmatism to oppose the heady idealism of the inexperienced Blair; and there were no dearth of such people on offer. The best of these was the former Chancellor, 'Ken' Clarke. A shrewd and intelligent man, Clarke had carefully cultivated the *persona* of a bluff, cigar smoking, pint quaffing 'good bloke' with a taste for good jazz and scuffed suede shoes. A minister of immense experience, he had been a highly successful and respected Chancellor, and he would have made a formidable leader of the Opposition; he was the only Tory who worried New Labour. But they could rest easy because, for all his attractions and talents, Clarke bore the mark of Cain as far as many Tories were concerned – he was a Europhile. As in 1945, defeat had reduced the party to its heartland – which was pretty uniformly eurosceptic, and, in the first sign of things to come, MPs preferred to go for ideological purity rather than *Realpolitik*. For those who felt that Europe mattered more than anything else, John Redwood offered a re-run of his 1995 bid for power. The former Social Security Secretary, Peter Lilley, stood because Portillo could not, and announced that he had charisma; it was as well he told MPs, for they had not noticed it before. The other heavyweight figure to enter the lists was the former Home Secretary, Michael Howard, a eurosceptic and right-winger who was loathed by those on the political left. The latter were delighted by the vicious attack launched on him by his former junior at the Home Office, Ann Widdecombe, who accused him of having 'something of the night' in his character. That left the youngest and least experienced of the candidates, William Hague, who had entered the Cabinet in the post Redwood had vacated in 1995. At 36, the balding Hague positioned himself as the candidate of the future: pragmatic and unscarred by the Major years.

For the first time since the Tories had begun the practice of electing a leader, the ballot went to the third round; the whole process showed how little the media pundits understood the Conservative Party – and how little the latter understood the new political landscape. Redwood, who had been written off as an unelectable 'Vulcan', went into the second round instead of Lilley and Howard who, in pique, threw their weight behind Hague; eliminated at the second hurdle, Redwood found himself cast as king-maker. Then, in a move worthy of the best traditions of the Fox-North coalition or the Molotov-Ribbentrop pact, Clarke and Redwood made an unexpected alliance designed to scupper Hague. For a brief moment it looked as though *Realpolitik* might win the day, but with Lady Thatcher throwing her weight decisively behind Hague the commentators were confounded as 'William the Younger' came home by 92 to 70 votes. It thus fell to William Jefferson Hague, at the age of 36, to lead the Conservative Party out of the Conservative century – and the wilderness into which it now found itself.

Hague's victory was a triumph for the new managerialism which the Thatcher years had spawned; the answer to the party's difficulties lay in getting the structures right. For those, like Clarke, who felt that the answer was to get stuck into the Labour Government whilst it still lacked experience, this was the signal to go to the backbenches and concentrate on their business careers. This left the road open to Hague and his modernisers. Before winning election to Parliament in 1987, Hague had worked for the management consultants, McKinsey, and this showed in his plans to reform the structures of the party – the main plank in the 'Fresh Future' he promised his followers. As a first step, Hague brought in Archie Norman, a former colleague at McKinsey, as vice-chairman of the party. Newly elected to Parliament for Tunbridge Wells, Norman's rise was unusual, but not unexpected. As Chief Executive, then chairman of ASDA, Norman had turned around the fortunes of the supermarket chain, and it was hoped that he might be able to do the same with another 'damaged brand' – the Conservative Party. A speech by Hague, outlining his plans, was circulated to all party members; it was the first of a series of gestures designed to demonstrate that the party was 'listening' to its members; whether this was a good idea was another matter. In addition, Hague, aware that the voluntary party had expressed a preference for Kenneth Clarke, held a plebiscite of party members to vote on his leadership, as well as on a set of six broad principles. An unkind observer might have commented that as leadership ballots went, this one was a little lacking in democracy: Hague was the only candidate; and since his six principles were that the Party should be 'fresh, open, clear, clean, outgoing and listening',[3] it appeared unlikely that anyone would contest them; Labour's spin doctors hardly needed to point out the implication – which was that the party as it currently stood was none of these things.

There are advantages in getting off to a flying start; but when the traumas were as great as those the Tories had been through, there were some serious disadvantages. Because there had been no time to weigh up what lessons might need to be learned, and because the party was still in a state of shock, it was a moot point whether the suggested reforms were the ones needed; the leadership's determination to press on with them – whilst being seen to 'consult' and 'listen' – meant that they would be debated and decided upon at the party's 1997 Conference. That was always likely to resemble a wake; the fact that it was held in the northern seaside town of Blackpool – a venue unpopular with most Conservatives, simply added to the gloom that was already enveloping the party.

Hague easily won the ballot on his leadership, and went on to present a more concrete series of reforms. Although not immediately apparent, the debate on the reform of the method of electing the leader was to prove the most important of these debates. The mood of the conference over this was dark; almost one of fury. Archie Hamilton, Chairman of the 1922 Committee, was booed as he suggested that MPs should retain a preponderance of the vote in electing the leader. Jeffery Archer, the novelist, Tory peer and supreme opportunist, his eyes on a return to frontline politics, spoke in favour of the members having half the votes in any leadership election – and was roundly cheered. Thoroughly alarmed, the Committee decided to give all members an equal say in the selection of the leader – albeit only after the MPs had narrowed the field to two. An interesting side-effect of the reform was that it helped Hague. Although the new system was touted as offering more power to the ordinary members, it actually bolstered the security of the sitting leader, since it now required 15 per cent of MPs to trigger a leadership challenge (it had been 10 per cent). Moreover, unless the leader failed to win a simple majority in a vote of no confidence, there would be no election at all; under that system, Mrs Thatcher could not have been toppled. The system provided for two ballots of MPs, in order to narrow the field, and then a long delay as the membership were balloted; it might almost have been designed to avoid having a leadership contest – which begged the question of its utility whenever it would have to be used. Perhaps with a leader in his thirties, no one thought of that; but it is more likely that in sheer funk the leadership capitulated to what the party activists wanted. It would not be the last time this would happen, and if it allowed the party pause to pat itself on the back for being very democratic, it also showed a worrying tendency to veer towards the party's basic instincts.

For the first time, a corporate entity known as the Conservative Party came into existence, this replaced the ancient tripartite structure of the Parliamentary party, its professional organisation and the voluntary associations in the country; to the evident bewilderment of many of the latter, membership cards were introduced – with a charge for those joining the party for the first time; it seemed to some a perverse way of attracting new members. At the same time as tidying up these historical anomalies, the party also showed worrying signs of misreading its own history. In speaking on the 'Green Paper' for reform, the Deputy Chairman, Michael Trend, and others, mentioned the Butler reforms with great frequency; it was as if they believed that all the party had to do after a Labour landslide was set about a programme of structural change, and the voters would automatically flock back to its banner. This was politics by management consultancy, and whilst it was understandable that a party which had just taken such a drubbing in the polls should have less than full confidence in its instincts, it was beginning to look as though the baby was departing with the bath water, an impression strengthened with Hague's introduction of 'weekends away' for the Parliamentary party.

The 'away day' idea, popular in management theory, inevitably (given the party's recent scandals) gave rise to jokes about 'have it away days', and produced the unlikely spectacle of sweater-clad Conservative MPs trying to prove that they were 'regular guys'; the pictures served to suggest that they were anything but that, and the only ones to emerge with credit were those like Churchill's grandson, Nicholas Soames, who grandly refused to attend such a vulgar event. As an attempt to improve the image of the Conservative party it was a risible failure.[4]

One of the great ironies of Hague's leadership was that whilst obsessing with the latest management theorems, he was actually best at the old-fashioned stuff of traditional politics. As a speaker, both on the platform and in the House, he was simply superb. People who attended his meetings always expressed surprise at his great height. For reasons best known to themselves, cartoonists portrayed Hague as a midget; in fact he was a good six foot tall, and his athletic build made him appear even taller. He was adept at reaching out to his audiences in language they understood, and it was a mark of his success that even after he had ceased to be leader of the party he remained a great draw at constituency functions; it was little wonder that David Cameron was to make him Shadow Foreign Secretary in 2005. In Parliament, he proved an able adversary to Blair at Prime Minister's Questions. Commentators described the new Conservative leader as that rare thing in modern politics, an orator. One former minister, however, complained that he 'lacked the killer instinct'.[5] That was a little harsh, perhaps, but Hague's real problem lay elsewhere – in the nature of modern politics.

The sad fact was that few people listened to Prime Minister's Questions, which in any case Blair reduced to one session a week. Whatever else one could say of the new Prime Minister, his eye for what would play with the public was second to none, and the fact that he hardly bothered attending the House, even to vote, showed how marginal what happened on the floor of the Commons had become. The rest of the Shadow Cabinet proved transitory, and by 1999, only William Hague and George Young remained of the Cabinet that had gone into the 1997 election. Clarke remained on the backbenches, while Hague's other rivals for the leadership had managed to discredit themselves sufficiently for him to drop them quietly. The plain fact was that the party, still stunned by their rejection by the electorate, was being run ragged by Blair, who proved himself a politician of genius.

On the one hand the new Prime Minister talked about a 'new Britain', but on the other he was so clearly a respectable, moderately conservative middle-class barrister that it was useless to try to present him as some kind of revolutionary socialist. Where he did prove radical, in constitutional matters such as devolved assemblies for Scotland and Wales, and reform of the House of Lords, he disturbed few voters although, on this last issue, he did succeed brilliantly in destabilising the Conservatives. One of the few successes in Hague's Shadow Cabinet was the leader of the House of Lord, the latest bearer of the historic name of Lord Cranborne. An able and energetic former MP, Cranborne was determined to ensure that Blair's policy did not result in the total removal of the hereditary peers. Rightly suspicious of Blair's claim that the abolition of the 'hereditaries' was just the first in a two stage reform of the Lords, Cranborne wanted to keep some element of the principle upon which the House was founded; Blair proved willing to negotiate on the issue, and Cranborne secured the retention of 92 hereditary peers to be chosen by ballot. This was the politics of pragmatism, as he himself admitted. Perhaps, he had publicly mused in happier days, to die in the last ditch might sound romantic, but then ditches are not pleasant places to die in.[6] However, by some oversight, Cranborne had forgotten to inform his leader of his involvement in this scheme. This was to prove particularly unfortunate, for Hague, learning of the plan, attempted to taunt Blair for abandoning his principles over it, only to be informed that his leader in the Lords was the main begetter of the compromise. After a stormy series of meetings, and amidst scenes that smacked of farce, during which the entire Conservative front bench in the Lords came close to resigning, Cranborne agreed to be sacked.[7] To the press, he explained that he had run in 'like an ill-trained spaniel'. While Cranborne went, the deal stayed in place, an admission that it was the best that could have been expected. That this episode did not damage Hague says much about the indifference of the country to the antics of the party.

Hague had lost an experienced and wily politician, and looked, more than ever, like the only man of talent on his own Front Bench; this was not a good thing because, despite his own very considerable abilities, he suffered from the most appalling public image. He had first come to national attention as a 16-year-old schoolboy, when he had addressed the 1977 party conference. This 'Tory boy' image still clung to him, although he was balding and 20 years older. He seemed, in the eyes of many, to have passed from nerdish adolescence to fogeyish middle age without ever having been young. Not even his marriage in 1997 to the glamorous blonde Ffion Jenkins, formerly a Civil Servant at the Welsh Office, could dispel this image. Stunts designed to show he was young and modern served only to make him seem ridiculous. The decision to visit a 'theme park' was bad enough, but to do so whilst wearing a baseball cap embroidered with his name, was to invite the ridicule he received. The person responsible for sending him and Ffion to the Notting Hill carnival deserved the sack; she, as ever, looked gorgeous, even casually dressed; he looked like a banker having an uncomfortable 'dress down Friday'.

The over-reliance on Ffion's glamour also led to some moments best forgotten. Her decision to wear a 'daring' dress to the Party Conference dance seemed too much like trying too hard, and it is best to draw a veil over the 'revelation' that the couple were going to share a bed at the party conference.[8] These attempts to present Hague as a 'normal bloke' came to an end, thankfully, in 1998 when professional advice was sought. Instead of 'casual smart' Hague began to wear Jermyn Street shirts and well-cut dark suits, as well as having what was left of his hair cut short.[9] While there were occasional slips in this image, such as Hague's boast to a men's 'lifestyle' magazine about his teenage alcohol intake, these were rare in comparison to the early stories. Whether a bald man with a Yorkshire accent could ever have matched the slickness of Mr 'I'm a pretty straight sort of a guy, call me Tony' Blair, may be doubted; but Hague's bad start put him at a permanent disadvantage.

Had politics been conducted in the fashion of a previous age, without the broadcast media, Hague's undeniable presence on a political platform would have made these stunts unnecessary, but in the media age, the fact was that the Conservative Party did not know exactly what to do with its leader. He was undeniably talented, but he also seemed 'odd.' Appointing media people, such as former *Daily Express* managing editor Amanda Platell might have had the same effect as the appointment of *Mirror* journalist Alistair Campbell had on Labour – but that would have required her to be of his calibre. Imitation may be the sincerest form of flattery; it is not necessarily good politics. Perhaps sensing where his strengths lay, Hague had a go at reviving the mass meeting, with 'Road shows' such as the 'Battle For Britain', a campaign against Labour's constitutional changes, and his 'Keep the Pound' rallies and the 'Listening to Britain' exercise. This last campaign was based on the Republicans 'Listening to America' exercise that had taken place after the 1992 defeat of President George H. Bush, and was felt to have contributed to their victory in the 1994 elections.[10] The danger with these was that, being largely held for Conservative audiences, they became less dialogue than internal monologue, and turned into opportunities for Hague to display his undeniable talents as an orator in a private setting.

Hague went to great trouble to seem to be consulting his party's members; but the utility of listening to people who were, themselves, out of touch with Blair's Britain seemed both contrived and of doubtful utility. The cosmetic nature of these exercises was cruelly exposed by the much-trumpeted 'consultation' over the contents of the Conservative manifesto for 2001; a few days after the launch of the exercise the press published the contents of the manifesto – which rather underlined the cosmetic nature of the 'consultation'. But the wider question, of whether the membership of the Party was the right group from which to be taking advice, was seldom asked; and yet, as the continuing obsession over 'Europe' (always spoken thus) showed, it was a highly relevant one.

The question of Europe continued to haunt the Conservatives, and their old commonsense approach to political issues flew out of the window on this one; for all the tendency of the Europhiles to categorise the eurosceptics as 'nutters', their own behaviour hardly suggested a balanced and sane approach. The decision by Ken Clarke and Michael Heseltine to appear on the same platform as Blair as he launched a campaign to promote Britain's entry into the single European currency, suggested that they cared more about that issue than they did about party unity; no doubt it never entered into Blair's mind that this might make the Tories look terminally divided. Naturally, this brought the froth to the mouths of the eurosceptics, who agitated for a firmer line to be taken, and for the 'pound' to be 'saved'. To most of the electorate the Tories looked as though they were both divided and unbalanced on this issue; since this was uncomfortably close to the truth, perhaps, for once, appearance were not deceptive. The Euro-elections of 1999, then, to be held under a system of proportional representation for the first time, were to be a serious test of Hague's leadership. They were also to prove a trap.

The change to Proportional Representation meant that every sitting Conservative MEP had to be reselected. Among these were a number of extreme pro-Europeans who, facing a hustings of ordinary members, failed to be selected high enough up the party lists to actually gain election. Some, like Robin Kellett-Bowman in the South-East, grinned and bore it. Others, including John Stevens and Brendan Donnelly, decided to form their own 'Pro-Euro Conservative Party'. Arguing that Britain should join the Single Currency as soon as possible, they attacked Blair for not possessing enough resolution to sell the euro to the British People. Their main target, however, was William Hague. If they could prove that enough Conservatives favoured British membership of the euro, or at least a more pro-European line than that suggested by the Conservatives' 'In Europe: Not Run by Europe' slogan (suggested by William Hague himself),[11] they might be able to change Conservative policy, even unseat William Hague: 'We foresee no improvement in the electoral fortunes of the Conservative Party until it reverts to its traditional positive view of Europe and European policy ... Every vote cast for us will be a powerful signal to the Conservative leadership that it is destroying the Conservative Party.'[12]

On the eurosceptic side, while the Referendum Party had died with its founder, Sir James Goldsmith, the United Kingdom Independence Party (UKIP) had inherited the mantle of Elijah. Initially founded by LSE historian Alan Sked, UKIP had been taken over by millionaire Michael Holmes, who saw in the Euro-elections a perfect opportunity to push his agenda of withdrawal from the European Union. The Conservatives under Hague ran a very real risk of being squeezed from both sides. The BBC gave the Pro-Euro Conservatives a high profile in its reporting, presumably awed by the very establishmentarian tone of the party leaders – and the fact that their views coincided with those which the Corporation's reporters thought normal and respectable.

Since European elections have never attracted the attention of a majority of the electorate, opinion polls are hardly reliable, still, the eventual result stunned observers. The Conservatives gained the largest number of seats, 36, with 34.5 per cent of the vote; the UKIP won three seats, and the Pro-Euro Conservatives got precisely nowhere. Hague's leadership, which had reached its lowest point, was greatly strengthened, and his instincts seemed to be vindicated. Reshuffling his Shadow Cabinet, Hague sacked Peter Lilley, by now Deputy Leader, who had alienated some on the Party's right wing by criticising the Thatcher legacy.[13] Now backed by the eurosceptic press, Hague embarked on a new series of 'Keep the Pound' rallies, identifying the Conservatives with the currency, even bringing out a set of merchandise emblazoned with pound signs (although Ffion Hague's appearing with a sterling silver pound sign on her necklace backfired when it was discovered that the pendant had not been paid for). It seemed that the Conservative eurosceptics were vindicated in their belief that a strong campaign against European integration was the road back to power.

When elected leader, William Hague had promised that the Conservative Party would 'reach out' to society, including those sections not traditionally identified as Conservative. However, his core instincts were more traditional than his appearance at the Notting Hill carnival might have suggested. One issue, which would return to haunt the party, was homosexuality. When the Labour Party proposed to repeal section 28 of the Local Government Act, 1988, which prohibited the promotion of homosexuality by Local Education Authorities, Hague vowed to oppose the move. Given that the measure was largely symbolic, having never applied to schools, the battle was always going to be more symbol than substance. Even so, Shaun Woodward, a rising star on the liberal wing of the party defected to the Labour party over the issue, which saw the Conservative Party align itself with evangelical Christians in an alliance more typical of the United States than the United Kingdom. Hague imposed a three-line whip on Conservative MPs to vote against repeal.[14] The image of a right-wing party in hock to its own bigots was to prove difficult to shake off in any event; but this hardly suggested that Hague wanted to try to do that.

In the wake of the Euro-elections, Hague began to formulate policy for the General Election, expected in May 2001. A series of consultations with party members produced *The Common Sense Revolution*, a 'pre-manifesto' setting out the broad details of Conservative policy in a number of areas. Billboard posters attacked the Labour Party's record on delivering public services. But basing himself on the Euro-election results, Hague preferred to hammer away of the issue of 'sovereignty' and 'Europe'. Addressing the Conservative Party's Spring Forum at Harrogate in March 2001, he delivered a stinging attack on the Labour Party, warning that its pro-European policies risked turning Britain into 'a foreign land. ... Our currency gone forever ... . The Chancellor returning from Brussels carrying instructions to raise taxes still further.'[15] Towards the end of this speech, Hague referred to immigration and asylum, leading to allegations from Labour and the Liberal Democrats that his remarks were racist,[16] while pro-Europeans in the Conservative Party, such as Michael Heseltine attacked the remarks as 'xenophobic'.[17] Hague was far from being a xenophobe – but his comments played straight into the Labour strategy of presenting the Tories as terminally old-fashioned, out of touch, and more than a shade unpleasant on issues such as sexuality and race.

The General Election of 2001 was delayed from May to June following the outbreak of Foot and Mouth Disease. In the run up to the election, Conservative posters asked: 'You Paid the Money, where are the Nurses/Teacher/Police?'[18] The Conservative Manifesto, *Time for Common Sense*, laid out a raft of policies aimed at 'setting the people free', such as freeing schools from Local Education Authority control and allowing Patients and GPs to decide whether patients should be treated at NHS or private hospitals. However, as the election campaign progressed, the Labour Party maintained a solid lead in opinion polls – to the confusion of activists, who felt sure that the British People must have rumbled Blair. William Hague concentrated on the one issue he knew had energised the people: Europe. Arguing that Labour would use an election win to take Britain into the European Single Currency, despite Blair's promise to hold a referendum before Britain joined, Conservative campaigners were instructed to stress that only the Conservatives would keep the Pound. Those constituencies that declined to have much to do with the campaign slogans of Central Office showed much wisdom.

The electorate had not forgiven the Tories for John Major, and they did not see why, after only four years, they should sack that nice Mr Blair and replace him with a bald Yorkshireman with a pretty wife. In the election, held on Thursday 7 June 2001, the Conservatives made a net gain of exactly one seat. Until the declaration of the Isle of Wight late on Friday 8 June, the Conservative Party faced the prospect of having achieved precisely nothing. In the circumstances, William Hague had little choice but to step down, having seen the sun glinting on the long knives. Thus William Jefferson Hague became the first Conservative leader since Austen Chamberlain to have never been Prime Minister; he was the first of many.

What went wrong? In the first place, while everyone had been very definite that the Conservative Party needed to change in order to win, there was no real indication of exactly what that change should be. Organisational change was easy: that was why it was the first item on the agenda after the defeat of 1997; but organisational change alone was not enough. Here, the misreading of their own history misled the Tories; had it not been for the palpable exhaustion of the Atlee Government in 1950, the reorganised Conservative Party would have stood as little chance as it did in 2001. Equally, while the Labour government of 1945 had presented a clear set of policies for the Conservative Party to adapt to, Blair proved more of a Baldwin than an Attlee, a master of mood music rather than substance. Hague and the Conservative leadership had assumed the public would 'see through' Blair, as they had; it did no such thing – it would take another two terms and a disastrous war in Iraq for that to happen. The Tories gave the impression of having lurched to the political right in the hope of shoring up their core vote; they gave no sign of having connected with the public mood Blair exploited so successfully; and so the public declined to connect with them.

In the leadership election which followed, the bookies' favourite, with the support of more than half the Shadow Cabinet, was Michael Portillo, who had become Shadow Chancellor following his election for Kensington and Chelsea in the November 1999 by-election following the death of Alan Clark.[19] In many ways Portillo's personal evolution reflected what the party should have done after 1997. He had spent his time out of the House making some very public recantations of his old right-wing views, and through the medium of print and television he had softened his image almost as much as he had his famous hair-style. This was a new 'softer', more 'caring' Portillo. He may still have been uncompromisingly hostile to a single currency for Europe, but on issues of sexuality and race, his message was a liberal, compassionate one; finally, a leading right-wing Conservative had twigged that it was a bad idea to insult large numbers of the electorate; after all, even back-woods squires had sons who might be homosexual, or daughters who produced heirs without benefit of clergy. Those who suggested that Portillo's change had more to do with tone than substance missed the point; it was precisely the tone adopted by the Conservative Party that made it unelectable.

Portillo's shift in position made him vulnerable to an assault from the right-wing of the party which, in a peculiarly dim re-run of Labour's experience in the early 1980s, went round suggesting that the people had voted for Blair because the Tories had not been right-wing enough.

Michael, now Lord, Heseltine, suggested that as the party had been foolish not to have chosen Kenneth Clarke the last time around, it should take this opportunity to rectify its mistake; neither he, nor his critics, had learned anything across the previous four years. After Shadow Home Secretary Ann Widdecombe discovered that she might well not get enough support to even make the first ballot, the field narrowed to Kenneth Clarke, Michael Portillo, Party Chairman Michael Ancram, former Europe Minister David Davis and Shadow Defence Secretary Iain Duncan Smith, Norman Tebbit's successor at Chingford. Portillo was the clear favourite, and his campaign gave every impression that he knew it too well. In his speeches, Portillo referred to the need for the party to modernise. He also, in what was viewed as an embrace of the 'confessional culture', told interviewers that he had had 'homosexual experiences' at University in Cambridge. His advocacy of modernisation and his apparent assumption that he would win alienated a number of his colleagues.

The first round of voting saw Michael Ancram and David Davies tie for last place, each receiving 21 votes. Although Portillo topped the poll, his 49 votes were well short of a decisive lead, meaning that the election was likely to be a long and bruising fight.[20] The second round showed that the worst had not passed, with Portillo gaining only one extra vote. Thatcherite champion Iain Duncan Smith and Kenneth Clarke increased their totals by three votes each, decisively (as events turned out) taking the wind out of Portillo's sails;[21] an attempt to revive his fortunes by claiming Mrs Thatcher's backing went disastrously wrong when she denied it.[22] The ballot to select the two candidates who would face the party members saw Portillo eliminated, receiving 53 votes, only one vote behind Iain Duncan Smith; Kenneth Clarke moved into the lead with 59 votes. Michael Portillo announced that he would quit frontline politics and would not seek re-election.[23]

The final dénouement was now inevitable, as the most formidable election-winner in the history of democratic politics now decided to shoot itself in both feet. Clarke remained what he had been in 1997: a man of formidable experience, political skills of a high order, and a figure feared by Labour; but he remained wedded to a Europhile position. A party serious about power would have paid the price of accepting his views of Europe – views which, in any event, he would have been unable to enforce on his party at large; but the Conservatives were, by now, lost in their own solipsistic madness. The MPs having made the mistake of offering the membership Duncan Smith instead of Portillo were duly rewarded for their want of judgement when the party members voted overwhelmingly for him. Duncan Smith looked like the membership; indeed, every local association had their own version of him, and very useful they were as party treasurers and providers of large gardens in which fund-raising parties could be held; but to elect one of these nice grey men as the leader of the party was rank folly. On 13 September 2001, Iain Duncan Smith became leader of the Conservative Party. The news was barely noticed amid the continuing coverage of the horrific terrorist attacks on New York two days earlier (which had caused the date for the announcement, originally set for 11 September, to be moved).

If William Hague's election as leader had taken some by surprise, almost no one had expected Duncan Smith to become leader. He had entered Parliament at the 1992 General Election, but had remained on the backbenches, participating in the rebellions over the Major government's European policy. BBC News Correspondent Nyta Mann commented: 'Iain Duncan Smith's election as Conservative leader is a remarkable turn in the political career of a man previously best known for destabilising his own government.'[24] Only after the 1997 election had he joined the Front Bench, and then in the relatively lowly position of Shadow Social Security Secretary. In 1999, he had become Shadow Defence Secretary, an appropriate post for one who had served in the Scots Guards. He had stood for the party leadership as a representative of the right-wing of the party, those who believed that the party must continue to promote Thatcherism, and who wished to punish Portillo for his perceived betrayal of Thatcherism. As leader, however, Duncan Smith struck a more conciliatory note.

Duncan Smith had supported John Redwood in 1997 and was a prominent member of the 'No-Turning Back' group of MPs. Yet among his first actions was the suspension of the right-wing Monday Club's affiliation to the party. While Duncan Smith's Shadow Cabinet was dominated by figures from the right of the party, Michael Howard returning as Shadow Chancellor after Portillo's decision to leave front-line politics, the new leader was aware that Kenneth Clarke had received more votes from the Parliamentary party than he had, and he was never able to command the full loyalty or respect of his colleagues. Accordingly, it often seemed that Duncan Smith was ruling the party as a man who believed Portillo had actually won. He took the party in a slightly more liberal direction than his supporters wanted; for example, his decision to decline membership of the Carlton Club because that institution did not admit women. This inclusive tone had its limits, however. May 2002 saw Duncan Smith adopting a policy of opposition to proposals for allowing homosexual couples to adopt children, a policy decision which caused the resignation of John Bercow, MP for Buckingham, from the Front Bench, in events faintly reminiscent of Hague's opposition to the repeal of Section 28. While condemned as 'homophobic' by Liberal Democrat and Labour spokesmen, this position was hardly surprising, given Iain Duncan Smith's Roman Catholic faith.[25]

Yet Smith's early leadership was also marked by signs of hesitancy. A vocal complaint led to his making very little impact in the Commons, while the party's performance at the Ipswich by-election saw the party only narrowly holding on to second place in a seat the party had held from 1987 to 1992, as disaffected Labour voters switched to the Liberal Democrats. Conservatives began to worry that the Liberal Democrats would continue to benefit from Labour woes. The local elections of May 2002 saw some encouraging signs, as the Conservatives became the largest party in local government. However, the Conservative Party still seemed becalmed. From July of 2002 a number of former ministers, including Nicholas Soames, Sir Malcolm Rifkind and Michael Heseltine criticised the leadership, Heseltine calling on the party to sack the new leader. Lacklustre performances at Prime Minister's Questions did nothing to help Duncan Smith, who came across as diffident and out-of-touch. In one notable exchange, he revealed that, in connection with the fire-fighters' strike of late 2002, he had personally called the fire-fighters' leader, rather than getting an official to do it for him.[26] Conservatives were heard to observe that at least Hague had performed well against Tony Blair. By the conference of October 2003, Iain Duncan Smith seemed increasingly embattled, with the journalist Andrew Rawnsley referring to him as 'dead man talking'.[27] It was at this conference that, in his closing speech, Duncan Smith, who had dubbed himself 'the quiet man' a year before, declared, in an attempt to shore up his position: 'The quiet man is here to stay and he's turning up the volume.' This won him a long-standing ovation in the hall, but outside the hall, the vultures were still gathering. A speech can only buy time. Duncan Smith would have to follow that with actual results, and these were slow in coming.

By Tuesday 28 October 2003, Duncan Smith was facing a vote of no confidence in his leadership, opponents having gathered the necessary 25 names from Conservative MPs. He initially attempted to brazen it out, appearing on the steps of Conservative Central Office to welcome the opportunity to end speculation about his leadership.[28] Under the rules introduced by William Hague, all Iain Duncan Smith had to do to stave off a challenge was win a simple majority of the votes of MPs. But it was not to be; the final result saw 90 MPs voting against their leader and 75 supporting Duncan Smith. Under the rules governing the contest, Iain Duncan Smith had no choice but to resign and take no further part in the leadership election that had to follow.

Iain Duncan Smith's leadership had revealed the problems of a system for electing a leader which allowed for the possibility that a man might become leader of the Conservative Party while not commanding the support of a majority of Conservative MPs. Perhaps if he had demonstrated a flair for leadership, he might have been suffered to continue to the next election. But he had not, and with that ruthlessness peculiar to the Conservative Party, he had been dispatched. If Hague had been the first Conservative leader since Austen Chamberlain to fail to attain the premiership, he was clearly not going to be alone for very long. As 'the Quiet Man' faded away into silence, the Conservative Party was left in the unusual position of having to replace a leader in mid-Parliament.

Swiftly it emerged that the Parliamentary party had no taste for another leadership contest. That would take several months, all the while allowing Labour to make sport of the Opposition, as Iain Duncan Smith soldiered on, in spite of having been dropped by the party. It was an impossible position, and the answer the party came up with was, to say the least, improbable: having embraced 'one member one vote' democracy, the party was going to return to the 'magic circle'. David Davis and Tim Yeo, two of the men most strongly implicated in Iain Duncan Smith's political demise, threw their support behind the former Home Secretary, Michael Howard, as did other potential leadership candidates such as Oliver Letwin; then Shadow Home Secretary.[29] The ousted leader stated that he would not back any of the candidates in the leadership contest, but this was unnecessary. By the close of nominations on 6 November, there was only one name before the party – that of Michael Howard. The man who had possessed 'something of the night about him' in 1997 had become the party's saviour in six years. During the campaign, Michael Howard had said that, like Hague, he wanted his leadership endorsed by the party membership.[30] However, after his 'emergence', Howard decided that this was unnecessary as well as expensive. Behind this was a dissatisfaction with the Hague reforms to the party's methods of electing its leaders. The democratic method had produced a weak and uninspiring leader who had lacked the support of the parliamentary party. Of course, members might object that the choice they had been given in 2001 was an unfair one, with Michael Portillo, the most popular candidate, having been eliminated in the early stages.

Michael Howard's initial task as Conservative leader was to restore some of the party's credibility, which had been undermined during the Duncan Smith leadership. Given his unopposed return by the party, he possessed the ability to quiet some of the discontent within it, and his aggressive performance at the Dispatch Box heartened Conservative MPs. In a change of tone over the war in Iraq, Michael Howard stated that he would not have voted for military action there, an action which earned him the enmity of the Republican administration in the United States, a rift which widened further when Howard refused to congratulate President George W. Bush on his re-election in November 2004. With Bush seeing Blair as a key ally in his 'War Against Terrorism', links between the Conservatives and the Republicans were at their lowest level for decades, in contrast to the close working relationship Mrs Thatcher had possessed with Ronald Reagan.

The European election results of 2004 saw the Conservative Party again gaining the most votes; but at 27 per cent, their lowest total since 1832, this was nothing to celebrate. The real story was the doubling of the vote for UKIP, who gained 16 per cent. While some of this was due to the voters becoming more comfortable with proportional representation, and Labour suffered a similar loss of support, it was still no platform for victory in the next General Election, despite the usual speech stating that this 'laid the foundation for a great victory'. This was the first UK election in which the two parties between them had failed to win more than half the vote.[31] It was not the sort of result likely to support the Conservative leader; indeed, had it not been for the lack of desire for a new leadership battle within the party, the performance of UKIP might have reopened the splits over Europe.[32] Still, there were siren voices saying that the Conservatives should stress their anti-European credentials in the run-up to the General Election if they were to win.

The run-up to the 2005 General Election saw the Conservatives facing yet another Labour landslide. The polls predicted a majority of around 130 for Labour, while the Conservative campaign had started badly, with Howard Flight, MP for Arundel and South Downs, being sacked as a candidate after suggesting that the Conservative Party had secret plans to slash spending. As the campaign continued, Howard was dogged by claims that the party's 'Are You Thinking What We're Thinking?' campaign slogan was designed to appeal to the worst instincts of the electorate while not making this explicit (called 'Dog-Whistle' campaigning by its opponents).[33] Only on the election night did it become clear that the result was going to be very different. Exit polls indicated that the election was likely to be much closer than things at first appeared, with early results in the South-East showing a strong swing towards the Conservatives. David Mellor's former seat of Putney was won by Justine Greening, and gains in Ilford and Enfield Southgate seemed to confirm this trend. However, the swing was not uniform. While the South-East, where house price inflation and worries over the economy were current, turned back towards the Conservative Party, northern England was not so convinced. The Conservatives failed to gain any of their target seats in the West Midlands, losing Solihull to the Liberal democrats, and it was a similar story in the North, with Westmoreland and Lonsdale moving into the Liberal camp. In Scotland, where major boundary changes had taken place, Peter Duncan, Shadow Scottish Secretary and the party's only Scottish MP, failed to secure re-election, and only the election of David Mundell in Dumfriesshire, Clydesdale and Tweeddale kept the party from suffering another wipe-out north of the border. In Wales, a Tory-free zone since 1997, three Conservatives were elected, two on the slenderest of majorities.

When the shouting had died down, Labour was left with a majority of 66, greatly reduced but more than adequate. The Conservatives gained 33 seats, at 198 just short of 200, while the Liberal Democrats, who had gambled on making greater gains than were actually realised, calling a number of South-Eastern seats, such as Eastbourne, for themselves, began to turn on their leader, Charles Kennedy. As for Michael Howard, while it was widely recognised that he was unlikely to be still leading the party by the time of the next election, expected for 2009, most commentators felt that he had done well enough to stay on for the time being, sparing a repeat of the 2001 leadership race (viewed as damaging if only because it had produced Iain Duncan Smith); however, as he went to address a meeting of the party at Putney, the first Conservative gain of the night, Michael Howard had already decided to stand down. Speaking at Putney, he declared that it was better for him to 'stand aside sooner rather than later', but announced that he would stay on to allow the party to re-think the Hague reforms to the mechanism for choosing a leader.[34]

The party opted not to change the rules, handing Michael Howard a humiliating rebuff and teaching the leadership that power, once given up, can seldom be reclaimed. Many party members felt unfairly criticised by MPs who blamed them for choosing Duncan Smith; after all, if the MPs had offered them a choice between a Europhile and a eurosceptic, they were always going to go for the latter – even if it was in the form of Duncan Smith; so it was that the leadership contest took place under more or less the same rules as had obtained in 2001.[35] However, there was to be one difference: the ballots were to take place after the October Conference, to be held, once again, at Blackpool.

For the first time since Macmillan's resignation in 1963, the Party Conference became a sort of American-style convention – except American Conventions no longer choose the candidate. All the candidates were there, and the press was watching eagerly to see what would happen next. There were five candidates this time, after Shadow Chancellor Oliver Letwin announced that he intended to leave the Front Bench to concentrate on his business interests, and Shadow Transport Secretary Alan Duncan withdrew before the conference after discovering that he could not possibly win. Malcolm Rifkind, newly returned for Kensington and Chelsea, which seemed to have become a gateway for former MPs to return to Westminster, was the 'moderate but still eurosceptic' candidate; Kenneth Clarke was the Kenneth Clarke candidate, declaring that the party had to have him as leader or remain in the wilderness; Liam Fox, Shadow Foreign Secretary, was the candidate of the right; Shadow Home Secretary David Davis, the firm favourite, with his working-class background, toughness and emphasis on taking the fight to Labour; and last, David Cameron, Shadow Education Secretary since September 2004, a relative unknown, and an MP since 2001.

The election was perceived as largely David Davis's to lose; accordingly the front-runner was cautious – and lost it. His speech at Blackpool was seen as pedestrian and lacking in inspiration.[36] Like Butler and Hailsham in 1963, he had stumbled at the first and, as events were to prove, crucial hurdle. At the same time, commentators agreed that Kenneth Clarke's speech had been a good pitch for the leadership, showing his customary bonhomie.[37] However, given that Clarke had tried and failed twice to win the ultimate prize, more importance was attached to the performance of the outsider, David Cameron, who had gone into the conference with William Hill giving odds of 10–1 on his winning. His speech, delivered without notes, served to dispel much of the unease at the 'posh' background of the old Etonian Cameron (who was also a member of White's), while emphasising his compassionate credentials. Cameron was compared to Blair in his personal style, his photogenic (and pregnant) wife Samantha joining him on the platform after his speech.[38] At the end of the week, the odds on Cameron becoming leader had shortened to 9–4. Shortly after the conference, Malcolm Rifkind withdrew from the race, backing former Cabinet Colleague Kenneth Clarke. At the same time, former Party Chairman Michael Ancram endorsed David Cameron.[39]

When the voting began, on 18 October 2005, it was Kenneth Clarke, much to the dismay of just about everybody, who was the first to be eliminated, gaining only 38 votes. Many of his supporters from 1997 were no longer in Parliament, and it was observed that his refusal to accept Front-Bench office after 1997 had not helped his profile, while his relaxed attitude to campaigning had seen him take too many votes for granted. David Davis did worse than expected at 62 votes, while Cameron came in second with 56, more than predicted. In the words of *The Times*: 'The big winner of the day was Mr Cameron, who had clearly taken the lion's share of undeclared MPs and persuaded others to defect from Mr Clarke. Mr Cameron's star has soared since his relaxed and confident performance at the party conference two weeks ago when he presented himself as the man to lead the Conservatives through a period of reform.'[40]

The second round saw right-winger Liam Fox eliminated, while Cameron moved into the lead with 90 votes. By this point Cameron had become the favourite to lead the party at odds of 3–1. As the vote moved to the ordinary members, and the candidates embarked on a series of local 'hustings', Davis hoped to recover some of the momentum lost at Blackpool, while Cameron's team hoped their candidate would hold steady. Despite rumours of drug use at University, and a reinvigorated performance by David Davis, Cameron won more than half the votes in the final stage with 134,446 votes, compared to 64,398 for David Davis. George Osborne, a close political ally some had declared his 'Gordon Brown', became Shadow Chancellor, while William Hague returned to the Front Bench as Shadow Foreign Secretary. Setting out his stall in a victory speech at the Royal Academy, Cameron declared: 'We need to change the way we feel. No more grumbling about modern Britain. I love this country as it is, not as it was, and I believe our best days lie ahead.'[41]

The party now moved ahead of Labour in the opinion polls for the first time since 1992. In the local elections of May 2006, the party gained 11 councils, including a majority of London Boroughs; however, the party only narrowly held onto Bromley and Chislehurst in a by-election in June of the same year.[42] David Cameron's institution of an 'A-List' of candidates which would be more broadly representative of the British population also met with mixed results. While the list is half female and 10 per cent ethnic minority,[43] the Bromley and Chislehurst seat selected a female candidate from the list, which has been attacked as discriminatory by others for disadvantaging male candidates.[44] Cameron sought to broaden Conservative appeal, speaking out on social and environmental issues, projecting a more 'compassionate' image, taking his lead from continental conservatives such as Sweden's Fredrik Reinfeldt, rather than American neoconservatives, moving the party onto traditionally centre-left territory in order to win.[45]

With a fresh young charismatic leader opposing a Blair who seemed well past his political sell by date, Conservatives hearts once more rose. Blair had already made it clear that he would not go on beyond his tenth anniversary, which came in June 2007, and Tory strategists looked forward to the change to Gordon Brown. Despite the Iraq war, and despite signs of a growing public distrust of him, Blair remained the most formidable election winner since Mrs Thatcher; the Tories, having failed to find a way to fight him, were reduced to awaiting his departure from the political stage. It was widely held that Brown, a grumpy obsessive Scotsman, would be an easier target against which to aim. As usual with Tory strategic thinking, this was wrong. Brown turned out to be an obedient apprentice to the image makers, and with a good hair cut, better fitting clothes, and Blair out of the way, bloomed in power. The fact that their expectations had been dashed pushed the Tories back into their habitual panic.

From the start, Cameron had faced the same dilemma as his three predecessors: how to win support from the centre ground of politics whilst retaining his core support; by staying ahead in the opinion polls he managed this fairly effortlessly until Brown's arrival. With his own and the party's poll ratings taking a dip during the summer of 2007, the grumblers came back out of their caves and started demanding a return to core values. There was much speculation that under pressure, Cameron would follow the line taken by his predecessors, and when he began to talk about crime, immigration and Europe at the end of the summer, there were those who thought they detected just such a shift to the right; the party's deputy treasurer, the little-known John Eliasch, resigned at the beginning of September in protest at what he saw as the abandonment of the centre ground.[46] There was much speculation that Brown might cash in on Cameron's difficulties by calling a snap election in the autumn, and his no doubt kindly meant suggestion that 'politics as usual' should be abandoned in favour of a more consensual approach, posed real problems for Cameron, who could not be seen to reject it, but who hardly welcomed attempts to hoover up two of his more semi-detached colleagues into Labour 'commissions of inquiry.'

Cameron was not lacking in advice that he must revert to stressing core values and 'listen' to his party, but there was, scare stories notwith-standing, little to suggest that he would follow his predecessors and move to the right. Cameron was instinctively a liberal conservative, and he had a healthy appetite for power; nothing suggested it would be found down that road. His best bet was to follow the path he had set on coming to the leadership; if the right-wing wished to depose him, it lacked a challenger of any stature, as well as any credibility; none of which stopped it sniping at the party's only chance of returning to power in the reasonably near future. The odds remained on a Labour victory whenever the election took place, but if Cameron remained on the course he had set himself, there was at least the hope that 'one more push' would do it.

Notes and References

(The place of publication is London unless otherwise stated.)

Notes to Chapter 1: The Conservative Tradition

1. R. Blake, *The Conservative Party from Peel to Major* (1997).
2. Daniel Finkelstein, 'Now the elephant's left the room, what next?' *The Times*, 4 July 2007.
3. B. Disraeli, *Lord Geoge Bentinck* (1905, edn), pp. xiv, xvi.
4. Robert Stewart, *The Foundation of the Conservative Party* (1978), p. 184.
5. J. Brooke, *The Prime Minister's Papers: Gladstone II: Autobiographical Memoranda* (1972) p. 272.
6. W. F. Monypenny, *The Life of Benjamin Disraeli*, volume II (1912), p. 314.

Notes to Chapter 2: Stanley and the Protectionists

1. A. Macintyre, 'Lord George Bentinck and the Protectionists: A Lost Cause?', in *Transactions of the Royal Historical Society* (1989), p. 141.
2. B. Hilton, *Corn, Cash and Commerce, the Economic Policies of the Tory Governments, 1815–1830* (1977); *The Age of Atonement* (1988); 'Peel: A reappraisal', in *Historical Journal*, 1979, pp. 585–614.
3. A. Gambles, *Protection and Politics: Conservative Economic Discourse, 1815–1852* (1999), p. 57.
4. Brooke, *Gladstone II: Autobiographical Memoranda*, p. 279.
5. G. P. Gooch (ed.) *The Later Correspondence of Lord John Russell*, vol. I (1925) p. 93.
6. Ibid., p. 100.
7. R. Stewart, *The Politics of Protection* (Cambridge, 1971), p. 49.
8. B. Disraeli, *Lord George Bentinck* (1905 edn.), p. 25.
9. Macintyre, 'Lord George Bentinck', p. 152.
10. Ibid.; M. Lawson-Tancred, 'The Anti-League and the Corn Law crisis of 1846', *Historical Journal*, 1960, pp. 162–83.
11. Brooke, *Gladstone: III Autobiographical Memoranda*, p. 21.
12. Stewart, *Politics of Protection*, p. 55.
13. J. Vincent (ed.) *Disraeli, Derby and the Conservative Party: The Political Journals of Lord Stanley, 1849–1869* (1978), 28 December 1852, p. 94.
14. Earl of Malmesbury, *Memoirs*, vol. I (1888), p. 169.
15. Brooke, *Gladstone: III Autobiographical Memoranda*, p. 267.
16. Brooke, *Gladstone: III Autobiographical Memoranda*, pp. 32–3.
17. Gambles, p. 205.
18. Stewart, *Politics of Protection*, p. 124.
19. Ibid., p. 132.
20. Ibid., p. 136.

Notes to Chapter 3: Derby's Conservatives

1. A. Hawkins, *Lord Derby*, 2 vols; G. Hicks, *The Conservatives and Europe 1846–1866* (2007).
2. Stewart, *The Politics of Protection*, p. 126.
3. R. Blake, *Disraeli* (1965), pp. 71–2.
4. Stewart, *The Politics of Protection*, p. 136.
5. Vincent, *Disraeli, Derby and the Conservative Party*, 20 March 1849, p. 1.
6. Stewart, *Foundation*, p. 234.
7. Stewart, *Politics of Protection*, p. 150.
8. Gooch, *Later Correspondence of Lord John Russell, vol. I*, pp. xxx–xxxi.
9. *Disraeli Letters, vol. V*, p. 369.
10. *Stanley Journal*, 22 February 1851, p. 44.
11. Brooke, *Gladstone: III Autobiographical Memoranda*, p. 73.
12. *Stanley Diaries*, 27 February 1851, p. 49.
13. Gooch, *Later Corr. of Lord John Russell, vol. II*, p. 107.
14. *Stanley Journal*, 15 December 1852, p. 89.
15. *Stanley Journal*, 28 December 1852, p. 94.
16. G. E. Buckle, *Life of Disraeli, vol. III* (1924), p. 483.
17. Ibid., p. 483.
18. Stewart, *Foundation*, pp. 299–300.
19. Buckle, *Disraeli III*, pp. 560–1.
20. Stewart, *Foundation*, p. 312.
21. Ramsden, *Pursuit of Power*, pp. 86–7.
22. *Hansard*, House of Lords, 9 July 1866, col. 744.
23. *Stanley Journal*, 17 June 1861, p. 173.
24. Stewart, *Foundation*, p. 352.
25. Buckle, *Life of Disraeli IV*, p. 424.
26. N. Johnson (ed.), *The Diary of Gathorne Hardy 1866–1869*, p. 11.
27. Buckle, *Life of Disraeli IV*, p. 441.
28. Disraeli Papers, Hughenden Mss. B/CC/S/366, Derby to Disraeli, 27 September 1866.
29. Disraeli Papers, Hughenden Mss. B/CC/S/367, Derby to Disraeli, 9 October 1866.
30. *Stanley Journal*, 4 December 1866, p. 277.
31. Disraeli Papers, Hughenden Mss. B/CC/S/410, Derby to Disraeli, 25 February 1867.
32. C. Whibley, *Lord John Manners and his friend, vol. II*, Journal of Lord John Manners, 2 March 1867, p. 125.
33. Buckle, *Life of Disraeli IV*, p. 527.
34. Ibid., p. 584.

Notes to Chapter 4: Disraeli on Top

1. P. Smith, *Disraeli* (1996), p. 217.
2. Hicks, *The Conservatives and Europe*, passim.
3. John Charmley, *Splendid Isolation? Britain and the Balance of Power, 1874–1914* (1999), ch. 1.
4. *Hansard*, House of Lords, 3rd series, clxxxiv, cols 738–7.
5. *Stanley Journal*, 23 December 1869, p. 347.
6. Richard Shannon, *The Age of Disraeli, 1868–1881* (1992), pp. 111–13.

7. Johnson, *Diary of Gathorne Hardy*, 3 February 1872, p. 149.
8. Buckle, *Life of Disraeli V*, p. 274.
9. *Splendid Isolation?* p. 15.
10. What follows is based on my *Splendid Isolation?* Where full references will be found.
11. *Diary of Gathorne Hardy*, p. 281.
12. J. Vincent (ed.) *The Derby Diaries, 1869–1878* (1994), 12 August 1876, p. 318; a most important entry is 21 January 1877, pp. 368–9.
13. *Derby Diaries*, 4, 19, 22 October 1876, pp. 331, 335–6.
14. Ibid., 23 October 1876, p. 337.
15. Ibid., 23 September 1877, p. 439.
16. *Splendid Isolation?* p. 105.
17. *Derby Diaries*, 1 January 1878, p. 475.
18. Randolph S. Churchill, *Winston S. Churchill, vol. II Companion volume 1* (1969), pp. 242–4.
19. Dudley W. R. Bahlman (ed.), *The Diary of Sir Edward Walter Hamilton, volume II* (Oxford, 1970), p. 431.
20. E. H. H. Green, *The Crisis of Conservatism, 1880–1914* (1995), ch. 3.
21. Winston S. Churchill, *Great Contemporaries* (1974 edn), p. 35.
22. J. A. Grenville, *Lord Salisbury and Foreign Policy* (London, 1964).
23. Blake and Cecil, pp. 157–8.
24. Quoted in M. Fforde, *Conservatism and Collectivism, 1886–1914* (1990), p. 44.
25. Ibid., p. 55.
26. Ibid., p. 70.

Notes to Chapter 5: Balfour in Trouble

1. Lady Gwendolen Cecil, *Life of Robert, Marquis of Salisbury, vol. II* (1921), p. 3.
2. Julian Amery, *Life of Joseph Chamberlain, vol. IV* (1951), p. 478.
3. Amery, *Chamberlain IV*, p. 496.
4. Ibid., p. 464.
5. John Charmley, *Lord Lloyd and the Decline of the British Empire* (1987), p. 10.
6. Richard A. Rempel, *Unionists Divided* (1972), p. 9.
7. E. H. H. Green, *The Crisis of Conservatism 1880–1914* (1995), p. 67.
8. Ibid., p. 3.
9. Amery, *Chamberlain IV*, p. 470.
10. Harcourt-Williams, *Salisbury-Balfour Correspondence*, introduction by Hugh Cecil, p. xv.
11. J. Vincent (ed.), *The Crawford Papers* (Manchester, 1984), 10 February 1905, p. 60.
12. Sir C. Petrie, *The Life and Letters of Sir Austen Chamberlain, vol. I* (1939), p. 142.
13. *Crawford Papers*, 10 April 1902, p. 66.
14. D. Dutton, *His Majesty's Loyal Opposition* (Liverpool, 1992), pp. 10–11.
15. British Library, Balfour Papers, Add. Mss. 49729, Lansdowne to Balfour, April 1905.
16. Amery, *Chamberlain VI*, p. 784.
17. Petrie, *Chamberlain I*, p. 157.
18. Green, *Crisis of Conservatism*, p. 137.
19. Randolph S. Churchill, *Lord Derby: King of Lancashire* (1959), pp. 89–90.
20. Balfour Papers, 49729, Lansdowne to Balfour, 28 January 1906.
21. *Crawford Papers*, 5 February 1906, p. 90.
22. Ibid., 5 February 1904, p. 70.
23. Amery, *Chamberlain VI*, pp. 717–18.

24. Balfour Papers, 49729, Lansdowne to Balfour, 4 February 1906.
25. Amery, *Chamberlain VI*, pp. 855–8.
26. Ibid., pp. 909–11.
27. John Ramsden (ed.), *Real Old Tory Politics* (1984), p. 27.
28. Amery, *Chamberlain VI*, p. 861.
29. British Library, Balfour MSS., 49737, letter to Balfour, 25 January 1906.
30 John Ramsden, *The Age of Balfour and Baldwin 1902–1940* (1979), p. 23.
31. Rempel, *Unionists Divided*, pp. 112–13.
32. Ramsden, *Age of Balfour and Baldwin*, p. 30.
33. Green, *The Crisis of Conservatism*, p. 138.
34. John Campbell, *F. E. Smith* (1983), pp. 127–31; for Liverpool politics see P. Waller, *Democracy and Sectarianism: A Political and Social History of Liverpool 1868–1939* (Liverpool, 1981).
35. Green, pp. 137–40 for an analysis.
36. For a convenient and up-to-date summary of an often confusing debate see K. Laybourn, 'The Rise of Labour and the Decline of Liberalism: The state of the debate' in *History*, June 1995, pp. 207–26. See also G. R. Searle, *The Liberal Party – Triumph and Disintegration, 1886–1929* (London, 1992), pp. 107–20.
37. Balfour MSS., 49736, Chamberlain to Balfour, 24 October 1907.
38. See G. Phillips, *The Diehards* (Princeton, 1979), especially ch. 1.
39. Churchill, *Derby*, p. 125.
40. Amery, *Chamberlain VI*, p. 795.
41. Ibid., p. 937.
42. Sir Austen Chamberlain, *Politics from Inside* (1936), pp. 298–311.
43. Petrie, *Chamberlain I*, p. 269.
44. Ramsden, *Age of Balfour and Baldwin*, pp. 38–41; Dutton, *His Majesty's Loyal Opposition*, pp. 99–103.

Notes to Chapter 6: The Unknown Bonar Law

1. Robert Blake, *The Unknown Prime Minister* (1956), p. 31.
2. Alan Clark (ed.), *A Good Innings* (1974), p. 118.
3. D. Dutton, *His Majesty's Loyal Opposition*, p. 170.
4. Blake, *Unknown Prime Minister*, p. 130.
5. *Crawford Papers*, p. 298.
6. Blake, *Unknown Prime Minister*, pp. 115–16.
7. Ramsden, *Age of Balfour and Baldwin*, p. 69.
8. Blake, *Unknown Prime Minister*, p. 227.
9. D. Gilmour, *Curzon* (1994), p. 436.
10. Petrie, *Chamberlain II*, p. 23.
11. G. D. Boyce (ed.), *The Crisis of British Unionism ... 1885–1922* (1987), p. 128.
12. For this, see G. R. Searle, *Corruption in British Politics* (1987).
13. R. Self (ed.), *The Austen Chamberlain Diary Letters* (1995), p. 147.
14. M. Gilbert, *Winston S. Churchill IV. Companion vol. 3* (1977), letter to Churchill, 8 April 1921, p. 1434.
15. Self, letter, 24 September 1922, p. 197.
16. There are good accounts in the following: K. O. Morgan, *Consensus and Disunity* (1979), ch. 14; Cowling, *Impact of Labour*, ch. 11; and M. Kinnear, *The Fall of Lloyd George* (1973), chs 5–6.

Notes to Chapter 7: Scalped by Baldwin

1. P. Williamson, *Stanley Baldwin* (Cambridge, 1999), p. 2.
2. David Marquand, *Ramsay MacDonald* (1977), p. 243.
3. Maurice Cowling, *The Impact of Labour* (Cambridge, 1972), pp. 65–88.
4. Ibid., p. 84.
5. Ibid., p. 1.
6. 'A Gentleman with a Duster' (pseud. Harold Begbie), *The Conservative Mind* (1924), p. 47.
7. R. Brent, *Historical Journal*, 1986, p. 768.
8. John Charmley, *Lord Lloyd and the Decline of the British Empire* (1987), p. 67.
9. Ibid., p. 73.
10. Gilmour, *Curzon*, passim.
11. S. Ball (ed.), *Parliament and Politics in the Age of Baldwin and MacDonald: The Headlam Diaries, 1923–1935* (1992), pp. 11, 34.
12. Rush H. Limbaugh III, *See, I Told You So* (New York, 1993), p. 34.
13. David Dilks, *Neville Chamberlain, vol. I* (1984), p. 339.
14. Philip Williamson (ed.), *The Modernisation of Conservative Politics: The Diaries and Letters of William Bridgeman, 1904–1935* (1988), pp. 168–70.
15. Keith Feiling, *Neville Chamberlain* (1946), p. 109.
16. Feiling, *Neville Chamberlain*, p. 108; Blake, *Conservative Party*, pp. 220–2.
17. John Campbell, *F. E. Smith* (1983), chs 21 and 23.
18. R. Grayson, *Austen Chamberlain at the Foreign Office* (Unpublished Oxford DPhil, 1995) is the most comprehensive as well as the best study of this important but neglected subject.
19. Charmley, *Lloyd*, p. 69.
20. Ball, *Headlam Diaries*, 1 March 1927, p. 113.
21. Williamson, *Bridgeman Diaries*, pp. 233–4.
22. British Library, Cecil of Chelwood papers, Add. MSS. 51084, Irwin letter, 7 June 1927.
23. Philip Williamson, *National Crisis and National Government* (1992), pp. 106–17.
24. S. Ball, *Baldwin and the Conservative Party* (1988) for what follows.
25. Charmley, *Lloyd*, pp. 166–7.
26. Ball, *Baldwin and the Conservative Party*, passim; Williamson, *National Crisis and National Government*, pp. 122–7.
27. John Charmley, *Duff Cooper* (1986).
28. Ball, *Headlam Diaries*, 20 February 1930, p. 185.
29. Ramsden, *Age of Balfour and Baldwin*, pp. 316–17; Williamson, *National Crisis and National Government*, pp. 277–9.

Notes to Chapter 8: Chamberlain in Charge

1. Ball, *Headlam Diaries*, 24 August 1931, p. 213; Williamson, *National Crisis*, chs 9 and 10 for the best modern account.
2. Marquand, *MacDonald*, pp. 664–5.
3. Ibid., pp. 662–5.
4. Ibid., p. 671.
5. Charmley, *Lloyd*, p. 177.
6. John Charmley, *Churchill: The End of Glory* (1993), p. 275.

7. Charmley, *Lord Lloyd*, p. 185.
8. Ball, *Headlam Diaries*, 22 January 1932, p. 227.
9. Ramsden, *The Age of Bonar Law and Baldwin*, p. 331.
10. R. A. Butler, *The Art of the Possible* (1972), p. 30.
11. Marquand, *MacDonald*, pp. 696–700 for the sad story.
12. Ball, *Headlam Diaries*, 23 November 1933, p. 252.
13. Charmley, *Lord Lloyd*, pp. 180–2.
14. David Dilks's 1982 biography has been crucial here.
15. R. A. C. Parker, *Neville Chamberlain and Appeasement* (1994); D. C. Watt, *How War Came* (1989) and John Charmley, *Chamberlain and the Lost Peace* (1989) for the different views.
16. Charmley, *Chamberlain*, pp. 82–3 for the evidence.
17. Ibid., p. 82.

Notes to Chapter 9: Churchill's Consensus

1. Franklin D. Roosevelt Library, Private Secretary's File, Box 49, letter, 15 September 1942.
2. Paul Addison, *The Road to 1945* (1975), pp. 230–1.
3. Trinity College, Butler MSS., G11/180, letter, 22 December 1940.
4. Andrew Roberts, *Eminent Churchillians* (1994) for their comments.
5. Birmingham University Library, Neville Chamberlain MSS., NC 13/17/57, letter, 10 May 1940.
6. NC 13/17/68, letter, 13 May 1940.
7. J. Barnes and D. Nicolson (eds), *The Empire at Bay: The Leo Amery Diaries 1929–1945* (1988), p. 754.
8. Barnes and Nicolson, *Amery Diaries*, 15 June 1940, p. 624.
9. Birmingham University Library, Avon MSS., AP 20/1/23, diary, 12 July 1943.
10. Barnes and Nicolson, *Amery Diaries*, 19 February 1943, p. 777.
11. Addison, *The Road to 1945*, pp. 230–1.
12. Barnes and Nicolson, *Amery Diaries*, 30 November 1942, p. 848.
13. C. Barnett, *The Audit of War* (1986), p. 47.
14. AP 20/10/679, letter to Eden, 18 February 1943.
15. Addison, *The Road to 1945*, p. 232.
16. Lord Hailsham, *A Sparrow's Flight* (1990), p. 210.
17. John Ramsden, *The Making of Conservative Party Policy* (1980), p. 99.
18. Paul Addison, *Churchill on the Home Front* (1992) for this.
19. Charmley, *End of Glory*, p. 435.
20. K. Jeffreys (ed.), *Labour and the Wartime Coalition … diary of James Chuter-Ede* (1987), p. 119.
21. R. A. Butler, *The Art of the Possible* (1971), pp. 80–125.
22. Barnes and Nicolson, *Amery Diaries*, 22 April 1943, p. 883.
23. AP 20/1/23, diary, 23 September 1943.
24. Jeffreys, *Chuter-Ede Diary*, p. 54.
25. Barnes and Nicolson, *Amery Diaries*, 27 February 1944, p. 969.
26. AP 20/1/21, diary, 29 April 1941.
27. Addison, *The Road to 1945* (1977 edn), p. 155.
28. Ibid., p. 155.
29. Ibid., pp. 155–6.

30. Ibid., pp. 249–50.
31. Jeffreys, *Chuter-Ede Diary*, p. 122.
32. B. Pimlott (ed.), *The War Diaries of Hugh Dalton* (1986), 18 February 1943, p. 555.
33. AP 20/1/20A, diary, 6 September 1940.
34. Barnes and Nicolson, *Amery Diaries*, 20 April 1943, p. 883.
35. AP 20/1/24, diary, 18 January 1944.
36. AP 20/1/24, diary, 18 February 1944.
37. Addison, *The Road to 1945*, pp. 257–8.
38. Pimlott, *Dalton Diary*, 9 March 1942, p. 391.
39. Bodleian Library, Oxford, Woolton MSS., Vol. 20, fo. 19, undated note from the election period.
40. Woolton MSS., Vol. 20, note to Beaverbrook, 31 May 1945.
41. Barnes and Nicolson, Amery Diaries, 4 June 1944, p. 1046.
42. AP 20/1/25, diary, 6 June 1945.

Notes to Chapter 10: The New Model Tory Party?

1. Bodleian Library, Conservative Party Archives, Papers of the Conservative Research Department [CRD], 2/53/1, fo. 363, letter to Rab Butler, 5 August 1945.
2. Butler, *Art of the Possible*, p. 133.
3. Jeffreys, *Chuter-Ede Diary*, 29 October 1942, p. 103.
4. See John Ramsden, ' "A Party for Owners or a Party for Earners?" How far did the British Conservative Party really change after 1945?', *Transactions of the Royal Historical Society*, 1987, pp. 49–63.
5. AP 20/14/34, letter to Eden, 9 August 1946.
6. Cockett, *Dear Max*, p. 58.
7. Butler, *Art of the Possible*, p. 134.
8. Cockett, *Dear Max*, pp. 58–9.
9. Lord Woolton, *Memoirs*, p. 418.
10. AP 20/14/34, letter to Eden, 9 August 1946.
11. Cockett, *Dear Max*, p. 59.
12. J. Hoffman, *The Conservatives in Opposition* (1963), pp. 39–40.
13. AP/20/1/26. diary, 4 June 1946.
14. Hoffman, *The Conservatives in Opposition*, pp. 139–40.
15. Ibid., pp. 142–4.
16. Cockett, *Dear Max*, p. 58.
17. Lord Woolton, *Memoirs*, (1957), pp. 331–6.
18. AP 20/1/25, diary, 27 July 1945.
19. AP 20/1/25, diary, 2 August 1945.
20. Ball, *Headlam Diaries*, 15 February 1933, p. 259.
21. Ramsden, *TRHS*, 1987, p. 58.
22. AP 23/9/29, Eden to Lord Birkenhead, 29 January 1970.
23. AP 20/1/25, diary, 6 June 1946.
24. Ramsden, *Conservative Party Policy*, pp. 109–15.
25. Story told to me by the late Lord Lloyd.
26. Paul Addison, 'The Road from 1945', in P. Hennessy and A. Seldon (eds), *Ruling Performance* (1989), p. 7.
27. C. Barnett, *Audit of War* (1988) for this, but Maurice Cowling would seem to share this view.

28. Sir Ian Gilmour, *Inside Right: A Study in Conservatism* (1977).
29. See, e.g., Simon Heffer, 'Centenary of a double-crosser', *Spectator*, 5 February 1994, pp. 8–10.
30. See the debate in *Contemporary Record*, vol. 1, no. 3, Autumn 1987.

Notes to Chapter 11: A Conservative Consensus?

1. Dennis Kavanagh, *Politics & Personalities* (1990), p. 62.
2. A. Seldon, *Churchill's Indian Summer* (1981), p. 426.
3. Andrew Roberts, *Eminent Churchillians* (1994), p. 258.
4. Seldon, *Churchill's Indian Summer*, pp. 154–5.
5. A. Cairncross (ed.), *The Robert Hall Diaries 1947–1953* (1989), p. 177.
6. Roberts, *Eminent Churchillians*, p. 258.
7. A. Horne, *Harold Macmillan, vol. I* (1987); Seldon, *Churchill's Indian Summer*, pp. 250–9.
8. Cairncross (ed.), *Robert Hall Diaries*; Lord Birkenhead, *The Prof in Two Worlds* (1961), pp. 284–9; K. O. Morgan, *The People's Peace* (1989), pp. 119–22.
9. Morgan, *The People's Peace*, p. 122.
10. Roberts, *Eminent Churchillians*, pp. 253–4.
11. For example, Ian Gilmour, *Inside Right* (1977).
12. Lord Hailsham, *The Case for Conservatism* (1947), p. 22.
13. Michael Bentley, 'Liberal Toryism in the Twentieth Century', in *Transactions of the Royal Historical Society*, 1994, esp. pp. 187–91.
14. Dennis Kavanagh, 'Is Thatcherism Conservative?', *Politics & Personalities* (1990), pp. 64–77.
15. The *locus classicus* of this is now Margaret Thatcher, *The Downing Street Years* (1992); but see also Patrick Cosgrave, *Margaret Thatcher: A Tory and her Party* (1978) and *Thatcher: The First Term* (1985).
16. See Chapter 10.
17. Kavanagh, *Politics & Personalities*, pp. 42–4.
18. T. E. Utley, *Enoch Powell* (1968), p. 66.
19. Roy Lewis, *Enoch Powell: Principle in Politics* (1979), pp. 48–51 for an analysis.
20. Lord Moran, *Churchill: The Struggle for Survival* (1965); see Seldon, *Churchill's Indian Summer*, pp. 42–54, for some common sense.
21. Shuckburgh diaries, *passim*.
22. Rhodes James, *Eden*, pp. 355–89.
23. See the correspondence in *The Times* in June 1980 on this subject.
24. John Grigg, 'Churchill: Crippled giant', *Encounter*, vol. XLVIII, no. 7, 1977.
25. Seldon, *Churchill's Indian Summer*, p. 51.
26. Rhodes James, *Eden*, pp. 392–5.
27. Private information.
28. Anthony Howard, *RAB* (1987), p. 222.
29. John Charmley, *Churchill's Grand Alliance* (1995); David Carlton, *Anthony Eden* (1979); Diane Kunz, *The Economic Diplomacy of the Suez Crisis* (1991) for all of this.
30. Bernard Levin, *The Pendulum Years* (1969).
31. See Simon Heffer, 'Centenary of a Double-Crosser', *Spectator*, 5 February 1994, pp. 8–10.
32. Enoch Powell, 'Macmillan: The Case Against', *Spectator*, 10 January 1987, p. 15.
33. Margaret Thatcher, *The Path to Power* (1995), p. 118.

34. Harold Evans, *Downing Street Diary* (1981), p. 22.
35. Heffer, 'Centenary of a Double-Crosser', p. 9.
36. Julian Amery, ' ... And the Case For', *Spectator*, 10 January 1987, p. 16.
37. Heffer, 'Centenary of a Double-Crosser', p. 9 for the last; Alistair Horne, *Macmillan vol. II* (1989), p. 5, for the first.
38. Horne, *Macmillan II*, pp. 64–5, but also G. Hutchinson, *The Last Edwardian at No. 10* (1979).
39. Horne, *Macmillan II*, pp. 71–8 surveys both sides of the argument; see also Lewis, *Powell*, pp. 55–7.
40. Heffer, 'Centenary of a Double-Crosser', p. 10.
41. Amery ' ... And the Case For', p. 16.
42. Enoch Powell, 'Macmillan: The Case Against', *Spectator*, 10 January 1987, p. 15.
43. Horne, *Macmillan II*, p. 62.
44. Bevan, awkward as always, did not adopt these positions.
45. D. E. Butler and Anthony King, *The British General Election of 1964* (1965), pp. 303–4.

Notes to Chapter 12: Decline and Fall

1. Horne, *Macmillan II*, p. 253.
2. Thatcher, *Path to Power*, p. 114.
3. Evans, *Downing Street Diary*, p. 118.
4. *Contemporary Record*, vol. 1, no. 1, 1987, interview with Anthony Seldon, p. 27.
5. Thatcher, *Path to Power*, p. 114.
6. Ramsden, *Conservative Party Policy*, p. 229.
7. Eden MSS, AP 20/60/46, Salisbury to Eden, 26 February 1960.
8. Butler and King, *General Election of February 1964*, p. 79.
9. Horne, *Macmillan II*, p. 256.
10. R. Lamb, *The Macmillan Government: The Emerging Truth* (1995) for the most recent account.
11. Horne, *Macmillan II*, p. 449.
12. Evans, *Downing Street Diary*, p. 286.
13. Horne, *Macmillan II*, pp. 529–30.
14. Lord Home, *The Way the Wind Blows* (1976), p. 182.
15. Evans, *Downing Street Diary*, pp. 298–9.
16. Howard, *RAB*, pp. 304–5.
17. Ibid., pp. 313–14.
18. Rhodes James, *Anthony Eden* (1986), p. 599.
19. Butler and King, *General Election of February 1964*, pp. 24–5.
20. Ibid., p. 84.
21. Ibid., pp. 88–91; Ramsden, *Conservative Party Policy*, pp. 220–4.
22. Butler and King, *General Election of February 1964*, pp. 303–4.
23. Ramsden, *Conservative Party Policy*, pp. 225–6.
24. D. R. Thorpe, *Selwyn Lloyd* (1989), pp. 394–6.

Notes to Chapter 13: From Heath to Thatcher

1. Patrick Cosgrave, *Thatcher: The First Term* (1985), p. 9.
2. Ramsden, *Conservative Party Policy*, p. 236.

3. Robert Blake, *The Conservative Party from Peel to Thatcher* (1985), p. 300.
4. Ramsden, *Conservative Party Policy*, p. 234.
5. Ibid., p. 241.
6. Thatcher, *Path to Power*, p. 133.
7. Timothy Raison, *Conflict and Conservatism* (1965).
8. Utley, *Powell*, p. 96.
9. Ibid., p. 98.
10. Ibid., p. 190. The full text is to be found on pages 179 to 190.
11. Ramsden, *Conservative Party Policy*, p. 275.
12. See D. E. Butler, *The British General Election of 1970* (1971); D. E. Schoen, *Enoch Powell and the Powellites* (1977); Roy Lewis, *Enoch Powell, Principle in Politics* (1979).
13. Philip Norton, *Conservative Dissidents* (1978), pp. 36–8.
14. Ibid., p. 38.
15. Cosgrave, *Thatcher: The First Term*, p. 23.
16. John Ramsden, 'The Conservatives since 1945', in *Contemporary Record*, vol. 2, no. 1, 1988, p. 21.
17. There is some dispute over how many Conservative supporters followed his lead; the present author can think of at least one who did.
18. G. R. Searle, *Country before Party* (1995) for this.
19. Letter from Sir Alfred Sherman in *Contemporary Record*, vol. 1, no. 2, 1987, p. 6.
20. 'Escaping from the chrysalis of Statism', Anthony Seldon interview with Sir Keith Joseph, *Contemporary Record*, vol. 1, 1987, pp. 28–9.
21. *The Independent*, 5 January 1993.
22. Thatcher, *Path to Power*, p. 195.

Notes to Chapter 14: The Iron Lady

1. Kavanagh, *Politics and Personalities*, pp. 70–1.
2. Simon Jenkins, 'An Indigestible pill', *The Times*, 14 June 1995, p. 16.
3. John Campbell, 'Defining Thatcherism', *Contemporary Record*, vol. 1, no. 3, 1987, p. 3.
4. Cosgrave, *Thatcher: The First Term*, p. 34.
5. Angus Maude, 'The Conservative Crisis – 1', *The Spectator*, 15 March 1963.
6. Nigel Lawson, *The View From No. 11* (1992), p. 249.
7. Thatcher, *Path to Power*, pp. 362–4.
8. David Butler and Dennis Kavanagh, *The British General Election of 1979* (1980), p. 151.
9. Thatcher, *Path to Power*, p. 448.
10. Butler and Kavanagh, *British General Election of 1979*, p. 354.
11. Ibid., pp. 390–5.
12. Cosgrave, *First Term*, ch. 3.
13. Hugo Young, *One of Us* (1989), pp. 138–40.
14. Cosgrave, *First Term*, p. 38.
15. *Now!*, 5–11 October 1979, pp. 5, 57.
16. John Vincent, 'The Thatcher Governments', in Hennessy and Seldon (eds), *Ruling Performance* (Oxford, 1987), pp. 274–5.
17. See, especially, Hugo Young's *One of Us* and Andrew Gamble's 'Thatcherism and Conservative Politics', in S. Hall and M. Jacques (eds), *The Politics of Thatcherism* (1983); see also William Keegan, *Mrs Thatcher's Economic Experiment* (1984).

18. See, for example, John Vincent, 'Margaret Thatcher: Her Place in History', in *Contemporary Record*, vol. 1, no. 3, 1987, pp. 23–4 and his piece in Ruling *Performance*, and also Cosgrave's *Thatcher: The First Term*. John Campbell, *Margaret Thatcher: Volume II* (2003), pp. 80–8 is the most sensible view on all of this.
19. *Now!*, 5–11 October 1979, p. 57.
20. Jock Bruce-Gardyne, *Mrs Thatcher's First Administration* (1984), p. 58.
21. Margaret Thatcher, *The Downing Street Years* (1993), p. 122.
22. See David Sanders et al., 'Government Popularity and the Falklands war: A reassessment', *British Journal of Political Science*, vol. 17, pp. 281–314.
23. Thatcher, *Downing Street Years*, p. 181.
24. Ibid., p. 184.
25. Mrs Thatcher, when she saw the pictures on TV, uttered 'Oh, the poor shopkeepers!' At the time, it was seen by the media as parochial – but it would now be more and more the gut reaction of most of the public.
26. Simon Jenkins, 'An indigestible pill', *The Times*, 14 June 1995, p. 16.
27. Quoted in Cosgrave, *Thatcher: The First Term*, p. 213.

Notes to Chapter 15: High Tide and After

1. Peter Riddell, 'Mrs Thatcher's Second Term', *Contemporary Record*, vol. 1, no. 3, 1987, p. 17.
2. Vincent, in Hennessy and Seldon (eds), *Ruling Performance*, p. 279.
3. Nicholas Ridley, *My Style of Government* (1991), p. 23.
4. Ibid., p. 24.
5. Thatcher, *Downing Street Years*, pp. 711–13.
6. Alan Clark, *Diaries*, p. 343.
7. Ibid., p. 345.
8. Thatcher, *Downing Street Years*, p. 846.
9. Clark, *Diaries*, p. 366.
10. 'Hurd is best suited to take on Thatcher's mantle', *Daily Telegraph*, 24 November 1990, p. 12.
11. 'Whatever happened to Thatcher's Economic Miracle?', *The Times*, 23 November 1990, p. 5.
12. Charles Moore, 'A farewell to a great prime minister', *Daily Telegraph*, 23 November 1990, p. 19.
13. This was the theme of a lecture by Professor Andrew Gamble at the Institute of Contemporary British History's Annual Summer Conference in July 1995.
14. Moore, 'A farewell to a great prime minister', p. 19.
15. Thatcher, *Downing Street Years*, p. 151.
16. Campbell, *The Iron Lady*, ch. 18 gives a good flavour of this.
17. See the *Sunday Telegraph*, 25 November 1990, p. 12 for the reaction.
18. *Daily Telegraph*, 23 November 1990, p. 3.
19. *Sunday Telegraph*, 25 November 1990, p. 22.
20. *The Times*, 26 November 1990, p. 3, and interview with Simon Jenkins, p. 12; *The Times*, 28 November, p. 18.
21. *Daily Telegraph*, 23 November 1990, p. 23.
22. *The Times*, 26 November 1990, main headline, 'Thatcher backs Major'.
23. 'Major wins the battle for No. 10', *The Times*, 28 November 1990, p. 1.
24. *The Times*, 28 November 1990, p. 4.

Notes to Chapter 16: After the Ball was Over

1. Alan Clark, *Diaries*, p. 377.
2. *The Times*, 29 June 1991, p. 1.
3. *The Times*, 1 April 1992, poll analysis by Professor Ivor Crewe, p. 7.
4. *The Times*, 2 April 1992, p. 9 – the hapless Professor Crewe yet again!
5. Maurice Cowling, *Sunday Telegraph*, 25 November 1990, p. 22.
6. *The Times*, 2 April 1992, p. 9, report by Robin Oakley.
7. *The Times*, 10 April 1992.
8. *The Times*, 11 April 1992, p. 1.
9. 'We must return to traditional Tory values', *Sunday Times*, 11 June 1995, p. 3.
10. Ian Lang, *Blue Remembered Years* (Politico's, 2002), p. 246.
11. 'Excluded brethren', leader by Charles Moore, *Sunday Telegraph*, 9 July 1995.
12. 'Is Labour the true heir to Thatcher?', *The Times*, 17 July 1995, p. 17.
13. 'Blair next?', *The Sunday Telegraph*, 16 July 1995, p. 27.

Notes to Chapter 17: No Direction Home?

This chapter is heavily based upon work done by my son, Gerard Charmley, who, as a participant in some of the events described, gave me the benefit of his own reflections; to which I have added my own as a sometime Chairman of a local Conservative Association and Election Agent. My gratitude to Gerard is immense.

1. Julian Critchley and Morrison Halcrow, *Collapse of Stout Party* (Gollancz, 1997), p. 181.
2. John Major, *Autobiography* (HarperCollins, 1999), pp. 726–7.
3. Quoted in Jo-Anne Nadler, *William Hague: In His Own Right* (Politico's, 2000), p. 192.
4. Ibid., p. 211; Julian Critchley, Letter, *The Spectator*, 8 November 1997.
5. Lord Roberts of Conwy, *Right From the Start* (Cardiff: University of Wales, 2006), p. 337.
6. Remarks to a meeting of the *Politeia* think-tank at Carlton House Terrace, 1998.
7. Nadler, *William Hague*, pp. 257–63.
8. Ibid., p. 214.
9. Ibid., pp. 219–20.
10. Ibid., p. 252.
11. David Butler and Martin Westlake, *British Politics and European Elections 1999* (Basingstoke: Palgrave Macmillan, 2000), p. 55.
12. BBC News: Election '99: Parties and Issues: Pro-Euro Conservative Party
13. Butler and Westlake, *British Politics and European Elections 1999*, p. 184.
14. BBC News Online, Tuesday 25 January 2000.
15. 'William Hague's "Foreign Land" speech', *Guardian Unlimited*, Sunday 4 March 2001.
16. Benedict Brogan, 'Kennedy Attacks "Powellesque" Hague Over Asylum', *Telegraph Online*, 7 April 2001; Hugo Young, 'Weeping for the Country', *Guardian Unlimited*, 6 March 2001.
17. Sarah Womack, 'Hague in retreat over talk of "Foreign Land" ', *Telegraph Online*, 7 April 2001.
18. Dennis Kavanaugh, 'How William Hague Lost the Election', *Independent Online*, 30 December 2006.
19. 'Portillo Launches Leadership Bid Today', *Guardian Unlimited*, 13 June 2001.
20. 'Portillo Falters in Chaotic Vote', *Guardian Unlimited*, 11 July 2001.

21. 'Stalled Portillo Hustles for Votes', *Guardian Unlimited* 13 July 2001.
22. 'Furious Thatcher Rounds on Portillo', *Guardian Unlimited*, 16 July 2001.
23. 'Clarke Takes Pole Position as Shocked Portillo Quits the Race', *Guardian Unlimited*, 18 July 2001.
24. BBC News Online, 13 September 2001.
25. BBC News Online, 20 May 2002.
26. Matthew Tempest, 'Quiet Times', *Guardian Unlimited*, Tuesday 24 December 2002.
27. Andrew Rawnsley, 'Dead Man Talking', *Guardian Unlimited*, Sunday 12 October 2003.
28. BBC News Online, Tuesday 28 October 2003.
29. BBC News Online, Wednesday 29 October 2003.
30. BBC News Online, Friday 31 October 2003.
31. BBC News Online, Monday 14 June 2004.
32. Nick Assinder, 'Tories' Euro-Blow', BBC News Online, Monday 14 June 2004.
33. Cheryl Kernot, 'The Master of the Dog Whistle', *Guardian Unlimited*, Wednesday 27 April 2005; Andrew Grice, 'The Week in Politics', *Independent Online*, 29 January 2005.
34. BBC News Online, Friday 6 May 2005.
35. Leadership Archive: 'MPs Set to Reject Michael Howard's Leadership Election Process – But Can't Agree on Alternative.'
36. *Guardian Unlimited*, 'Davis Licks Wounds After Media Bruising', Friday 7 October 2005.
37. *Observer* Special Report, Carole Cadwallader, Sunday 9 October 2005.
38. BBC News Online, Tuesday 14 February 2006.
39. 'Rifkind Quits to Back Clarke, leaving Tory Ballot Wide Open', *Times Online*, 12 October 2005.
40. 'Clarke knocked out of Tory Leadership Contest', *Times Online*, 18 October 2005.
41. 'The Great Gamble', *Times Online*, 7 December 2005.
42. Bromley and Chislehurst, *Guardian Unlimited*, 30 June 2006.
43. BBC News Online, Wednesday 20 May 2006.
44. Anne Jenkin, 'Tory A-List is Working', *The Express on Sunday*, 12 November 2006.
45. 'Sweden's "Cameron" offers an electable right-wing', *Independent Online*, 30 December 2006; Tory Diary, 'Cameron Abandons Dog-Whistle Politics', *ConservativeHome.com*, 18 December 2005.
46. 'Blow for Cameron as treasurer quits over party's "swing to the right" ', *The Times*, 3 September 2007.

Bibliography

(The place of publication is London unless otherwise stated in Notes and References.)

1 General

Standard Works

The standard narrative history of the Conservative Party is:

Lord Blake, *The Conservative Party from Peel to Thatcher* (1989)

The best single volume on the party from 1900 to 1939 is:

John Ramsden, *The Age of Bonar Law and Baldwin* (1979)

Part of the Longman *History of the Conservative Party*. Other volumes are:

Robert Stewart, *The Foundation of the Conservative Party* (1978)
Richard Shannon, *The Age of Disraeli* (1992)
John Ramsden, *The Age of Churchill and Eden* (1995)
John Ramsden, *The Winds of Change: Macmillan to Heath 1957–1975* (1996)

These should now be supplemented by:

A. Seldon and S. Ball (eds), *The Conservative Century* (1994)
John Ramsden, *An Appetite for Power: A History of the Conservative Party Since 1830* (1998)
A. Clark, *The Tories: Conservatives and the Nation State 1922–1997* (1998)
M. Francis and I. Zweininger-Bargielowska (ed.), *The Conservatives and British Society 1880–1990* (Cardiff, 1996) contains some useful and interesting articles on Conservative policy.

Monographs

P. Addison, *The Road to 1945* (1975)
S. Ball, *The Conservative Party 1900–1951* (1994)
S. Ball and A. Seldon, *The Heath Government 1970–74* (1996)
M. Cowling, *The Impact of Labour* (1971)
M. Cowling, *The Impact of Hitler* (1975)
D. Dutton, *His Majesty's Loyal Opposition* (1992)
M. Fforde, *Conservatism and Collectivism 1886–1914* (1990)
E. H. H. Green, *The Crisis of Conservatism 1880–1914* (1995)
S. Hall and M. Jacques, *The Politics of Thatcherism* (1983)
P. Hennessy and A. Seldon (eds), *Ruling Performance* (1989)
J. Hoffman, *The Conservatives in Opposition* (1963)
D. Kavanagh, *Politics and Personalities* (1990)
K. O. Morgan, *The People's Peace* (1990)
P. Norton, *Conservative Dissidents* (1978)

J. Ramsden, *The Making of Conservative Party Policy* (1980)
R. A. Rempel, *Unionists Divided* (1972)
A. Roberts, *Eminent Churchillians* (1994)
G. R. Searle, *Party Before Country* (1995)
A. Seldon, *Churchill's Indian Summer* (1981)
G. Stewart: *Burying Caesar: Churchill, Chamberlain and the Battle for the Tory Party* (1999)

2   Diaries

Those students who want to get close to the original source material are excellently served by the superb series produced by The Historians' Press. For some reason or other, Conservatives seem to keep better diaries than their opponents – a great boon for historians of the party. The ones currently published and used here are:

S. Ball, *Parliament and Politics in the Age of Baldwin and MacDonald: The Headlam Diaries, 1923–1935* (1992)
G. Boyce, *The Crisis of British Unionism: The Domestic Political Papers of the Second Earl of Selborne, 1885–1922* (1987)
G. Boyce, *The Crisis of British Power: The Imperial and Naval Papers of the Second Earl of Selborne, 1895–1910* (1990)
R. Cockett, *My Dear Max: the letters of Brendan Bracken to Lord Beaverbrook, 1925–1958* (1990)
J. Ramsden, *Real Old Tory Politics: The Political Diaries of Robert Sanders, Lord Bayford, 1910–1935* (1984)
P. Williamson, *The Modernisation of Conservative Politics: The Diaries and Letters of William Bridgeman, 1904–1935* (1988)

To these can be added:

G. Brandreth, *Breaking the Code: Westminster Diaries* (1999)
J. Barnes and D. Nicholson, *The Leo Amery Diaries, vol. I* (1981)
J. Barnes and D. Nicholson, *The Empire at Bay: The Leo Amery Diaries 1929–1945* (1988)
A. Clark, *A Good Innings: The Papers of Lord Lee of Fareham* (1974)
A. Clark, *Diaries* (1993)
A. Clark, *Diaries: Into Politics* (2000)
A. Clark, *The Last Diaries: In and out of the Wilderness* (2002)
R. Self, *The Austen Chamberlain Diary Letters* (1995)
J. Vincent, *The Crawford Papers: The Journals of David Lindsay, twenty-seventh Earl of Crawford and tenth Earl of Balcarres, 1871–1940* (1984)

3   Memoirs

Churchill set what some might consider to be an unfortunate precedent by writing his memoirs in many volumes; of his successors only the most recent have failed to follow suit, and perhaps the market for autobiographies of Hague, Duncan Smith and Howard is a little limited. What follows is just a selection of the more useful memoirs:

R. A. Butler, *The Art of the Possible* (1971)
Duff Cooper, *Old Men Forget* (1953)
A. Eden, *The Eden Memoirs*, 3 vols (1959–1962)
E. Heath, *The Course of My Life* (1998)
M. Heseltine, *Life in the Jungle: My Autobiography* (2000)

Lord Home, *The Way the Wind Blows* (1976)
G. Howe, *Conflict of Loyalty* (1994)
D. Hurd, *Memoirs* (2003)
N. Lamont, *In Office* (1999)
I. Lang, *Blue Remembered Years* (2002)
N. Lawson, *The View from No. 11* (1992)
H. Macmillan, *Memoirs*, 6 vols (1968–1972)
John Major, *Memoirs* (1999)
N. Ridley, *My Style of Government* (1991)
Lord Roberts of Conwy, *Right From the Start* (2006)
Gillian Shephard, *Shephard's Watch* (2000)
Margaret Thatcher, *The Downing Street Years* (1993)
Margaret Thatcher, *The Path to Power* (1995)
Lord Woolton, *Memoirs* (1957)

4 Biographies

The historian of the party is almost embarrassingly well-served in this field – despite the attitude of some historians who (not having tried the task usually) tend to dismiss the art.

Prime Ministers/Conservative leaders

Disraeli is still best served by Robert Blake, *Disraeli* (1965).

Salisbury is still best served by the official life in 4 volumes published by his daughter: Lady G. Cecil, *The Life of Robert, third Marquis of Salisbury* (1921–1932). This is now supplemented by: David Steele, *Lord Salisbury: A Political Biography* (1998), and Andrew Roberts, *Salisbury: Victorian Titan* (1999). Lord Blake and H. Cecil (eds), *Salisbury: The Man and his Policies* (1987) is invaluable.

Balfour continues to elude his biographers as he did contemporaries. The authorised life by his niece has some useful material and has been unfairly neglected, perhaps because of its publication date: B. E. C. Dugdale, *Arthur James Balfour*, 2 vols (1939). Neither Kenneth Young's *Balfour* (1963) nor Sydney Zebel's *Balfour: A Political Biography* (1973) get much further. The same is true for Lord Egremeont's *Balfour* (1980). Ruddock F. Mackay, *Balfour: Intellectual Statesman* (1985), deals mainly with his influence upon imperial policy.

Bonar Law has not, despite Beaverbrook's efforts, proved an attractive subject for biographers – bores seldom do. The paucity of biographers may also owe something to the fact that Lord Blake said it all so well in the one and only existing biography: Robert Blake, *The Unknown Prime Minister: Bonar Law* (1955). R. J. Q. Adams, *Bonar Law* (1999) has since been published, and is not bad.

Austen Chamberlain has the dubious distinction of being the only leader in this period not to have been Prime Minister. His official biography by Sir Charles Petrie (2 vols, 1939) is better than its descent into obscurity suggests. David Dutton, *Austen Chamberlain: Gentleman in Politics* (1985), is an excellent modern study.

Baldwin has also largely eluded his pursuers. J. Barnes and K. Middlemas, *Baldwin* (1969), is very long and very uneven. G. M. Young, *Baldwin* (1952), was written by a critic and it shows. More modern studies by H. Montgomery-Hyde (1973) and Kenneth Young (1976) do not add much. Roy Jenkins, *Baldwin* (1987), although short and a little light-weight, is very strong on perceptions. Philip Williamson, *Stanley Baldwin: Conservative Leadership and National Values* (1999) is a thematic study, examining the man in depth, and finding much below the surface.

Neville Chamberlain has not lacked biographers, but most of them have naturally concentrated on his foreign policy. Once more there is much to be said for the official biography: K. Feiling, *Neville Chamberlain* (1946). D. Dilks, *Neville Chamberlain*, vol. 1 (1984), only takes the story to 1929. J. Charmley, *Chamberlain and the Lost Peace* (1989), is mainly concerned with foreign policy and is contentious.

Winston S. Churchill is the only modern British Prime Minister with a whole magazine devoted to his life and works (*Finest Hour*, published by Richard Langworth). Biographies pour from the presses in an unstoppable stream, to which this author has contributed – at least he had something different to say! The official biography (1966–1990) runs to 8 massive volumes and (so far) 11 companions. Volumes 1 and 2 are by Randolph S. Churchill, the other 6 by Sir Martin Gilbert. R. R. James, *Churchill: A Study in Failure* (1970), stops in 1939 but is brilliant. Recent biographies worth reading include: P. Addison, *Churchill on the Home Front* (1992); J. Charmley, *Churchill: The End of Glory* (1993); J. Charmley, *Churchill's Grand Alliance* (1995); C. Ponting, *Churchill* (1994); N. Rose, *Churchill: An Unruly Life* (1994). There have been many recent biographies saying what the others have said, but since to list them would be as tedious as it was to read them, I shall spare the reader.

Anthony Eden has been well served. The case against is marshalled with great skill and not a little malice by D. Carlton, *Anthony Eden* (1979). The case for is ably presented in R. R. James, *Anthony Eden* (1986). You pays your money and you takes your choice. D. R. Thorpe, *Anthony Eden* (2003) has since appeared, as has David Dutton, *Anthony Eden: A Life and a Reputation* (1996).

Harold Macmillan is equally well-served. The official biography is A. Horne, *Macmillan* (2 vols, 1987 and 1989). J. Ramsden, *Macmillan* (1994) is very useful.

Sir Alec Douglas-Home had had nothing worth reading written about him when the first edition of this book was published; this has now altered thanks to D. R. Thorpe's excellent *Alec Douglas-Home* (1996), a favourable look at the 14th Earl. The same was true for Ted Heath before John Campbell's recent (1992) biography, which is, like all his work, splendid.

Margaret Thatcher has suffered the attention of liberal journalists such as Hugo Young in *One of Us* (1990) (and numerous editions), but if one wants a balanced view one is out of luck. From the other side, Patrick Cosgrave has written intelligently about her in *Margaret Thatcher: A Tory and her Party* (1978) and *Thatcher: The First Term* (1985). John Campbell has since written a biography in two volumes, *The Grocer's Daughter* (2000) and *Iron Lady* (2003), which should be read by anyone wishing to see how this sort of thing ought to be done. We await Charles Moore's authorised biography, which, given his political instincts and unique vantage point, should be worth the wait.

John Major. Anthony Seldon's *Major: A Political Life* (1997) takes the story up to 1997. Other short studies such as Hywel Williams' brilliant and feline *Guilty Men* (1998) look at the collapse of the Major Government; in Hywel Williams' case from a fiercely pro-Redwood position. Julian Critchley and Morrison Halcrow, *Collapse of Stout Party* (1997) is a stridently pro-European diary of the period, concluding with William Hague's victory in the leadership election.

William Hague has had one published biography, Jo-Anne Nadler's *William Hague: In His Own Right* (2000), which takes the story past the Euro-Elections. It is more political profile than full biography. Simon Walters' *Tory Wars: The Conservatives in Crisis* (2001) takes the reader up to the 2001 election.

Cabinet Ministers

J. Amery, *Joseph Chamberlain*, vols IV, V and VI (1951, 1953, 1969)
Lord Birkenhead, *FE: The Life of the first Earl of Birkenhead* (1959 edn)
Lord Birkenhead, *The Prof in Two Worlds* (1951)
Lord Birkenhead, *Lord Halifax* (1966)
J. Campbell, *F. E. Smith* (1983)
J. Charmley, *Duff Cooper* (1986)
J. Charmley, *Lord Lloyd and the Decline of the British Empire* (1987)
Randolph S. Churchill, *Lord Derby, King of Lancashire* (1959)
P. Cosgrave, *The Three Faces of Enoch Powell* (1985)
J. A. Cross, *Lord Swinton* (1980)
D. Gilmour, *Curzon* (1994)
Simon Heffer, *Like The Roman: A Life of Enoch Powell* (1998)
Morrison Halcrow, *Sir Keith Joseph* (1989)
A. Howard, *RAB: The Life of R. A. Butler* (1987)
A. Roberts, *The Holy Fox: Lord Halifax* (1990)
A. J. P. Taylor, *Beaverbrook* (1972)
D. R. Thorpe, *Selwyn Lloyd* (1989)
T. E. Utley, *Enoch Powell* (1968)

One could go on for ever, rather like some memorialists, but I shall stop here, with apologies to the tribe of those who continue to produce biographies of high quality.

Index